ANALYZING TEXT
and DISCOURSE

Sara Miller McCune founded SAGE Publishing in 1965 to support the dissemination of usable knowledge and educate a global community. SAGE publishes more than 1000 journals and over 800 new books each year, spanning a wide range of subject areas. Our growing selection of library products includes archives, data, case studies and video. SAGE remains majority owned by our founder and after her lifetime will become owned by a charitable trust that secures the company's continued independence.

Los Angeles | London | New Delhi | Singapore | Washington DC | Melbourne

ANALYZING TEXT
and DISCOURSE

Eight Approaches for the Social Sciences

Kristina Boréus
Göran Bergström

Los Angeles | London | New Delhi
Singapore | Washington DC | Melbourne

Los Angeles | London | New Delhi
Singapore | Washington DC | Melbourne

SAGE Publications Ltd
1 Oliver's Yard
55 City Road
London EC1Y 1SP

SAGE Publications Inc.
2455 Teller Road
Thousand Oaks, California 91320

SAGE Publications India Pvt Ltd
B 1/I 1 Mohan Cooperative Industrial Area
Mathura Road
New Delhi 110 044

SAGE Publications Asia-Pacific Pte Ltd
3 Church Street
#10-04 Samsung Hub
Singapore 049483

Editorial Arrangement © Kristina Boréus and Göran
Bergström 2017
Chapter 1 © Göran Bergström and Kristina Boréus 2017
Chapter 2 © Kristina Boréus and Göran Bergström 2017
Chapter 3 © Kristina Boréus 2017
Chapter 4 © Mats Lindberg 2017
Chapter 5 © Alexa Robertson 2017
Chapter 6 © Kristina Boréus and Göran Bergström 2017
Chapter 7 © Anders Björkvall 2017
Chapter 8 © Göran Bergström, Linda Ekström and Kristina
Boréus 2017
Chapter 9 © Kristina Boréus and Göran Bergström 2017

First published 2017

Editor: Jai Seaman
Assistant editor: Alysha Owen
Production editor: Tom Bedford
Copyeditor: Catja Pafort
Proofreader: Aud Scriven
Indexer: Cathy Heath
Marketing manager: Sally Ransom
Cover design: Shaun Mercier
Typeset by: C&M Digitals (P) Ltd, Chennai, India
Printed by CPI Group (UK) Ltd, Croydon, CR0 4YY

Library of Congress Control Number: 2016944506

British Library Cataloguing in Publication data

A catalogue record for this book is available from
the British Library

ISBN 978-1-4739-1374-5
ISBN 978-1-4739-1375-2 (pbk)

Contents

About the Editors and Contributors

About the Editors

Göran Bergström is Assistant Professor in Political Science, Department of Political Science, at Stockholm University, Sweden. For a long time he was Director of Education. He has studied ideological change in Education Policy with a particular focus on the Swedish Labour Party. Recent publications include articles in pedagogical content knowledge, more specifically how the relation between content knowledge and pedagogical content knowledge is developed in social science/civics research projects (with Linda Ekström, Nordidactica – *Journal of Humanities and Social Science Education*, 2015). He has also recently studied how a central core value in the Swedish educational system has been interpreted among school leaders (with Linda Ekström, *Utbildning & Demokrati* 2016). Göran Bergström has published *Textens mening och makt* (with Kristina Boréus, Studentlitteratur), a Swedish textbook, third edition 2012.

Kristina Boréus is Professor of Political Science at Uppsala University, Sweden. She has studied ideology and ideological change, discrimination against migrants and racialized employees at Swedish workplaces, and right-wing populism in Austria, Denmark, and Sweden. Her publications in English include 'Patterned inequalities and the inequality regime of a Swedish housing company' (with Ulf Mörkenstam, 2015, in *Nordic Journal of Working Life Studies*); 'Nationalism and discursive discrimination against immigrants in Austria, Denmark and Sweden' (2013, in Wodak, R., KhosraviNik, M. and Mral, B. (eds) *Right-Wing Populism in Europe*) and 'Discursive Discrimination: A Typology' (2006, in *European Journal of Social Theory*). She takes an interest in different kinds of textual analysis as method and theory and has published *Textens mening och makt* (with Göran Bergström, Studentlitteratur), a Swedish textbook that appeared in its third edition in 2012.

About the Contributors

Mats Lindberg is professor in Political Science at Örebro University. For three decades he has been lecturing (at several Swedish universities) on the history of political ideas, as well as on social and political theory and philosophy of science. His dissertation (Uppsala University, 1979) was a theory-critical analysis of Karl Marx's *Capital*. He has made a widely read ideology-critique of the Swedish Social Democracy (1975) and has made theory-critical analyses of the Marxist Theory of the State (1982, 1985) and the concepts of Civil Society (1995) and Local Self-Government (1999). (All in Swedish.) He is one of the introducers of Jürgen Habermas to the Swedish public (1984) and the initiator of The Swedish Network in Political Theory (since 1993). At Lund University he is currently leading a research project on the renowned Swedish political scientist Herbert Tingsten, dominant liberal chief editor in the late 1940's and the 1950's. Mats Lindberg's latest publication is the new *Introduction* to the Swedish edition of Marx' *Capital* (2013). In the public debate Mats Lindberg has defended a left liberal or social democratic position of reformist rational argument against more fundamentalist views, both to the left and to the right.

Alexa Robertson is Professor of Media and Communication studies at Stockholm University. The red thread running throughout her work is the question of how media representation is conceived and effected in a world of diversity and transborder flows, with a particular focus on global television news. Her books include *Media and Politics in a Globalizing World* (Polity, 2015); *Global News: Between Conflict and Cosmopolitanism* (Peter Lang, 2015); and *Mediated Cosmopolitanism* (Polity 2010). Her current research compares (tele)visual narratives of dissent across time, space, media culture and genre (see screeningprotest. com for more information).

Anders Björkvall is Professor of Swedish Language at Örebro University, Sweden. He has published widely within the fields of multimodality, social semiotics, discourse analysis, literacy studies, and the ethnography of artefacts and texts. Recent publications include 'Places and spaces for multimodal writing in "one-to-one computing"', in *Multimodality in Writing: The State of the Art in Theory, Methodology and Pedagogy* (2015); 'Practices of visual communication in a primary school classroom: Digital image collection as a potential semiotic mode' (*Classroom Discourse*, 2014); 'Practical function and meaning: A case study of IKEA tables' in *The Routledge Handbook of Multimodal Analysis* (2013); and 'Multimodality' in *Handbook of Pragmatics* (2012). Anders has also published a Swedish handbook of multimodal analysis (*Den visuella texten: Multimodal analys i praktiken*, 2009), introducing the analysis of multimodal texts to a Scandinavian audience.

Linda Ekström has a PhD in political science and is currently employed as a researcher at the Swedish Institute for Educational Research. Previously she has held a postdoctoral position at the Department of Humanities and Social Science Education at Stockholm University. She has studied meaning making processes regarding questions of gender and power from a discourse analytical perspective, and together with Göran Bergström studied the implications of the use of different qualitative methods within the growing field of civics didactics. In their latest publication, Ekström and Bergström analyse school leaders' understanding of the contested concept of 'equity' from a discourse psychological perspective.

Companion Website

All of the texts on which the chapter exercises for *Analysing Text and Discourse: Eight Approaches for the Social Sciences* are based can be found at: https://study.sage pub.com/boreusandbergstrom.

1

Analyzing Text and Discourse in the Social Sciences

Göran Bergström and Kristina Boréus

A university lecturer wakes up in the morning. After her hot shower she quickly registers a few headlines in the daily paper before she puts it down on the breakfast table and turns on the radio morning news which also presents sports results. Uninterested, she turns the radio off and cannot avoid reading about the qualities of her cereals on the package while having breakfast. On the Underground she stares at an ad for electronics which claim to be very suitable as Christmas presents. Walking from the metro station to the university she is presented with a leaflet about a new exhibition and passing through the corridors to her office she registers pieces of texts on posters, information boards and cafeteria menus. During most of her workday she will be working with texts, consuming and producing them, while in lots and lots of other workplaces people will also read and write, speak and listen to others, all day long.

1.1 Texts in the study of power and other social phenomena

Before her workday has even begun the fictive lecturer above has been exposed to a large number of texts – some of which she has chosen to read, others that are just there as unavoidable parts of her surroundings. As this little story is meant to illustrate, texts are crucially important in modern societies. For that reason, they are also important objects of analysis for the social sciences. Through its different disciplines, people in societies are researched. The objects of study include power, politics, families, oppression, governments, equality, inequality, crime, economic markets, traditions, migration, conflict, consensus and many other social phenomena. Obviously when such phenomena are studied, texts are crucial artefacts.

Just to illustrate the importance of texts with an example from the list of social phenomena: take governments. They take decisions formulated in texts and express their proposals textually to parliaments. There are texts that regulate what governments may and may not do. In government departments, large amounts of texts circulate every day. Governments are criticized in texts. Not only do texts need to be studied by those who want to learn about governments, it is also difficult to imagine studies of governments that would not use texts as part of their materials. It is indeed hard to think of any social phenomena the study of which would not need the analysis of texts in the wide sense of 'text' that will be explained in this chapter. Before we turn to what a text is, we will exemplify how textual analysis might be applied when the object of study is the first one in the list above: power. Power is very often examined in social research and power-related issues will be used throughout the book to exemplify how texts can be analyzed in the social sciences. The examples here illustrate how the complex objects of study of the social sciences are constructed in different ways and how these differences imply different tasks for textual analysis.

There are several different ways of conceptualizing power. Steven Lukes (2005) describes it as having three dimensions (or faces). According to the **first dimension of power**,[1] power is about making somebody do what they would not otherwise have done. A typical example is when a decision is taken by a political body and those in opposition have to yield to the majority. In using such a concept of power texts like voting protocols and texts that express opinions could be analyzed. The **second dimension of power** is broader: the usage of **non-decision making**, when some issues are never put to a vote, perhaps due to shifty agenda-setting techniques, is also power. In this case, crucial texts can exist outside the arenas of decision making and could include statements or petitions from groups whose issues are excluded from the decision-making process. The **third dimension of power**, according to Lukes, is about manipulating people to want things that are not really in their interest. When such power over the minds and souls of people is studied, other texts become relevant. It might be assumed, for instance, that mass media play an important role in making people hold certain beliefs. In this case, mass media texts would be important to study. Pictures might be interesting to analyze from all the mentioned perspectives, but presumably most important for the third dimension of power. Images can influence us in partly unconscious ways, avoiding our shield of critical thinking – which is why they are so important in advertising.

The social sciences also use other concepts of power, such as that formulated by Michel Foucault. According to Foucault, studying power is not about finding out which agents have power over others, the way Lukes conceptualizes power studies. In Foucault's conceptualization, individuals do not have power – they are

---

[1]Note that the first time a term is explained or discussed in the book it will appear in bold.

instead **locations of power** (Foucault, 1980). Power is diffused, always shifting and present, almost everywhere, not least in the details – what Foucault refers to as the **micro-physics of power**. Power exists between people and within people as self-discipline. When studying power, one should analyze how it is exercised, its technologies – is it exercised e.g. by weapons, by linguistic means or through different forms of surveillance and control? The way power is institutionalized should also be investigated: institutions like families, prisons and mental hospitals create different conditions for power (Foucault, 1994: xv–xvi). An example of how texts can be used to study technologies of power and their institutionalization is provided when Foucault, in one of his major studies, *Madness and Civilization* (2001 [1967]), examines the shifting meaning of 'madness' in European culture, law, medicine and other contexts from the Middle Ages until the end of the nineteenth century. He uses not only texts that describe madness but also texts that describe how those considered mad were treated during different periods. Thus, Foucault uses reports by inspectors of the institutions where 'the mad' were confined that describe how they were treated – which can be understood as descriptions of the technologies of power used within institutions – to interpret how madness was understood. Such descriptions could give us important clues about how people with mental diseases were conceptualized at different points in time: e.g. as criminals that needed 'correction' or as animals that could not be corrected but needed to be locked away.

According to a conceptualization of power based in **critical realism**, a theory of science referred to by Norman Fairclough as related to CDA, critical discourse analysis (see Chapter 8), power is a potential: defined as possibilities created within the social structures in which agents (individuals or groups) act. Analyzing texts becomes a first necessary step in assessing how power is reproduced and how it changes (Fairclough, 1992: 113). If the project is to study how power changes in academia, we need to analyze policy documents and texts in which universities describe what they do and ask how the content of such documents and texts has changed over time. We also need to study which groups are allowed to influence important decisions in academia, such as the distribution of research grants and the content of the education (see Fairclough, 2015: 73–6). To analyze the texts is to study the 'empirical' domain (Bhaskar, 1978/2008: 56), which is necessary to get at the mechanisms that affect power relations which are to be found in the 'real' domain. Fairclough has often referred to the shifts in power relations between university staff, politicians, students and commercial interests as a result of changes in capitalism (Fairclough, 2015: 63–7).

As the examples show, texts can hardly be avoided in the study of power or other social phenomena. They are not the only things that ought to be analyzed: social practices need to be studied through observations of how people go about doing things; it might be necessary to ask people and to study other artefacts of societies, such as buildings. It might also be indispensable to study the distribution of goods such as money, arms or the ownership of the means of production. But text studies of one kind or the other are crucial to the sciences of people and societies.

A view of textual analysis as a method for the social sciences we would like to promote is that texts in one way or another relate to people and groups of people. People have created the texts and people are their addressees. Texts mirror conscious ideas as well as unconscious ones. They might reproduce, strengthen or challenge power and they also do myriads of other things in social settings. They can be studied in the quest for learning about relations between individuals or groups of people. It is in this way that texts become interesting from a social scientific point of view. They might also be highly interesting for other reasons, like stylistic or aesthetic ones, but that is not what this book is about.

As with any method, a student who wants to learn to use text studies will need to get a grasp of the basic ideas and techniques. The aim of this book is to function as a guide in such a learning process. The rest of this chapter is meant as a manual for reading and using the book. To begin with we explicate the central concepts of sign, text, genre and discourse.

1.2 Sign, text, genre and discourse

A basic concept in textual analysis is that of the sign. **Semiotics**, as elaborated by Charles Sanders Peirce and Ferdinand de Saussure (the latter of which used the word **semiology**), is the science of signs within human communication. A **sign** in language is conceptualized as the combination of a **concept** and a **sound-image**. When talking about trees we utter the word that is pronounced/triː/ in British English, and it has a written image: tree. 'Tree' is the sound-image of the sign. The sound-image is called the **signifier** and it signifies the concept of trees – the general idea of what trees are that we carry with us – which is the **signified** part of the sign. Figure 1.1 is a diagram based on Ferdinand de Saussure's definition of a sign.

Parts of the sign	Example
Sound-image (signifier)	'tree', 'träd', 'árbol', 'Baum', 'puu'…
Concept (signified)	The concept of trees

Figure 1.1 The sign, according to Saussure (Source: based on Berger, 2014: 8)

The relationship between the signifier and the signified is arbitrary: the concept of a tree could well be signified with other written or spoken words – which it is in other languages. This is the basic problem of interpretation: there is no natural connection between the words read or heard and the concepts they refer to. The meanings of signifiers are learned by individuals as social beings in relation to shared cultural understandings but not once and for all:

Anyone who communicates uses associations between signifiers and signifieds all the time. Because in real life the relationships are arbitrary and change rapidly, one must be on one's toes all the time. Signifiers can become dated and change their significance all too quickly. (Berger, 2014: 8)

Apart from words a vast amount of other phenomena have meanings and thus function as signs: when it comes to people, their clothing, hairstyles, brands of sunglasses, gestures, facial expressions and a lot else carry meaning. These become signs and obtain their meaning through culture and communication. Semiotics is not only about how meaning is created, but also about relations between signs. In semiotics all kinds of meaningful systems of signs are referred to with the word **text**: written documents, pictures, films, advertisements, parades, plays and other cultural products. In this book we use this wide concept of text that includes not only written text but also pictures, film, spoken text (such as speeches by political leaders) and other cultural products. The book is thus about how to analyze not only different kinds of texts, including written texts and images, but also **multimodal** ones – texts comprising different forms of communication – such as written messages and images which interact in conveying meaning.

Written texts are distinguished from random lists of letters or words by being coherent, communicative and cohesive. Being **coherent** means that they have themes that are rationally organized and can be followed in given cultural contexts. Being **communicative** refers to having a message, being meaningful to someone and requiring some kind of reaction from a person reading the text. **Cohesive** refers to how texts are delimited and internally kept together through linguistic means such as lexical repetition or referencing within the text (see Halliday and Hasan, 1976). Pictures and other non-written texts are also coherent (even though coherence in pictures is interpreted differently from that in written texts), communicative and to some extent cohesive through, for instance, uses of similar colour schemes in composite images.

Languages and other systems of signs, and therefore texts, can be understood to have three main functions, two of which are of particular importance for this book (see Fowler, 1991: 68–70; Halliday and Hasan, 1976). First, language is used to express thoughts and ideas. The **text producer** (author, speaker) uses language to reflect, to express their ideas about the world around them and their inner experiences. Such ideas are expressed in texts. This aspect is referred to as the **ideational** or **content aspect** of texts. Second, we use language in our social relations with others, e.g. to express an opinion, inform somebody about something, ask a question, greet somebody, give an order, or joke. Language is thus used not only for reflection but also for action. This aspect is called the **interpersonal aspect** of language. (The third function is the **textual** one that connects the other two functions into interpretable, communicative texts. Put differently, the textual metafunction has to do with how words and clauses are combined into coherent and cohesive texts.) If we take this book as an example, we, the authors, have spent a lot of work on its ideational aspect. We have, for instance, wanted to express a particular view of how textual analysis ought to be used within social sciences and how to explain methods clearly. We have also considered the interpersonal aspects of the text and asked ourselves questions such as who it is we are writing for, what function do we want the book to fill in academia, and what kind of reactions would we like to get. Related to these questions we have considered how to write clearly, what style and tone are appropriate, and so on.

Texts follow given conventions with regard to how they are both produced and consumed. They belong to different **genres**. Texts like news stories in daily papers, articles in journals of anthropology, children's school essays, emails and this book belong to different genres. Also texts that are not written – a telemarketer's interaction with a potential customer, a romcom movie, or a photo of a convict in a police file – can be said to belong to particular genres. Genres develop over time and in particular contexts. Texts in different genres have different purposes and uses. A recipe is meant to guide cooking, not to amuse or convince people to take certain political action. This is taken for granted both by the authors of cookbooks and someone who wishes to make a sponge cake at home. Genres can also be recognized by their special content, what they are about (McQuail, 2010: 370). Recipes are about quantities of ingredients and how to mix and treat these to obtain a certain result. They are also structured in a genre-specific way, often beginning with a short description of the dish to be made, and thereafter listing ingredients and what quantities to use, followed by a step-by-step description of how to make the dish.

We have now travelled from signs, the building blocks of texts, to genres or text types. The fourth basic concept to be introduced in this section is that of **discourse**. In Chapter 8 on discourse analysis there is a detailed explanation of different concepts of discourse. Here we will simply point to some common characteristics. Common to concepts of discourse used in the social sciences is that they refer to some kind of **social practice** as regards language use or the use of other sign systems in particular social contexts. Social practices are ways in which humans do things: patterns of action, habits and conventions that follow more or less explicit rules. Examples of social practices at universities are how teaching is carried out; how students interact at lunch breaks; which routines are followed when the university buildings are cleaned; and how staff wages are decided. In people's social practices, language use is crucial. Discourses are wholly or partly made up of language use as part of wider social practices. According to a narrower definition of 'discourse', discourses are merely the linguistic aspects of the wider social practices; according to other definitions 'discourse' refers to more aspects of social practices than only what is said or written. Both the narrower and the wider discourse concepts, in one way or another, connect rules and conventions for how people speak and write to other ways they act in societies. According to the narrow definition the discourse of university teaching would include how lecturers speak when they lecture or lead seminars, what they talk about (and what they keep silent about), which terms they use, the content of pictures and other material they use in teaching, and how that material is composed. According to the wider definition, the teaching discourse could also include the way lecturers move about (or stand still) in lecture halls, where students sit in relation to their teachers, and which software and equipment are used in teaching, from PowerPoint slides to microphones. Texts are concrete manifestations of discourses, such as a particular lecture given by a particular teacher or what they have noted on the whiteboard.

1.3 Approaches to textual analysis

To analyze something is to identify and scrutinize its components. Different approaches to textual analysis are about identifying and studying different parts of texts, different phenomena that relate to the two basic aspects of texts mentioned above, the ideational and the interpersonal. The book presents eight broad, partly overlapping, approaches.

Content analysis is used both within the humanities and social sciences. By conducting content analysis a student might make comparisons based on quantifications of different elements in texts, which may be useful, for example, if the purpose is to study changes over time. If it is found that the frequencies of certain words in certain genres, such as editorials, change over time, this could be a sign of ideological change. Content analysis might focus on both the ideational and the interpersonal aspects of texts. The approach is sometimes divided into qualitative and quantitative content analysis, respectively. In this book we treat these varieties as different in degree rather than in kind.

Argumentation analysis, which focuses on the structure of argumentation, is also in use in both the social sciences and the humanities and comes in several varieties. It might be of interest to study aspects of what different agents are arguing for or against, and with which arguments. Argumentation analysis is about the ideational aspect of texts since it studies certain ideas expressed in texts. Argumentation is used for persuasion. But people will use other means than arguments when trying to persuade, such as addressing someone's feelings rather than their intellect. Argumentation analysis is related to the wider approach of **rhetoric**, which is seen as an approach to the interpersonal aspect of attempts to persuade.

Qualitative analysis of ideas and ideological content is an approach with methodological roots and a long and venerable ancestry of studies in theology, history, philosophy, law, literature and political science. The key concepts are ideology and its component single ideas; the focus is on intentional action. Ideologies are analyzed as consisting of ideas which guide the actions and interactions that make up society with its institutions, social relations and power relations. The aim is to identify, interpret, describe and classify the ideological content in thought and language not only in existing institutions and social fields, but also in the debates, movements and organizations striving for preservation or change of the social order.

From its origins as a method used almost exclusively by historians, **narrative analysis** has spread to all branches of the social sciences and beyond. It involves the explication of stories as a way of gaining insights into ideological power and 'common-sense' understandings of the way the world works. A student might be interested in which components constitute a narrative, in what order different kinds of events take place and what roles there are in the story. Or they might want to study how something is narrated, e.g. whether the story-teller keeps their distance from the characters in a story or if they seem engaged with their destinies. The ideational aspect is most central in narrative analysis.

In the chapter on **metaphor analysis** and **critical linguistics** we have brought together two approaches to textual analysis with their roots in different fields of linguistics: metaphor analysis, as it is conducted within cognitive linguistics, and critical linguistics. Both approaches can be used to uncover less explicit ideological content in texts. The kind of metaphor analysis explained in this chapter is about the ideational aspect of texts, the idea being to reveal how people conceptualize abstract and complex social phenomena by studying which metaphors they use. Researchers who depart from critical linguistics claim that both grammar and choice of words in a text convey information about the world view expressed in that text. The ideational aspect of texts is central here, too.

In the chapter on **multimodal discourse analysis** we present tools for analyzing many visual resources and their ideational and interpersonal aspects. Images of all kinds, like written texts, can be manifestations of discourses. Interest in studying both pictures as such and multimodal texts, e.g. how writing and pictures interact on a website, has been growing lately. Although both verbal language and pictures can represent reality and are used to create and maintain social relations, they do so in different ways. In verbal language aspects such as the composition of a clause are used to express offers or demands; in pictures an important way in which this is done is by humans' different ways of looking at the viewer.

Discourse analysis – henceforth often DA – is also used both within humanities and the social sciences. As explained above, a way to understand a discourse is either as linguistic practice in context or as linguistic and other kinds of social practice. Aspects of discourses that might be studied are the frames for what ought (not) to be said in a particular context, which categories are in use and what is taken for granted but not explicitly expressed. The overarching purpose of DA is often to study issues related to power, an example being how different categories of people (like 'the mad' in Foucault's analysis referred to above) are linguistically constructed and how this might affect their possibilities to act. Discourse analysis is used to study the ideational aspects of texts.

The different approaches presented in this book have grown out of different academic traditions, and studies inspired by them are more or less clearly anchored in particular theories of science. In some of the chapters we discuss issues to do with the theory of science. We deal with two general aspects, epistemology and language. In the next section we introduce a few basic ideas that will be revisited in coming chapters.

1.4 Textual analysis, language and learning about the world

The theory of science deals with **ontology**, i.e. the issue of what is real and what exists, and **epistemology**, issues regarding knowledge and how we can know things. A number of epistemological questions will be brought up in the following chapters. Central epistemological questions are whether it is possible to know anything about reality and how we can obtain knowledge. One position here is that it is, at least in principle, possible to reach true knowledge. The **empiricists**, close to the school of **logical positivism** that was active from the late 1920s (Carnarp, 2002 [1928]), claimed that it is possible to gain knowledge by using our senses and that scientific knowledge can be reached using a **neutral observation language**, a language for scientific descriptions that would be neutral and objective in the sense of being related to the sensory experiences common to human beings (Kitcher, 2002). This neutral observation language would relate to reality and refer to its parts in exact ways. More modern scholars influenced by the empiricists consider these ideas too simplistic but still stress the relationship to sensory impressions and the distinction between reality and language.

The possibility of a neutral observation language is rejected by other approaches. They treat language as central and often claim that our knowledge is based in language. According to a **constructivist** view of language and reality, the two cannot be separated. We cannot meaningfully speak about reality without language working as a lens that makes us see things in certain ways. While the idea about the neutral observation language implies that it is possible to construct a language that adequately represents reality, this is impossible according to the constructivist idea. At least when it comes to ourselves as human beings and the societies we inhabit, there cannot be anything like neutral representation. Our minds create, through language, ways of seeing the world. It is meaningless to speak about realities other than those that we create for ourselves in our societies (Barthes, 1993 [1970]; Berger and Luckmann, 1966).

Yet another epistemological position is the above mentioned critical realism, developed by Roy Bhaskar, which can be considered a position in between the somewhat simplistic empiricist ideas on how to gain knowledge about reality and constructivism. According to critical realism it is possible to obtain knowledge about the **real domain** of social mechanisms by studying phenomena in the **empirical domain**, which is accessible through our sensory experiences and by studying processes that take place in what is referred to as the **actual domain**. While it is possible, according to critical realism, to gain knowledge about reality, data must be considered as dependent on our theories (Bhaskar, 1978/2008: 56–7; Collier, 1994: 52–4). Bhaskar's epistemology differs from positivism, which he sees as the dominating theory of science of our time – 'an ideology', as he refers to it. He does not accept the idea that we would be able to constitute an empirical world simply through our senses: reality cannot be reduced to a series of events that could be represented more or less automatically. Critical realism, however, also rejects positions that are often considered to be typical for constructivism, e.g. its inherent scepticism towards scientific knowledge and that all knowledge should be of equal worth (Bhaskar, 1986: 228–30).

Poststructuralist approaches emphasize the role of language and deny given meanings of social phenomena. Constructivism is one of their keystones, meaning that knowledge can never be neutral. In post-structural traditions such as some kinds of discourse analysis the term **essentialism** is used to question the empiricist way of understanding how knowledge can be gained. Poststructuralists criticize the tendency for social sciences to take categories like 'women', 'man' or 'class' as givens (Butler, 2007; Laclau and Mouffe, 1985). The category 'man' has no previously existing essence but is created in discourse. The category is differently constructed in different societies and at different times. It might also be differently constructed within different social groups in the same geographic setting. Thus poststructuralism defends anti-essentialism. Anti-essentialists argue for a pluralist approach to science (e.g. Rorty, 1995).

The poststructuralist emphasis on the unique role of language in understanding reality has been criticized from several standpoints. The current theory of **new materialism** comprises a critique aimed both at the idea that nature is reflected in language and the idea that language is the basis for our concept of reality (Barad, 2003; Åsberg et al., 2011). Another critique of poststructuralism aims at its unclear ontological and epistemological positions, sometimes described as relativistic. This kind of critique has also been aimed at poststructuralist discourse-analytical approaches. An attempt to meet this challenge is made by Howarth and Glynos (2007) who try to develop a stringent philosophy of science for discourse theory, i.e. the kind of discourse analysis primarily based on the writings of Chantal Mouffe and Ernesto Laclau (Laclau and Mouffe, 1985; 2008). As stated above, another variety of DA, critical discourse analysis as developed by Norman Fairclough, starts out from critical realism (Fairclough, 2010).

1.5 Textual analysis and interpretation

The verb 'to interpret' has two meanings in this book. On the one hand, it refers to the fact that texts must be interpreted: they must be understood, the meaning of what is stated must be drawn out of the text; signifiers must be related to particular signifieds. On the other hand, it refers to the step in the research process that follows the textual analysis where the meaning of the results is interpreted, i.e. their significance for the social scientific problem that the analysis was meant to shed light on. In this section we will only discuss interpretation in the first sense.

Both written texts and pictures need interpretation. Regardless of how the text is analyzed – through argumentation analysis, narrative analysis or other approaches – it has to be interpreted. Interpretation is a more or less complex process. The complexity is due to the research problem one is working on, the nature of the text itself and the kind of analytical approach chosen. In a content analysis where words are encoded, interpretation problems might not occur. In a discourse analysis in which both explicit and implicit meaning are important, the interpretation problems are likely to be more challenging.

We will begin with the interpretation context most relevant for the reader of this book: interpreting texts in order to conduct a social scientific study. This context is different from many others in which interpretations are made: e.g. reading a novel for pleasure or when people interpret each other's body language in everyday encounters. In this particular context of interpretation there are a number of crucial elements: the text, the discourse that the text is a manifestation of, the context in which it occurs, the text producer, the primary receiver or addressee of the text and the interpreting analyst, i.e. the researcher. The text producer might be a single person or an organized group of people, like an NGO, a board or a government. The interpreting analyst is a receiver, too, but a particular one. Firstly, because they do not interpret a text – say an advertisement – in exactly the same way as the addressees the advert was originally meant for, referred to here as the **primary addressee**. Secondly, because the analyst might have a particular interest, namely to interpret the primary addressee's understanding of the advert, hence they are interpreting an interpretation.

From these elements we will develop four strategies of interpretation: one that primarily relates the interpretation to the analyst, one that relates it to the producer of the text, one that relates it to the primary addressees and one that relates it to the discourse without focusing on particular agents. Neither of these strategies is pure: normally one does a little bit of everything but with different emphasis. In this context we will introduce a fundamental insight from **hermeneutics**, the art and theory of reading and interpreting, namely the role of the prejudices with which every reader approaches a text.

According to the **analyst-oriented strategy** the text means what the analyst reads into it. Hans-Georg Gadamer (1900–2002) stresses that every reader comes to a text with prejudices (Gadamer, 1989). The analyst is interpreting a text from their particular historical horizon. Without prejudices, interpretation is not possible. Our individual experiences, our understanding of the world, the social context in which we exist, our education, our knowledge of the genre of the text, our language, all influence our interpretation. Gadamer describes the analyst's own historically and socially conditioned prejudices as the starting point from which it is at all possible to appreciate texts from other times and cultures. The meaning of the text changes, since different readers interpret it differently in different historical contexts. It is impossible to reconstruct exactly what the author wanted to say with the text, hence also how other addressees have interpreted it. The text and we as socially and historically conditioned interpreters are what matters. Understanding texts is a never-ending process; the horizon of the interpreter is always integrated with other historically-determined horizons (Gadamer, 1975). The Gadamerian strategy can be described as putting the analyst at the centre. Most important, in our understanding, is awareness of the prejudices that always exist: we never meet a text as clean slates.

A variety of this interpretative strategy occurs when the analyst uses special tools or interprets with particular purposes related to the study that would be foreign to both the text producer and the primary addressees. To interpret Jean-Jacques Rousseau's texts with the help of game theory does not teach us a lot either about what Rousseau wanted to express or about how contemporary readers understood the text (see Hermansson, 1992 for such an interpretation). Rousseau was an eighteenth-century philosopher while modern game theory was developed in the twentieth century. But such an interpretation can be of value for other purposes, e.g. to generate new ideas or to show logical relations between elements in texts. It shows a new reading made possible by the new tools. This interpretation strategy can thus be seen as an extreme variety of Gadamer's way of reading.

The **producer-oriented strategy** is primarily focused on the meaning of the text at its production, not at its reception. The meaning of the text is decided by what the person or the people that formulated it meant it to mean. In hermeneutics Friedrich Schleiermacher (1768–1834) is often referred to as a researcher who considered interpretation to be a reconstruction of what the text producer meant, a form of interpretation that Gadamer opposed (Schleiermacher, 1998). Historians of ideas often use this way of reading when studying texts by dead authors. Art might also be interpreted that way.

In relation to this kind of interpretation Quentin Skinner gives us some sophisticated advice, the essence of which is, firstly, that it is essential to understand what kind of **speech act**[2] – what is *done* by this act of using language – has been carried out by producing the text. Did the author write a piece of social satire, a scientific report, a political pamphlet or something else? To be able to decide one has to be familiar with the kind of speech acts that were, or are, usually carried out by producing texts of that particular kind. What is an author of news articles, economic reports or medical records supposed to be writing (Skinner, 1988a)? Secondly, the meaning of the text must be interpreted in relation to the given author's language use and way of arguing. Skinner (1988b) stresses the importance of not reading one's own (the interpreter's) meaning into the terms used in the text. This is crucial when studying old texts, but the vocabulary does not need to be that old for

---

[2]The concept of speech act is drawn from linguist J.L. Austin (1975) but Skinner's use of the concept is wider than is usual in linguistics.

the interpreter to fall into linguistic traps. Thirdly, knowledge of context is very important for good interpretations. The context should, however, not be seen as decisive for what is expressed in texts but rather be of help for determining the frames inside which reasonable interpretations can be made.

Stuart Hall (1994) also has advice to offer to those interpreting texts from the perspective of the text producer. He is less interested in particular individuals (such as Mary Wollstonecraft, John Stuart Mill or whatever author's texts are being interpreted) and more interested in societal structures and the positions created by them for different agents. He concentrates on what resembles Skinner's first point. What might – say – a journalist on a TV channel in a particular part of India in the mid-2010s be doing when publishing a TV news report? What frames are created by technical issues, format of the news programme, owners of the TV channel and other social structures? What are the production routines, professional ideologies and the news producers' conceptions of their audience? Here Skinner's third advice for interpretation should be remembered, that the frames are just frames inside which great variation is possible.

When interpreting images we also use knowledge about conventions to understand what the text producer wanted to convey. We know that text inside a balloon above somebody's head in a comic tells us what the person says and that the cartoonist wants to convey that the person is in pain and dizzy when they draw a ring of little stars around the head of a character that has for example just been beaten over the head. This example illustrates the importance of a knowledge of conventions, in particular text genres, for the interpretation of texts, while the genres in themselves partly decide what speech acts are possible.

The purpose of the **addressee-oriented strategy** is to understand which meaning a particular text might have for its primary audience. The meaning of the text is determined by its reception, just as stated by Gadamer. In media reception studies it might be asked how certain groups of people – the poorly educated, the highly educated, people in blue- or white-collar jobs, female, male, young or old – tend to interpret a certain news item. Hall explains that different social groups interpret what they read, hear and watch from different frames of interpretation and sets of values. This interpretation strategy is thus about learning about the prejudices of others and how they meet with texts. Of relevance to some studies in this context is the concept of **preferred reading** (Hall, 1994), which refers to the reading that a text producer intended the addressees to make, or, more loosely, to a dominant reading that most people would have made at the time. But people also interpret messages in ways other than those intended by text producers and might produce oppositional readings, using alternative frames of reference.

According to the **discourse-oriented strategy** the text receives its meaning from a wider discourse in which agents are not the primary focus. In discourse analysis this is the most common strategy of interpretation. The meaning of a particular text is thus understood through other texts that it is related to and from discourses that the texts manifest. It works the other way round as well: the discourse as a whole is interpreted and understood from interpretations of many single texts. Discursive patterns – such as how categories are used, and the claims and evaluations that are made when particular subject matters are treated in particular contexts – are studied in a systematic fashion and these patterns are related to a wider social reality. An example of an interpretation of patterns in discourses not primarily interested in agents is Fredric Jameson's the **political unconscious**. He creates Marxian interpretations of fiction written in certain social conditions and finds in them expressions of social contradictions being symbolically processed in narratives (Jameson, 1989). This interpretation strategy is also used for images, symbols and multimodal texts. Recurrent images of the nation's flag as well as photos of triumphant members of the national team lifting the victory trophy towards the sky may be interpreted as **banal nationalism** (Billig, 1995), i.e. an everyday recurrent message that 'we' belong to the same nation which we naturally feel is ours, which we esteem and want to defend. Individual images of flags could not be interpreted in this way: every single image gets its potential meaning by being part of a social practice in which flags and other national symbols are often depicted.

Table 1.1 summarizes the four interpretation strategies. In practice, interpretations normally focus on several aspects.

To what degree the different interpretation strategies should be kept apart depends on the study. The meaning of the text encoded by the producer and how it is interpreted by its addressees will often overlap if they share a society and culture.

Table 1.1 Interpretation strategies

Interpretation strategy	Whose meaning is in focus?	What aspects should be studied?	Example of use
Analyst-oriented strategy	The analyst's as an addressee with special interpretative purposes	Patterns and particularities in texts available using particular interpretative tools	Specialized kinds of interpretations
Producer-oriented strategy	The text producers' as individuals or groups of people	The producer's particular social position and the speech acts likely to be performed in certain genres from that position; the addresser's normal language use; context	The history of ideas; interpretations of art and literature
Addressee-oriented strategy	The primary addressee's	Addressees as agents in particular social positions	Media reception studies
Discourse-oriented strategy	Meaning created through discourse	Discursive patterns regarding particular subject matters in particular contexts and the discourse in relation to its social context	Discourse analysis

The analyst might also be part of the same social context. In practice, many of the same steps should be taken whichever interpretation strategy is chosen.

We will end the discussion of interpretation with a practical example of interpretation in line with the producer-oriented strategy, which might easily be tilted towards the discourse-oriented strategy.[3] The example shows practical tools that will serve in most cases of interpretation. The text to be interpreted is a short passage from a well-known ideological text, *The Communist Manifesto* (1848) by Karl Marx and Friedrich Engels, namely the preamble. The first goal is to interpret its meaning according to its authors.

> A spectre is hunting Europe – the spectre of Communism. All the powers of the old Europe have entered into a holy alliance to exorcise this spectre: Pope and Czar, Metternich and Guizot, French Radicals and German police spies.
>
> Where is the party in opposition that has not been decried as Communistic by its opponents in power? Where the opposition that has not hurled back the branding reproach of Communism, against the more advanced opposition parties, as well as against its reactionary adversaries?
>
> Two things result from this fact:
>
> I. Communism is already acknowledged by all European powers to be itself a power.
>
> II. It is high time that Communists should openly, in the face of the whole world, publish their views, their aims, their tendencies, and meet the nursery tale of the Spectre of Communism with a Manifesto of the party itself.
>
> To this end, Communists of various nationalities have assembled in London, and sketched the following Manifesto to be published in the English, French, German, Italian, Flemish and Danish languages.

To start at the word-level, we do not think that the prejudices of a modern reader would make them, as Skinner warns, fall into traps. The word usage is rather modern and there is no need to consult an English dictionary from the time of the text production. Yet the text includes several words that need to be interpreted in their historical context to make sense to a modern reader. We find words that refer to historical persons, events or situations like the 'holy alliance', 'Metternich', 'Guizot', 'French Radicals', 'the nursery tale of the spectre', 'police spies'. These words are all void of meaning without specific background knowledge that must be obtained from encyclopedias, historical or political research, or textbooks.

Another kind of words whose interpretation might cause problems are 'Communism' and 'Communists'. What do they refer to? Do the authors have specific movements or ideologists-philosophers in mind? These questions could possibly be answered in the following parts of the *Manifesto*, or in other related

---

[3]This part of the chapter was written with Mats Lindberg.

texts by the authors. Another complicated term is 'the party', with a definite article, where we should avoid the pitfall that Skinner warns against, inferring ideas of what a party is from our own present word use. In 1848 in Europe there was no such thing as the modern party system. So what kind of entity does 'the party' refer to – something already existing or something hoped for?

Background knowledge gained from previous literature is thus indispensable. In some cases we will also need more textual material from the authors to be able to understand their usage of single words. We might also need to consult other relevant texts of the time. Lastly, we will need at least some knowledge of the historic situation to understand what the authors were saying. Just in the short preamble of the Manifesto several prominent statesmen representing different governments and diverse political movements are mentioned. Movements or political tendencies of the time were the monarchist, the national republican, the liberal radical, the reformist, and the socialist 'parties'; all lining up in different camps and with different power resources in the shattering turmoil of the upcoming revolution of 1848. Thus, knowledge about the social context in which the authors produced the text, as well as about their standard use of language, is indispensable. More knowledge about the particular speech act – what the authors were doing when launching a manifesto – would also help.

Thus, a successful interpretation focusing the producer's meaning normally needs four kinds of textual material: 1) the chosen text itself; 2) the relevant surrounding textual **corpus** (i.e. collection of texts of a certain kind) of the authors; 3) relevant texts by other authors and 4) texts that provide necessary information about the social and political situation at the time.

In a discourse-oriented interpretation strategy the goal is to understand the *Manifesto* through patterns in the discourse of which it is a textual manifestation, so we would need more material that informs us about the discourse, about the relevant linguistic practices in relation to wider social practices. In the case of *The Communist Manifesto* the relevant context involves numerous agents that all produced essays, pamphlets and articles in the political press. We would also presumably need to consult more material regarding the relevant context in which the discourse developed. These conditions involve the institutions of and the privileges of the church and the clergy as well as of the monarchy and the aristocracy.

Informed interpretation is a prerequisite for good textual analysis, but it is not sufficient. In the next section we discuss what more it takes.

1.6 What is a good textual analysis in a social scientific study?

A good textual analysis for the purposes described in this book is an analysis that casts light on a social scientific research problem. A good textual analysis as such is not necessarily relevant for such research problems. It is perfectly possible to analyze a political text from certain linguistic perspectives, answering questions of interest within the field of linguistics that lack relevance for politics as studied within political science. Such an analysis might reveal something about the language of the text without telling us much about politics. For an analysis to be relevant to the social sciences, it needs to ask questions relating to the study objects of these disciplines. Methods for answering such questions might be borrowed from linguistics' solid techniques of analyzing text and language or from other disciplines.

To answer research questions, methodological tools are needed. It is important both to know how to use different tools and to choose the right ones for the task. When wood needs to be chopped it is probable that the clumsiest axe-user will do a better job than an expert user of sewing machines. But unlike the woodcutter who can fall back on centuries of experience of wood cutting during which axes of all sorts were developed, the social scientist who wants to analyze texts lacks precise tools to choose between for particular research questions. There is nothing like an offer of readymade axes for different chopping purposes to choose from. Instead there are more general tools that in most cases need to be honed to precision and often combined with other available tools. This is important to keep in mind when reading this book.

The tool metaphor illustrates the aspect of a good study that is referred to as **validity**. In the empiricist perspective a method is valid if – and only if – it measures what is intended to be measured in a particular study. Is frequency of mosque visits a valid way of measuring the strength of religiosity in a community? Presumably in many cases but in others not at all, as in a predominantly Christian community. To turn to a real research example, Robert Putnam, in a renowned study, investigated to what extent **social capital**, i.e. social, trust-generating connections between people, generates democracy and economic growth (Putnam, 1993). He compared southern Italy with northern Italy. An indicator used for the existence of social capital was the proportion of people who read daily papers. Critical questions regarding the validity of the extent to which people read daily papers as a way of measuring social capital could well be posed.

To turn to textual analysis, take the research question of whether the views on 'madness' or mental illness differed between two points in time in a particular place. This could be analyzed by comparing two corpora including texts from the same genre and kind of context from the different points in time. There are more or less valid methods for making this comparison. Should we compare the lengths of sentences in the texts in the two corpora in a simple content analysis? Or perhaps use narrative analysis to compare in what order events are told in narratives that might possibly be found in the texts? There is reason to doubt that either of these strategies would be valid: why would they tell us anything about the views on mental illness expressed in the texts? We should start by going through some of the texts in search of a suitable method. Comparing how 'madness' or people categorized as mad are described, what treatment is proposed for them and what evaluative expressions are used about them might be more valid methods.

Yet another aspect of validity is the choice of texts to analyze for answering a particular research question. If, for example, one wants to conduct textual analysis to pin down the positioning of a political party in a particular policy area – say foreign policy – there will be a vast choice of texts to study: party manifestos, internal party publications, leaflets, webpages, private bills or propositions from a party that has been in government, minutes of parliamentary debates, documents from party conferences, texts from its youth organization if there is one, and many more. What texts ought to be analyzed to answer the question? The choice should be well motivated.

Theoretical ideas also play a part when it comes to validity. Is it sufficient to investigate who got a majority for their propositions and who was voted down to know who exercised power in the university board? *Yes it is, it is a valid method for analyzing power*, an adherent of power's first dimension would answer. *No, it is not*, someone who prefers the second or third dimension of power would argue, *that is not a valid way of measuring power*.

The meaning of the concept of validity in relation to a constructivist take on research is more complex. Some authors claim that the issue of validity changes if the terms used in the social sciences do not refer to objects that researchers can study and judge regardless of their own prejudices. When questions about power, oppression, criminality or any other social scientific object of study are asked, the researcher is not just an outside observer. On the contrary, they are involved in shaping the study objects and their own prejudices limit the possible answers to the research questions. For that reason not only the research tools but also the researcher with their historically and socially influenced prejudices must be taken into account when evaluating validity. If researchers widen their understanding of their own prejudices, e.g. by learning more about the culture of science in which they have been trained and the social context in which their research takes place, validity can be improved (see Salner, 1989).

Good validity is not enough to make a study credible. Even though it might be preferable to use an axe clumsily to trying out a sewing machine on wood, some ability to handle an axe is necessary to get the wood chopped. It is, for example, crucial to hit the wood rather than other nearby objects. In other words, there is a need for precision. This is true also for the research study. This aspect is referred to as **reliability**. When this concept is used in the context of an empiricist view of science the way of obtaining high reliability is to be sufficiently accurate in measuring and counting. The concept may also be used in a broader sense and refer to operations other than measuring and counting. It then refers to being accurate and precise in all steps of the study and to eliminating sources of error as far as possible. For most textual analyses interpretation is a matter of reliability. Whatever interpretation strategy is used, the reading must be careful enough for the purpose.

A way of testing reliability is to compare the results of independent studies of the same phenomenon which were carried out in the same way. If different persons conduct them and reach the same results, they have a high **intersubjectivity**.

How strongly intersubjectivity is emphasized varies with the theory of science. The empiricist ideal states that it should be possible for different researchers to use the same type of analysis of the same material (e.g. a text corpus) and reach exactly the same results. This is an ideal based on the idea of a neutral observation language. In social sciences and humanities that use interpretation of human communication and activities, this ideal is controversial. Even if complete intersubjectivity is seen as an impossible ideal, good research should still be transparent and the results well argued for. The reader should be able to reconstruct the steps taken by the researcher to reach the conclusions. For this to be possible, interpretations of written texts should be argued for with the help of quotes and records of the texts. The interpretation of pictures can be argued for by using descriptions of the image, references to its context and the meaning that certain camera angles, for instance, have in a particular genre.

Another aspect of reliability is **intrasubjectivity**. Good intrasubjectivity implies that the same person gets the same results from the same kind of analysis of the same material at different points in time. The purpose is to guarantee that the researcher is judging consistently. This is particularly important when comparisons are made. If the differences found between corpora from different points in time are best explained by the researcher having judged the texts of the corpora in different ways, there is a reliability problem at hand. In that case the result is due to differing researcher judgments and not to differences in the texts.

Texts and documents that function as **sources** ought to be handled in particular ways. A source is a text that is invoked to extract particular pieces of information, which contributes to accepting this piece of information as true; i.e. a text used to verify data, thereby taking a part in the production of evidence. Minutes, interviews and research articles are common sources in research. A first step in evaluating sources is to answer the question: is this source authentic? This is sometimes known as **external criticism of sources** and deals with whether the document is genuine: is it what it is claimed to be (Tosh, 2015: 102)? The next step in evaluating sources is **internal criticism**, which involves an assessment of the credibility of the text content. If one wants to reconstruct a course of events by the use of texts, such an evaluation is indispensable. What kind of information did the text producer have access to? Did they have an interest in lying, idealizing, understating or overstating? From what perspective, what position, did the text producer view what happened? What could and could not be known from this position? Is the text a primary or secondary source?

Table 1.2 summarizes what has been stated about good research above.

The description above should not be taken to mean that we look upon the research process as compartmentalized into neat units that follow a particular order: a research question is asked, it is decided how it should be answered, the material for the study is selected, relevant theory is chosen, the analytical tools are developed, the analysis is conducted and the results reported. This is not the way things usually work out. When these steps are described in a research article it

Table 1.2 Criteria for good textual analysis for social scientific purposes

Criterion	Aspects and meaning
Posing of good research questions about the study objects of social sciences	
Choice of appropriate methods	Might include adapting analytical tools found in the literature to suit the particular study
Informed interpretation of text content	Awareness of which interpretation strategy is used
Validity	• Choice of right method to answer each particular research question • Well-motivated choice of appropriate texts for answering each research question
Reliability	• Being accurate and precise in all steps, including counting, measuring and interpreting texts • Intersubjectivity (= the possibility for other researchers to repeat the study and reach the same results; particularly important from an empiricist view of science) • Intrasubjectivity (= the result of the researcher themselves having judged all parts of a corpus consistently)
Transparency	In all methodological steps, including interpretation
Well-argued results	
Appropriate handling of texts that function as sources	• External criticism (= judging whether the source is genuine) • Internal criticism (= credibility assessment of text content)

is normally not a description of how the research process actually developed. The process is usually much messier than that: one tries to develop the research questions and the analytical tools simultaneously, perspectives and research questions change throughout the process, coincidences lead to new ideas. In some ways inspired cooking is a good metaphor for the research process. The actual result depends on the time and cooking utensils at the cook's disposal, previous cooking experience and available ingredients. An inspired cook does not always follow given recipes but can draw an advantage from the cookbooks they read and the cooking courses they attended previously.

It is our hope that this book will be used like a cookbook by an inspired cook. We explain how food processors, sharp knives and different kinds of pans might be used and provide examples of how others have used such utensils. The purpose is not that you should slavishly follow recipes however.

1.7 How to use this book

Apart from this introductory chapter the book contains seven more chapters, each of which presents an approach to textual analysis, as well as a chapter with suggested solutions to the exercises included in the other chapters. The approach chapters are all organized in the same way. To begin with there is a 'Background' section that provides an overview and puts the approach in perspective. Sometimes this part relates the approach in question to other approaches, sometimes it explains key concepts. In some chapters the background section is fairly long since we wanted to shed light on a theoretical issue.

The purpose of the 'Analysis' section – which is at the heart of each chapter – is to demonstrate how the methodological approach can be used in social science studies. These demonstrations are very hands-on and their objective is to make it possible for readers to use the analytical tools in their own studies. To show how they might be used in a detailed fashion, we present existing studies or parts of studies; in some cases we have constructed the examples ourselves for the purpose of the book.

After 'Analysis' follows a section entitled 'Critical reflections', which is meant to deepen the understanding of each approach and be of help both to those who have already decided to use the method in question and to those still hesitant about whether or not to use it. This section frequently points out the pros and cons of the practical usage of the method. Sometimes it discusses more theoretical issues, e.g. questions to do with epistemology, language or interpretation; in some chapters issues of reliability and validity are brought up.

The section '… analysis and the study of power and other social phenomena' has been included to stress the importance of always asking whether a particular method is relevant for studies within the social sciences. Not surprisingly we have only included methods that, in our opinion, are suitable for social science studies. Suitability is, however, always a matter of which methods are relevant for answering particular research questions. In this section we sometimes discuss the approach as such while sometimes we refer to studies in which it has been used.

Every chapter has a 'Summary' in two parts. The first part examines for what the approach is and is not useful, the second summarizes the central elements of an analysis according to the approach in a step-by-step fashion. The summary can be used either as a way for a reader to check whether they have missed an important part of the chapter or be read at the beginning to gain an overview of the content of the chapter.

A section 'Suggested reading' contains commented suggestions for those readers who want to broaden their understanding of the method or dig deeper into certain aspects.

A student who really wants to learn to use the methods and not only get an orientation about them should work with the exercises included in each chapter. The exercises are all about trying out the methods on real texts. A 'Suggested analysis' for each exercise is provided in the concluding chapter. The analyses we suggest are also examples of how the different kinds of textual analysis can be conducted and can be used as such after reading the approach chapters. A reader who tries the analysis out before comparing it with our suggestions will get the best value out of the exercises.

The book, like most textbooks, ends with a list of all the references and an index for the many terms explained in the different chapters.

This book is primarily meant for college and university students and researchers. It should be useful not least for thesis writing. For those who choose to analyze different kinds of texts in doing research for their Bachelor's or Master's theses this book will presumably be sufficient as a methodological basis. If needed some of the literature recommended under 'Suggested reading' can be added. For PhD students and other researchers not very familiar with textual analysis the book can be used as an overview of methods and a gateway to further reading. The seven approach chapters can be read separately, but this introductory chapter should be read first.

Before we enter the maze of text analytical paths, we want to stress an important point: that research starts with problems, with research questions about a subject matter. Methods – in this book various kinds of textual analysis – should not become aims in themselves and should be considered and used in relation to research problems as well as theory.

Suggested reading

Berger (2014) is a basic and accessible introduction to semiotics and how it could be used in media analysis.

Introductions to the theory of science can widen one's theoretical understanding of language, text and power. Alan Chalmer's introductions to the question of what characterizes science are important (1990; 1999). For a deeper understanding of critical realism its best known representative (Bhaskar, 1978/2008) or an introduction to critical realism (Collier, 1994) can be consulted. Rorty advocates a completely different approach, exemplified in *Philosophy of Hope* (1999).

Robert Audi's extensive introduction to epistemology (2010) can be recommended, as could *The Oxford Handbook of Epistemology* (Moser, 2005). Both present different epistemological positions, such as varieties of constructivism and empiricism. John Searle's (1997) work on constructivism has been seminal. Bruce Aune's (1970) *Rationalism, Empiricism and Pragmatism: An Introduction* is a standard work for argumentation about rationalism (knowledge through reason) and empiricism (knowledge through sensory experience).

A number of journals in different disciplines publish hermeneutic and empirical studies in which different models for interpretation are used (e.g. Carpenter, 2003; Kinsella, 2006; Lee, 1994). There are a number of works by Gadamer himself and about his writings and hermeneutics to choose from. One of his most important works is *Truth and Method* (1989), another one is *The Relevance of The Beautiful and Other Essays* (1986), which presents his general ideas on hermeneutic thinking. There are about 30 works on Gadamer in English, e.g. Silverman's *Gadamer and Hermeneutics* (1991), Weinsheimer's (1985) *Gadamer's Hermeneutics: A Reading of 'Truth and Method'* as well as Wiercinski's (2011) *Gadamer's Hermeneutic and the Art of Conversation*. After Gadamer's death in 2002, *The Gadamer Reader* (Grondin, 2007) was published.

2

Content Analysis

Kristina Boréus and Göran Bergström

2.1 Background

In 1743, a collection of 90 hymns called *Songs of Zion* appeared in Sweden. Although the collection passed state censorship it was later accused of undermining the clergy of the Swedish state church and of being dangerously popularized and benefitting an oppositional religious group. A number of scholars got involved in a controversy over whether the songs really had a subversive content. They began counting some religious symbols in the suspect songs and the same symbols in established songbooks but found no difference. This is probably the first well-documented content analysis (Dovring, 2009). In the late 1800s, what was referred to as 'quantitative newspaper analysis' was already conducted in the United States. The sociologist Max Weber (1864–1920) predicted in 1910 that researchers would now start to measure quantitative changes in newspaper content (Weber, 2009). During the Second World War the British intelligence service used content analysis of Nazi Germany's propaganda directed at the German people to draw conclusions about the new German weapons of mass destruction – the results were good (George, 2009). During the second half of the twentieth century, the new medium of TV sparked an interest in the analysis of more than written text: pictures and film sequences could also be studied! In the 1950s what came to be referred to as 'qualitative', in contrast to 'quantitative', content analysis was developed (Schreier, 2014). In the twenty-first century, the development of computer software and the existence of large amounts of text in digitized form have created new opportunities.

2.1.1 Quantitative and qualitative content analysis

Content analysis, in other words, has a long history. All content analysis uses **coding** to systematically break down, categorize and describe the content of texts. Some authors define 'content analysis' as a quantifying method (e.g. Shapiro and Markoff, 1997). Others, like Schreier (2014), make a distinction between quantitative and qualitative content analysis. The basic concept of **quantitative content analysis** is then that it is a method for counting or measuring something in texts because it is thought that the frequencies, or that the fact that there is more or less of something in texts, are indications of something outside the texts. This definition of content analysis has its roots in an empiricist view of science. Manifest aspects of texts, i.e. what is explicitly stated, are searched for. The method is predominantly deductive in the sense that the research questions, often generated from some theoretical notion rather than from the texts themselves, are the basis for working out the tools for analyzing the texts.

Qualitative content analysis sometimes refers to textual analysis where nothing is counted or measured. Schreier describes this as "a method for systematically describing the meaning of qualitative data [performed by] assigning successive parts of the material to the categories of a coding frame" (2014: 170). She also describes it as a method that is at least partly inductive (data-driven), meaning that although the researcher might start from broader themes or research questions when analyzing the material, the text is coded directly, with categories growing out of that coding. The label 'qualitative content analysis' is also frequently used for analyses in which quantification is part of the analysis but more complex interpretations must be made (see for example the description of 'summative content analysis' as one kind of qualitative content analysis in Hsieh and Shannon, 2005). In this chapter we describe several different kinds of content analysis where some kind of counting – whether simple or more advanced – takes place.

A fruitful way of understanding the distinction, we claim, is that the difference between quantitative and qualitative content analysis is relative. If the counting or measuring involved is more prominent and complex, the content analysis is more quantitative than if counting and measuring are less prominent methods. Another way of making this distinction is to state that more qualitative analyses use complex interpretations of texts while less qualitative ones use simpler interpretations. Seen this way, the most quantitative studies have counting or measuring at their heart and interpretation becomes so simplified that a computer application can encode the text. The most qualitative studies use complex interpretations that can only be done by humans and use very simple ways of counting how many times something occurs in a text. Then again, many studies conduct both qualitative and quantitative content analysis on the same material. Luckily it is not important to be able to categorize a study as either quantitative or qualitative or to draw the line between the methods: what is important is, as always, to be able to describe how the results were obtained.

2.1.2 The uses of content analysis

Content analysis is used in several subjects in the social sciences and humanities, not least in media studies. Qualitative content analysis especially has become popular in health science. Recent developments in **corpus linguistics** – the study of langue as it appears in corpora of real world texts – have brought this linguistic sub-discipline closer to social sciences by engaging with language in its social use. Many of the techniques used by corpus linguists are also useful for content analysis.

Any kind of text may be content analyzed: reality TV shows, advertising, editorials, novels, stamps, comics, filmed psychologist–patient communication, textbooks, religious scriptures, tourist brochures ... Virtually any element in texts could be categorized, counted or measured, e.g. the presence of certain words or expressions, metaphors, arguments of a particular type, headline size or how often a particular phenomenon is referred to. One may want to examine both textual aspects mentioned in Chapter 1. Most common, at least in the social sciences, is to study the ideational aspect: what does the text state? The interpersonal aspect of texts could also be explored by using content analysis. How, for example, do different texts speak to their recipients: asking, pleading, or demanding? The examples in this chapter focus on the ideational aspect.

When aspects of texts are counted or measured this is done because the researcher understands that these aspects are indications of something else. In the sample studies in this chapter the presence of certain words in party manifestos is seen as an indication of the party holding a particular policy position (Laver and Garry, 2000); the number of articles reporting on particular types of crime is taken to reflect the newsworthiness of such crimes (O'Connell, 1999); the presence of certain ideas in party manifestos is seen as another indication of the parties' policy positions (Laver and Garry, 2000), as is the expression of certain ideas in parliamentary speeches (Boréus, 1997); while different aspects of a cartoon strip (like who the characters are and what they say) are thought to indicate the political leaning of the cartoon (Shannon, 1954).

Content analysis is suitable for finding patterns in larger bodies of materials, such as multiple letters to the editor, party election manifestos, ads, novels, or larger transcriptions of interview material. The approach can be used with broad categories, as when one goes through the foreign reporting in newspapers for a certain period in order to find out how many articles were published on a particular region of the world, or for more complex classifications, as when one records a particular type of metaphor in a corpus.

Content analysis is very useful for *comparing different corpora*, like the methods explained in Laver and Garry (2000) that can be used to compare the manifestos or other policy documents of different parties. For this reason the approach is also good for *analyzing changes over time*, which can be done by comparing the same kind of text from different time periods, as in Boréus (1997) in which ideological change is detected through a comparison of the expression of certain ideas in political speeches. Given that the possibility to generalize and to examine overall societal patterns and changes over time is central to the social sciences, quantitative content analysis provides a kind of general information that the other analytical approaches presented in this book – with the exception of corpus linguistics, briefly introduced in Chapter 6, and critical discourse analysis when using corpus linguistic techniques (see Chapter 8) – are rarely capable of.

Content analysis is not only used for comparing different corpora or for studying changes over time. One may also wish to examine *the attention paid to a particular topic*. One can count how frequently news articles on a particular theme occur or how many TV news broadcasts during a time period deal with a particular topic. An additional kind of analysis suitable for print media is to measure column centimetres reporting on the theme, or make a word count. Columns about a particular topic can also be counted. A further standard method is to study the location of articles, such as what is selected as front-page news. In one sub-study (that we do not account for further) of the study on crime reporting in the Irish press that is used as a sample study in this chapter, the number of words was used as a measure of newsworthiness (O'Connell, 1999).

A study of the attention paid to a topic might be the backdrop to studies that aim at *making a comparison with data pertaining to conditions in the wider society*. This was done in the research project 'Ideas and Images on Television' (von Feilitzen et al., 1989) on Swedish public service television content from transmissions in 1982. One of the project's theoretical notions was that groups in the population that were strongly underrepresented on television were often underrepresented because they were rated lower in society. This invisibility was thought, in turn, to contribute to these groups being disparaged. Corresponding US studies had found significant underrepresentation of working-class people, ethnic minorities, women, the elderly and children on TV. The Swedish project, too, showed that women, children, people above the age of 65 and working-class persons were rather heavily underrepresented in relation to their proportion of the population. Perhaps surprisingly, people of Swedish nationality were also underrepresented in drama programmes (von Feilitzen et al., 1989). The explanation for this was hardly Swedish nationals' low rating in society but that a large proportion of fiction programmes were imported (mainly from the US and UK). Studies of this kind might be of interest to understand cultural patterns.

Often one is not interested solely in how frequently a topic occurs but more in *how it is evaluated or portrayed*. The researcher might want to examine the extent to which something is valued positively or negatively and/or whether there is any difference in such evaluations between different sources or whether the same source makes different evaluations of a phenomenon. Negative or positive statements about or descriptions of something might be counted in more quantitative content analyses; more qualitative analysis might also be used. One of the studies explored further in this chapter uses open questions to be answered by coders about the content of a US cartoon strip to bring out its political content (Shannon, 1954).

2.2 Analysis

In this section, we first go through general steps in the analysis and present some key concepts of the method before we discuss possibilities for using software in content analysis and take a detailed look at the sample studies.

2.2.1 Analytical steps and key concepts

Starting out from a research question that might be answered with the help of content analysis, one of the first tasks is to choose and collect the texts to be analyzed. It is advisable to start by examining a small number of texts in order to get an idea of which kinds of texts can provide the relevant information. If it is going to be a media study a number of choices still remain: which parts of a newspaper or what TV programme genre will be analyzed, which particular papers or programmes will be included, from which time period will the sample be drawn? These should all be decided in relation to the purpose of the study. If one intends to study newspaper content over a long period of time, one might need to reduce the material further by taking samples. Texts sourced on the Internet provide particular selection challenges (McMillan, 2009). The materials selected should be representative of the corpus under investigation. The importance of having good reasons for the choice of texts is not specific to content analysis. Chapter 6 in Krippendorff (2013: 112–25) gives a detailed account of sampling methods.

The next step in the process lies in constructing an analytical instrument that shows what should be noted and counted in the material. Such an instrument is usually referred to as a **coding scheme** in manual quantitative content analysis. The word 'code' has to do with elements in texts, e.g. certain words, being recorded by means of a numerical code (see Table 2.3). When the coding scheme has been developed it should tell us exactly what to note in the analyzed texts. More complex coding schemes are often accompanied by a separate **coding instruction**, which describes how the assessments should be made in unclear cases. An analytical tool for computer-based content analysis is a **dictionary** that tells the software which words or phrases should be noted in a text corpus. In qualitative content analysis the sorting tool is often referred to as a **coding frame** (Schreier, 2014). Coding frames used in qualitative content analysis might be amended during the analysis.

Before constructing this kind of analytical tool it is wise to first become familiar with the material by reading all of it (if its size is manageable) or going through parts of it (if the corpus is too big to be read in its entirety). Just as with any textual analysis, some genre awareness is indispensable. Knowledge of the discourse of which the texts are manifestations and of the social context in which they were produced is also necessary in almost all cases. It was stated above that quantitative content analysis is often thought of as a deductive method, where the coding scheme is constructed on theoretical grounds and then used on texts, while in qualitative content analysis the coding frame grows out of inductive coding, starting with the text content. We recommend a combination of a deductive and an inductive approach in the construction of this analytical tool.

After the coding scheme and the coding instruction have been sketched out, they need to be tested on parts of the material. This process almost always reveals a need for modification of the coding scheme and for clarification of the instructions. This normally needs to be done several times. It is also appropriate to conduct some double coding (see below) at an early stage in order to check whether the analytical tools are sufficiently well developed to enable consistency in the assessment of the material. Letting someone else use one's analytical tools at the design stage can also reveal oddities that you as a researcher had difficulty detecting yourself.

Constructing coding schemes means deciding what to count. The phenomena to be first noted and then counted are called **coding units** or **recording units** (Krippendorff, 2013) and can be references to certain phenomena words, metaphors, themes, kinds of arguments or anything else that might be identified in texts. The characteristics of coding units 'vary'. Phenomena can for instance be spoken of in a neutral, appreciative or derogatory way. The varying characteristics of coding units are sometimes referred to as **variables**.

The **context unit** (Krippendorff, 2013; McMillan, 2009) is the unit of text that is treated separately and where notations for the presence of a coding unit are made. A coding instruction can for example state that the expression of certain ideas should be noted once for each political speech in a corpus consisting of such speeches. But the speech can also be broken down so that each section or each sentence constitutes a context unit. A context unit on the Internet can be a website, which requires further clarification, particularly of how many levels should be analyzed (McMillan, 2009: 65–6).

Once functional tools have been developed, a **pilot study** of a small part of the corpus should be conducted. This involves carrying out content analysis of a text sample exactly in accordance with the principles developed for the entire study. Sometimes the pilot study leads to the identification of additional problems with the analytical tools that will have to be dealt with. Sometimes one finds no problems; in that case the pilot study results can be part of the overall results. Once the pilot study has been conducted and possible adaptions to the tools of analysis made, the entire corpus can be analyzed.

As the goal of the analysis is to find patterns in a corpus it is important that the coding scheme or frame is used consistently. If the purpose is to compare a set of texts to another, it is important that the two sets are analyzed in exactly the same way, otherwise the differences found might reflect differences in judging rather than differences in the actual corpora. To ensure a reliable outcome, researchers coding alone will usually conduct a **double coding** with themselves to ensure intrasubjectivity, i.e. the correlation between one's own coding of the same texts at different points in time (see Chapter 1). This involves re-coding parts of the material and comparing the results of the two coding rounds. In order for the coder to forget how the individual assessments were done the first time, sufficient time should elapse between the two coding rounds. If one remembers exactly what assessments were made the first time the double coding does not test the clarity of the coding instructions but merely one's memory. If the results do not agree well, this is an indication of inconsistent assessments. The remedy then becomes to clarify the coding instructions. Another possibility is to merge two categories that prove difficult to distinguish. Since the tools of analysis may need to be reworked, it is important that double coding is implemented at an early stage.

With more than one coder it is important to check that all coders make similar assessments, i.e. that the intersubjectivity is satisfactory. Otherwise different results for different parts of a corpus might be due to coders making different judgments rather than reflecting differences in the corpus itself. To check consistency, all coders can code the same selected small parts of the corpus.

In addition to striving to ensure that all coders assess the material in the same way, an often stated reason for the performance of double-coding is that it should be in principle possible for another researcher to reach the same results using the same tools on the same texts. This is sometimes a reason to let someone else double-code parts of the corpus even if there is only one coder. The purpose is then to check whether the coding scheme and instruction are unambiguous enough for someone else to reach the same results. This aspiration stems from ideas on general scientific intersubjectivity and the **cumulativity of science**. The notion of intersubjectivity relates to the idea that there is an objectively assessable reality that we, with our human senses, perceive similarly, thus, with an empiristic view of science (see Chapter 1). The ideal of scientific cumulativity is that it should be possible to relate each piece of research to other studies so that the body of knowledge accumulates. If it is possible to repeat a content analysis and get the same results, it is also possible to make analyses with the same coding schemes and coding instructions on other corpora, so that the results can be compared.

What is considered to be an acceptable level of deviation between different coders or between different codings by the same person depends on the extent to which discrepancies in the assessment would influence the results one is interested in. If one needs relatively precise figures, high intra- or intersubjectivity should be sought. If one is after a rough measure of difference, such as which newspaper contained the most articles on a given theme and, in addition, one finds that the difference between the papers is large, a higher degree of mismatch can be accepted. For such a result to be biased it would take more serious problems with the intra- or intersubjectivity. There are various conventional ways to calculate the correlation between different codings, but little agreement on which measures are best suited (see Krippendorff, 2013: Chapter 12). The main idea is often to seek to determine how large a proportion of correspondences in the assessments is unlikely to be the result of chance. Simpler calculation methods are also used. QDA applications (see below) might have built-in intra-/intersubjectivity tests.

Sometimes it happens that the coder's assessments during the process of analysis – such as the judgment of how clearly something must be stated to be deemed to express a particular idea – gradually tip over in a particular direction. This creates a reliability problem. A way to minimize the effect of such unintended systematic shifts in assessment is to consider the order in which one analyses the texts in a corpus. If two sets of texts from two different periods are compared, one should not analyze one set first and then the other. If there is any systematic drift in the assessment it can affect the outcome so that the two sets of texts are analyzed according to different principles. If the coder instead goes back and forth between the corpora, such systematic slippages in the analyses are less important to the outcome.

When the entire material has been analyzed, the results of the quantitative content analysis are processed. A common and easy way is to calculate the frequencies of the coding units, i.e. adding all occurrences. One may also be interested in the relationships between codes, e.g. correlations. More advanced statistical analyses, such as factor analysis, can be created from the results, which assumes that the coding has been planned so that this is possible. At this stage, the results of manual coding can be further processed with the help of computer software. When the results of the content analysis have been processed in this way it remains to interpret the results in relation to the research questions posed.

In qualitative content analysis, the coding frame – which represents an interesting way of categorizing the content of the material – might be the main result in itself. The frame might then be presented together with quotes that illustrate the different categories (Schreier, 2014).

2.2.2 Content analysis and the usage of software

Software might come in at different stages of the analysis and in different ways. Firstly, there are applications to assist with manual coding; secondly, there is special software developed for computerized content analysis, i.e. where the application does the coding; and thirdly, SPSS, Stata or similar applications are needed if more advanced statistical calculations will be part of the study.

If possible, we recommend that qualitative data analysis (QDA) software should be used for any manual coding task that is more complex than just counting words. Software packages like NVivo, MAXQDA and Atlas.ti have very handy coding functions which allow one to save, rework and organize one's coding in time-saving and creative ways. The content analysis remains 'manual' when such software is used in the sense that – contrary to a computerized analysis – all texts are read by the coder, and exactly the same kind of interpretation and the same coding decisions are made as when one works with pen and paper. Compared to marking different parts of the texts in a pile of paper with different coloured pens (which is not an uncommon method), working with QDA software means enormous gains in both time and reliability in that it keeps materials orderly and makes precise comparisons possible. This goes for all larger projects (like writing a PhD thesis) and for all researchers who plan to analyze large numbers of texts again in future research. For students writing a Bachelor's or Master's thesis, utilizing complex QDA applications like the ones mentioned above might not really be an option for two reasons. Firstly, not all departments give their students access to these applications, while buying them is not an option for many a student wallet. Secondly, these applications only provide time savings in the long run. They take time to learn and it is hard to avoid some disheartening experiences like losing files and codings during the learning process; a Bachelor or Master student probably does not have the time both to learn how to use QDA software properly and to write their thesis. The remaining option for coding units larger than words might be coloured pens after all.

When it comes to coding words only, there are options other than the specialized software developed for content analysis mentioned above, namely applications used for corpus linguistics, such as WordSmith Tools. There are also freeware applications – AntConc probably being the best known of these – that perform similar tasks and also suit the purposes of content analysis.

Box 2.1

QDA software suitable for coding and software for statistical analysis of coding results

AntConc	http://www.laurenceanthony.net/software/antconc/
ATLAS.ti	http://atlasti.com
MAXQDA	http://www.maxqda.com
NVivo	http://www.qsrinternational.com/product
SPSS	http://www.ibm.com/analytics/us/en/technology/spss/
Stata	http://www.stata.com
WordSmith Tools	http://www.lexically.net/wordsmith/

Next, we present a number of studies along the continuum from more quantitative to more qualitative content analysis. We start with a study in which words were counted by computer software, moving to a study in which references to certain phenomena were coded in a rather straightforward way that did not necessitate complex interpretations, continue with two studies in which expressions of ideas were counted – the first in a way that demanded less complex interpretations than the second – and end with a study that used rather complex interpretations but very simple calculations.

2.2.3 Counting words as indications of policy positions

The first study we present involves a count of word frequencies. Two political scientists wanted to develop methods for estimating the policy positions of political parties through content analysis of party manifestos (Laver and Garry, 2000). They developed two methods: a computer-based word count and manual coding in accordance with a strictly structured coding scheme. In this section we describe the computational method; in Section 2.2.5 we return to the manual coding method.

The coding units for the computer-based analysis were specific words. To this purpose, a computer dictionary was constructed. The words in this dictionary were then systematically associated with certain coding categories representing particular political ideas (e.g. a positive approach to state regulation of the economy). The software then counted the number of words or phrases associated with each coding category. To make the connection between the presence of certain words and certain coding categories a credible one, the dictionary had to be carefully constructed. Specific terms were sorted into particular coding categories partly on the basis of the researchers' general knowledge of the political language, partly through an empirically-based procedure. This procedure included a calculation of the relative frequency of words in the British Conservative Party and the Labour Party manifestos of 1992. The word 'taxes' was, for example, used 22 times in the Conservative manifesto but only once in the Labour manifesto. Based on knowledge of the Conservative party rhetoric this word was then made an indicator of the category 'Reduce state involvement in the economy'.

This study represents a distinctly quantifying analysis with strictly standardized techniques that enable the processing of large bodies of materials. If properly set up, the computer-based word count is 100% reliable. There are validity problems associated with letting occurrences of single words measure policy positions. We will return to this at the end of the chapter. The next section presents a quantitative content analysis in which the coding was manual but needed a low level of interpretation.

2.2.4 Counting references to crime as indications of newsworthiness

Social psychology researcher Michael O'Connell (1999) analyzed crime reporting in the Irish press. The starting point was that the Irish, despite the fact that the Republic at the time of the survey was among the European countries with the lowest reported crime rates, were worried about high criminality, perceived that there had been a disastrous rise in the crime rate and wanted to see a clampdown on criminals. Could this – perhaps excessive – anxiety be explained by tendentious and sensationalist mass media crime reporting, wondered O'Connell. To investigate this, he carried out a content analysis in which crime reporting was compared to police crime statistics.

We will look closely at one of the studies in this project. The material consisted of crime reporting in four Irish newspapers during a two-month period. The newspaper selection was intended to be representative for both 'quality' and evening papers. The chosen period directly preceded a major opinion poll on attitudes to crime, i.e. the reporting could conceivably have had an impact on public opinion. The total number of articles was 2,191.

The texts were collected by a number of coders who went through the newspapers, picked out what was crime reporting and then coded the selected articles according to a coding scheme. For each article, they made a number of notations. In the sub-study we refer to here it was the type of crime the article reported that was noted.

--- **Box 2.2** ---

Coding scheme for a study of crime reporting in newspapers

1) Murder and attempted murder
2) Abduction and attempted abduction
3) Child sexual abuse/indecent assault of children
4) Rape, marital rape, sexual assault (on adults)
5) Manslaughter and hit and runs leading to killings or very serious injuries, assaults leading to death
6) Malicious wounding
7) Armed robbery
8) Arson, malicious damage
9) Assaults against the person – physical assault, affray, mugging, child physical abuse, causing bodily harm
10) Serious drug offenses – smuggling, trafficking, supplying
11) Possession of dangerous weapon, threats, intimidation, stalking
12) Car theft and joy riding
13) Serious thefts – burglary, breaking and entering, robbery
14) Serious fraud – embezzlement, handling stolen goods, blackmail, sabotage, forgery, smuggling
15) Cruelty to animals
16) Minor thefts – larceny from a person, larceny from a vehicle, shoplifting, tree-theft, cattle-rustling
17) Obscenity – indecent behaviour involving exposure, selling or passing obscene materials, public indecency

(Continued)

(Continued)

18) Minor fraud – bogus callers, obtaining money by deception, loan sharks, spreading false information, poteen distilling, using illegal fishing nets
19) Minor drug offenses – growing and possession (cannabis)
20) Serious driving offenses – drink-driving and dangerous driving
21) Criminal justice offenses – contempt of court, unlawfully at large, resisting arrest
22) Public disorder offenses – drunk and disorderly, criminal damage (vandalism) disorderly behaviour, after hours drinking, breach of peace, prostitution
23) Minor driving offenses – driving without insurance, other minor driving offenses, careless driving, speeding

(Source: O'Connell, 1999: 208)

The article does not make it clear which, if any, classification problems occurred in the coding process and no results of control codings are presented. It can be assumed, however, that sorting articles according to which legal offences they referred to would not have been all that difficult.

The results of this study were presented as a comparison between the type of crime frequently reported by these newspapers and official crime statistics.

Table 2.1 Results from a study of crime reporting in the press (Source: Table 1 in O'Connell, 1999: 196).

A comparison of offense frequency between sampled newspaper data and the Garda[1] crime figures for 1993.

Offence	Percentage from sample	Percentage from Garda figures	Ratio of sample to Garda figures
Murder	12.3	0.004	3,075.00
Manslaughter	4.6	0.003	1,533.00
Abduction	3.0	0.005	600.00
Malicious wounding	6.0	0.010	600.00
Child sexual abuse	3.1	0.006	517.00
Arson	4.2	0.011	382.00
Possession of dangerous weapons	2.5	0.007	357.00
Armed robbery	15.8	0.090	176.00
Assaults	8.4	0.079	106.00
Rape	6.7	0.077	87.00
Serious drug offences	4.7	0.122	38.00
Cruelty to animals	0.5	0.045	11.00
Serious frauds	5.1	0.631	8.08
Car theft	2.2	0.320	6.87

Offence	Percentage from sample	Percentage from Garda figures	Ratio of sample to Garda figures
Minor drug offences	1.1	0.485	2.27
Minor frauds	1.0	0.605	1.65
Serious thefts and burglaries	8.2	5.132	1.60
Obscenity	0.3	N/A	N/A
Serious driving offences	2.0	1.865	1.07
Criminal justice offences	0.9	N/A	N/A
Public disorder	3.1	5.461	0.57
Larcenies	2.1	6.349	0.33
Minor driving offences	2.2	73.412	0.03

[1]The Irish national police force

'Ratio' in the far right-hand column shows the relationship between the proportion of crime in Ireland reported in the press and the proportion in official statistics, which can be said to be a measure of each crime's news value. Murder was reported in the press at 3 075 times the rate of murders in the official statistics (12.3 / 0.004 = 3 075). This result, argues the author, shows that extreme and violent crimes were overrepresented in crime reporting in the press. While the typical crimes in the Irish press rarely figured in the official crime statistics, statistically typical crimes were rarely reported in the press. The results support the hypothesis that newspaper crime reporting gave rise to a distorted and overly negative picture of actual criminality.

The next studies we look at counted something arguably more difficult to interpret: political parties' policy positions as expressed through political ideas in party manifestos or in parliamentarian speeches.

2.2.5 Counting expressions of ideas as indications of policy positions

We now return to the article by Laver and Gary (2000). As their second method, they constructed a complex coding scheme.

The coding scheme was hierarchical. At the top level broad policy domains were distinguished, in this example 'economy'. Other such domains were the political system, the social system, foreign relations and a general domain. The domain 'economy' had four branches: to increase the role of the state in the economy; to reduce the role of the state in the economy; to be neutral on the role of the state in the economy; and to display a general concern with economic growth. On each of the first three branches there were four new branches indicating how the state may intervene in the economy: through the state budget, through state ownership of

Table 2.2 Part of a coding scheme for the analysis of party manifestos (Source: partially based on Table 1, Laver and Gary, 2000: 623).

```
1   ECONOMY
Role of state in economy
  11   ECONOMY/+State+
       Increase role of state
     111   ECONOMY/+State+/Budget
           Budget
       1111    ECONOMY/+State+/Budget/Spending
               Increase public spending
               11111   ECONOMY/+State+/Budget/Spending/Health
               11112   ECONOMY/+State+/Budget/Spending/Educ.& training
               11113   ECONOMY/+State+/Budget/Spending/Housing
               11114   ECONOMY/+State+/Budget/Spending/Transport
               11115   ECONOMY/+State+/Budget/Spending/Infrastructure
               11116   ECONOMY/+State+/Budget/Spending/Welfare
               11117   ECONOMY/+State+/Budget/Spending/Police
               11118   ECONOMY/+State+/Budget/Spending/Defence
               11119   ECONOMY/+State+/Budget/Spending/Culture
       1112    ECONOMY/+State+/Budget/Taxes
               Increase taxes
               11121   ECONOMY/+State+/Budget/Taxes/Income
               11122   ECONOMY/+State+/Budget/Taxes/Payroll
               11123   ECONOMY/+State+/Budget/Taxes/Company
               11124   ECONOMY/+State+/Budget/Taxes/Sales
               11125   ECONOMY/+State+/Budget/Taxes/Capital
               11126   ECONOMY/+State+/Budget/Taxes/Capital gains
```

industry and services, through state regulation, as well as through direct action. On the branch 'State budget', policy may relate to increased public spending, increased taxation and increased budget deficit and so on into more branches.

Table 2.2 shows a part of the branch of economy that expresses a positive attitude towards state intervention in the economy. An expression of the idea that the state should spend more on defence should thus be coded as 1 1 1 1 8; a demand for higher taxation on capital as 1 1 1 2 5. The coding scheme had more than 300 categories in total. The authors point out that new branches can be added on to include new policy issues on the agenda or if local circumstances so require. The unit of context used was 'quasi sentences' – word strings that were either complete sentences or part of sentences that could have been complete if the writer had chosen to use a complete sentence – on average ten words long. The advantage of using quasi sentences as the context unit instead of entire sentences is, according to the authors, that the result of the coding is not affected by the sentence length in the text. Each ten-word string was attributed to one and only one category.

The authors compared the results of this coding method with their own word count method and other methods using Pearson's r correlation and found good coherence, particularly for the coding of British parties. In a latter article the methods were used to include German party manifestos in the analysis (Laver et al., 2003).

2.2.6 Counting expressions of ideas as indications of ideological shift

Now let us turn to another study in which the expressions of ideological positions were noted, but in a less tightly structured way, which demanded more complex interpretations, something that arguably places this study closer to a qualitative content analysis than the studies referred to so far. We use this study to show in detail how a coding scheme can be constructed and how it can be used, together with coding instructions, to code a particular text.[1] The object of study was the 'shift to the right' in Sweden, defined as a change in the public debate according to which values, ideas and concepts became consistent with various right-wing ideologies (Boréus, 1997). This was an ideological shift – away from a political climate dominated by social democratic and left liberal ideas – which had originated in the late 1970s.

The Swedish shift to the right was, in its turn, related to an international ideological shift that started among economists who turned away from Keynesian economics towards neo-liberal free-market economics, soon to be followed by policy changes. The United States at the time of Ronald Reagan's presidency and the UK in the Margaret Thatcher era were in the lead. Central to the ideological shift were demands for 'rolling back' the welfare state, lowering taxes, cutting state spending, and refraining from state regulations of the markets. These ideological and economic changes had far-reaching social impacts world-wide. Some authors – like Naomi Klein whose text on climate change is analyzed in the next chapter – claim that they play a crucial role for the chances we have today of mitigating global warming (Klein, 2014). (For an account of various meanings of the term 'neo-liberalism' and the ideology's development across the global geographical space, see Chapter 1, 'Neoliberal Worlds', in Peck, 2010: 1–38).

To capture this shift in Sweden, material from the public debate from the late 1960s to the late 1980s was analyzed. One of the questions addressed was how comprehensive the ideological shift in public debate was. This was examined through a content analysis of the extent to which 'right-wing ideas' came to replace other kinds of ideas. Ideal-type models of neo-liberalism and other right-wing ideologies were constructed. The model of neo-liberalism was a compilation of central ideas from literature usually referred to as neo-liberal in political philosophy, social sciences and economics (examples include works by James Buchanan and Gordon Tullock; Milton, Rose and David D. Friedman; Robert Nozick; and Ayn Rand). Variables in the coding scheme were constructed

---

[1] This section builds on Boréus (1997) which includes parts of the coding scheme used. The coding instructions are only found in Swedish in Boréus (1994: 366–70) and the piece of text coded here is included in neither.

based on this model. A number of right-wing ideas, primarily neo-liberal ones, were formulated for different policy areas. For each right-wing idea an 'alternative idea', mostly of a social democratic, Marxist or social-liberal kind, was constructed. If only the expression of right-wing ideas had been counted an increased frequency of such ideas could just as well have indicated a polarization of the debate: the frequency of ideas that contradicted right-wing ideas could also have increased.

The coding scheme included a total of 24 variables, each divided in an a-variable, which was the expression of a right-wing idea, and a b-variable, an expression of an alternative idea. The coding scheme was divided into three main parts that covered issues regarding 'state, market, capitalism', 'the individual and the collective', and 'values', respectively. A part of the coding scheme is shown in Box 2.3.

Box 2.3

Part of coding scheme for studying ideological change

[Note: 'society' in points 4a/b could also have been translated as 'the public sector']

1a) The market is superior in regulating such economic activity as the setting of prices or determining what should be produced/Selective state regulations of markets are generally something bad/Abolish state attempts to regulate the market with such instruments as price subsidies or regulations stipulating who is allowed to produce what/In favour of 'free enterprise'/Against planned economy.

1b) The state should interfere in the free play of the market by imposing certain controls on market forces, certain regulations, such as subsidies/Introduce more or harder state regulations of the market/Maintain existing regulations. [...]

4a) It is not society which has the (main) responsibility for welfare or employment, neither for all citizens nor for groups of people.

4b) It is society which has the (main) responsibility for welfare/employment.

5a) The welfare state is too expensive/The public sector is too big/Reduce the size of the public sector/public expenses/The extension of the welfare state is a cause of the economic crisis.

5b) Add to/improve the public sector/Against cuts/Suggestions for specific public spending. [...]

8a) Taxes and employers' contributions are theft/an imposition/a burden.

8b) Taxes described as a mechanism that provides society or some groups in society with something valuable.

(Source: Boréus, 1997: 280).

The coding scheme was developed a step at a time while being tried out on the material. A fairly extensive coding instruction grew out of the problems that emerged when the analysis was tried out. Box 2.4 shows a part of these instructions.

Box 2.4

Part of coding instructions for a study of ideological change

Introduction

The variables are meant to indicate various things in a text: that *a claim of a specific kind about social reality* is made, that an *ethical evaluation* of a certain kind is presented, that particular *policy demands* are made, or that a special *definition or interpretation of a concept* is created. What matters is what a piece of text is about, not its linguistic form. The ideas can be expressed in several ways. Variable 1a, for example, is about the market's superiority in relation to the state and should be coded both when a claim is made that expresses this and when it is demanded or proposed that the market should take over more, or that the state should keep out, etc. The variable descriptions in the coding scheme exemplify different formulations of certain ideas. [...] The context unit is the speech/article. Each variable is thus encoded at a maximum once per text [...].

Code in the following way:

- Read the entire speech or article once. [...]
- Review the speech/article paragraph by paragraph, or a piece at a time, and judge whether any of the variables are applicable. Note all the variables that apply to the speech/article, e.g. 1b; 11a; 12a. Explanations of some of the individual variables follow below.

I. The State, market, capitalism

Variables 1a and 2a refer to the critique of state regulations of markets for goods and services (ignore regulations of credit and money markets!) and of private enterprises, production and marketing, as well as to arguments for the benefits of free market forces. 1b is coded e.g. when support of distressed private companies and press support are advocated (both measures counteract the market mechanism). [...]

The welfare state variables 4-7 are about public services in the reproductive sector and communications, culture and environmental protection, education, healthcare, childcare and eldercare, railways, libraries, sewage-treatment plants and so on.

(Source: translated from Boréus, 1994: 366-70).

The coding scheme was used for two types of public material: 'debate articles'[2] in two leading Swedish dailies, and the speeches made by the Social Democrats, the right-wing Moderate Party of Sweden and the Liberal Party leaders in particular parliamentary speeches; 840 articles and 63 speeches were analyzed. We will illustrate how the coding was done by giving an example. The following is a quote from a speech by the Liberal Party leader in the year 1973. Parts of the text that have been crucial for the coding decisions are underlined.

> Sure, the state and the municipalities can do a lot for more sensible social planning, for the expansion of childcare. But we are not finished with social care that way. [...]
>
> How do we as politicians utilize the funds of idealism and willingness to personal responsibility that exist in this society? We have a chance to take advantage of the willingness to show responsibility in non-profit organizations and religious communities, when it comes to the expansion of preschool. We have another chance to give the Swedish Sports Movement better economic conditions. And we can lighten the tax burden for Christian communities which they cannot compensate for in the way commercial entities can. Precisely because public responsibility must grow, it is particularly necessary that the individual has the feeling of a respite, but also the feeling of being protected against being abused by a state apparatus that risks transforming itself step-by-step from a servant of the public to its ruler.
> (Translated from Parliamentary protocol 1973: 127, pp. 13-14)

This extract expresses the liberal public views of the time nicely: the public sector should be expanded, but it is important to look after individual freedom and initiatives. This short text gave rise to notations for variables 4b, 5b and 8a: 4b is motivated by the phrase 'Precisely because public responsibility must grow...', which has been interpreted as a support for the claim that public responsibility should grow, thus that society/the public is in fact responsible for welfare. This interpretation is consistent with this party's (and other parliamentary parties') rhetoric at the time, something that should remind us of the importance of contextual knowledge. That 5b was noted is motivated by the first sentence, which expresses consent to the expansion of (public) childcare facilities. The talk about giving the Swedish Sports Movement better terms should probably be interpreted as the party leader advocating more public spending there, but that is less certain. Recording 8a was motivated by the expression 'lighten the tax burden for Christian communities ... '.

The speeches held in the latter years of the analyzed period contained considerably more a-variables.

The result of the content analysis of the parliamentary speeches is presented in Figure 2.1 below. The figure shows that for all three parties the proportion

---

[2]Many Swedish newspapers have special pages for general debate, on which 'debate articles' (= opinion pieces) appear daily. The authors of these articles almost all belong to society's middle or elite strata and often represent big organizations, political parties, NGOs etc.

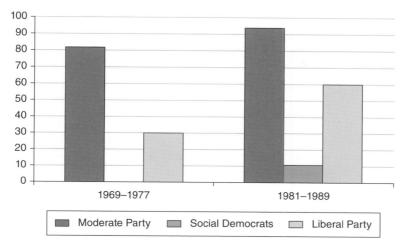

Figure 2.1 Percentage of expressions of right-wing ideas in political speeches in the Swedish parliament in a study of ideological change.

of right-wing ideas to alternative ideas grew in the period 1981–89 compared to 1969–77. The Liberal Party, for example, which showed the clearest swing, went from expressing 11 right-wing and 26 alternative ideas in in the first period, to 25 right-wing ideas and 16 alternative ones in the second.

The next step in the analysis was the interpretation of these results. Could they be used to draw the conclusion that the Swedish public debate had taken a turn to the right? In the original study a number of reasons for and against such a conclusion were tested. It was argued that together with other results from the broader study it was reasonable to see the outcome of the content analyses of parliamentary speeches as an indication of a right-wing shift in the Swedish public debate.

As for reliability, only intrasubjectivity – i.e. the consistency in the coding of the entire material by the same coder – was tested. The result indicated that it was difficult to code the speeches in an exactly equal manner all the way through. The proportion of notations for right-wing ideas was, however, the same in the second coding as in the main coding, which indicates that the intrasubjectivity was satisfactory for the purpose of the study.

The last study we will present is an even clearer example of a qualitative content analysis that used open-ended questions which would have demanded fairly complex interpretations by the coders.

2.2.7 Counting various aspects of content as a way to analyze ideological leaning

Below we show some details from a content analysis of a US comic strip, an analysis referred to by Schreier (2014) as 'a classic', using a presentation of some of the study's results in Shannon (1954). The analysis can be said to belong to the ideology critical tradition (see Chapter 4). The cartoon strip, 'Little Orphan Annie', created by Harold Gray, was very popular but also controversial. It ran between 1924 and 2010 in the US press and was read by more adults than children. The time period analyzed in the article, 1948–50, occurred not long after the Second World War and during the early days of the anti-communist campaign carried out in the US during the Cold War.

The author of the study analyzed what she found to be expressions of a conservative social idealism of a US middle class and of capitalist values as well as anti-communism. In the beginning of the article, Shannon describes the overall content of the strip using examples outside of the analyzed material to illustrate some points. The following quote (from a strip published on January 13, 1946) illustrates the cartoon's concern with foreign spies, in this case trying to obtain US secrets about the atom bomb. Warbucks is one of the characters, a benevolent capitalist and Annie's friend. 'The child' or 'da brat' in the German's broken English, is the heroine, Little Annie. Tidnab ('bandit' backwards), the German and the Japanese are holding Annie prisoner. That the crooks are a Japanese and a German, leaning on Nazi ideas, in a cartoon strip that was published less than a year after the war ended, was no coincidence:

Japanese:	"But Baron... is-sss it certain that Warbucks possesses the great secret?"
German:	"Vell, if he does not possess it he can get it – Ya! and *he will!*"
Japanese:	"Yess... Warbucks is of the decadent soft American race... he is a sentimental fool..."
German:	"Ya! Not like der master race... for da brat he would do anything."
Japanese:	"Hee-hee! When Mr. Tidnab sends him one of the child's ears... what a surprise!"

(Shannon, 1954: 170)

The sample for analysis consisted of a period from April 1948 to July 1950, about 116 weeks. The context unit (although not referred to with that term in the article) was the strip that appeared on any particular date, meaning that whatever was counted was only counted once per strip. The coding instrument used was a set of questions regarding different aspects of the cartoon:

Box 2.5

Coding questions used for a content analysis studying ideological leaning

1   Which villains are pursuing Annie; which persons are in opposition to her?
2   What is the occupation, overt and covert, of the persons mentioned above?

3   Which opponents are killed or injured, how and by whom?
4   Who are Annie's friends?
5   What is the occupation, overt and covert, of the persons mentioned above?
6   Which friends of Annie are killed or injured, how and by whom?
7   What goals in life are approved by Annie and her friends?
8   What means and methods for reaching these goals are suggested by Annie and her friends?
9   What symbols are approved by Annie and her friends?
10 What symbols are condemned by Annie and her friends?

(Shannon, 1954: 173)

Two coders answered the questions independent of each other, and the author of the article, after reading the entire series, collated the two answer sheets obtained, thus "arriving at a third set of answers which represented a consensus of three persons' answers to the questions" (1954: 173).

There was therefore no attempt made to measure reliability by a double coding. Instead the quality of the coding was improved by the method described. From such a procedure little can be said about the possibilities for other coders or researchers to reach the same conclusion. Careful proceeding should, however, diminish the risk of personal inclinations by individual coders influencing the results in a way that would skew them compared to how other readers would have understood the cartoon.

Apart from the presentation of the results of the coding, an overall description of the series during the analyzed period is provided in the article. Thirty-nine of the 110 weeks were spent by Annie in conflict with foreign agents with names such as Ivan, Andrei and Alex. Another 15 weeks were spent in conflict with young gangsters in the protection racket. Thus half of Annie's time was devoted to conflict with specific causes, "preservation of capitalism in the struggle against Communism and aid to small, honest, decent businessmen having difficulty with young hoodlums engaged in the protection racket", while the rest of her time was devoted to helping the poor (1954: 173–4). As the author states, Annie interacted with people in extreme walks of life, such as spies, gangsters and millionaires. She did not interact with coal-miners, steel-workers or other working people. The poor that she helped were not the ordinary workers who strove to make means meet ends but those who were poor because they were lazy or lacked initiative. Their misfortune thus depended on themselves, not on how a capitalist USA was organized.

The results of the coding were then presented in commented tables and numbers. Table 2.3 below shows some of the results.

The most common kind of opponents that Annie met were foreign spies and their radical US counterparts. They were often disposed of with the help of Annie's friend Kansk or the magician Punjab. Sometimes they were drowned, shot, hanged or had their necks broken. Among her friends were millionaire

Table 2.3 Results drawn from content analysis studying ideological leaning (partially based on Tables 1 and 2 in Shannon, 1954: 175–6).

Annie's opponents

Number of appearances	Annie's opponents and who they are	What happens to them
9	Axel – head of foreign spy ring	sent away on ship by Kansk
7	Max – handyman and chauffeur, member of spy ring	sent away on ship by Kansk
6	Ivan Ichalotski – foreign agent	sent home in box by Warbucks
4	Peter and Pola Petard – run secondhand store, members of Axel's spy ring	sent away on ship by Kansk
3	Andrei – foreign spy with Alex	pushed into sewer by Annie
1	Axel's messenger – foreign spy	neck broken by Kansk
1	Michail – scientist, gives secrets to foreign agent	sent away by Punjab
1	unnamed foreign agent who gets secrets from scientist	sent away by Punjab
1	three foreign agents pursuing Warbucks	stumble into quicksand – Annie misleads them

Annie's friends

Number of appearances	Annie's friends and who they are
19	Daddy Warbucks – millionaire industrialist
13	Punjab – Warbucks' giant assistant
6	Patrick Puddle – millionaire steel man
5	Mrs. MacBond – former hasher come rich on oil wells
5	Mr. Locust – Annie's lawyer
4	Kansk – counter espionage agent from Eastern Europe
4	Kurt Kolly – small town sheriff
2	Two uniformed sympathetic policemen
2	Mr. Starr – plainclothes policeman who enjoys seeing Annie's gang beat up their opponents

leaders of industry and professional and middle-class people. Small business men also appeared fairly often.

The author's analysis of this is that the world presented in the cartoon was "one in which the hard-working captains of industry struggle against a vicious and uncompromising underground in order to protect capitalism, earn large profits and thus assume their social responsibilities, i.e., be charitable to the needy" (Shannon, 1954: 177). The article is a short one and we think it would have been possible to create a more in-depth analysis of the ideological content of 'Little Orphan Annie'. Nevertheless we find the methodology and analysis thought-provoking and inspiring.

2.3 Critical reflections

Like other research methods, content analysis has its limitations and challenges to meet and working with content analysis means making certain choices.

2.3.1 Not everything can be quantified

The idea behind counting something that occurs in texts is generally that a higher frequency (or more) of something means that this something is more important or more dominant in a particular context. This is not always true. The content of a single political statement can have far-reaching consequences despite, or precisely because of, differing strongly from what is usually expressed. In many contexts, it is not important *how many times*, but *in which way*, something is expressed. There are simply many research questions that cannot be answered with statements about 'more' or 'less'.

2.3.2 The invisible is not counted

Another limitation of quantitative content analysis is that it shows the explicit rather than the implicit, i.e. it is the manifest content of texts that is coded. This is a truth with modification: Kleinnijenhuis et al. (1997) demonstrate a study in which implied, but not stated, content of texts is analyzed. Wiebe and Bruce (2001) show possibilities for using computer-based content analysis to examine implicit text content. Yet to obtain good reliability non-explicit content must be implied very clearly to enable coding. In their study, Wiebe and Bruce (2001) noted logical implications of manifest text content. Implicit meaning can be of many different kinds, though, and at different levels of clarity, and need not be logical. That something is not stated might be a sign of it being unimportant in the context, but it might also mean that it belongs to the realm of the 'obvious' that is not in need of being stated, exactly because it is obvious and by no means unimportant. These two cases cannot be kept apart by content analysis alone; discourse analysis might do a better job. Based on a more complex picture of what is said and not said it is often possible to make inferences regarding the conditions for those statements.

A related problem is that differences over time or between corpora might be missed which were not captured by the coding scheme. The coding scheme makes it difficult to be open to the material, to 'let the text speak'. Or the texts speak to the researcher only about what they have already decided to investigate. The problem is thus not only that what is actually invisible (the implicit) is difficult to count, but also that a precise and targeted analytical tool tends to make even manifest text content that might have attracted the attention of the researcher in a more open kind of analysis invisible. It is possible to reduce the problem by getting a good overview of the text content and by beginning the study by reading at least parts of the text material in an open way. Doing parts of the coding inductively is also a remedy.

2.3.3 Validity issues

Evaluations of validity can only be made of individual studies and the question to pose is how well their design and method fit the research questions. The validity of the study of the Irish crime reporting (O'Connell, 1999) does not appear to be particularly problematic: the number of articles dealing with specific offenses in relation to official crime statistics seems to be a good measure of the news-worthiness of various types of crime, as well as a tendency for the entire crime reporting to emphasize these types of crime. The validity of the study that measured policy positions with the help of computerized word counts in party manifestos might be more problematic (Laver and Garry, 2000). The main validity problem of this study – as in many others – was due to the fact that the coding units (in this case single words) were taken out of context. Policy positions can be expressed in a virtually unlimited number of ways and with different words. Recognizing a position expressed in a way it has not been expressed before cannot – at least not yet – be done without manual coding (see Shapiro, 2009).

A particular type of validity problem created by a lack of consideration for the context in an investigation like Laver and Garry's is that a word, say 'taxes', may occur both in argumentations for higher and for lower taxes. The authors' defence against this criticism was that the appearance of particular words is more determined by the context than one thinks. If the word 'taxes', they say, is coded into a category that contains arguments to cut taxes, this will result in few erroneous coding decisions: the number of times the word appears in such a context will be significantly larger than the number of times it occurs in contexts where the standpoint is that taxes ought to be raised (Laver and Garry, 2000). The argument, then, is that certain text genres use quite specific vocabularies to express particular ideas during certain time periods.

There are also other validity problems associated with the word count, one being that words can be ambiguous. Examples in English are 'bank', 'rock' and 'plain'. Each of these words has two or more distinct meanings. There are also ambiguous words with different but related meanings, e.g. 'bed' as in a river bed or referring to a piece of furniture. It is rare that a content analysis in social sciences is interested in a word apart from its meaning. This problem is not very difficult to handle, however. One can either avoid ambiguous words in coding or back a computer analysis up with a manual coding of such words. If software of the kind used in corpus linguistics is at hand, creating a concordance (see Chapter 6) will be helpful for this task. Laver and Garry (2000) also point out that one meaning of an ambiguous word usually dominates the others in specific genres. When an word 'banks' occurs in political manifestos, it very rarely refers to river banks but almost always to financial institutions.

Vague words are more problematic, i.e. those that have diverse but not clearly defined meanings. Most of the terms in the social sciences are of this kind. This applies in particular for evaluative words whose meaning is contested (see the discussion on essentially contested concepts in Connolly, 1983). What does 'democracy' mean? Most likely a form of governing that the text producer evaluates positively. But what 'democracy' refers to varies. For one text producer, it may be a political system where the majority make far-reaching decisions about finances and other aspects of social life, for another a form of government that just meets certain criteria regarding periodical elections, the freedom to form political parties and an absence of media censorship. To determine the meaning of such a term for a particular text producer (if it is at all possible to determine) often requires relatively complex interpretations and comprehensive discourse knowledge. If nuances of meaning are important to one's research problem, a computer-based analysis does not suffice and one has to be prepared to invest considerable time in the interpretation process, which limits the amount of material that can be analyzed.

One further problem is that the meaning of words both differs between text producers and changes over time. If the frequency of certain words is used to determine ideological change or stability over time, important information is lost if such changes-of-meaning are not taken into account, especially if the study involves a longer time period or an ideological transition. Changes over time in the frequency of terms like 'freedom', 'democracy' and 'equality' in political debates seem to indicate ideological change. But many political terms have a 'left-wing' and a 'right-wing' meaning. 'Freedom' is a positively charged term in political rhetoric and might therefore be the subject of an ideological tug of war. In left-wing rhetoric 'freedom' tends to mean what in political theory is termed **positive liberty**, i.e. freedom as a genuine opportunity to realize one's projects, which implies that some basic needs, like available education and health care, are fulfilled. In right-wing rhetoric the word tends to mean that other actors, primarily the state through taxation, should not stand in the way of individual projects, which is referred to as **negative liberty**. Since ideological change might mean both changed frequencies and changes in the meaning of certain words, one needs to be observant.

2.3.4 Interpretation issues

What is really 'there' in a text? In the case of simple assessments such as whether or not a certain word is there, this is rarely a problem. When it comes to counting the expressions of certain ideas, however, one immediately runs into questions about interpretation. What might it mean that I find certain ideas expressed in a text? It could mean that I, as the researcher and person I am, tend to interpret certain phrases as the expression of certain ideas. But if I am concerned primarily with something outside of myself, this may not be particularly interesting. Here the different interpretation strategies presented in Table 1.1 become relevant. In the studies referred to above, these matters are hardly discussed. Laver and Garry (2000) argue that their way of interpreting party manifestos is similar to that of an 'ordinary' reader, or, in the words of Table 1.1, they use an addressee–oriented interpretation strategy. Such a reader is assumed to reach a conclusion on what attitude is expressed on a particular issue on the basis of the sum of neutral, positive and negative statements on the issue in the manifesto. There is cause for questioning this reasoning; it is not supported by references to research on how people actually embrace and interpret political messages.

2.3.5 Working with content analysis

A particular feature of content analysis performed by manual coding as compared to some of the other analytical approaches presented in this book is that one cannot make great changes to the research design during the study. Once the coding scheme/frame has been elaborated and used to analyze substantial parts of the material one cannot change it: too much time and resources have then already been invested. In computer-based analysis this is less of a problem. The equivalent of the coding, i.e. the computer processing of the texts, is generally a subordinate and quickly completed part of the work, which means that you can go about it again and again if the first attempts do not provide the information expected.

2.4 Content analysis and the study of power and other social phenomena

How can content analysis be used in the study of power, politics, oppression or other subjects of interest to the social sciences? Some ways are shown by the sample studies. In O'Connell's study of Irish crime reporting it was argued that such reporting provided a distorted picture of crime in society, which led to demands for tougher law enforcement. In November 1996 an overwhelming majority of Irish voters voted in a referendum in favour of a law that restricted the right to be released on bail for certain offenses. This was seen by some as a further step in an ongoing erosion of civil rights (O'Connell, 1999: 92). The study was thus relevant to social phenomena like attitudes to and treatment of those convicted of crime, and society's allocation of resources and civil rights.

Other content analytic studies too have been motivated by an interest in media power and influence. Some studies regard the media's power to set the agenda. McCombs and Shaw (2009) analyzed newspapers and television influence on what voters considered the most important themes in the presidential campaign in the United States in 1968, and demonstrated a strong connection between the themes that the media highlighted and which issues voters deemed most important. Another drastic example of mass media influence was provided by a study of the positive relationship between the extent of news coverage of murder-suicide (i.e. when people deliberately kill others when committing suicide) and pilots who purposely crashed passenger planes in various states in the USA (Phillips, 2009).

Summary

On the usefulness of content analysis

- The chapter has reviewed the principles of quantitative and qualitative content analysis of texts, i.e. analyses in which elements of texts are categorized, counted or measured with particular research purposes.
- The approach is especially suitable for finding patterns in larger corpora, for categorizations and comparisons, and may be complemented with other types of analyses.
- If the texts to be studied are available in a database or can be scanned, very large quantities of material may be analyzed by computer software.
- Manually conducted content analysis makes more advanced judgments and interpretations possible, but leads to the processing of less material than computer-based analysis.
- A consequence of choosing manually-conducted content analysis is that the researcher becomes locked into one approach relatively early.
- Not all interesting aspects of texts can be counted or measured.
- Content analysis is poorly suited for studying the unspoken and implied.
- Content analysis is insensitive to the context in which units like words are counted, which could reduce validity.

How to go about doing it

- The selection of texts should be made with regard to the research question. Selection and sampling always need justification.
- The researcher should become familiar with the material at an early stage, read parts of it, if possible all of it, learn about the text genre and about the social context.
- An analytical tool called a 'coding scheme' for manual coding (sometimes a 'coding frame' for qualitative analysis) and a 'dictionary' for computer-based analyses are constructed. More or less detailed coding instructions are usually also necessary. In quantitative content analysis the codes are often deductively formulated. In qualitative content analysis one option is to begin from a more general research problem and code the material inductively.
- Before the final coding tool with instructions is put together, it should be tried out several times on portions of the material and a pilot study conducted. It is an advantage if someone apart from the researcher can try out the tools.
- There are special applications for computer-based quantitative content analysis. If possible, QDA software should be used for manual coding.
- The coding units (what is counted, such as words or references to something) can be of many different kinds, as can the context unit (a particular text, a sentence, etc.). Both should be determined by the research question.

- Consistency in coding should be ensured: intrasubjectivity is about how consequent the same coder is in the assessment of the whole material, good intersubjectivity means that different coders code the same way. Double-coding can be used to check intra- or intersubjectivity. Reliability can also be improved by taking into account the order in which different parts of the material are analyzed. Reliability is not a problem in computer-based analysis.
- The results from a quantitative content analysis can be presented in charts, in tables or otherwise. Content analysis of a more qualitative kind can also be presented that way or as a presentation of the different frames found, illustrated by typical quotes. The results should then be interpreted and related to the research problem.

Suggested reading

Schreier (2014) provides a good introduction to qualitative content analysis.

Krippendorff (2013) is a very thorough book, which defines and delimits quantitative content analysis as a method and goes through all the steps of what he considers to be good content analysis. He provides a detailed review of different types of reliability tests and includes a chapter on computer-based methods. Grbich (2013) reviews software useful for manual coding in Chapter 21 and presents a number of applications that can also be used for content analysis in Chapter 22, which discusses some concerns related to the usage of software in qualitative analyses. Walberg et al. (2001) also deal with the usefulness of various kinds of software for quantitative content analysis. Roberts (1997), an anthology, presents studies conducted with different types of quantitative content analysis. The book distinguishes between thematic, semantic and network textual analysis. Another substantial anthology is Krippendorff and Bock (2009). In more than 50 contributions various aspects of quantitative content analysis are presented, such as its history, selection of texts, issues of reliability and validity, questions about inference from analyses of material to contexts and computer-based versus manual coding. The book contains many interesting examples of content analytic studies of texts in different genres.

Laver (2001) presents a number of contributions on how to systematically study political actors' positions through both manual and computer-based content analysis and discusses methodological issues. The extensive research carried out by the Manifesto Research Group (http://manifestoproject.wzb.eu/), which has coded election manifestos from 1945 to the present for more than 1000 parties in over 50 countries, is referred to in several of the contributions.

Exercise

Neo-liberalization of the UK Labour Party?

In his book *New Labour, New Language?* (2000) critical discourse analyst Norman Fairclough describes how the ideological change that the British Labour Party underwent in the 1990s - referred to as the party choosing the 'Third Way' - is intertwined with changes in the party's language use. (Some detailed examples from Fairclough's analyses are presented in Chapter 8 of this book.) The Third Way is described by Fairclough as a partial acceptance of neo-liberalism by the party. Thus Fairclough's study covers 'neo-liberalization' in Britain, which had an earlier breakthrough than the shift to the right in Sweden analyzed in Boréus (1997). In Sweden, Block (1984) showed how the frequency of certain political terms like 'freedom'/'liberty' ('frihet'), 'equality' ('jämlikhet') and 'democracy' ('demokrati') changed during the period 1945–75 in a way that mirrored the ideological shift to the left that took place in the Swedish public sphere in this period. The terms 'equality' and 'democracy' became more frequent and the term 'freedom' less frequent. The opposite trends for these three words were shown in the later shift to the right. During this period 'justice'/'fairness' ('rättvisa') was also shown to become more frequent and 'solidarity' ('solidaritet') less (Boréus, 1997: 271, Table 3).

The task

The exercise is about empirically analyzing this kind of change by comparing two corpora: one that includes the Labour manifestos for the general elections in 1970 and in February 1974, and one that includes manifestos for the general elections in 1997 and 2001. Choose either a quantitative or a qualitative analysis. Formulate one or more research questions that can be answered, or formulate hypotheses that can be tested by content analysis. A simple coding scheme/frame with instructions should be constructed and used.

A more quantitative content analysis might consist of counting frequencies of words, and testing some hypothesis about what kind of change could be expected. Such an analysis could be conceived of as a pilot-study for a larger study on change in the political vocabulary caused by, or being an integrated part of, neo-liberalization. A freeware like AntCont will be very helpful for working with this task. (Even Microsoft Word can be used for this assignment if the documents on the companion website (**https://study.sagepub.com/boreusandbergstrom**) are used.)

A qualitative analysis could take an inductive coding of the documents as its starting point, or address open-ended questions about differences in content between the manifestos in the two corpora.

(After working with this exercise you can check the suggested analysis in Chapter 9.)

The texts

The texts for this exercise are found, together with many other British party manifestos, in a pdf format at http://www.politicsresources.net/area/uk/e01/man/lab/lab01.htm (accessed 23 August 2016). Four Labour manifestos in Word format can be reached on the companion website (**https://study.sagepub.com/boreusandbergstrom**). The excerpt below is drawn from the first manifesto to work within this exercise, and exemplifies the rhetoric of the early 1970s:

> Our purpose is to create, on the firm base of a steadily growing economy, a better society for all the people of Britain: a strong, just and compassionate society, one where the handling of complex problems may be a source of pride to ourselves and an example to the world.

> Our appeal is to those who have faith in the capacity and humanity of their fellow-men, and to those who are not solely moved by the search for profit or the hope of personal gain.

(Continued)

(Continued)

First, we believe that Britain's potential for improvement is enormous. Science, technology and the general growth of knowledge present great opportunities for social and economic advance. With foresight, intelligence and effort - with planning - we can harness the new technologies and the powerful economic forces of our time to human ends.

But, without planning, with a return to the Tory free-for-all, people become the victims of economic forces they cannot control.

(Source: The 1970 Labour Manifesto. For the full text to analyze, please visit the companion website at **https://study.sagepub.com/boreusandbergstrom**.)

3

Argumentation Analysis

Kristina Boréus

3.1 Background

When I take the commuter train to work, advertisements try to persuade me that I need a new mobile phone deal by telling me how much money I could save. At the university my colleagues I and write academic articles in which we try to convince other academics that our results are interesting and sound. In politics not only political parties but also think tanks, lobby groups and NGOs strive to make people see society in particular ways and therefore support certain policies rather than others. Persuasion is an important part of social communication and a crucial aspect of trying to persuade is by arguing. Therefore social scientists need tools to both describe and evaluate argumentation. This chapter will provide such tools.

3.1.1 Rhetoric and argumentation analysis

Rhetoric, the study of persuasion, was developed by Greek and Roman scholars during antiquity. Rhetoric takes a broad grip on attempts to persuade by speech or writing in particular situations and can be defined as the "systematic study and intentional practice of effective symbolic expression" (Herrick, 2013: 8). The three central concepts of rhetoric are logos, ethos and pathos. **Logos** is the part of the attempt to persuade that appeals to the rational capacities of the audience or readership. Argumentative texts in which logos dominates appear factual and contain few evaluative words and expressions. **Ethos** might be defined as the character or personality that a speaker wants to ascribe to themselves in order to win the interest and confidence of the audience. If ethos is pronounced in texts, the speaker or writer appears strongly present. **Pathos** is the aspect of strong feelings and passions that a speaker or writer tries to awaken. A text with a strong pathos appears passionate and uses many evaluative expressions.

Argumentation analysis is a development of rhetoric that focuses on logos rather than ethos or pathos. The study of logos in argumentations has, since antiquity, been related to logic. The logical relations between claims are used to describe or model the argumentative content of texts. Since the late 1950s argumentation analysis has broadened from rhetoric and logic to become more interdisciplinary (van Eemeren and Houtlosser, 2005: 1).

Text genres are more or less argumentative. Political speeches, parliamentary motions and editorials are highly argumentative genres, while poetry and recipes rarely contain argumentative structures. The proportion of logos, ethos and pathos in argumentative texts is also genre-specific. A scholarly text such as an article in a scientific journal is expected to be driven by logos, while in journalistic works more pathos is allowed but logos is also expected to be well developed. Ethos is nowhere as important as in spoken texts where the speaker is heard and seen.

3.1.2 Aims of argumentation analysis

Argumentation analysis can have at least three objectives. First, there is a *descriptive* aim. The researcher needs to reconstruct the arguments and the relations between them in single texts or debates. This is a task as such: arguments do not jump out of texts by themselves and texts often do many things apart from arguing. Thus, the argumentation structure needs to be 'found' or 'reconstructed'.

The second objective that the analysis might have is to be *evaluative*. Argumentations might be assessed from different perspectives, one of which is to judge how strongly an argumentation speaks for or against a standpoint. In order to make this judgment it is necessary to first carry out a descriptive analysis. In judging the credibility of an argumentation it might also be helpful to examine **argumentation fallacies**.

Such fallacies can also be the focus of research. The objective might be to formulate standards for good argumentation, which avoids argumentation fallacies, a *prescriptive* aim. Several different norms for good argumentation have been formulated. Some of them concern objectivity and rationality. The purpose of an "effective discussion", according to Arne Næss (2005: 97), is the "exchange of cognitive contents in a manner that facilitates the greater consistency and proper understanding of those contents". One of his norms for effective discussion is that *"one should keep to the point, even if one is aware that it harms one's own interests to do so"* (emphasis in the original), which is a way of avoiding the fallacy of "tendentious references to side issues". In the approach to argumentation analysis referred to as **pragma dialectics**, a similar ideal of good argumentation is formulated, the intention being to find the best way of arguing when the aim is to solve contentions between parties. Among the rules proposed are that the parties must not stop each other from stating or questioning claims and that a party that has made a claim has a duty to defend it, if the other party so demands (van Eemeren and Grootendorst, 1992).

This chapter focuses the first two aims of argumentation analysis, the descriptive and evaluative ones. Descriptive argumentation analysis is useful for reconstructing the argumentation of single texts as well as entire debates. The tools proposed here might be used for reconstructing the entire argumentation of texts and debates or for capturing only the most important arguments and standpoints. Argumentation analysis might also be used together with other kinds of textual analysis and used as an overarching way of structuring a text corpus. Once it has been discovered what people are arguing for or against and which reasons they cite, other kinds of analysis can be employed.

Evaluative argumentation analysis can be used in critical research and as a part of critical discourse analysis (see Chapters 4 and 8).

3.1.3 What do different approaches to argumentation analysis have in common and how do they differ?

There are several approaches to argumentation analysis – or **argumentation theory** – apart from pragma dialectics. In this chapter I draw on three: on the pro et contra model as formulated by Næss (2005), on Stephen Toulmin's way of structuring argumentations (Toulmin, 2003 [1958]), and on a recent development within discourse analysis, referred to by Isabela Fairclough and Norman Fairclough (2012) as political discourse analysis (PDA).

These three approaches all have their roots in logic. Several textbooks take that starting point and differentiate between two basic parts of arguments: **premises** and **conclusions**. In a sound argument the premises taken together will lead to the conclusion. Confronted with the premise "If drivers on cell phones have more accidents, then drivers should be prohibited from using them", together with the premise "Drivers on cell phones *do* have more accidents", one should accept the conclusion "Therefore, drivers should be prohibited from using cell phones" (Weston, 2009: 38). Whether we are inclined to accept the conclusion depends on several things, among them whether we could think of reasons for allowing drivers to use their mobile phones even if it might be dangerous, thus not accepting the first premise, and whether we believe that the second premise about what actually causes accidents is true. If we accept both premises we are logically compelled to accept the conclusion. (See also Chapter 4 on premises and conclusions in practical argumentation.)

The three approaches to argumentation analysis are grounded in this basic understanding of drawing conclusions but have different ways of further classifying the cornerstones of argumentations and emphasize them differently.

In relation to the simple model of premises and conclusions, Næss focuses on the central conclusion in a text or debate, and organizes all the reasons for and against it in a hierarchical model, while Toulmin treats all conclusions in the same way but takes a particular interest in premises that are implicit rather than explicit. Fairclough and Fairclough provide a more detailed classification of different kinds of premises. They also specify the context of argumentation more than the other authors, constructing a particular model for analyzing **practical argumentations**, i.e. argumentations in which the conclusion is that something should be done.

Another difference between the approaches is that they provide different models for the visual representation of argumentations (through numbers, boxes and arrows employed in different ways).

3.2 Analysis

Before going into detail about how to analyze argumentation I will introduce three texts about what is arguably one of the most important political issues ever: climate change. The problem is global but the text sample is drawn from a North American setting. The sample texts, all drawn from longer texts, will be used for explaining the techniques of argumentation analysis throughout the rest of the chapter.

3.2.1 Argumentation about climate change

The first sample text comprises parts of a political speech held in August 2015 in which the US president Barack Obama introduced a plan for cutting America's carbon emissions, referred to as the Clean Power Plan:

> ... I am convinced that no challenge poses a greater threat to our future and future generations than a changing climate. And that's what brings us here today.
>
> Now, not everyone here is a scientist – (laughter) – but some of you are among the best scientists in the world. And what you and your colleagues have been showing us for years now is that human activities are changing the climate in dangerous ways. Levels of carbon dioxide, which heats up our atmosphere, are higher than they've been in 800,000 years; 2014 was the planet's warmest year on record. And we've been setting a lot of records in terms of warmest years over the last decade. One year doesn't make a trend, but 14 of the 15 warmest years on record have fallen within the first 15 years of this century. [...]
>
> The Pentagon says that climate change poses immediate risks to our national security. While we can't say any single weather event is entirely caused by climate change, we've seen stronger storms, deeper droughts, longer wildfire seasons.

Charleston and Miami now flood at high tide. Shrinking ice caps forced National Geographic to make the biggest change in its atlas since the Soviet Union broke apart. [...]

And today, we're here to announce America's Clean Power Plan – a plan two years in the making, and the single most important step America has ever taken in the fight against global climate change. (Applause.)

Right now, our power plants are the source of about a third of America's carbon pollution. That's more pollution than our cars, our airplanes and our homes generate combined. That pollution contributes to climate change, which degrades the air our kids breathe.

> (Source: Barack Obama, 3 August 2015, 'Remarks by the President in Announcing the Clean Power Plan')

All political attempts to reduce carbon emissions have been met with resistance in the USA. Climate change science has been disputed and forces that are hostile to climate policy have enjoyed influential access to the policy machinery (Hayes and Knox-Hayes, 2014: 83; see also Oreskes and Conway, 2010). A climate change counter-movement consisting of at least 118 organizations, funded by 140 or more foundations and with a total income exceeding seven billion US dollars during the period 2003–10, has tried to persuade politicians and the public that no climate change caused by human activities is taking place and/or that political measures that limit power plants' possibilities to pollute should not be taken. Conservative think tanks, trade associations and advocacy organizations are the key components of this well organized counter-movement that first appeared in 1989 (Brulle, 2014). The Heritage Foundation was a major recipient of funding among the climate change counter-movement organizations. The following criticisms of the Obama government's Clean Power Plan are drawn from an article on its homepage:

> This summer, the Obama Administration will finalize climate regulations for new and existing power plants under the Clean Air Act. While the regulations largely target coal-fired power plants, the costs of more expensive energy will be borne by all Americans. Higher energy bills for families, individuals, and businesses will destroy jobs and strain economic growth – and it will all be for naught. No matter one's belief on the climate effects of man-made greenhouse emissions, the regulations will have a negligible impact – if any – on global temperatures.

> The regulations for both new and existing power plants will face a number of legal challenges, and rightly so. However, waiting on the outcomes of legal battles would likely mean that states will already be on an irreversible path toward shuttered power plants, increasing energy bills, and lost opportunity. Furthermore, by placing the entire onus on the states to devise their own carbon-cutting plans, the Environmental Protection Agency (EPA) evades all accountability to Americans and leaves state officials to take the political heat for executing power plant regulations that are all economic pain and no environmental gain.

> Both Congress and the states need to step forward and reject these regulations entirely, not succumb to the executive branch's coercion.
>
> (Source: Nicolas D. Loris: 'The Many Problems of the EPA's Clean Power Plan and Climate Regulations: A primer', Backgrounder, 7 July 2015)

The third sample text contains arguments on the causes of the inefficient handling of the climate crisis and what needs to be done. It is drawn from an article by Canadian journalist and author Naomi Klein who has argued that the power of private big enterprises in neo-liberalized market economies effectively blocks the necessary steps towards mitigating global warming:

> To have even a 50/50 chance of hitting the 2° target (which, they [referring to two climate experts at the Tyndall Centre for Climate Change Research, Kevin Anderson and Alice Bows] and many others warn, already involves facing an array of hugely damaging climate impacts), the industrialized countries need to start cutting their greenhouse-gas emissions by something like 10 per cent a year – and they need to start right now. But Anderson and Bows go further, pointing out that this target cannot be met with the array of modest carbon pricing or green-tech solutions usually advocated by big green groups. These measures will certainly help, to be sure, but they are simply not enough: a 10 per cent drop in emissions, year after year, is virtually unprecedented since we started powering our economies with coal. In fact, cuts above 1 per cent per year "have historically been associated only with economic recession or upheaval", as the economist Nicholas Stern put it in his 2006 report for the British government. [...]
>
> If we are to avoid that kind of carnage while meeting our science-based emissions targets, carbon reduction must be managed carefully through what Anderson and Bows describe as "radical and immediate de-growth strategies in the US, EU and other wealthy nations". Which is fine, except that we happen to have an economic system that fetishizes GDP growth above all else, regardless of the human or ecological consequences, and in which the neoliberal political class has utterly abdicated its responsibility to manage anything (since the market is the invisible genius to which everything must be entrusted).
>
> So what Anderson and Bows are really saying is that there is still time to avoid catastrophic warming, but not within the rules of capitalism as they are currently constructed. Which may be the best argument we have ever had for changing those rules.
>
> (Source: Naomi Klein: 'How science is telling us all to revolt', *The New Statesman*, 29 October 2013)

Below I present different models for describing or reconstructing argumentation, first in single texts, then in entire debates, and describe ways of classifying arguments. This presentation of the descriptive approaches is followed by an account of evaluative argumentation analysis. I start by introducing a number of key concepts and the analytical steps common to the three approaches presented in more detail below.

3.2.2 Key concepts

Argumentation

The word **argumentation** has a rather technical meaning here, a meaning more accessible through many languages other than English. The counterparts of the English 'argumentation' in many European languages (among them Dutch, French, German, Italian, Portuguese, Spanish and Swedish) differ from the meaning in English. In these languages the corresponding words often refer to argumentation as a certain kind of structured content of a text: 'The argumentation in this article is not very convincing'. In these languages the words for argumentation also lack the quality of strife or quarrel that 'argumentation' can have in English uses (van Eemeren, 2010). In this chapter, a piece of structured content of a text, "a constellation of reasons put forward by a speaker or writer in defence of a standpoint" (2010: 26) is what is referred to by 'argumentation', a constellation that includes the standpoint argued for or against.[1] Argumentations might be about facts, about normative issues and about how to act. The last kind is referred to as 'practical argumentation'.

Claims

Claims are the building blocks of argumentations. A claim is something proposed or alleged to make somebody believe or accept it. Obama claims in his speech, among other things:

- that the levels of carbon dioxide are higher than they have been in 800,000 years
- that 2014 was the planet's warmest year on record
- that the Pentagon says climate change poses immediate risks to US national security

Issue expressions

Claims play different roles in argumentations, which brings us to the next key concept. Næss assigns a particular status to the central claim of a text or debate, a claim (or sometimes a few claims), which is not a reason, i.e. is not there to support or undermine other claims, but tells us what the controversy is about. He refers to such a claim as an **issue expression,** sometimes called a **thesis**. Issue expressions come in different kinds: prescriptive, normative and descriptive. **Prescriptive issue expressions** urge us to act in particular ways. Such issue expressions are particularly common and important in politics. Fairclough and Fairclough (2012) call them **claims for action**. If one reads the entire Obama speech it becomes evident that his mission is to present the Clean Power Plan, but also to sell it, so to speak. He never utters the words 'Support the Clean Power Plan!', but it would still be safe to conclude that that is the prescriptive issue expression, the claim for action, of his speech. The Plan should be supported because there is dangerous

---

[1]The standpoint is not included in the definition of 'argumentation' used in van Eemeren (2010).

climate change that can be mitigated by cutting carbon dioxide emissions, so the argumentation goes.

Issue expressions might also be **normative**, i.e. express evaluations. Prescriptive issue expressions can be reformulated as normative ones, such as 'You ought to support the Clean Power Plan'. They might also express moral evaluations, such as 'Climate change increases global injustice'.

Descriptive issue expressions are about what are considered to be facts rather than values, e.g. "To have a 50/50 chance of hitting the 2° target, the industrialized countries need to start cutting their greenhouse-gas emissions immediately by approximately 10 per cent a year". This claim made in Klein's article does not in fact function as the article's issue expression – I interpret her issue expression as being a prescriptive one (see Figure 3.2 below) – but could well be one in another context where it could be supported by various arguments, e.g. drawn from the writings of the scientists she refers to.

Arguments

Another key concept is that of **argument**. 'Argument', confusingly, has several related meanings in English. The word might refer to a verbal fight, to a submission of evidence, or to the body or main part of a written work. It might also refer to what is labelled 'argumentation' here, namely a set of reasons put forward in support of a standpoint. In this book 'argument' has the precise meaning of a claim made in support of or against another claim; a reason. Toulmin (2003 [1958]) refers to such claims as **data** but this chapter uses the term 'argument'.

Arguments are normative or descriptive. In my interpretation of the Klein article what is argued for is a claim for action, namely that we must change the rules of capitalism (see Figure 3.2). A reason for this is that "The neoliberal political class has abdicated its responsibility to manage anything"; clearly a **normative argument**.

There are plenty of **descriptive arguments** in the texts, for instance Loris's claim that higher energy bills will strain economic growth. This is meant as a reason for us to support what I have interpreted as a normative issue expression of that piece of text, namely that Congress and the states should reject the Obama administration's climate regulations for new and existing power plants (see Box 3.2 below).

Arguments in support of a claim are referred to by Næss as **pro arguments** and those against as **contra (counter**, sometimes abbreviated **con) arguments**, which are the terms that will be used here.

In his speech, Obama makes the claim that human activities are changing the climate in dangerous ways. Even though there is now massive scientific support for that claim, this is still sometimes questioned in the US public sphere. That fact, together with an effort to make people accept the Clean Power Plan, are probably why he uses other claims to support the claim about the dangers of particular human activities. Each of the following claims is used as a pro argument for the claim that human activities are changing the climate in dangerous ways. They are reasons provided for us to believe that this is true:

- that it has been shown by good scientists for years
- that levels of carbon dioxide are higher than they have been in 800,000 years
- that 14 of the 15 warmest years on record have fallen within the first 15 years of this century

In many genres, not least political speeches, contra arguments are rarely formulated in single texts. What is common, however, is that arguments against central claims are found in *debates*. The issue expression, as I interpret it, in Obama's speech is that the Clean Power Plan should be supported. Against this it is claimed by Loris in the Heritage Foundation text that "[b]oth Congress and the states need to step forward and reject these regulations entirely".

Arguments are said to be of different orders. Arguments for or against what is argued for, the issue expression, are arguments of the first order. Arguments for or against arguments of the first order are of the second order, those for or against second order arguments are of the third order, and so on.

Premises

The last key concept to be introduced is that of **premises**. Premises were said above to be the steps that lead to a conclusion in logical reasoning. Real-world argumentations resemble logical reasoning only partly, and 'premise' in argumentation analysis has a more limited meaning, namely something taken for granted, a presupposition for an argument. Between a claim (that might work as an argument or as an issue expression in an argumentation) and another claim that supports the first claim (a pro argument) or contradicts it (a contra argument) there is a third claim, explicit or implicit, that functions as a bridge between the first two claims. For the claim expressed as "It has been shown by good scientists for years" to be a pro argument for the claim that human activities are changing the climate in dangerous ways, something else has to be assumed. The assumed claim is the premise. It should be interpreted something like the following:

- if good scientists make repeated claims of something being true there is reason to believe it is true

This was not explicitly stated in the speech, which makes this premise an implicit one. Sometimes claims found in texts are explicit premises rather than arguments and should be listed as such in the reconstruction of the argumentation. Toulmin's bid for modelling argumentations demands that implicit premises should always be taken into account. He labels them **warrants** but I will use the term 'premise' throughout. He also takes an interest in claims made in support of premises, labelling them **backing**. In this chapter they are referred to as **premise arguments**. Table 3.1 summarizes the key concepts of argumentation analysis.

Table 3.1 Key concepts in argumentation analysis

Term used in this book	Alternative labels in the literature	Definition in this book	Types	Functions in argumentations
Argument-ation	argument	an issue expression and a constellation of reasons put forward by a speaker or writer in defence of that issue expression	argumentations can be divided into those about facts, those about normative issues and those about how to act (called practical argumentations)	
Claim	standpoint	something that is proposed, alleged, in order to make somebody believe or accept it		claims are used as arguments, as issue expressions and as premises
Issue expression	thesis claim for action (PDA name for prescriptive issue expression)	the central claim(s) argued for or against in a single text or a debate	issue expressions can be divided into prescriptive, normative and descriptive ones	what the argumentation is all about
Argument	data (Toulmin) premise (in the logical set-up only differentiating between premises and conclusions) contra arguments can be called counter arguments or abbreviated as con arguments backing (Toulmin's label for 'premise argument')	a reason for or against a claim	arguments can be divided into pro arguments and contra arguments arguments can be divided into normative and descriptive ones	arguments can be put forward for or against an issue expression, other arguments or premises arguments can be of a first, second, third… order depending on their role in argumentations
Premise	warrant (Toulmin's name for implicit premise)	a claim taken for granted, a presupposition for an argument	premises can be divided into explicit (stated) or implicit (only presumed) ones	each argument has explicit or implicit premises

3.2.3 Analytical steps common to the three approaches

A first step in all three approaches to argumentation analysis is to find the important claims in the texts or debates under investigation. Claims made in texts must be interpreted. The same claim might be expressed in different ways. The same or very similar claims – that the US Congress and different states should refuse to accept the regulations – are made in different parts of Loris's text: "Congress and the states should intervene and reject these regulations entirely" and "Both Congress and the states need to step forward and reject these regulations entirely". There are also other potential ways that the claim that the US Congress and different states should refuse to accept the regulations could be expressed in English or in other languages.

Words and sentences that read the same can also express different claims, depending on the context. Take the sentence 'She sees the light at the end of the tunnel'. As discussed in Chapter 6, different claims would be made depending on whether the expression were intended to be understood metaphorically or literally.

It might help to *mark or list all claims* that are not too peripheral in a text. Listing claims means interpreting text content. Language might be vague and it might be necessary to clarify sentences to be able to find the argumentation structure, i.e. to make more **precise** interpretations of what is claimed.

Another sometimes helpful move is to *split sentences up* into the different claims that might be expressed in the same sentence. An example of a sentence that should be split up to make the argumentation structure easier to grasp is drawn from a part of Loris's text not included in the quote above: "Known as the Clean Power Plan, these regulations have garnered bipartisan concern at all levels of government due to the threats the Clean Power Plan poses to the economy, quality of life, reliability of the national power grid, and constitutional separation of powers". Several claims are made here. They could be separated in the following way:

- the Clean Power Plan regulations have garnered bipartisan concern at all levels of government
- the concern is due to the threats the Clean Power Plan poses
- the Plan poses threats to the economy
- the Plan poses threats to the quality of life
- the Plan poses threats to the reliability of the national power grid
- the Plan poses threats to the constitutional separation of powers

The point of the splitting-up exercise is that these different claims might be argued for separately in the text. It is also common that the same or very similar claims appear several times in a text. They could then be *reduced to one claim*, as exemplified above.

The second analytical step consists of relating the important claims of a text to each other, finding out which claims are put forward as reasons for or against other claims. This is more or less clear in texts. It is for example quite clear that Loris uses the claim that more expensive energy (which will, according to him, be a result of adopting the Clean Power Plan) is meant as a reason, an argument, against accepting the plan. Sometimes it takes more interpretative work to grasp the relations between different claims. After this step the three approaches depart.

3.2.4 Reconstructing argumentations in single texts according to the pro et contra method

Næss (2005) relates *pro et contra dicere* (to speak for and against) as a method to the ancient Greek philosopher Carneades (ca. 214–129 BC). To reconstruct the argumentation of a particular text, according to this technique, means to find the issue expression and all pro and contra arguments that bear on it. The first step in reconstructing the argumentation of a single text is to find the issue expression. In Loris's article for the Heritage Foundation I interpret it to be:

> IE: Congress and the states should reject the Obama administration's climate regulations for new and existing power plants

The reason this particular claim was interpreted as being the issue expression was that, when considering other claims, it could be decided that they were arguments in support of this claim. Furthermore, it is common that prescriptive claims are what is being argued for or against in a text, which makes such a claim a likely candidate from the outset.

Apart from the claim interpreted as the issue expression, the following claims are made in the quote by Loris (some of which could be broken down further if needed):

--- **Box 3.1** ---

Claims made by Loris on the Heritage Foundation webpage

- the Obama Administration will finalize regulations for new and existing power plants under the Clean Air Act this summer
- the costs of more expensive energy will be borne by all Americans even though the regulations largely target coal-fired plants
- higher energy bills will destroy jobs
- higher energy bills will strain economic growth
- the regulations will have a negligible or no impact on global temperatures
- the regulations will rightly face a number of legal challenges
- waiting on the outcome of legal battles would likely mean that states will be on an irreversible path towards shuttered power plants, increasing energy bills and lost opportunity
- by placing the onus on the states to device their own carbon-cutting plans the EPA [United States Environment Protection Agency] evades accountability to Americans and leaves state officials to take the political heat

While the first and the sixth claims only explain what the argumentation is about, the others can rather straightforwardly be organized into a hierarchical structure with an issue expression and arguments supporting it:

Box 3.2

Organization of claims into an issue expression with supporting arguments

IE: Congress and the states should reject the Obama administration's climate regulations for new and existing power plants

P1: While the regulations largely target coal-fired plants, the costs of more expensive energy will be borne by all Americans

P2: Higher energy bills for families, individuals, and business will destroy jobs

P3: Higher energy bills will strain economic growth

P4: The regulations will have none or a negligible impact on global temperatures

P5: If waiting on the outcome of legal battles, states will take the path toward shuttered power plants, increasing energy bills and lost opportunity

P6: The EPA evades accountability to Americans

   P1P6: The EPA places the entire onus on states to devise their own carbon-cutting plans

---

The indications P1–P6 tell us that the arguments so designated are six different pro arguments of the first order, i.e. they support the issue expression directly. The order between them, i.e. which one is designated as P1, P2, P3…, is unimportant. I have just listed them in the order they appear in the text. The last one, P1P6, is an argument that does not support the issue expression directly, but P6. It is the first pro argument for the sixth pro argument for the issue expression. If one wants a reason for the claim made that the EPA is not accountable to Americans, the claim that the EPA puts the obligation on the different states (that are only accountable to people living in them) makes sense.

Next, I return to the Obama speech to demonstrate how the restructuring can include contra arguments and premises. I claimed above that the issue expression of the entire Obama speech was a prescription to support the Clean Power Plan. Box 3.3 is a reconstruction of the argumentation in the sample text, related to this issue expression. I interpret the argumentation as containing three first order arguments for the issue expression: that climate change is dangerous, that it is really taking place and that the Clean Power Plan is an important means of mitigating it. In the part of the speech quoted here, Obama expends some energy on arguing for the first two of these arguments – i.e. he also presents lower order arguments for them. I only found one contra argument (my emphasis):

> 2014 was the planet's warmest year on record. [...] *One year doesn't make a trend*, but 14 of the 15 warmest years on record have fallen within the first 15 years of this century.

That 2014 was the warmest year so far is meant as an argument for the claim that human activities have been changing the climate (although, strictly, it is only an argument in support of the claim that climate is changing, not of what has caused the change), but is directly countered by the claim that one year does not make a trend, implying that one warm year might not be a sign of climate change but just happened to be warm. That implication is the premise: for the claim that one year doesn't make a trend to be a contra argument to the claim that there is dangerous climate change going on, something of that sort must be implied. In the pro et contra list below the Greek sign 'ϕ' (pronounced 'fy' or 'fee') is used to designate a premise and '(ϕC1P2)' designates that it is a premise for the argument C1P2. C1P2, in its turn, is the first (and only) argument against P2, which is the second pro argument for the issue expression. The brackets are there to show that the premise is implicit. It is common in political speeches to disarm the few counter arguments to one's own issue expression put forward. This is what Obama does by formulating a contra argument against (ϕC1P2), namely that the temperatures of 2014 are in fact difficult to explain by natural variation, since 14 of the 15 warmest years on record have fallen within the first 15 years of this century.

Box 3.3

Pro et contra list with pro and contra arguments and premises on first, second and third level

IE: You ought to support the Clean Power Plan
P1: No challenge poses a greater threat to our future and future generations than a changing climate
P2: Human activities are changing the climate in dangerous ways
    P1P2: It has been shown by good scientists for years
    P2P2: Levels of carbon dioxide, which heats up our atmosphere, are higher than they have been in 800,000 years
    P3P2: 2014 was the planet's warmest year on record
    C1P2: One year doesn't make a trend

(φC1P2): The record is due to a normal variation in temperature and is not a sign of human activities changing the climate
   C1(φC1P2): 14 of the 15 warmest years have fallen within the first 15 years of this century

P1P1: Climate change poses immediate risks to our national security
   P1P1P1: The Pentagon says so
   P2P1P1: We've seen stronger storms, deeper droughts, longer wildfire seasons
   P3P1P1: Charleston and Miami now flood at high tide
   P4P1P1: Shrinking ice caps forced National Geographic to make the biggest change in its atlas since the Soviet Union broke apart
   P5P1P1: Climate change degrades the air our kids breathe

P3: The Clean Power Plan is the single most important step America has ever taken in the fight against global climate change
   P1P3: Our power plants are the source of about a third of America's carbon pollution, which contributes to climate change

Next the Toulmin model for restructuring argumentations will be demonstrated.

3.2.5 Reconstructing argumentations in single texts according to Toulmin

Stephen Toulmin's model for reconstructing argumentations, developed in *The Uses of Argument* (1958), differs from the pro et contra model by highlighting other aspects of the logical relations between claims. What is shown below is a modified version of his scheme.

In Toulmin's analysis there are two imagined parties to the discussion. When someone makes a claim, somebody else is thought to be there, pressing the first person for their reasons. This person would ask the first one what they have based the claim on and the first person is thereby challenged to provide reasons, to formulate arguments. The person challenging the initial claim-maker might well accept the claim of the argument then provided for the first claim made but still question whether the argument really supports the claim. They will then ask for the bridge between the argument and the initial claim, thus demanding that the premise be clarified.

The premise is also a claim and can, like other claims, be argued about. As an example, take the argument P1P2 "It has been shown by good scientists for years", in Box 3.3, which is meant to support P2 "Human activities are changing the climate in dangerous ways", in the Obama speech. I formulated the implicit premise above as "If good scientists make repeated claims of something being true there is reason to believe it is true". This claim could, in its turn, be argued for or against.

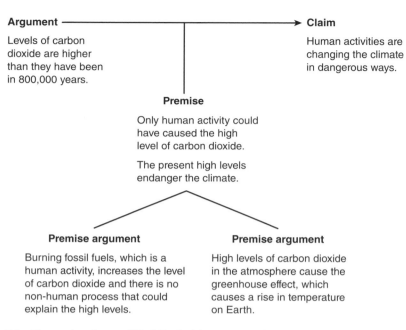

Figure 3.1 Elements of a modified Toulminian scheme.[2]

Argumentations are laid out graphically in a Toulminian analysis. In Figure 3.1 one of the arguments of the first order (P2) found in the Obama speech is taken as the starting point and one of the second order arguments supporting it (P2P2) is shown, together with the implicit premise with likewise implicit arguments supporting it.

The premise, in my interpretation, consists of two claims: one being that there is no other reasonable explanation for the high levels of carbon dioxide in the atmosphere than that it has been caused by humans, the other being that these levels affect the climate in a dangerous way. That there are two claims needed to formulate the premise is because P2 actually consists of two claims: that human activities are changing the climate and that the change is dangerous. Once the premise has been formulated, it becomes clear that we have arrived at the natural science part of the argumentation, which, in the Obama speech, is partly implicit. Since the two premise arguments are what the world's scientists state in their Intergovernmental Panel on Climate Change reports, summarized for example in the 'Summary for policy makers' (IPCC, 2014), this is a very likely interpretation of how Obama would have backed the premise if challenged to do so or of how

---

[2]In Toulmin (2003 [1958]), what is here referred to as 'argument' is called 'data', 'premise' is labelled 'warrant', and 'premise argument' is called 'backing'. Toulmin also includes two more elements: **qualifiers**, referring to the certainty or force with which the data confer the claim in virtue of the given warrant, and **rebuttals** that indicate circumstances in which the general authority of a warrant would be rejected (2003: Chapter III).

he could have argued for it, given the body of knowledge he seems to be drawing on in his speech.

The advantage with the Toulminian model is also what makes it more challenging to use than the pro et contra model: it needs the formulation of implicit premises. This demands more complex interpretations while drawing attention to the unsaid, something that is often important in discourse analysis. The third model for restructuring argumentation that will be explained was created specifically to be used in discourse analysis.

3.2.6 Reconstructing argumentations in single texts according to PDA

To reconstruct a practical argumentation according to **political discourse analysis**, PDA, one should look for claims that have particular tasks in the argumentation. Fairclough and Fairclough (2012) refer to all these claims as 'premises', taking departure in the logical model of arguments referred to above according to which all steps leading to a conclusion are called 'premises'. In the vocabulary of this book some of them would be arguments and some would be premises.

The issue expression – labelled **claim for action** in this model – should be found. The claim for action is meant to help someone reach a particular **goal**. Formulations of that goal should be looked for in the text: for what reason is it stated that a particular course of action should be chosen? A special kind of argument often explicitly stated is called **means-goal** in the model, which refers to claims made to convince the reader that the course of action proposed in the issue expression will actually lead to the stated goal.

Another common and important kind of claim in practical argumentations is in regard to the **circumstances**. The action argued for is supposed to transform the circumstances referred to in a way that makes the goal come true.[3]

The goal is often related to certain **values**. These restrict the set of actions that might lead to the goal of actions that are compatible with these values. (Even if Obama knew of a way of closing down all US power plants immediately he would, as a leading US politician, be very unlikely to propose this, since it would compete with values regarding private property, economic growth etc.)

To illustrate this model for reconstructing argumentations I now turn to the article by Naomi Klein. All elements stand out quite clearly in the text. Klein claims that we need to change the rules of capitalism since there is no other way to obtain the economic "de-growth" needed for the quick and radical reduction

---

[3]Fairclough and Fairclough (2012) differentiate between kinds of circumstances brought up: these might be natural (e.g. about carbon dioxide and greenhouse effects) or institutional (about political actors or to do with political or economic institutions, for example). I have skipped that step here.

of emissions that is necessary to save the world from catastrophic warming. The crucial circumstances are those about the relationship between emissions of greenhouse gases and climate change that the quoted scientists refer to, and circumstances to do with the economic system. Klein also argues that cuts in greenhouse-gas emissions as big as those that are now necessary have hitherto only been the result of economic recession or upheaval. There is most likely a set of unstated values about human wellbeing that are the basis for her argumentation. Most of these cannot be deduced from the text. The only formulation that resembles an explicit value statement is that the kind of "carnage" that recessions or upheavals lead to should be avoided; thus a planned "de-growth" is preferable. Figure 3.2 shows this interpretation of the practical argumentation in the text.

These particular kinds of claims – claims about what action to take, claims that the action proposed actually will lead to the goal, claims about what the circumstances are – are typical for practical argumentations, according to Fairclough and Fairclough (2012) and should be sought in texts. These claims are related to particular implicit or explicit goals and values. Using this model instead of either of the other two might be particularly helpful for analyzing political or other practical argumentations, though it is not suitable for argumentations based on descriptive issue expressions and only for such normative issue expressions that say we ought to act in a particular way, which are a kind of claim that the prescriptive claim in this example could easily be reformulated into, i.e. 'We ought to change the rules of capitalism'.

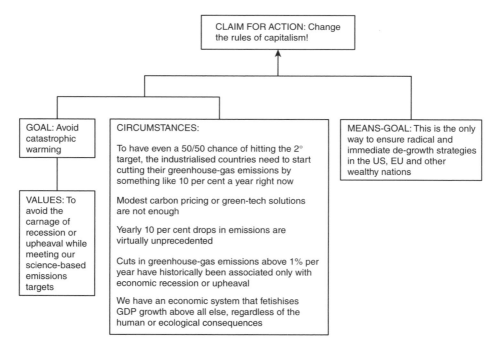

Figure 3.2 Reconstruction of a practical argumentation according to PDA

So far the focus has been on the reconstruction of single texts. Now I will turn to the task of analyzing debates which include several texts.

3.2.7 Reconstructing debates

Vedung (1977; my translation of the terms) proposes different ways to reconstruct the argumentation of entire debates, two of which are shown here: the **agent-oriented model** in which the arguments are grouped according to which agents put them forward, and the **substance-oriented model** which focuses on the subject matter of the controversy. (There are also other ways of organizing the argumentations of debates; see for example Kopperschmidt, 1985.)

In the case of the debate about the Obama government's Clean Power Plan, a reconstruction in accordance with the agent-oriented model could take Obama's issue expression that the Plan be supported as the issue expression of the debate and then list all pro and contra arguments put forward by different agents in relation to this issue expression. If used to reconstruct the first two sample texts but sorting only the first order arguments it would look like this:

Box 3.4

Reconstruction of part of a debate applying the agent-oriented model

IE: You ought to support the Clean Power Plan

Barack Obama:

P1: No challenge poses a greater threat to our future and future generations than a changing climate
P2: Human activities are changing the climate in dangerous ways
P3: The Clean Power Plan is the single most important step America has ever taken in the fight against global climate change

Nicolas Loris:

C1: While the regulations largely target coal-fired plants, the costs of more expensive energy will be borne by all Americans
C2: Higher energy bills for families, individuals, and business will destroy jobs
C3: Higher energy bills will strain economic growth
C4: The regulations will have none or a negligible impact on global temperatures
C5: If waiting on the outcome of legal battles, states will take the path toward shuttered power plants, increasing energy bills and lost opportunity
C6: The EPA is not accountable to Americans

All that was done was that the enumeration of Loris's arguments as interpreted in Box 3.2 was changed. In the above list all central arguments by important agents could be included. Arguments of lower orders could be included to the extent needed for the research purpose. Once the central arguments put forward by different agents have been listed, it is easy to relate these to the chosen issue expression.

When the substance-oriented model is used to reconstruct the first order arguments of the debate into one pro et contra list – which demands some renumbering of the arguments – it becomes immediately clear that in the sample texts, few arguments contradict each other. Obama and Loris relate to different topics when they speak for and against the Clean Power Plan. There is just one central disagreement: the president claims that the Plan is very important for mitigating climate change while the Heritage author states that it would have next to no effect.

Box 3.5

Reconstruction of part of a debate applying the substance-oriented model

IE: You ought to support the Clean Power Plan
P1: No challenge poses a greater threat to our future and future generations than a changing climate
P2: Human activities are changing the climate in dangerous ways
P3: The Clean Power Plan is the single most important step America has ever taken in the fight against global climate change
  C1P3: The regulations will have none or a negligible impact on global temperatures.

C1: While the regulations largely target coal-fired plants, the costs of more expensive energy will be borne by all Americans
C2: Higher energy bills for families, individuals, and business will destroy jobs
C3: Higher energy bills will strain economic growth
C4: If waiting on the outcome of legal battles, states will take the path toward shuttered power plants, increasing energy bills and lost opportunity
C5: The EPA is not accountable to Americans

The difference between the two ways of reconstructing the argumentation of a debate is minimal in the example but would be greater with more participants and with the arguments of lower orders included. While the agent-oriented model shows the arguments different agents have made in relation to a particular issue expression, the substance-oriented model lists the pro and contra arguments as they logically relate to each other. The first model is useful for gaining an overview of how agents have positioned themselves in relation to the subject matter and each other. The latter model is more useful when the purpose is coming to a conclusion on a contentious issue.

The last tool that will be demonstrated here before turning to evaluative analysis is the grouping of arguments into categories.

3.2.8 Classifying arguments

Arguments can be classified according to their general kind or in regard to their specific content. When arguments are classified according to their general kind, the classification is a matter of what function the premise linking them to an issue expression fulfils. There are several ways of classifying arguments according to the purpose of their premise. A **causal argument** is exemplified in Figure 3.3 below and a **generalizing argument** in Figure 3.4.

The other way of classifying arguments, according to their content, is often more useful in the social sciences. The arguments are grouped together according to their subject or theme. In Box 3.6 some of the arguments found in the sample texts from the North American climate debate are grouped according to content.

Box 3.6

Arguments classified according to content

(O = Obama, K = Klein, L = Loris)

Arguments supporting the claim that climate change is dangerous:

- No challenge poses a greater threat to our future and future generations than a changing climate. (O)
- Climate change poses immediate risks to our national security. (O)
- Even if the 2° target is hit, there will be an array of hugely damaging climate impacts. (K)

Arguments supporting the claim that carbon reduction must be managed through radical and immediate de-growth strategies in the wealthy nations:

- To have even a 50/50 chance of hitting the 2° target the industrialised countries need to start cutting their greenhouse-gas emissions by something like 10 per cent a year immediately. (K)
- According to Anderson and Bows this target cannot be met with modest carbon pricing or green-tech solutions. (K)
- A 10 per cent drop in emissions, year after year, is virtually unprecedented since we started powering our economies with coal. (K)

(Continued)

(Continued)

Economic arguments against state regulations of emissions:

- The costs of more expensive energy will be borne by all Americans. (L)
- Higher energy bills for families, individuals, and business will destroy jobs. (L)
- Higher energy bills will strain economic growth. (L)

Texts by further agents who have taken part in the North American climate debate would yield more arguments that could be listed under these headlines and several other headlines that would group central arguments together could be thought of.

3.2.9 Evaluative argumentation analysis

Argumentations might be evaluated in different ways according to the researcher's perspective. According to a logical perspective, the goal could be labelled **rational persuasiveness**, meaning that the issue expression argued for should be justified: good and sufficient reasons and rational support should be provided (Fairclough and Fairclough, 2012: 52). This form of evaluation does not ask whether an issue expression is true or tenable but whether it is well supported. An issue expression might be true despite the fact that it is part of a very weak argumentation. Pragma dialectics focuses on argumentation as a procedure for testing the acceptability of a standpoint and **reasonableness** is an ideal. Rules for ideal 'argumentative conduct' are developed with the goal of reaching reasonable resolutions for differences of opinion. These rules for good behaviour are contrasted with different unreasonable or fallacious argumentative moves (2012: 53). The **effectiveness** of an argumentation could be evaluated according to a rhetorical perspective on argumentation (that includes not only logos but also ethos and pathos): how persuasive is it?

What is described in this section is the kind of evaluation which asks whether an argumentation in rationally persuasive, what Næss (2005: 75) refers to as "'surveys' of arguments for and against a standpoint". How strongly do the arguments taken together speak for or against the issue expression? There are four steps involved in this kind of evaluation. First, the tenability of the arguments is evaluated. Second, their relevance is scrutinized. Third, one should search for potential arguments that are of importance for the claim of the issue expression but which are not present in the argumentation. Fourth, the arguments with their respective degree of tenability and relevance must be weighted against each other.

Tenability
The degree of **tenability** of an argument is a question of its credibility. In the case of descriptive arguments evidence is asked for in the same way as one questions any

kind of factual data. President Obama claimed that 2014 was the planet's warmest year ever recorded. Is it true that it was the warmest year ever recorded? According to which reports, what scientific evidence? Are there conflicting opinions on the matter?[4] To evaluate the tenability of his argument "We've seen stronger storms, deeper droughts, longer wildfire seasons", we would really need more precision: we do not know what part of the world Obama refers to, or what time periods he compares. We might assume that he is talking about the United States – a plausible interpretation considering that he refers to the US in the sentences both before and after the one in which the argument is made – and presume that he is speaking about the last few decades. With this interpretation at hand we can ask whether there are research and records to support this argument.[5]

Normative arguments that contain moral claims must be examined in other ways. Towards the end of his speech (a part not included in the text sample above) Obama says:

> I don't want my grandkids not to be able to swim in Hawaii, or not to be able to climb a mountain and see a glacier because we didn't do something about it. I don't want millions of people's lives disrupted and this world more dangerous because we didn't do something about it. That would be shameful of us.

"Shameful" implies that it would be morally wrong for us not to act: if we do not "do something about it" we ought to be ashamed of ourselves. I interpret the statement as a first order argument for the issue expression about supporting the Clean Power Plan. A gut reaction of many would be that Obama is right: that would in fact be wrong. But why? The reaction that normative arguments cannot be argued about because they are 'only a matter of opinion' or since 'norms are relative' would be unsatisfactory when in fact much of our arguing is about what is morally right and wrong (see Chapter 11 on moral arguments in Feldman, 1999). Instead we could take some of the ways to argue about moral issues described in normative theory, a branch of philosophy, as our starting point.

One way of reasoning about moral issues is that we should choose the actions that have the best consequences, a moral doctrine referred to as **consequentialism**. The consequences that should be regarded are often the happiness or wellbeing of sentient beings; according to **utilitarianism**, as expressed by the eighteenth-century philosopher Jeremy Bentham, we should always act so as to maximize the total sum of welfare for those affected by our doings. An action is wrong if, in the situation, there was an alternative to it, which would have resulted in a larger sum total of welfare in the world (Tännsjö, 2002: 17–19). To judge whether or not

---

[4]In this case Obama (or his speech writers) could for instance have referenced the NASA page on global climate change (http://climate.nasa.gov/vital-signs/global-temperature/) that at the time would have shown 2014 as the hitherto warmest year.

[5]Again, Obama could have utilized the NASA site: http://climate.nasa.gov/effects/

supporting the Plan is something we ought to do in a moral sense, we need to evaluate the consequences of accepting or rejecting. There are also other possible intuitions underlying moral judgment, for instance that certain kinds of action are always wrong and that people have rights that ought not to be transgressed, which motivates other kinds of tenability assessment of normative arguments.

To test the tenability of any kind of argument is to judge to what extent it is true, likely to be true or reasonable. As in real life it is often difficult to be sure about the answer and one often has to settle for something less than certainty.

Relevance

Arguments might be as solid as a rock without strengthening an argumentation's reasonable persuasiveness. To do so they also need to be **relevant**, meaning that they actually fulfil their purpose in the argumentation, namely to support or contradict the issue expression, another argument or a premise. In many cases it would be easy to check the tenability of the claim 'It's a quarter to eleven'. It is easy to think of contexts in which this claim supports the issue expressions 'We need to hurry' or 'It's time for you to go to bed'. In such cases we would consider the arguments to be relevant. But it would be farfetched to see it as a relevant argument for the issue expression "Congress and the states should reject the Obama administration's climate regulations for new and existing power plants". We simply do not understand what the time of day has to do with the issue of the Clean Power Plan. Indeed, we would have difficulty seeing that claim as an argument in the context. The difference to the first two issue expressions is that it is easy to think of premises that bridge the arguments and what they claim, e.g. in the first case in a causal argumentation whose premise is a causal claim, a claim about cause and effect (as in Figure 3.3).

Figure 3.4 illustrates a generalizing argument in which the claim of the premise is that the case at hand can be related to a general rule or pattern.

That the relevance of these arguments seems high at first glance is no guarantee that it stands up to further scrutiny. If the train station is nearby and the train leaves at three o'clock the argument in Figure 3.3 might still be irrelevant.

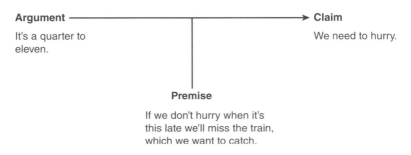

Argument ——————————————————→ **Claim**

It's a quarter to
eleven.

We need to hurry.

Premise

If we don't hurry when it's
this late we'll miss the train,
which we want to catch.

Figure 3.3 Causal argumentation whose relevance seems high

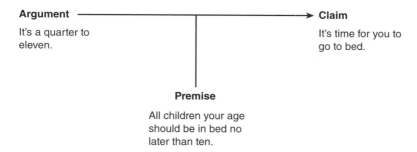

Figure 3.4 Generalizing argument whose relevance seems high

Relevance testing is often not as easy as in the example with the 'It's a quarter to eleven' argument. The premises to be tested might be both complex and controversial. Take Loris's argument P3 and its implicit premise (Figure 3.5).

The tenability of the argument would be more likely to be questioned in the US debate than its premise. Economic growth as a goal has been dominating world politics for a long time. To see it questioned, one has to go either to authors who claim that economic growth as such is not desirable, or to those who claim that it is desirable in most cases but that growth based on today's high level of production and consumption is undesirable since the mitigation of climate change is more important.

Thus the first and second steps in an evaluation of an argumentation consist in evaluating the tenability and relevance of all important arguments. This is not enough – one should also look for tenable and relevant arguments for or against the issue expression that do not appear in the argumentation: is there anything of importance to the issue at hand that is not brought up for discussion? In the last step, the arguments on either side are weighted. Although some authors propose that each argument be given points according to its degrees of tenability and relevance, after which the numerical sums of pro and contra arguments should be compared, there is no way to avoid a degree of subjectivity in the judgment.

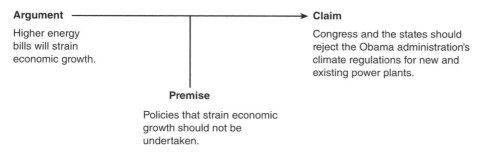

Figure 3.5 Argument with a contentious premise

Evaluating practical argumentations

Fairclough and Fairclough (2012) propose a different way of evaluating argumentations. They call attention to the fact that a proposal for action can be acceptable even if the reasons that support it are neither tenable nor relevant, i.e. even if the argumentation as such is not reasonably persuasive (2012: 66). They list a number of critical questions, relating to different parts of their model for reconstructing argumentations. The list below is based on the discussion in Fairclough and Fairclough (2012: 62–8). The primary aim of posing them is to evaluate the claim for action – should it be chosen or not? – but they are also good for evaluating the reasonable persuasiveness of the argumentation.[6]

One question to ask is in regard to the description of the *circumstances*:

1. Are the circumstances rightly assessed?

It should, for instance, be true that the situation really involves a problem that needs to be solved. The *means-goal* claims also need to be addressed:

2. Does the action or policy proposed really lead to the goal?

It should be noted that a conclusion of the evaluation might be that the action proposed is not sufficient or adequate for the goal but that this does not prove the claim for action false: there might be other good reasons for the action. The *claim for* a particular course of *action* should also be scrutinized:

3. Are there better courses of action for reaching the goal?

Again, even if better alternatives for reaching the goal are identified, it does not follow that the course of action should not be taken: there might be other strong reasons for choosing it instead of the alternatives. It should also be asked whether there are other problems with the claim for action:

4. Does the proposed course of action undermine the goal or other goals that are or ought to be important to the agent?

If the claimed course of action undermines the goal it is supposed to enhance, that is a strong reason to rebut the claim. If it has negative consequences for other goals those have to be weighed against the positive outcomes of taking the course of action.

There are also questions to pose regarding *values*:

5. Are the values that motivate the action acceptable?
6. Should other values be considered?
7. Do the stated values conflict with other values?

---

[6]In Fairclough and Fairclough (2012) the questions are not formulated exactly as I have chosen here and they are not numbered.

In real-world practical argumentations all the elements are not always spelled out in texts and debates. In a critical evaluation of a course of action all the elements are important to consider all the same.

Now that the different tools for describing and evaluating argumentations have been demonstrated I shall turn to a short critical discussion and some examples of their usage in research.

3.3 Critical reflections

The researcher runs into at least two kinds of interpretation problems when conducting argumentation analysis. The first has to do with a tension between different interpretation strategies. Trying to interpret the text producer's argumentation seems an obvious step, adhering to the producer-oriented strategy in Table 1.1. Yet reconstructing an argumentation sometimes comes close to constructing a more coherent argumentative structure than the text producer has actually been aware of. This approaches the analyst-oriented strategy, according to which the analyst interprets the text with particular tools or from particular perspectives that might reveal patterns in the text that neither the producer nor primary addressees would be aware of. As argued in Chapter 1, such readings might be justified as long as it is not claimed that they are merely an interpretation of the producer's text.

The second and related problem is that the interpretation – or reconstruction – of the argumentation structure forces the analyst to make precise interpretations of claims to be able to reconstruct the argumentation structure. What is really claimed by different sentences in texts? The decision is often difficult since rhetorical texts are notoriously unclear in parts, and often purposely so. The decisions become even more difficult in Toulminian analyses in which implicit premises need to be reconstructed. The way to handle this difficulty is, just as in other text studies, to argue for interpretations that are not obvious.

3.4 Argumentation analysis and the study of power and other social phenomena

The practice of argumentation analysis is more common in philosophical and linguistic works on argumentation theory than it is in empirical social scientific work. It is, however, possible to use for studies of all kinds of social phenomena. It is hoped that the sample studies described in this section will show that the approach can be useful for the social sciences and the study of power-related issues such as citizenship rights and discrimination.

3.4.1 Argumentation analysis in a study of citizenship

In the first study the classification of arguments in accordance with their content was a central method. Albert Hirschman (1991) classifies arguments in *The*

Rhetoric of Reaction in which he analyses "Three Reactions and Three Reactionary Theses" (1991: 3) against the backdrop of 200 years of progressive development of citizenship in a number of European countries. The analysis sets out from T.H. Marshall's (1965) division of this development into three stages, each of which saw an ideological battle. The first battle took place during the eighteenth century and regarded the institutionalization of civil citizenship: freedom of thought, speech and religion, even-handed justice and other kinds of individual rights. In the nineteenth century the battle was about political citizenship, the right for citizens to take part in the exercise of political power. This right was strengthened with the extension of the franchise to new groups. The third battle took place in the twentieth century when citizenship was widened to the social and economic spheres, with the welfare state's recognition that a certain level of education, health care, economic wellbeing and security is necessary to enable citizens to exercise their civil and political citizenship.

All these steps in the development of citizenship met with what Hirschman refers to as reactionary waves. The institution of civil rights was met by reactionary propaganda, not least in connection to the French revolution. Edmund Burke's *Reflections on the Revolution in France* (1790) includes a polemic against the Declaration of the Rights of Man. The second reactionary wave opposed universal suffrage. From the last third of the nineteenth century up until after the First World War a broad literature appeared which formulated every conceivable argument against giving 'the masses' political power. The third wave of reaction was the neo-liberal demands for 'rolling back' the welfare state (see Chapter 2 of this book) that were voiced during the late twentieth century.

Hirschman's analysis consists of reconstructing typical contra arguments that were found in all the waves of reaction. He recognizes three recurrent argument types that he calls Perversity, Futility and Jeopardy. While he refers to these as 'theses' they are arguments according to the vocabulary of this book. The **Perversity thesis** claims that every act aimed at improving some aspect of the political, social or economic order will have the opposite effect: the attempt to push society in a particular direction will result in making it move the opposite way. According to the **Futility thesis**, the attempt to create change is futile, it lacks effect. The third kind of argument, or the **Jeopardy thesis**, states that the proposed policy risks destroying something that has been achieved previously.

I illustrate Hirschman's analysis with the Futility thesis and a few of his examples of this way of arguing. In the first (belated) wave of reaction Alexis de Tocqueville (1856) argued that almost all of what was described as achievements of the French revolution had already existed during the Ancien Régime. The revolutionary attempts to reform France were thus futile. This argumentation was then developed by other authors. An example of the Futility thesis from the second wave of reactions was the economist Vilfredo Pareto's claim that every society remains divided between a ruling elite and those that are ruled, regardless of its surface organization. For that reason the widening of citizens' formal possibilities to influence is futile.

An example from the third wave of reactions is the claim made by the economists Milton and Rose Friedman that many welfare programmes that aim at reaching the poorest in the USA are futile:

> Many programs tend to benefit middle- and upper-income groups rather than the poor for whom they are supposedly intended. The poor tend to lack not only the skills valued in the market, but also the skills required to be successful in the political scramble for funds. [...] Once well-meaning reformers who may have helped to get a welfare measure enacted have gone on to their next reform, the poor are left to fend for themselves and they will almost always be overpowered. (Milton Friedman and Rose Friedman (1979), quoted in Hirschman, 1991: 65)

3.4.2 Argumentation analysis in a study of discrimination

The second sample study used a combination of the pro et contra technique and a Toulminian focus on premises together with a classification of arguments (Boréus, 2006). These techniques were employed as part of an analysis of the discursive treatment of people referred to as 'mentally deficient' in interwar Swedish public elite discourse. Many of those referred to as mentally deficient would today be called persons with 'intellectual' or 'general learning' disabilities. This group was particularly prominent in Swedish elite discourses and in general perceptions in the early 1930s (Söder, 1978). One ideological current making the 'mentally deficient' interesting to discuss was the race biological or eugenic one that swept Europe and North America at the time. By the early part of the twentieth century, eugenics as a science of human hereditary improvement had arisen in more than 30 countries (Adams, 1990). The 'mentally deficient' were seen as carriers of inferior genes and as such a threat to the national stock of people. Sterilization was the most prominent point in the political programmes of the eugenic movements in many countries.

At the time when the analyzed Swedish debate took place, Denmark, one Swiss canton, a province of Canada and 27 of the states in the USA already had sterilization laws. In Sweden the adoption of a law had become a political issue. A sterilization law was first officially proposed in 1922. After several years of investigations and discussions a law was accepted in 1934 by the Swedish parliament. It allowed for the sterilization of mentally deficient persons without their consent under certain conditions.

The analyzed corpus consisted of all central documents in the Swedish parliamentary decision process between 1922 and 1934, of entries to do with 'mental deficiency' and related topics in encyclopedias from the 1920s and 1930s, as well as of some other publicly available texts produced by political or scientific elite authors.

The main purpose of the study was to analyze to what extent and in what way discursive discrimination – defined as unfavourable treatment by linguistic means of people due to their (alleged) membership of a certain group – against the 'mentally deficient' took place. The group were severely marginalized and often harshly and cruelly treated in the institutions where many of them lived, often against their will. The discursive treatment was found to be clearly discriminatory, not least in the sense that this group of people were excluded from taking part in the discussion of politics of relevance to them – even though the debate harboured the understanding that "[t]here are mentally deficient for whom not only general medical knowledge but specialized medical knowledge is needed to judge their condition", and potentially affected persons were writing "addresses, petitions, and letters", as stated by a member of the First Chamber in 1934 (Boréus, 2006: 447).

Argumentation analysis was a way of structuring the discourse but was also used to analyze another kind of discursive discrimination, called objectification, referring to, among other things, a denial of subjectivity, i.e. people being treated as if they lacked experiences, feelings and desires, or as if these did not need to be considered.

In a first step, the arguments in the entire political debate for and against the adoption of the sterilization law were found and organized in a pro et contra list, arranged in accordance with the substance-oriented model. In line with the Toulmin model explicit and implicit premises were also interpreted and analyzed. The arguments and premises were sorted according to content, which made for an overview of the debate.

The argumentation analysis showed that the debate was almost completely objectifying in the sense explained above: all the central arguments related to alleged societal interests rather than the interest or wellbeing of the people considered for sterilization. Box 3.7 shows parts of the reconstructed debate.

Box 3.7

Part of a pro et contra list arranged according to the substance-oriented model with arguments and premises classified according to their content.[7]

IE: A sterilisation law aimed at the mentally deficient should be adopted

The eugenic argument:

P1: By sterilising the bearers of bad genes in large enough numbers, the proportion of the inferior could be reduced in coming generations

---

[7]The labels for the elements of the argumentation have been adapted to the usage in this chapter. (Source: Part of Table 1, Boréus, 2006: 452–3.)

P1P1: Many mentally deficient people give birth to children who are themselves abnormal

> **P1P1P1:** Case stories [of 'mentally deficient' children born of 'mentally deficient' mothers] are presented

The burden to society premise:

ϕ**P1:** The existence of a large number of psychologically inferior individuals is a burden to society

> **P1ϕP1:** Such individuals are usually not of any social value
>
> **P2ϕP1:** They must usually be supported by society and result in substantial costs for society

To summarize, the function of the argumentation analysis in this study was, first, to structure the fairly large material consisting of state reports, legislative proposals, private bills, minutes from parliamentary debates etc. Argumentation analysis is particularly useful for text genres that are overtly argumentative, such as in this case. Second, the conclusion about objectification was based on the scrutiny for arguments that would take the interests and subjectivity of the targeted group into consideration.

Summary

On the usefulness of argumentation analysis

- Argumentation analysis can be used to describe and evaluate the argumentative content of single texts or debates. An evaluation of the rational persuasiveness of argumentations might be a method used in critical discourse analysis.
- Argumentation analysis is focused on the part of argumentation that speaks to logos, our intellectual capacities. Descriptions and analyses of other aspects of attempts to persuade other analytical tools, such as those offered by rhetoric, are needed.
- Argumentation analysis generates a tension between a producer-oriented and an analyst-oriented interpretation strategy. The researcher should be aware of what kind of interpretation they are aiming at.

How to go about doing it

- Three methods for reconstructing argumentations in single texts were described: the pro et contra list, the Toulminian analysis and PDA.
- The reconstruction according to all three models starts by finding the central claims in the text and analyzing their relation to each other.
- In the pro et contra analysis the next step is to find the issue expression and then arrange the other claims hierarchically in relation to the issue expression. There might be pro as well as contra arguments of the first, second, third (and so on) order.

- Some claims in a text might be premises and should be included in the pro et contra list as such. Sometimes implicit premises will need to be made explicit in the list. Some of the claims found in a text might be arguments related to a premise.
- In the Toulminian model the analyst finds arguments for claims and should always formulate the premise for the argument, whether or not it is explicit in the text. Premise arguments should also be laid out.
- PDA reconstructs the argumentation structure by finding the claim for action, the goal that the proposed action is claimed to lead to, claims about means-goal, i.e. about how the proposed action would lead to the goal, claims about relevant circumstances, and values related to the goal.
- Debates can be restructured in their entirety (or in parts) and the claims organized according to the substance-oriented or the agent-oriented model.
- Arguments can be classified in accordance with their general type or their content.
- In an evaluation of the rational persuasiveness of argumentations the tenability and relevance of the arguments are scrutinized and it is asked whether there are unstated arguments that should be taken into account.
- The tenability of descriptive arguments is evaluated in the same way for all descriptive claims, while normative arguments of a moral kind can be judged in relation to different normative theories.
- Evaluating the relevance of an argument is the same as evaluating the tenability of its premise.
- Evaluating the rational persuasiveness of an argumentation is not the same as evaluating the tenability of the issue expression.
- In PDA evaluations of argumentation critical questions regarding the claimed circumstances, means-goal claims, values and alternatives and outcomes of the proposed course of action should be posed.

Suggested reading

There are several guides to logically sound argumentation and on how to recognize and avoid argumentation fallacies, such as Sand (2000) and Weston (2009). They are good for those purposes but of limited value for learning how to analyze real world argumentation.

The basics of pragma-dialectics are explained in van Eemeren and Grootendorst (1992) and further worked out by the same authors (2004). The latter work develops the relations to speech act theory. Pragma-dialectics is a broad approach with an expanding literature and should be consulted by those interested in the aim of argumentation analysis only briefly treated in this chapter: the description of how we ought to argue if we want to solve controversies in constructive and rational ways. Ways of describing real-world argumentation are also developed within pragma-dialectics, for instance in van Eemeren and Houtlosser (2005).

The approach of Fairclough and Fairclough (2012) has been simplified for the purpose of this chapter and students who want to understand their take on PDA in full should read their book. It is, however, not particularly accessible for students who are not well read in argumentation analysis or logic. (It is not for nothing that the sub-title is 'A method for advanced students'.)

Herrick (2013) surveys the history of rhetoric and explains various currents, ideas and terms in an approachable way. Uhr and Walter (2014) demonstrate several analyses of contemporary Australian political speeches and texts using a rhetorical approach.

Tännsjö (2002) is an accessible introduction to moral theory for readers who want to gain a better basis for arguing about moral claims. It presents more normative theories than utilitarianism and suggests which philosophers to read in order to take the next step in learning about moral theory.

Exercise

The US tobacco industry argues for its own benefit

In the mid-1980s a critique was put forward in the USA that tobacco companies were advertising to children in order to replace adult smokers who had given up smoking or died (van Eemeren, 2010: 20). This presumably created the incentives for the tobacco industry to defend itself.

The task

Think of this exercise as part of a broader research project in which the reactions of the US tobacco industry to the critique are analyzed.

1 Reconstruct the argumentation of the text and evaluate it. Is the argumentation rationally persuasive or not, and in which ways?
2 What is a likely reason for the tobacco company having produced an argumentation of this kind? Consider whether using the rhetorical concepts of ethos or pathos, and not just logos, could be of help in answering the question.

(After working on this exercise you can check the suggested analysis in Chapter 9.)

The text

The text and part of the suggested analysis are drawn from van Eemeren (2010: 20-2) who uses the example to argue for an extension of the pragma-dialectical analysis. The text is an 'advertorial' from a tobacco company that appeared in the US in the mid-1980s:

> Some surprising advice to young people from R.J. Reynolds Tobacco:
>
> Don't smoke.
>
> For one thing, smoking has always been an adult custom. And even for adults, smoking has become very controversial.
>
> So even though we're a tobacco company, we don't think it's a good idea for young people to smoke.
>
> Now, we know that giving this kind of advice to young people can sometimes backfire.
>
> But if you take up smoking just to prove you're an adult, you're really proving just the opposite.

For the full text to analyze, please visit the companion website (**https://study.sagepub.com/boreusandbergstrom**).

4

Qualitative Analysis of Ideas and Ideological Content

Mats Lindberg

4.1 Background

Terms like 'ideas' or 'ideologies' are commonplace in ordinary language. In a news programme the question may be raised as to what kind of *ideology* is guiding the Labour party, or the Tories, in the UK. A documentary can state that Nazi Germany of the 1930s was imbued with nationalist *ideas*. At a demonstration we can get to hear an anti-globalist speaker arguing that the media of today are full of pro-capitalist *ideology* turning the consumerist lifestyle and commercialised newspeak into natural common sense. And finally we can listen to one of our neighbours describe her workplace as full of wall-to-wall sexist *ideas*, while another neighbour complains about her husband's traditional *ideas* regarding housework.

In these five examples the words 'ideas' and 'ideologies' allude to *thinking that motivates and guides social and political action and interaction*. The thought content of action-guiding ideas, that is, the ideological content in social and political communication and discourse, is the object of analysis of the methodological approach in this chapter. Three strands of contemporary social science have informed the theoretical and analytical view presented here. The first strand is general social theory, starting with Max Weber's *Verstehende Soziologie*, where society is regarded as made up of *meaningful actions* and their *action-guiding thoughts*, whether 'traditional', 'emotional', 'value rational' or 'goal rational' (Weber, 1972 [1921]: 1–2).

See for example Lasswell and Kaplan, 1950; Parsons and Shils, 1951; Easton, 1971 [1953]; Habermas, 1984 [1981]; Giddens, 1984; Archer, 1995; Archer, 2000; Hedström, 2005.

The second is manifested in the manifold empirical studies in sociology and political science that emerged from this general social theory, concerning action-guiding *values, beliefs, attitudes and norms* in political culture, public opinion and electoral behaviour.

See for example Lipset, 1959; Campbell et al., 1960; Lane, 1962; Almond and Verba, 1965; Inglehart and Norris, 2003; Norris and Inglehart, 2011.

The third, which is the most sophisticated regarding the inner structure of idea systems, is the study of *political ideologies* in political science and historical studies.

For an overview, see Sabine and Thorson, 1973 [1937]; Oakshott, 1939; Adams, 2001; Heywood, 2007; Vincent, 2010; Ball and Dagger, 2011.

Habitual patterns of interaction, thought and language use are all around us in society. The habitual patterns of everyday life, for example, are integral parts of the institutions of the family, the workplace or the supermarket. They are transmitted by socialized traditions and patterns of discourse, and they are successively changed and renegotiated in our daily interaction and communication with others. They are also accompanied and renegotiated by role models in commercial advertising and media entertainment. Regarding institutions on the system level of society, we come across information and debates about education, healthcare, free trade, privatization, city planning or infrastructure investments; and sometimes about state-formation itself (Scotland's independence or the 'Brexit' issue). All these flows of communication, conversation, information and debate in fact display *various kinds of action-orienting and action-motivating thoughts*. I will use the common term **ideas** as shorthand for such action-guiding thoughts, in so far as they are inherent parts of, or relate to, the institutions in society (which most of them are), or are addressing the preservation or change of the institutions of society (which many of them do, either directly or indirectly).

4.1.1 Idea systems

But ideas normally do not appear on their own. In all the messages, communication and discourse around us they are combined into more or less coherent and more or less convincing **systems of ideas**, also called **belief systems** or **ideologies**. These are explicitly or implicitly upheld or propagated by opinion-holding or opinion-forming agents and networks, such as media companies, newspapers, think tanks, lobby groups, social movements or political parties. These agents are constantly targeting our preferences and views in various directions (traditional or modern, right or left, nationalist or internationalist, patriarchal or gender equal, consumerist or ecologist), hoping to influence our propensities for action.

Systems of ideas, or belief systems, or ideologies, have a common inner structure or a common morphological composition. They are composed of three interlaced dimensions of thought which are central to the methodological approach here: 1) the **value dimension**; 2) the **descriptive dimension**; and 3) **the prescriptive dimension**. (For an elementary presentation, see for instance Adams, 2001: 4; Heywood, 2007: 4–15; Ball and Dagger, 2011: 8–11.) When combined into a system of ideas, these three dimensions in combination make up the action-motivating, action-orienting and action-directing force of a text or a piece of spoken discourse. I will refer to this action-guiding force as **ideological content**. (We will return to these three dimensions below.)

4.1.2 A theoretical and methodological synthesis

As a methodological approach, the qualitative analysis of ideas and ideological content has a venerable ancestry. One bloodline reaches down to the *sacred hermeneutics*, the interpretative method of Jewish, Christian and Islamic theology and law. Another reaches down to Plato's critique of common opinion (**doxa**) and Aristotle's rhetorical and semantical analyses. (See for instance Jensen, 2007: 1–111; Crowley and Hawhee, 1999: 9–12.) Here I will present an up-to-date theoretical and methodological reconstruction and synthesis, based on the three strands of contemporary social science mentioned above.

The aim of qualitative analysis of ideas and ideological content is to identify, interpret, describe and analyse the specific ideas and the specific ideological content inherent in: a) *established modes of thought* residing in the language use of the media, public institutions, organizations or social fields; b) *propagated messages* from opinion-forming organizations or networks, trying to influence these modes of thought and language use; or c) *ongoing public debates* or ideational struggles (sometimes called 'culture wars') about whose ideas are 'the best', and whose language use and world-view shall prevail. This methodological approach may thus contribute to a better knowledge of the patterns of ideas and ideologies inherent in the communication and discourse around us; and hence of the cultural, social or political alternatives before us. Hence the overarching purpose of this methodological approach is to contribute to *enlightened understanding* among citizens, which is one of the fundamental values for a democratic political culture (see for example Dahl, 1989: 83–134; Dahl, 1998: 37). Furthermore, the results of this methodological approach may also be used as the basis for two other distinct methodological approaches close to it, which are also in the service of enlightened understanding, namely systematic *idea criticism* and systematic *ideology critique*. (See for example, Vedung, 1982; Majone, 1989: Chapters 2–3 and Figure 4.1 below.)

The reader is invited to follow a step-by-step presentation of my reconstruction and synthesis, leading up to a formal (morphological) model of *ideological content* consisting of the combination of values, descriptions and prescriptions; the V-D-P–triad, as I will call it (Figure 4.1). I will then present a *two level analytical scheme* for the (morphological) analysis of ideas and ideological content in established thought patterns and discursive patterns or in propagated messages or debates (Table 4.2). After that follow two illustrative examples of actual analysis; of the British Women's Equality Party, founded in 2015 (Table 4.3) and of the speech made by his Holiness Pope Francis to the UN General Assembly, also in 2015 (Table 4.4). Let us start, though, with some basic theoretical notions.

4.1.3 Ideas, actions and institutions

In social and political theory (see above), ideas and ideologies are regarded as parts of the communicative interactions in society. Patterns of communicative interactions – repeated and habitual thought, language use and action – make institutions and their social relations, including power relations, exist and persist over time. Specific patterns of *interactions* in specific *social relations* together with specific *ideas and language use* (discourse) and specific *material artefacts* make up specific institutions. Christmas celebrations are lacking without a Christmas tree and the action-guiding idea and discourse of 'Christmas'. And moving to a more comprehensive societal level: Left liberal political ideas will guide actions that are quite different from conservative ones, and suggest quite different institutional and cultural configurations in society. Furthermore, gender equal political ideas will suggest institutions and legislation that are quite different from the ones in patriarchal societies.

The renowned theorist in the political science knowledge tradition, Carl J. Friedrich, in his book *Man and his Government* (1963), makes the following summary:

> Ideologies are action-related systems of ideas [...] related to the existing political and social order and intended either to change or defend it. The ideas an ideology contains are as such action-related, and may or may not be very true and appropriate. (Friedrich, 1963: 89)

In Friedrich's political science world of pluralism and political realism there is always a *plural set of social and political ideologies* in societies. These are brought forward by a plural set of social or political agents or networks involved in a constant ideational strife and power struggle (see for example Lasswell and Kaplan, 1950; Duverger, 1966; see also Mann, 2012). As Friedrich points out, the truth or falsity of the ideas and ideologies is not important for their possibility of being effectual or operative. The key thing is that they are *subjectively held to be true* by their propagators and adherents.

4.1.4 Comprehensive and field-specific ideas and idea systems

I will refer to a system of ideas which suggests an institutional and cultural configuration for the whole society as a **comprehensive socio-political ideology**. In the European cultural sphere we experienced about a dozen of these in the so-called 'age of ideology' after the French revolution of 1789 (Bracher, 1984: 14–16; von Beyme, 2013a: 12–16). These comprehensive socio-political ideologies exist as self-proclaimed but rather loose *idea traditions* of canonical works and iconic deeds in epic situations or processes. During the nineteenth century the Liberal, Conservative and Cooperative Socialist idea traditions develop; later they are joined by Marx's and Engels' 'Scientific Socialism' and the Social Doctrine of the Catholic Church. In the twentieth century some new socio-political idea traditions emerge, intermeshed with rejuvenated versions of the old ones. Democratic Socialism (Social Democracy), Left Liberalism (Welfare Liberalism), Leninist Communism, Fascism and Nazism, Christian Democracy, Ecologism, Feminism and Islamism are such examples; all with important variants and sub-divisions. Based on a huge amount of detailed historical, political and biographical cases studies, these idea traditions are sifted and generalized in well-known classic and contemporary handbooks with titles like *Political Ideologies* (e.g. Heywood, 2007; Ball and Dagger, 2011), *The History of Political Theory* (Sabine and Thorson, 1973 [1937]) or *A History of Political Thought* (e.g. Coleman, 2000a, 2000b).

Ideal types
The stylized generalizations of the thought patterns of the different idea traditions are in fact morphological reconstructions – **ideal types**. Each of these has its own biased 'view of the world' or 'ideological tale', as well as a value-loaded system of core ideas and key concepts together with an ideologically coloured vocabulary and language use. Hence they describe, explain and interpret 'the world' differently. They all, though, have a common inner formal structure or morphological composition. They are all built up of ideas of the three dimensions of thought mentioned above: 1) fundamental moral values and philosophical views of man, nature and society; 2) general descriptions, criticisms, analyses, accounts and judgements of the times and the situation; together with 3) general principles and prescriptions for action. These three kinds of ideas differ, of course, between the various ideologies in question; for example, as we saw, liberal ideas differ from conservative ones, and feminist ideas from patriarchal ones. (For an elementary overview, see for example Sabine and Thorsson, 1973 [1937]; Oakshott, 1939; Bracher, 1984; Adams, 2001; Heywood, 2007; Vincent, 2010; Ball and Dagger, 2011.)

The accumulated knowledge of these handbooks serves the analyst as a guiding map and a preliminary classification and evolutionary scheme. As with all maps, you get a better overview from a distance and with stylized simplifications; but this simplification, of course, has to rely on profound knowledge of details. (For an impressive overview relying on detailed knowledge, see especially von Beyme, 2013a; 2013b; 2013c.) The classification scheme of the handbooks is the basis for the important *classificatory understanding* of the ideas and ideological content we meet in communication and discourse (liberal, conservative, socialist, feminist, patriarchal, nationalist etc.). Hence this accumulated knowledge and these schemes are central to the methodological approach presented here, investigating *ideas and ideological content.*

The comprehensive socio-political ideologies that arose since the French revolution in 1789, and the conservative and monarchical reaction against it, have been directly or indirectly involved in most of the developments of philosophy, science and humanities in European academic culture, even influencing religion. They also have parallels and offshoots in the cultural forms and *isms* of art, literature, music and architecture, which have all been directly or indirectly involved in the social criticisms or future hopes of the ideologies. And they have, of course, been involved in the struggles of the configuration of the institutions of society; political, economic, social and cultural.

Field-specific ideologies
But the comprehensive ideologies also have parallels and offshoots in ideas concerning more *partial domains or fields* of society. Hence we meet **field-specific ideologies**. These are as often involved in ideational struggles corresponding to the comprehensive ones. Concerning power in working life, for example, the ideas of capitalism or syndicalism, and of positions in between which suggest a shared influence, make up three typical field-specific ideologies of the workplace. Concerning family life, the ideas of patriarchy or equality between the sexes, or different standpoints on upbringing and children's rights, make up contesting field-specific ideologies. Such field-specific ideologies (and field-specific ideational struggles) can also be found not only in the realms of healthcare, education, housing, law, technology, and city planning, but also in religious communities, voluntary organizations and social movements. They make up intriguing objects of research in their own right.

Comprehensive respectively *field-specific* ideological thought is involved in the patterns of interaction, communication and discursive language use that make up the institutional and cultural configurations of society. Consequently the task for the methodological approach here, as we saw above, is to interpret and describe the *ideological content* of: a) established patterns of thought, language use and discourse in social domains or fields; b) the messages and discourses from opinion-forming agents and networks; and c) the main positions in ideational contest or public debate.

4.1.5 The three basic kinds of ideas: values, descriptions and prescriptions

The action-guiding *ideological content* in social and political communication and discourse is always build up from three dimensions of thought, as stated above. Hence we always meet three different kinds of *ideas.*

In the knowledge traditions of general social theory and empirical political sociology these three dimensions are commonly termed 'values, beliefs and norms', anchored in psychology and social psychology (see Inglehart and Norris, 2003: 8; see also Almond and Powell, 1965: 11–14). In the historical and political science tradition, which is anchored in language philosophy and political theory, we can run across terms like 'value judgements', 'descriptions and explanations', respectively 'recommendations' or 'normative conclusions'; and several others. From this terminological flowerbed I have chosen *values*, *descriptions* and *prescriptions* as basic names for the three kinds of ideas. But we must remember that ideas are action-guiding thoughts. As thoughts in actual communication and discourse (and in different genres of text and documents) they may be expressed in various vocabularies and varying language down to genre-specific composition, rhetoric style and sentence construction. We thus find:

1) **value-statements**, expressed in various ways (ideals, goals, preferences, interests or desired end-states); *values* for short (V);
2) **descriptive statements**, expressed in various ways (narrative accounts, descriptive assertions, situational analyses, evaluative assessments, explanations or judgements) (of objects, agents, ideas, events, issues, problems, solutions or processes in the surrounding world or of the actual situation); *descriptions* for short (D);
3) **prescriptive statements**, expressed in various ways (normative or practical conclusions, policy suggestions, recommendations, imperatives, orders, norms or rules); *prescriptions* for short (P).

For the political science tradition on this point, see for example Sabine and Thorson, 1973 [1937]: vii-ix, 3-9; Walsby, 1947: 141-9; Næss et al., 1956: 176-81; Lane, 1962: 13-16; Friedrich, 1963: 83-105; Levine, 1963: 12-30; Björklund, 1970: 28-30; Plamenatz, 1970: 72-76; Gregor, 2003 [1971]: 23-24, 336-9; Seliger, 1976: 102-121; Vedung, 1982: 181-205; see also Adams, 2001: 3-5; Heywood, 2007: 11-15; Ball and Dagger, 2011: 8-11.

Values, descriptions and prescriptions – taken alone – are not sufficient to guide actions. They need to be combined to acquire an action-guiding capacity or force. The members of the Society for Homeless Cats in Huddersfield, for example, are motivated by certain moral *values* or compelling emotions regarding suffering animals (V), and oriented by certain evaluative *descriptions* regarding the difficult situation for stray cats in the city (D). The V and the D in combination are logical grounds for the prescriptive conclusion 'Take care of stray cats!' (P).

Ideological content: a combination of values, descriptions and prescriptions
In this example the value, the description and the prescription are combined in a specific pattern; they form a quasi-logical sequence of *practical reasoning*. In a sequence of practical reasoning the argumentative premises (V and D) lead up to, or logically support, the practical conclusion (P). Such sequences of practical reasoning I will term **V-D-P–triads**. The V-D-P–triad is the kernel of *ideological*

content in all social and political communication and discourse. It is a central tenet of this methodological approach. (See Figure 4.1 below. See also Chapter 3 on premises and conclusions in argument and practical reasoning; the terminology here is somewhat different but the thought content is quite similar.)

Above we saw an example of a *field-specific ideology* based on practical reasoning, that of animal welfare in a charitable voluntary organization. That pattern of practical reasoning is also found in the comprehensive socio-political ideologies (see above). And moving from the political science tradition to general social theory, we can see that basically all social and political communication and discourse is made up of various combinations of the three kinds of ideas; as they are motivating, orienting and directing actions and interactions in society, whether in habitual patterns or in deliberate attempts at preservation or change.

> For the social theory tradition on this point, see for example Parsons and Shils, 1951: 3-29; Parsons, 2012 [1951]: 3-19, 348-55; Lane, 1962: 13-16; Therborn, 1980: 15-20; Habermas, 1984, vol. 1: 309; van Dijk, 1998: 8; van Dijk, 2006: 379-407; Simpson, 2004: 78; Hedström, 2005: 34-42.

Consequently qualitative analysis of ideas and ideological content has its methodological focus on identifying and describing: 1) *single ideas* of the three basic kinds V, D or P in communication and discourse; and 2) *combinations* of these ideas into V-D-P–triads of practical reasoning in communication and discourse.

4.1.6 The source material

The task for this methodological approach is to identify and describe the ideas and the ideological content irrespective of their truth or falsity. The analyst will work as a serious investigating journalist, making the best of the sources in order to present as truthful a picture as possible of the actual thinking and reasoning. The analyst, of course, can move a step further and start to scrutinize and criticize the ideas under investigation; a principal methodological move we will return to below (see Table 4.1).

The *source material* that can be used in the qualitative analysis of ideas and ideological content is varied and wide. The choice of sources depends, of course, on the chosen problem and the focus of the research. We can find action-guiding ideas and ideological content in cultural products like films and literature; in personal sources like letters or diaries; in schoolbooks, education policies or curricula; in political party manifestos or social movement platforms; in official government documents, public policy reports and parliamentary debates; in speeches and texts by political leaders, ideologues or theorists; or in the messages and discourses of the usual media flow. Besides, researchers also produce their own source material on ideas and ideological content when needed, using tools like questionnaires and interviews.

4.1.7 Five types of investigation in the study of ideas

Let us take a step back to put qualitative analysis of ideas and ideological content as a methodological approach in perspective. We will consider some principal methodological *types of investigation* in the study of ideas inherent in communication and discourse, stylized from a long row of works and summarized in a six-field table.

Content-oriented respectively functional–explanative studies
The horizontal dimension of the table (rows) displays two theoretical aspects of the modelled research object. On the one hand we find studies oriented at the *inner aspect,* the *thought content* or the *ideological content.* On the other hand we find studies oriented at the *external or contextual aspect;* the explanations of the existence of certain ideas in communication and discourse, or their geographical or social spread; the study of the *functions* or roles of specific ideas in society and history; or the study of the biographical, historical or cultural *origins* of specific ideas. As we saw above, the methodological approach in this chapter focuses on the inner aspect and the inner structure of thought. It is hence *content-oriented.* (See Vedung, 1982: 23–6.)

Descriptive, critical or normative modes
On the vertical dimension (columns) we meet three kinds of knowledge-seeking methodological orientations: **descriptive, critical** and **normative**. A study of the thought content of, say, a policy programme on domestic violence can be a *description* of its ideological content. Another study can be a *criticism* of the policy programme or some aspect. Yet another study can be occupied with the *normative* task of proposing new and better policy. These three orientations, of course, can also be mixed in the same study or blended into each other. A thorough *description* might seamlessly move over into the *critical* mode. (Besides, a detached and analytic description of an agent's ideas always places the investigated ideas in some critical light, or will highlight problematic or detrimental points, just by being analytic or coming from the outside.) In a similar way the combination of a *description* and a *criticism,* say, of the policy programme on domestic violence above, may seamlessly move over into the *normative* (prescriptive) mode, arguing for an allegedly 'better' solution for the perceived problem.

See Vedung, 1982: 123–80; see also Næss et al., 1956: 1-3; Geertz, 1964: 71-73; Skinner, 2002: 27-56; Fairclough and Fairclough, 2012: 78-80.

As in many taxonomic tables of this kind, one of the fields turns up empty; hence the six-field table displays only five types of investigation and analysis. We must also remember that the five types are stylized methodological types – *ideal types* – and that any actual investigation of ideas may use one or more of them in the same study. (See Table 4.1.)

Table 4.1 Five types of investigation and analysis in the study of ideas.

	Descriptive mode	Critical mode	Normative mode
Internal aspect of ideas (Content-oriented theoretical perspective)	**1. Idea analysis** of the ideological content in discourse and language, or the social or political meaning in social or public debate; in messages from opinion-forming agents and think-tanks; in messages from literature, film and art; in messages from social movements, political parties or public bodies	**2. Idea criticism** of the logical, moral or factual rigour of ideas in discourse of the propagandistic or rhetorical aspects critical assessment of values or goals, problem-formulations, concepts, descriptions and prescriptions systematic policy assessment and evaluation	**3. Normative suggestions** regarding fundamental social change regarding specific policy areas regarding the choice of fundamental values or operative goals
External aspect of ideas (Function/ explanation-oriented theoretical perspective)	**4. Historical and empirical studies** of the effects of specific ideas of the social origins of specific ideas of the actual social function of specific ideas of the social, ethnic, gender or regional spread of ideas	**5. Ideology critique** *Power-oriented:* of the social role of seemingly neutral ideas and ideologies legitimizing power and power relations *Psychological:* of actual drives behind actions, unknown to the agent *Strategic:* of the actual causes of strategic action, sometimes unknown to the agents themselves, or known but not openly displayed	6. _____

Idea analysis

At the junction of content-oriented and descriptive we meet **idea analysis**. It is here we find qualitative analysis of ideas and ideological content. Idea analysis is normally aimed at a synchronic investigation of the ideological content in a text from an agent (a person, an organization or a public body). But of course such investigations can be diachronic, trying to picture the *ideational change* of the agent. In that case the study settles for *describing* the change as interesting in itself and is not attempting to *explain* the change with some causal factor(s).

See for example Tingsten, 1973 [1941]; Lane, 1962; Levine, 1963; Schurmann, 1968; Larsson, 1970; Manning, 1976; Mott, 1992; Van Dyke, 1995; Gregor, 2005; Müller, 2011; Brekke, 2012.

In this first field of idea analysis we can also place studies of ideas using other methodological approaches, such as content analysis, metaphor analysis, narrative analysis, discourse studies or conceptual history, as long as the knowledge interest is descriptive and content-oriented.

Idea criticism

In the second field we find **idea criticism**. This is a content-oriented, yet critical, type of analysis whose aim is to scrutinize the logical, moral or factual rigour of the same ideas that were descriptively established in the first field. For idea criticism, the results of a descriptive idea analysis are indispensable as the first basic step; descriptive idea analysis establishes *the object for critical analysis* by laying bare the underlying single ideas and their combinations. A simple truth applies: before you can make a criticism you must have something specific to criticize.

See for example Myrdal, 1990 [1929]; Popper, 2003 [1945]; Lepague, 1978; Arnold, 1990; Ellis, 1998; Wolin, 2004; Lindberg, 2009; Judt, 2010; Streeck, 2014. Idea criticism is also the basic method of evaluation theory and systematic assessments of policy programmes - see for instance Vedung, 1982, 2000; Stone, 1988; Majone, 1989: Chs. 2-4.

Historical and empirical studies

Skipping the third field for a moment, we move to the fourth field where we find **historical and empirical studies**. This is a functional-explanation–oriented, yet descriptive, type of investigation; laying the main emphasis on the social and political *context*, not the *content*, of ideas in communication and discourse. In this field we find the main part of all qualitative empirical studies of the role of ideas, or the origin of ideas, made in the disciplines of history, sociology or political science.

See for example Moore, 1965; Letwin, 1992; Berman, 1998; Gregor, 2000; Köhler, 2000; Berman, 2006; March, 2013; Israel, 2014; Widfeldt, 2014.

We also find all the quantitative studies of values, beliefs and attitudes in comparative political culture, global value studies, or studies on electoral behaviour and political opinion here.

See for example Almond and Verba, 1965 [1963]; Inglehart and Norris, 2003; Inglehart and Welzel, 2005; Inglehart and Norris, 2011.

However, and this is important, all the explanatory investigations and empirical studies are dependent on qualitative analyses of the ideas and ideological content of the first field. It is essentially meaningless to try to explain the social function of, for example, 'Christian beliefs in life after death' or 'the idea of gender equality' – or to search for their origin, or to study the spread and significance of them – before you know *which thought content* (qualitatively seen) you are about to explain. Qualitative idea-analysis simply helps establish the *ideational research object* which is to be analysed or explained.

Ideology critique

In the fifth field we meet **ideology critique**. This label is borrowed from the Marxist tradition with its specific concept of ideology, a pattern of thought and language use legitimating class power behind a façade of common-sense. We find three basic kinds of ideology critique: power-oriented, psychological and strategic. The main method of ideology critique is to reveal the 'hidden social function', or the 'real causes', behind the expressed ideas and seemingly natural 'common sense'. (See the classic study by Lukacz, 1971 [1923]; Habermas, 1989 [1962]; Haug, 1987.) Ideology critique is the basic type of analysis in most Marxist, psycho-analytic, constructivist or poststructuralist studies of ideas, including critical discourse analysis (see Chapter 8). Ideology critique is very often intermeshed with moral or factual idea criticism, pointing to flaws in the argument. Like idea criticism, ideology critique is basically dependent on qualitative idea-analysis. As with idea-criticism, you need a systematic description of the ideological content in a text or a discourse before there is anything to be ideology-critical about. (See Vedung, 1982: 123–206; Majone, 1989: 21-23; see also Fairclough and Fairclough, 2012: 78–81.)

Ideology critique, however, has not only been made from the left. The same type of critical analysis has also been launched from a conservative or libertarian point of view. A prominent example is the neo-liberal Public Choice School with its thinkers like G. Tullock and J. Buchanan in the 1970s and 1980s. This school in launched a broad criticism, parallel to the Marxist one, against the then-dominant economic theories of Welfare Economics and Keynesianism. The Marxist critique saw a hidden interest of the monopolist capitalist class concealed in these theories, which suggested an expanding and system-supportive state apparatus (see for instance Miliband, 1972; Holloway and Piciotto, 1978; Gough, 1979). The Public Choice School instead saw a set of politicians and bureaucrats whose 'real interests' of votes or financing were cloaked in these legitimizing economic theories. There was an invisible causal chain, the Public Choice School argued, between 'welfare maximizing citizens', 'vote maximizing politicians' and 'budget maximizing bureaucrats', leading up to the ever expanding 'growth of public expenditure' or 'big government' with its accompanying and distasteful ever rising taxes (see for example the influential Lepague, 1978: Chapters 5-6).

Analytically seen, though, the borderline between *ideology critique* and *historical and empirical studies,* of the fourth respectively in the fifth field, is thin. Both types study the actual function of ideas or ideologies in society. And in practice, a well-conducted historical and empirical study of opinion formation by powerful think-tanks might not differ so much in mood and method from a corresponding ideology-critical investigation (or a critical discourse analysis). These both search for the (hidden) power agents or the hidden interests behind an established pattern of thought and language use (discourse); or the indirect consequences of such a pattern for the power structure in society.

> For prominent studies balancing on the edge of this border, see for instance Sutton et al., 1956; Foucault, 1977; Hobsbawn, 1990; Hobsbawn and Ranger, 1992; Losurdo, 2011; Stedman Jones, 2012; Hollis-Brusky, 2015.

Normative suggestions

Finally, in the third field, we find prescriptive **normative suggestions**. This is a mode where the descriptive and critical studies break into normative suggestions of the appropriate or desirable policy or social action. We can speak of social engineering or applied social science in government reports or policy analyses, as such studies are made in close contact with the public administration, political organizations or lobbying think-tanks. These kinds of studies, when based on serious factual analysis, are of great importance for qualified debate and enlightened understanding in society. We find them, for example, in issues of environment, immigration, citizenship or gender inequality, on a global scale or in a nation-state setting. (We could also add normative political philosophy or moral philosophy to this third field, with the discussion of fundamental values or alternative basic policy goals. See Brecht, 1959: Ch. 8; Majone, 1989: Ch. 2.)

My concluding point here is to highlight the specificity of *qualitative analysis of ideas and ideological content*. Firstly, it is placed within the first field of the table as content-oriented and descriptive *idea analysis*. Secondly, this methodological approach has a basic importance for all the other types of investigation in the study of ideas. Qualitative idea analysis stand in the centre – directly or indirectly – for studies of the other four types; *being logically indispensable as a first step for all the others*, bringing about the inherent pattern of thought content and language use for the others to analyze and work upon. At the same time none of the other types is indispensable for the pursuit of qualitative analysis of ideas and ideological content.

4.2 Analysis

4.2.1 The formal model of simple practical reasoning

We saw above that action-guiding ideological thought content – according to my suggested view – is made up of a three kinds of ideas: values, descriptions and prescriptions combined in the quasi-logical sequence of *practical reasoning*. I called this triadic combination the V-D-P–triad. The notion of practical reasoning as the kernel of ideological content in communication and discourse had a long intellectual history until it became established in analytical philosophy and the political science knowledge tradition.

> For the history of the notion of practical reasoning in the junction of analytical philosophy and political theory, see for example Tingsten, 1939; Tingsten, 1973 [1941]; Næss et al., 1956: 176-81; Anscombe, 1957: 56-87; Toulmin, 2003 [1958]: 87-105; Brecht, 1959: 117-35; Hampshire, 1959: 90-168; Gauthier, 1963: 24-49; Levine, 1963: 12-30; Björklund, 1970: 28-31; Seliger, 1976: 102-21; Vedung, 1982: 101-206; Majone, 1989: 21-41; Walton, 1990: 3-68; Richardson, 1994: 22-46; see also Fairclough and Fairclough, 2012: 35-77.

I will illustrate the general pattern of practical reasoning with an example from an elementary textbook in political science (from my time as a young student) written by the Swedish political theorist Stefan Björklund, *Politisk teori* [*Political theory*] (1970: 28–31). It comes at the argument from one side in the public debate about a local government reform in Sweden in the 1960s. It is put up as an argumentative quasi-logical deductive sequence and is somewhat reformulated here:

V: 'Citizens ought to have the greatest possible democratic influence on local government'

D: 'The old and small municipalities offer better possibilities for local democratic influence than the suggested new large ones'

P: 'Keep the old and small municipalities!'

In this example the prescription (P) derives from the value of local democracy (V). But how do we get from the value (V) to the prescription 'keep the old and small municipalities' (P)? As we can see the action-motivating force emerging from the initial value (V) is *as such void of direction*. What is needed is a specific ascertained descriptive assertion (D) of some kind, to situate and orient the actions needed. In this case the descriptive assertion that the old small municipalities offer better democratic possibilities for citizens than the suggested new large ones (if held as true) leads to the prescription (P), to keep the municipalities small. The imagined validity of the prescription (P) hence depends on the imagined or assessed truthfulness of the description (D). (See the example on the use of mobile telephones while driving, in Section 3.4.)

In the example above on local government we met a sequence of practical reasoning in its most simple form. It illustrates the *general formal pattern* of practical

```
┌─────────────────────────────────────────┐
│    ┌──────────────────────────────┐     │
│    │                              │     │
│    │  V (value premise)           │     │
│    │                              │     │
│    │  D (descriptive premise)     │     │
│    │                              │     │
│    │  ──────────────────          │     │
│    │                              │     │
│    │  P (practical conclusion)    │     │
│    │                              │     │
│    └──────────────────────────────┘     │
└─────────────────────────────────────────┘
```

Figure 4.1   A formal model of simple practical reasoning, the kernel of action-guiding ideological content, presented as a quasi-logical deduction

Source: Elaborated from Toulmin, 2003 [1958]: 87-105; Brecht, 1959: 117-135; Björklund, 1970: 28-31; Seliger, 1976: 102-121; Vedung, 1982: 181-205. Since the structure of practical reasoning is a logical conclusion, one could also write it as (V, D) → P. (See also Chapter 3 in this book.)

reasoning. We also met this pattern in the example regarding stray cats, above. In conclusion this general formal pattern can be presented in a model, as a quasi-logical (or pragmatically reasoned) deduction. (See Figure 4.1.)

4.2.2 In real life: Unorganized or fragmented practical reasoning

Sometimes the task of qualitative analysis of ideas and ideological content is easy. The pattern of practical reasoning presents itself in a text in a neat and well-ordered fashion. This is most often the case in openly argumentative texts. But in much communication and discourse in real life this is not the case, and even openly argumentative texts can be difficult to interpret. The sequence of practical reasoning, though, the formal model of the V-D-P–triad, is always a skeleton or a kernel which needs to be laid bare. The analyst should just be aware of how the sequence and its factors are sometimes explicit and obvious, sometimes diffuse or hidden.

In some cases the factors of ideological content, and the whole V-D-P–triad, may also be fragmented or dispersed throughout the text. Some Ps may hang loose, and the necessary connections to the value premise or the descriptive premise may be broken. In such cases it takes some delicate ameliorative interpretative work, and often several close readings, to sift out and assemble the fragments. In extreme cases a *reconstructive interpretative effort* might be needed in order to establish the meaning of a piece of communication or discourse. (See Vedung, 1982: 99-122.)

Whether a text is neatly organized or sadly unorganized (from the point of view of the eager analyst), the first step is still to discern and identify the *single ideas* (many or few) of the kind V, D or P expressed in claims, statements, metaphors, images, propositions or implied by narrative events or morals. *(Which single ideas do we find?)* The second step is to find or reconstruct the actual combination of these ideas into sequences of practical reasoning (many or few, major or minor), which make up the inherent action-guiding ideological content. *(Which combinations of values, descriptions and prescriptions do we find?)* As a third step comes the understanding and classification of the found ideological content. *(Which kind of ideological content is it? Which institutional or cultural configurations does the agent criticize respectively positively suggest? What are the relations, adverse or consenting, to other agents or ideas?)* These three steps will be more clearly illustrated below, in the two actual analysis examples.

4.2.3 In real life: Multi-layered, formally multifarious and long sentences

Multi-layered

In some texts the three kinds of ideas indeed are textually present, but fused in multi-layered meanings or flowering associations of the words and phrases making up statements or claims.

> For the semantic distinction between words (terms, symbols, signs) and their conceptual content (significance or meaning), see for example Locke, 1964 [1690]: 259-262; de Saussure, 1959 [1916]: Part One, Ch. 1; Ogden and Richards, 2013 [1923]: 1-47; Vedung, 1982: Ch. 3; Simpson, 1993: Ch. 1 and 5; Bunge, 1988, Vol. One: 63-82; Evans, 2009: 193-213; Sartori, 2009: 97-150.

The language use by an agent may be very natural or quite effective in front of an audience which shares the agent's language use and vocabulary, with its associative meanings and references. If the analyst is lucky, they are acquainted with the linguistic conventions of the time or the situation, in which case the interpretative effort might run smoothly. If the analyst is not familiar with the conventions, the multi-layered associative meanings and references can be hard to discern and lay bare; word by word, phrase by phrase, paragraph by paragraph. (Ask me! My doctoral dissertation was on Karl Marx's *Das Kapital! In the original German!*) It normally takes a thorough background knowledge of the vocabulary and language use (and a good dictionary) to grasp even very common meanings, associations and references of the time or the cultural context (this is an elementary difficulty in all interpretation). Often a laborious reading of *surrounding texts* is needed, by the same author-agent or by others in the intertextual discursive situation, in order to (at least hypothetically) get a reasonable hold of the thought content. And still you can never be completely sure of your suggested interpretative hypothesis; you can only try to check it again, and then try to argue for it.

Formally multifarious

It takes some time and training to be acquainted with the language use and vocabulary in a source material of a specific genre, a specific discursive situation or a specific agent. In reality, any of the three basic kinds of ideas V, D and P may be residing in sentences with multifarious syntactical forms. A value claim (V) in a text, for example, can be stated in seemingly descriptive sentences like 'Health is important' and still serve as value-statements in a sequence of practical reasoning. In another text one might simply meet the expression 'Health'. You might even meet value-claims in (rhetoric) questions like 'How can you put up with yourself without taking care of your health?', which in a specific discursive situation in fact may express the value-statement 'Health' (V). Hence it is not the sentence type, the syntax or the linguistic construction that decides *which basic kind of ideas* we deal with in action-guiding text or talk. Instead, it is the actual linguistic-pragmatic role of the expression that decides; that is, the *actual position of the statement in the actual and inherent structure of practical reasoning*. This means that the process of identifying values, descriptions or prescriptions in a text *is dependent on the V-D-P–triad as the analytical tool*. This discerning, identifying and interpreting of statements, using the V-D-P–triad as an interpretative guiding thread, demands both training and skill; and of course also substantial acquaintance with the genre, the intertextual discourse and the intentions and vocabulary of the agent-author. There are no shortcuts on the way to establishing a *reasonable interpretative hypothesis* of the actual action-guiding thought content – the ideological content – in a text.

I will bring in another example, from the United Nations' Universal Declaration of Human Rights, where the well-known first article says: "All human beings are born free and equal in dignity and rights". This grammatically descriptive sentence (present tense in the indicative) is of course downright wrong if it is interpreted as an empirical statement of facts (D) (most people on the earth are not born free and equal at all). On a closer look, though, we can see that this statement is not formulated on the empirical but on the philosophical level, and even more, that it actually is a value-statement (V). To make the actual character of a value-statement manifest, we might imagine some implicit 'We, the here assembled hold as our fundamental value that all human beings are born free ... etc.'; an interpretation which also is supported by the preamble to the articles in the Declaration.

To conclude, value-statements (V) can be expressed in formally multifarious sentences. The same also goes for prescriptions (P) which can be stated in a row of different syntactical constructions. Regarding descriptive statements (D), the pragmatic discursive variation is even greater, ranging from precise factual sentences to flowery metaphorical narratives. The guiding thread in discerning the three basic kinds of action-guiding ideas V, D or P is to use the formal model of simple practical reasoning (see Figure 4.1 above).

Longish sentences or verbose reasoning

Longish sentences or narrations need to be shortened and stylized to make the inherent action-guiding thought content visible. Such a shortening and clarification are part of the analytical process. It takes some experience to be good at these. Print-outs and a suitable reading protocol are helpful in the procedure to register different wordings. (We have already met such stylized statements in the examples of practical reasoning above.) In this process of reconstructive shortening and specification, the formal model of practical reasoning, again, is the guiding thread. The model demands precise and unequivocal statements to enable it to bring out the inherent kernel of *ideological thought content* of the text.

It is important to note that the formal model of practical reasoning suggests the search for the *argumentative inner skeleton*, which is not always directly accessible on the surface of the text. The V-D-P–triad is a modelled hypothesis of the *reasoned inner logic* in social and political communication, which resides in the flow of words and the agent-specific, field-specific or genre-specific vocabularies and discursive pragmatics.

4.2.4 In real life: Verbally incomplete

It is also common that a text involves only one or two of the three factors of the V-D-P–triad, and that consequently one or two of these are simply *not verbally present*. In such cases the sequence of practical reasoning might be *incomplete* on the surface of the text, but perhaps not in its implicit meaning. Then the analyst must try to find the missing factor(s) in two main ways. The first is to search for it in *implicit assumptions* or in *self-evident silent commonplaces*, inherent between the lines or behind the words. The second is to search for them in *other texts* of the author-agent (the textual corpus) or in the *intertextual discursive situation* or debate in other texts by contending or participating author-agents.

Especially common is the lack of explicit value claims. We can meet a text where an evident descriptive account (D) is present ('The Ebola-virus is spreading') and an equally evident prescription (P) is pronounced ('Start the vaccination at once!'). But why this is important might not be stated in manifest words. In such a case it might be possible to deduce backwards from the practical conclusion (P) to the *implicit value premise* (V) ('Health') using the quasi-deductive logic of the V-D-P–triad as the analytical tool. The formal model of practical reasoning always suggests the search for *the explicit or implicit presence of all three factors* in a text, or a textual corpus, at least somewhere, in order to be able to lay bare the actual and effective action-guiding thought content.

4.2.5 In real life: Situational descriptions and means-ends descriptions

There are two main kinds of descriptive accounts to be observed:

- accounts of the situation, of the objects of the situation, or of the problems (or possibilities) of the situation (D*sit*);
- accounts of means-ends relationships and means-ends methods to reach goals (D*me*).

Descriptions of situations (D*sit*), and of their objects, agents, limitations or possibilities are the most extensive parts of human action-guiding communication and discourse. We seem always to speak of what is 'out there'. You will find these everywhere in the text and talk of the workplace or in everyday life, making up the cognitive base or the stable ground, as it seems, for actions and action-guiding thought. Descriptions of means-ends relations (D*me*), on the other hand, are normally not so bulky, but still very important. As statements of causal relations or mechanisms they often hold central positions. They are very common in ordinary language. They state relations like 'booze → will destroy your life', 'equal parenting → makes it possible for women to advance in the workplace', 'more immigrants → will destroy public finances', or 'education for all → strengthens the economic competitiveness of the country'. Statements of means-ends relations (D*me*) often lead immediately to practical conclusions or direct prescriptions (P) like 'Stop drinking!', 'Strive for equal parenting'! 'Curb immigration'! 'Promote education for all'!

4.2.6 In real life: The double exposure of descriptions and evaluations

There is a further, more complicated aspect of descriptions (D). All descriptions carry a cognitive part and an attitudinal part. They have a double nature as simultaneously both *descriptive assertions and evaluative assessments*; making them at the same time both descriptions and evaluations. The attitudes to specific objects, to put it simply, are emotional loadings of like or dislike. Take the descriptive claim that 'Global warming is increasing' as an example. On the one hand it points to some observable or cognizable facts. On the other hand, there are one or more evaluative attitudes attached to it. Which attitudes really are present (in any descriptive statement) is sometimes easy to discern, sometimes a matter of closer analysis.

In the hands of the analyst the double exposure character of descriptive statements must be *broken apart into its two component parts*; one sheer *descriptive assertion* and one sheer *evaluative assessment*. Breaking apart the two aspects of any description and formulating these into separate statements is a fruitful way to bring out the hidden values which load the attitudes with emotions of like or dislike. If the evaluative attitude is difficult to discern – the example above was easy – the analyst can search for it in: a) other statements inside the text; or b) in other texts by the agent; or c) in surrounding texts in the intertextual discursive situation or debate. The key thing here is to note that evaluative statements are not in themselves value-statements or goal-statements; a point we now will examine more closely.

4.2.7 The tricky distinction between values and evaluations

Finally I want to highlight the analytical distinction between an evaluative descriptive statement (D) and a value statement (V). Compare these two statements regarding health: 'Apples are a healthy food' and 'Health is important'. The former is an evaluative assessment (an evaluation) expressed in a descriptive statement regarding the properties of a specific type of fruit (D); parallel to 'This car is fast'. The latter is a value-statement (V), expressing the value 'Health' of the speaker; parallel to 'Speed is important' or 'I love speed'. Here this distinction might seem rather harmless, but in more ardent or complicated matters this distinction can imply a whole world of differences. My daughter's statement 'Italy is great' (D), after her vacation there, differs very much from Benito Mussolini's statement 'The greatness of Italy' (V) in a political speech. The task of the analyst, as we saw, is to look through the formal linguistic expressions and their syntax, in order to discern and identify the effective ideas and their combinations in practical reasoning of social and political pragmatic discourse. At the same time the inherent bias of an evaluative descriptive statement like 'Apples are healthy food' of course reveals some latent or hidden value (in this case simply detected as 'Health') and suggests a search through the text for a more manifest and direct value-statement.

4.2.8 The two levels of ideological thought: The fundamental and the operative level

In all idea systems and all ideological content we find two main levels of thought. On the one hand lies the *fundamental level,* close to philosophical world views and fundamental moral values or ideals. On the other hand lies the more concrete and *operative level,* close to practical problems and practical goals.

See for example Tingsten, 1973 [1941]: 66; Hacker, 1961: 5; Apter, 1964: 16; Schurmann, 1968: 17–45; Seliger, 1976: 175–97; Heywood, 2007: 13.

The distinction between the fundamental and the operative level is fluid, though, and the levels themselves may have sub-levels.

The value-dimension divided into 'values' and 'goals'
Up to now we have been speaking of the 'value-dimension' of action-guiding thought and language (V). The distinction between the fundamental and operative level, though, demands a subsequent and parallel distinction within the value-dimension itself. On the one hand, we find values or ideals on the fundamental level, on the other hand we find specified goals and end-states on the operative level. The 'value-dimension' in a piece of discourse or debate thus might consist of both values and goals, depending on how the argument moves between the two levels. I will consequently speak of a principal difference between 'values' (V) (on the fundamental level) and 'goals' (G) (on the operative level).

Values are like general compass directions; they have no definite end point. The value 'Health', for example, is a value which, in itself, has no limit. You cannot have too much of 'Health'. The same goes for moral or political values like 'Justice', 'Freedom', 'Equality', 'God's will' or 'Nature' (for an overview, see classically Brecht, 1959: Ch. 8). Goals, on the other hand, are specified end-states, which can be reached. For example the specified goal 'a BMI about 20–25' (G) is situated on the operative level. After defining this goal (and holding it as relevant or valid), the agents become interested in detailed descriptions of the most effective means or methods (Dme) to reach it. This specific goal, and these specific means-ends descriptions of efficient methods (of diet and exercise), will accordingly lead to quite specific prescriptions (P) on the operative level. Depending on the imagined truthfulness of the Dme-statements the agents will accept the prescriptions (P) as valid. On the concrete and practical operative level we hence meet G-D-P–triads. These are the concrete and operative versions of the general logical pattern of practical reasoning.

Values and goals appear in chains from higher levels to lower ones

Consequently, values and goals appear in chains, from fundamental to operative levels of thought. The operative goal of BMI 20–25 is derived as one of the aspects of the more general value 'Health'. The chain consists of logical connections between levels, since the fundamental values are supportive as warrants for more concrete goals. These chains between levels are the systemic connections in a system of ideas. Similarly, there is also a systemic connection between general prescriptions (P) on a higher level and goal-statements (G) on a lower level. The high-level prescription (P) 'Take care of your health!' might serve perfectly as a general goal on the operative level, starting a new sequence of practical reasoning to more concrete prescriptions like 'Eat more apples!' or 'Mind your BMI!' (See Tables 4.2 and 4.3 below.)

... which also concerns descriptions

The distinction between the fundamental and the operative level, however, does not only concern values and goals, it also concerns descriptions (D). On the *fundamental* level we find philosophical, ideological or religious *descriptive assumptions* of human nature or the view of history, society and the state. (Optimistic or pessimistic, in progress respectively decline?) We can also meet *high-level general accounts* of the role of the family (the base for emotional security or neurosis?) or the market (welfare-bringing or poverty-bringing?). The *operative level*, on the other hand, involves more practical and concrete descriptions, informing of practical issues, problems or possibilities. Descriptive accounts of bodily health, on a general level (to return to that example again), can be combined with concrete descriptive accounts of specified detailed aspects of health on the operative level, down to minute expositions of bio-chemical mechanisms. These more specified Ds all lead to ever more specific prescriptions (P).

To conclude, all social and political ideas and ideological content in any communication and discourse may be fruitfully analyzed using these two dimensions. What we need, though, is a handy analytical scheme.

The two-level analytical scheme of ideological content

Combining the two levels of thought with the already known three basic kinds of ideas, we can construct a six-field table (Table 4.2) which makes up a *two-level analytical scheme of ideological content*. Consequently we can, in principle, handle a V-D-P–triad on the fundamental level and a G-D-P–triad on the operative level, and the connections between them as chains of sequences of practical reasoning.

The two-level analytical scheme can be used either to discern and identify single ideas of the six fields or to clarify the composition of a systematic and complete *idea system,* with connections between V-D-P–triads on both levels.

All of the six kinds of ideas may not be present in a text at the same time. The thing with the scheme, functioning as a two-level analytical model of ideological content, is that it makes it possible to *discern which kinds of ideas are present and which are not.* Some of them may be *implicit,* as we saw above. Some of them will have to be found in other adjacent texts. With this two-level scheme the analyst has a strong fishing net, or a forceful metal detector, to sweep over the verbal flow. Some texts will may consist of ideas and statements only on the fundamental level, while other texts will move only on the operative level, or on both. Which will be the case, and in what combinations, is an empirical question.

Table 4.2 The two-level analytical scheme of ideological content, and the possible six main kinds of action-guiding social and political ideas.

	Values	*Descriptions*	*Prescriptions*
Fundamental level	Moral, social, cultural or political *values* (V)	a) *Philosophical assumptions* of human nature, history or society, held to be true (D). b) *High level descriptive generalizations* of the state or the market, or other general institutional complexes (D) (held to be true or valid).	*General principles* of social and political action (P) (as suggested in the traditions of social and political philosophy, theory and ideology) (held to be valid or appropriate).
Operative level	Concrete situation-specific or problem-specific *goals* (G)	Concrete descriptive or evaluative accounts of the (imagined) situation or of the objects of the situation, or of the (imagined) issues, problems or possibilities of the situation (D*sit*), or of the means-ends mechanisms or methods in it (D*me*) (held to be true or valid).	Concrete, situation-specific or problem-specific or means-ends specific *prescriptions* for action (P) (held to be valid or appropriate).

Comment: See the text above on the relation between value-statements and goal- statements, and the 'double exposure' quality of descriptive statements.

4.2.9 Women's Equality Party (WE)

The Women's Equality Party (WE) in Britain was founded in 2015 with the purpose to 'bring about equality for women'. What is their ideology? Is this a revolutionary feminist project or one of gradual reformism? Is their main thinking a kind of radical feminism, socialist feminism or liberal feminism, or a mix of them all? Or, should even the label 'feminism' be questioned?

WE labels itself as "a focused mainstream party" (Women's Equality Party, 2015: 4); a network of women working in the tradition of gradual democratic reformism. They strive for parliamentary seats and cooperation with the established parties. It does not label itself 'feminist' even though its party platform suggests profound gender equality goals and profound institutional change, launching a heavy critique of the lack of gender equality in Britain. The institutions under attack range from informal habits to existing legislation and public policies. Hence the chosen strategy of the WE is a mix of 'awareness campaigns' and suggested new legislation. (I recommend downloading the Policy Document [Women's Equality Party, 2015] from the party's website at http://www.women sequality.org.uk/objectives, to enable you to follow and check the following analysis, and some later exercises.)

The six 'core objectives' of the party

The opening chapter of the party platform (after the preamble) is called "The WE model". There we meet the over-arching goal, the "remit", of the party, and its "six core objectives":

> The Women's Equality Party is a focused mainstream party. WE will never take a party line on issues outside our remit: *to bring about equality for women*. Our policies are designed to further these six core objectives:

- WE are pushing for *equal representation* in politics, business, industry, and throughout working life.
- WE expect *equal pay* and equal *opportunity* to thrive.
- WE are campaigning for *equal parenting and caregiving* and shared responsibilities at home to give everyone equal opportunities both in family life and in the workplace.
- WE urge an *education* system that creates opportunities for all children and an understanding of why this matters.
- WE strive for *equal treatment* of women by and in *the media*.
- WE seek an *end to violence* against women. (Women's Equality Party, 2015: 4; emphasis added)

The six 'core objectives' make up the headings of the six main chapters of the platform. Each chapter heading using the words italicized by me above is formulated as a catchy prescription or political demand: "Equal representation" (Prescription 1 (P1)), "Equal pay" (P2), "Equal parenting and caregiving" (P3) and so on. I will term them P1–P6. The party promises to "work for", "tackle", "press for", "enable", "urge", "seek", "strive for", "address" or "push for" specific actions and *specific institutional change* in the direction of the basic goal "equality for women". This structure in six chapters, under headings closely connected to the initially stated "six core objectives", makes the structure of the platform and the whole ideological message easy to grasp. (The objective of equal representation, though, stands first in the enumeration on p. 4 but is placed last in the actual text of the manifesto: see Women's Equality Party, 2015: 30.)

From where do the six core objectives come?

So far, so good. But here we must grapple with a puzzling fact. These six "objectives" are seemingly derived from the general goal *"to bring about equality for women"* (G). But why are they six, and why these six? Let us put on our analytical reading-glasses and take a closer look at the two opening sentences of the quotation. The connection between the general goal (G) and the "six core objectives" (P1–P6) is not linguistically visible or spelled out. There is a non-reasoned hole (or a logical gap) in the text between the general goal statement "to bring about equality for women" and the subsequent statement starting with "Our policies ..." (See the quote above.) This is a very important hole, though, filled with an underlying meaning, related to practical reasoning, which most people intuitively understand when reading it and hence do not bother to dig deeper into. In order to lay bare the underlying meaning of this hole we need the formal model of the V-D-P–triad as the analytical tool.

We know from above that a prescription (P), as a practical conclusion, needs to be anchored on two grounds, both in a value premise (V) and a descriptive premise (D). Six prescriptions ought to need six descriptive accounts. We have not seen these yet, but these non-outspoken six descriptive premises are imagined intuitively when reading the text about the six objectives. For the party manifesto to be argumentatively convincing, we need to find these six descriptions at least somewhere in the text.

The solution is close at hand. The missing D-factor of the opening is present in the following way: in the party platform, taken as a whole, each chapter is filled with factual information from *six different social domains*. Each chapter contains thorough descriptive assertions and evaluative assessments of *the situation of insufficient gender equality* (Dsit) in six social domains of British society, together with descriptions and evaluations of available means to reach the goal of gender equality in these six domains (Dme). The descriptions of the situations (Dsit) and the suggested political means (Dme) are supported by statistical numbers and known facts, making up six basic *descriptive complexes*, one in each chapter. I term them D1–D6. Together they make up a *comprehensive descriptive and evaluative account* of contemporary British society, from the point of view of a profound gender equality perspective. This account is the descriptive and evaluative kernel of the party message.

If I shorten and stylize the six descriptive complexes, they assert the following: there is no equal representation in the UK in politics, business and beyond

(D1); there is no equal pay between the sexes (D2); there is no equal parenting and caregiving of children and elderly parents (D3); the education system is unequal or has unequal effects (D4); the treatment of women in media is not only unequal but also degrading (D5); there is an appalling level of violence against women and girls in the British society, including rape, prostitution and trafficking (D6). Here I have simplified the six descriptive complexes to the bare bones, as ingoing descriptive factors in the sequence of practical reasoning of the party manifesto.

The kernel of practical reasoning in the platform (= the ideological content)

The puzzle of the non-reasoned hole (or logical gap) in the opening, the question of why there were initially 'six core objectives', thus is resolved by the fact that the comprehensive account of the substantial gender situation in Britain is modelled on six social domains bringing forth the six descriptive complexes D1–D6. These six descriptive complexes function as six distinct descriptive premises in each of the six chapters. We know from above that the value premise was the general goal "to bring about equality for women" (G) ranging over all six chapters. Together these premises, chapter by chapter, lead up to the six practical conclusions P1–P6 which are the six core objectives of the opening. *We have thus found the over-arching argumentative sequence of practical reasoning in the party manifesto.* We get the following V-D-P–triad:

> G: "To bring about equality for all women".
>
> D: "There exist unequal representation, unequal pay, unequal parenting, unequal education system...etc." (D1-D6).
>
> _____
>
> P: "Push for equal representation, equal pay, equal parenting, equal education ... etc." (P1-P6).

We can see that the six core objectives P1–P6 now appear as derived practical conclusions from the general goal (G) as the value-premise, on the one hand, and the six complexes D1–D6 as the descriptive premises, on the other. This is the major skeleton of practical reasoning on the level of the whole party manifesto. *It is the kernel of the ideological content in the political message of the Women's Equality Party.* The formal model of the V-D-P–triad has shown its strength in an actual analysis. (In the exercises below the reader is urged to investigate the ideological secrets of the manifesto further.) But there is more to come right here.

Digging still deeper: Finding the fundamental philosophical assumptions

We have not yet touched upon the fundamental level, which is hardly visible in the manifesto. Initially I mentioned a preamble which we have not yet examined. Let us take a closer look on it. It starts like this, in highlighted text:

Nowhere in the world do women enjoy *full equality*. This represents a shameful *waste of potential, for women and for the countries* that fail to harness their talents and the societies living at odds instead of mutual respect. This also represents a huge opportunity. WE believe that England, Scotland, Wales and Northern Ireland should not lag behind other countries but instead should take the lead and be the first countries in the world where all genders are equal. The policies set out in this document are a blueprint for enabling women and girls to *achieve their full potential*. (Women's Equality Party, 2015: 3; my emphasis)

In the first sentence, we actually seem to find a fundamental value, "full equality". But is this really the *most* fundamental intrinsic value? Does it not sound too similar to the general goal (G) we noted above? To be really fundamental, we ought to find a value which explains why "full equality for women" is important and should be valued. Reading close with our text-interpretative glasses on, we can actually find such a higher value in the preamble. The lack of equality for women in the world is said to be a "shameful waste of potential" for women (and for countries), and we get to know that the lack of equality hinders women to "achieve their full potential". Here we at last find a fundamental (politico-philosophical) higher value: *Every woman's achievement of her full potential* (V). If we jump over some interpretive and simplifying steps we arrive at the following sequence of practical reasoning on the *fundamental level*:

V: "Every woman's achievement of her full potential."

D: a) "Nowhere in the world do women enjoy full equality." (D*sit*)

   b) "This lack of equality is also found in Britain." (implied) (D*sit*)

   c) "The lack of equality for women in all countries (including Britain) → hinders women from achieving their full potential." (D*me*)

_____

P: "Bring about equality for women (in Britain)."

Bringing in the two-level analytical scheme
We thus have reached a result concerning both the operative level and the fundamental level of the manifesto. Let us combine them in the two-dimensional scheme to get hold of the inner structure of the *system of ideas*, or the *ideological content*, in the party manifesto of the WE. (See Table 4.3.)

As the reader will notice while working through the manifesto, or doing the exercises below, the manifesto is more complex than our rough analysis shows in Table 4.3. The fundamental level is in fact more complicated, and the operative level is distinctly divided into three sub-levels, that of manifesto, chapter and section. This will be pointed to in the exercises.

Table 4.3 The two-level structure of the ideological content of the WE party manifesto

	Values	Descriptions	Prescriptions
Fundamental level	'Every woman's achievement of her full potential' (V)	a) 'Nowhere in the world do women enjoy full equality' (Dsit) b) 'This lack of equality is also found in Britain' (implied) (Dsit) c) 'The lack of equality for women in all countries (including Britain) → disables them to achieve their full potential' (Dme)	'Bring about equality for women (in Britain)!' (P)
Operative level	'Bring about equality for women (in Britain)' (G)	'There exist unequal representation, unequal pay, unequal parenting, unequal education system...etc.' (D1 – D6).	'Push for equal representation, equal pay, equal parenting, equal education... etc.' (P1 – P6).

Comment: Elaborated into the two-level analytical scheme of this chapter (Table 4.3 above) from my analysis of the WE party programme (read 2016-01-15).

Summary: Understanding by classification and ideal type analysis

Initially I mentioned that the ideological content in communication and discourse often did not present itself in a neat and well-ordered fashion. In the example of the Women's Equality Party we have instead met an extraordinarily well-structured ideological text. Some (interesting) interpretative problems arose only concerning the *fundamental level* of the ideological content. Consequently we have laid bare a) the single ideas and b) the skeleton of practical reasoning. So far, so good. This is the first and the second step of analysis and a sufficiently interesting result. The knowledge achieved is *interesting in itself* as a comprehensive account of *the general goal and intention of the party* and the *institutional changes* it wants to bring about.

But which kind of ideology do we meet? With this question, our analysis reaches the third step, addressing the issue of *classificatory understanding*. As we know, the research community is in possession of a classificatory theory of the main comprehensive socio-political ideologies since 1789. This will be indispensable now. (See Section 4.1.3 above.)

At first glance, the WE appears as a feminist party with a feminist ideology. This is suggested from the initial delimiting of the scope, applying only to women. The party manifesto, however, never uses the word 'feminism'. It does not even make reference to feminist social or political theory. With the weight on the word "equality", as in the expression *"full equality for women"*, all the values and fundamental ideological statements seem to refer to *the equal value of human beings*. Gender equality, or equality between the sexes, then, is a derivative position rather than the fundamental starting point.

Feminism or extended liberalism?

The basic political-philosophic value "equality", especially when it is specified to "the individual´s achievement of their full potential", places the WE in a specific ideological tradition. This value is *the fundamental value of left-wing Liberalism*; in Britain not only the tradition of John Stuart Mill and the Liberal party (including thinkers such as John Maynard Keynes and William Beveridge), but also the tradition of modern *Social Democracy* from the Fabian Society and Eduard Bernstein's 'revisionism' onwards. This initial interpretation of mine (which can be contested) is also supported by the presence of another foundational value, "economic strength on the world market" (found in the preamble), and the heavy reliance on social engineering and the public sector as the basic socio-political means to achieve the goal of "full equality for women". To this left-liberal or social democratic tradition (they are very similar), though, is added the pervasive ideological element of *principled gender equality*, which I could easily have labelled 'feminist' had the terminological choice of the party itself not forbade it.

One could perhaps describe the party ideology as a house built of left-liberal floors and rooms, but full of gender equality furniture and carpets, and with some moved walls between some rooms and some new staircases between the floors. (For this kind of a gender equality political liberalism, as a position in political philosophy, see Nussbaum, 2000: 5, 4–11, referring to Rawls, 1993.)

In issues of public child care, the Nordic social democratic welfare states are seen as the models to follow. This is also the case regarding prostitution, an issue where the WE takes a (reluctant) stand in favour of the so-called 'Nordic model' of criminalizing the sex-buyer and not the sex-seller; like the decision in France in spring 2016. Being in the tradition of left liberalism or social democracy, with a profound gender equality element, the WE is distinctly relying on the public sector and increased public measures to attack the remaining gender inequalities. This represents a difference to right-wing liberalism and conservatism, whose support for the traditional private family sphere, in the eyes of WE, is support for continued gender inequality.

Being a 'mainstream party', though, accepting representative democracy and democratic gradualism, also means a demarcation against more militant leftist or feminist movements. WE does not argue explicitly against the more radical feminist positions, but the party's explicit urge to be regarded as mainstream, presenting the gender equality message as normal British common sense, implies an implicit, but strong, principal stance against such positions. At least the party is distinctly far from some earlier radical feminist stances, like the revolutionary feminism of Catharine MacKinnon, the mystical womanhood apartheid feminism of Luce Irigaray, or the post-structuralist notion of Judith Butler, where being a 'woman' is merely a linguistic social construction (see Lindberg, 2009: Ch. 2, 4 and 5).

4.2.10 His Holiness Pope Francis's address to the United Nations General Assembly (25 September 2015)

We shall now move on to another illustrative example of qualitative idea analysis. Let us travel to New York and that memorable day when His Holiness Pope Francis met world representatives at the United Nations.

This speech before the delegates of the General Assembly addresses the world situation, issues of environment and poverty, the important role and assignment of the UN, and the moral and political obligation inherent in the UN charter and the UN declaration of human rights. We meet a representative of an institution with an unbroken tradition of being a central diplomatic player in world affairs for almost two millennia. We also meet a representative who is elaborating on and developing the tradition of the Catholic socio-political comprehensive world-view. This is *The Social Doctrine of the Church* (2004) with its roots in the papal encyclical *Rerum Novarum* of 1891 and further back in the political philosophy of Thomas Aquinas and indirectly in Aristoteles (see for example Sabine and Thorson, 1973 [1937]: 236–49; Schmandt, 1960: 144–64; Finnis, 1998: 1–14, 132–79). On the one hand, the speech is very clear about its ideological content. On the other hand, it consists of several themes, partly interlaced with one another, which makes an attentive reading and interpretation necessary. Here we will concentrate on one main theme, the position on the environment and world poverty. (I recommend downloading the speech from the website of the Vatican; for the URL see Francis, 2015.)

The main theme, on environment and world poverty
Pope Francis starts out with a celebration of the UN and its efforts over 70 years. Those efforts and achievements are "lights which help to dispel the darkness of the disorder caused by unrestrained ambitions and collective forms of selfishness". Without the UN mankind would not "have been able to survive the unchecked use of its own possibilities" and would have been even more distanced from "the ideal of human fraternity".

Pope Francis's account of the contemporary world is thus signalled in outline. The economic and political elites of the world are pointed out as the main wrong-doers in the historical processes which have ended up in the contemporary "dramatic reality" of, on the one hand, the "misuse and destruction of the environment", and on the other, the "relentless process of exclusion" of the poor people of the world. The economic and political elites in both rich and poor countries have been driven by "a selfish and boundless thirst for power and material prosperity". All of this is "a complete denial of human fraternity". Pope Francis is very clear about "the baneful consequences" which follow in the wake of a global economy based on "environmental destruction" and "social and economic exclusion". Among these "scourges" are: "human trafficking, the marketing of human organs and tissues, the sexual exploitation of boys and girls, slave labour, including prostitution, the drug and weapons trade, terrorism and international organized crime". Furthermore the destruction of the environment and the exclusion of poor people are conceived as closely intertwined. The concept of "sustainable development", thus, is related to both environment issues and the issues of poverty and welfare in human societies. The solution of one problem presupposes the solution of the other. So much for the descriptive and evaluative account (D) in the address of Pope Francis, concerning this theme. After this description, the general normative prescription (P) is clearly stated: "We need to ensure that our institutions are truly effective in the struggle against all these scourges".

Further on Pope Francis specifies his urge in a row of prescriptions:

> ... government leaders must do everything possible to ensure that all can have the minimum spiritual and material means needed to live in dignity and to create and support a family, which is the primary cell of any social development. In practical terms, this absolute minimum has three names: lodging, labour and land; and one spiritual name: spiritual freedom, which includes religious freedom, the right to education and all other civil rights. (Francis, 2015)

Searching for the fundamental values

Which then are the values (V) that load the descriptive accounts (D) with so much evaluative force, and suggest such unequivocal normative prescriptions (P)? The values are not so difficult to find, even if they are intertwined with both descriptive and prescriptive statements. Both nature and humankind are seen as parts of God's creation. They are parts of his plan of the universe, and are hence *in themselves* regarded as intrinsic fundamental values. Pope Francis brings forward, in the line of St. Thomas and Aristotle, a fundamentally nature-centred, though deistic, world-view of God's creation:

> First it must be stated that a true 'right of the environment' does exist, for two reasons. First because we humans are part of the environment. We live in communion with it [...]. Man [...] possesses a body shaped by physical, chemical and biological elements, and can only survive and develop if the ecological environment is favourable. Any harm done to the environment, therefore, is harm done to humanity. Second, because every creature has an intrinsic value in its existence, its life, its beauty and its interdependence with other creatures. (Francis, 2015)

But neither nature in itself, nor humanity-in-nature in itself, suffice as fundamental values. The Pope continues to an even more profound philosophical level of his comprehensive socio-political ideology:

> We Christians, together with the other monotheistic religions, believe that the universe is the fruit of a loving decision by the Creator, who permits man respectfully to use creation for the good of his fellow men and for the glory of the Creator; he is not authorized to abuse it, much less to destroy it. In all religions, the environment is a fundamental good. (Francis, 2015)

Table 4.4   The structure of the ideological content of a central theme in His Holiness Pope Francis's speech to the UN General Assembly (25 September 2015)

	Values	Descriptions	Prescriptions
Fundamental level (I)	'The sacredness of God´s creation'(V)	'God´s plan for the creation. Nature is designed for humankind to live in and use' (D*sit*)	'Respect the sacredness of the environment!' (P)
		'God´s plan for the special existence of humans in which every human individual is a part of God´s plan' (D*sit*)	'Respect the sacredness of every human life!' (P)
Fundamental level (II)	'The Environment is a fundamental good' (V)	'By greed and lust for power, economic and political elites have produced environmental destruction' (D*sit*)	'Preserve and improve the natural environment!' (P)
	'The equal value of all humans' (V)	'There is a huge social, economic and cultural exclusion of humans in the world' (D*sit*)	'Put an end to the social, economic and cultural exclusion!' (P)
	'The right to life and development of every human' (V)	'A row of baneful consequences of this exclusion have occurred, driven by greed and lust for power of the powerful' (enumerated in the text) (D*sit*)	'Ensure that constant and effective measures are taken by our institutions against these scourges!' (enumerated in the text) (P)
		'Constant and effective steps by responsible and just institutions → may help repeal these scourges' (enumerated in the text) (D*me*)	

Comment: Elaborated into the two-level analytical scheme of this chapter (Table 4.2 above) from my analysis of the speech of His Holiness Pope Francis to the UN General Assembly (25 September 2015) (Francis, 2015).

This fundamental value of "the sacredness of nature" and all its creatures is combined with the fundamental intrinsic value of every human individual, as part of God's loving creation: "the sacredness of every human life, of every man and every woman, the poor, the elderly, children, the infirm, the unborn, the unemployed, the abandoned, those considered disabled…"

From this short account I dare to present the ideological content of this central theme in Pope Francis's speech in the two-level analytical scheme of ideological content. (See Table 4.4.)

As we can see, the speech resides only on the fundamental ideological level. The values are high-level compass directions (V), the descriptive accounts are broad generalizations (D) and the prescriptions are consequently very general principles of action (P).

4.3 Critical Reflections

4.3.1 The frequent error of idealism

The main limitations and difficulties in studies of ideas and ideological content, in my eyes, are the following. A first error, which is easily committed, is idealism.

Idealism is the mistake that culture, language or ideology – 'ideas' or 'language' – are seen as the self-sufficient ultimate reality in human society; or the ultimate causal factor, for instance the 'national spirit' or 'cultural heritage'. From the point of view of social science, though, there are no self-sufficient or ultimate causal factors. Nothing comes out of nothing. This means that the given ideas and ideologies (or 'language') of any given time or place are *historically produced by networks of acting persons* using and recombining already existing patterns or elements of thought and culture *in specific historical situations* in a structure-actor kind of social processes. Just think of the nationalist republicanism of the 'Young Turks' of 1908, or the 'New Left' of the 1960s or the 'New Right' of the 1980s. The analytical focus on the inner structure of an idea system is no excuse for forgetting the historically contingent and historically constructed character of the ideas, or their necessary structural and material context.

See the exemplary method of Tingsten, 1973 [1941]; Hobsbawn, 1990: 1-45; Hobsbawn and Ranger, 1992; Berman, 2006; Müller, 2011: Ch.1; Stedman Jones, 2012: 21-84; Mann, 2012, vol. 1: 1-33.

4.3.2 Mistaking the agent

A second typical error is to be vague about the agent, and hence who is the author, sender or speaker. This error often comes out of an unclear problem-formulation, and a corresponding badly considered choice of source material. It makes a lot of difference whether a political message comes from an official party conference, or from a diverging opposition within the party; or if the public document you are reading is a parliamentary report to be discussed, or a completed decision on new legislation.

It is all too common to find studies with imprecise research-questions about 'the view of the world in the 1960s', 'the political attitudes of immigrants', or 'attitudes to gender in the healthcare system'. The researcher, though, is bound to be precise, and know which texts from which agents are the relevant ones. If you are about to investigate attitudes to gender in the healthcare system, for example, you must specify both the agents and the source material, as well as the research problem and your basic analytical concepts.

4.3.3 The typical mistake of holism

A third error in the study of ideas is the mistake of holism. This mistake is close to the other two and concerns the study of a part and mistaking it for the whole. Holism comes in two version. The *consensus version* suggests that there exists only one dominant way of thinking, or only one worth mentioning, forgetting that there always is an ideational struggle in any organization or social field. Studies like 'The view of sex in the 1960s' ought to instead be titled 'The ideational struggle of the view of sex … etc.' The accompanying *elitist version* consists of forgetting the general public, implicitly making the ideas of the elite into the ideas of society or of the times. Studies like 'The view of insanity in the early twentieth century' in the elitist version normally involves a focus on academic and upper-class mentalities, ignoring other segments of the population as simply less interesting. The ideas of the elite (in literature, magazines or official documents) are presented as the ideas held by all people, while the actual ideas of the lower middle class, the workers, ethnic minorities, outsiders, the opposition or simply common men and women are not included in the investigation. The sad thing is, I would argue, that this is an in-grown or invisible *point of view*; a class-based prejudice in the academic community. (On non-conscious points of view and hidden values, see the classic account in Myrdal, 1944: vol. II, 1035–70.)

4.4 Qualitative analysis of ideas and ideological content and the study of power and other social phenomena

Having analysed both the party manifesto of the Women's Equality Party and Pope Francis's speech we shall return to Table 4.1 and the five types of investigations in the study of ideas. It is obvious that the results of analysis achieved here – using the tools of qualitative analysis of ideas and ideological content – is a fruitful starting point for other secondary analyses regarding ideas, and the use of ideas in power struggles and ideational struggles. I will put forward a few suggestions for such secondary studies.

- *Idea criticism.* A first type of questions arises in relation to the second field of Table 4.1. The explicit reasoned arguments of the WE or of Pope Francis invite critical examination and critical discussion. The scheme of analysis has broken down the ideological content into analysable items for critical scrutiny. Are the factual descriptions and the statistics correct? Are the descriptions of other agents and their hitherto undertaken public measures fair?
- *Empirical and historical studies.* Other kinds of interesting studies are waiting in the fourth field, first regarding WE. What are the similarities and differences between the WE and the other political parties in Britain? What are the similarities and differences between the WE and the other political feminist parties in Europe? Where does public opinion in Britain stand on gender equality issues? What is the thinking and what are the power resources of anti-feminist resistance? And moving to Pope Francis: What is the modern history of Catholic Social Doctrine? How has it been taking sides in the social and political struggles since the 1890s? Which ideational debates are actually going on in the Church regarding women in church service and on celibacy, as well as on family, divorce, contraceptives and abortion? What is the strategy of the Church in world politics, and who are its potential allies or enemies?
- *Ideology critique.* Another type of interesting study is suggested by the fifth field. Concerning WE the following questions may be raised: Is it possible to discern a (white) middle-class bias in the party ideology, which some commentators would suggest? Are the dimensions of class or ethnicity (together with gender) taken seriously enough? A closer analysis of the detailed policy suggestions on institutional change may be used to confirm or falsify such a hypothesis.
- *Normative policy suggestions.* A last kind of important secondary analysis is connected with the third field, normative policy suggestions. Do WE or Pope Francis suggest viable roads to the suggested goals? Are the suggested means too moderate to be able to make any difference? What does existing scientific knowledge say about the suggested policy goals and policy means?

Summary

On the usefulness of qualitative analysis of ideas and ideological content

- The primary aim of the approach is to single out the component ideas and the ideological content of: a) an established mode of thought, b) a propagated message, or c) an ongoing debate or ideational strife.
- The secondary aim is to clear the ground for the four other types of investigation in the study of ideas, as pointed to above (see Table 4.1).
- A more general aim is *to contribute to a more rational and enlightened discussion* on the existing and future social and political alternatives and normative tendencies.

How to go about doing it

- Choose the type of investigation according to Table 4.1. Note the central role of qualitative analysis of ideas and ideological content as the first step of analysis.
- State your research problem and the research questions clearly. Be self-critical of your analytical concepts and open about the limitation and the possible bias of your perspective.
- Specify the field, the agent or the debate to be investigated. Specify the source material central to the investigation and its representativeness.
- Do not forget other texts by the same author or agent, or the surrounding intertextual discursive situation; these might be needed in the interpretation and the analysis (as suggested above).
- Do not forget substantial background knowledge of the field, the agent or the debate, both historical and ideational.
- Read the text(s) carefully, two or three times. (Hence, do not choose a too-large corpus of source material!) Take notes of key formulations and the interpretative hints you get. Erect the two-dimensional analytical scheme, or a suitable variant of it. All six fields need not be filled to reach a result. If the scheme can only be half-filled, or less, this is also interesting.
- Start the search for values, descriptions and prescriptions in accordance with the analytical scheme. Do you find full V-D-P-triads? Are there holes in the argument or latent assumptions? Can you discern and identify even these implicit factors of ideological content?

Suggested reading

Methodological texts on qualitative analysis of ideas are rare. The closest is the extremely valuable Vedung (1982) as well as Majone (1989: Chapters 2-3) presenting a systematic method of idea-criticism, also informing the descriptive analysis of ideas and ideological content; Skinner (2002) of course is valuable as well. The usual handbooks of political ideologies (e.g. Heywood, 2007; Ball and Dagger, 2011) are indispensable as a substantial introduction and overview to the contemporary ideological universe.

For an introduction to Islamism I would suggest Esposito (2011), for Christian political thought Mott (1992). Regarding the variants of feminist ideas in contemporary political life and organization, a comprehensive overview is still missing; most comparative books

(Continued)

(Continued)

are focusing on feminist academic theory (see for example McLaughlin, 2003; and, more specialized, Lindberg, 2009). For other ideologies in European political life, see on the radical left March (2013), on right-wing extremism Widfeldt (2014), on Social Democracy Berman (1998, 2006). The remarkable Müller (2011) sketches the fragility of democratic ideas in twentieth-century European political and intellectual history. For the ideological patterns in American political life, that are normally hard to discern and identify, see the highly informative Van Dyke (1995).

Exercise

Digging deeper into the WE ideology

The following exercises are suited for individual as well as group discussions. We shall return to the party manifesto of the WE.

The task

The analysis above stated the overall pattern of practical reasoning on the programme level, with the six core political goals G1–G6 related to six descriptive complexes D1–D6 of six important policy areas of gender equality (see Table 4.3.). But how are these six chapters built up internally from the point of view of the V-D-P-triad? Let us choose the chapter on *sexual violence* with its goal "End violence against women and girls" (G6). We can see that this chapter is divided into five sections based on five aspects of the policy area "sexual violence". In each section we find a descriptive account of the aspect in question (D6: 1–5), making up the descriptive premise for a prescription (P6: 1–5) for policy and legislation in each of the aspects. The description in the first section of the chapter on sexual violence I suggest as "There is insufficient support and sanctuaries for women fleeing abuse" (D6: 1).

1 Which are the other four *descriptions* (D6: 2–5) in the chapter on sexual violence, shortened and stylized? And which are the five *prescriptions* for policy and legislation of these five aspects in this chapter (P6: 1–5)?
2 Construct the sequence of practical reasoning on the chapter level of this chapter on sexual violence. Establish the G6, the D6: 1–5 and the P6: 1–5 as a table. (Nota bene! Such a table is a part of the process of investigation and a support for clear thinking. Any mode of *presentation*, though, can look different, perhaps using only a running narration as in the humanities, or mixing narration with tables as in the social sciences.)

Now to another really interesting thing. Return to the preamble-page of the program where we found the fundamental value 'Every woman´s achievement of her full potential' (Table 4.4. above). Scrutinizing the formulations of the preamble page in repeated close readings there in fact appear *three other highest values*, as I see it. All of these are equally fundamental.

3 What are these other highest values? Hint: Paradoxical as it may seem, they are all tied to the idea of *Britain as a nation*.

4 The interesting thing is that all these three nationalist values are value premises leading up to the same prescriptive statement: 'Bring about equality for women (in Britain)!' as the first fundamental value did, of all women´s right to their 'full potential'. How is this logically possible?

5 Construct the four distinct V-D-P-triads on the fundamental level, starting with the four distinct fundamental values. Then add their respective general descriptive accounts (both D*sit* and D*me*) and check if they lead up to the same general prescription to 'Bring about equality for all women (in Britain)'.

6 Discuss possible ideological or strategic reasons for WE to include these four values and triads.

The text

The text below is from the first lines of the Women´s Equality Party Policy Document:

Nowhere in the world do women in the world enjoy full equality. This represents a shameful waste of potential, for women and for the countries that fail to harness their talents and the societies living at odds instead of mutual respect. This also represents a huge opportunity. WE believe that England, Scotland, Wales and Northern Ireland should not lag behind other countries but instead should take the lead and be the first countries in the world where all genders are equal.

The policies set out in this document are a blueprint for enabling women and girls to achieve their full potential.

(Source: The Women's Equality Party Policy Document [dated 20 October 2015], p. 3. Available from www.womensequality. org.uk/objectives [accessed 16 July 2016].)

For the full text to analyze, please visit the companion website (**https://study.sagepub.com/ boreusandbergstrom**).

5

Narrative Analysis

Alexa Robertson

This book begins with a story about a university lecturer and the large quantity of texts she is exposed to during an ordinary day. Many, but not all, of the texts she reads (or avoids reading) contain narratives. Like her, we are immersed in a flow of narratives from the moment we wake in the morning. The news we hear on the clock radio beside the bed or read on a tablet while eating breakfast tells us official or institutional stories of what is happening in the world. Our Facebook feed is replete with the stories of the private sphere that our friends relate to us in words and pictures, and of the public sphere that they share and comment on. On our way to class or work, and on our way home, we package our experiences and reactions to what we have been told into stories of our own, without even being aware of it. Stories not only entertain, they also teach lessons, socialize, and create community. According to a perspective that has grown exponentially since the mid-1980s (De Fina and Johnstone, 2015: 160), we are better understood as narrative creatures than as the rational actors who long enjoyed the attention of social scientists. It is through the stories we tell and are told that we make sense of society; it is through narratives that our situation in the political and cultural landscape, and that of everyone else, is reinforced. Making sense of our place in the scheme of things is not something that happens in a political vacuum, however. Meaning is made in context, not least in the context of certain constellations of power. The study of narratives thus provides insights into societal power dynamics. There are consequently good reasons for arguing that "a student of social life, no matter of which domain, needs to become interested in narrative as a form of knowledge, a form of social life and a form of communication" (Czarniawska, 2004: 2).This chapter provides an introduction to the terminology, assumptions and analytical approaches of scholars who study narrative. It is organized around answers to four sets of questions.

1. Why study narratives? What theoretical understandings and assumptions are entailed in this sort of research?
2. What are narratives, in scholarly terms as opposed to popular parlance?
3. How are narratives analyzed by scholars in different fields?
4. What are the implications of using a narrative approach to textual analysis?

An answer to the first question will be offered by giving an overview of the development of the field, highlighting its trans-disciplinary nature and the remarkable variation in narrativist research agendas. The ingredients of a narrative are listed, to answer the second question, in a section which also distinguishes between the structure or the 'what' of a story and its discourse or 'how' it is told. The section devoted to the third question, under the heading 'Analysis', surveys how researchers collect data, identify the object of narrative analysis, and organize their material. Two examples of narrative approaches are given, to the study of focus groups and to the analysis of television news stories. Answers to the fourth question will be offered in the section devoted to critical reflections on the narrative approach. As with the other contributions to this volume, the chapter ends with suggestions for further reading and an exercise.

5.1 Background

5.1.1 Why study narratives?

For a long time, it was mainly historians who used a narrative approach. They sorted out the chaos of past events, and were wont to fill in any blanks left by missing evidence, by organizing their primary source material into stories. This sort of work is sometimes referred to as the narrative mode of representing knowledge. Then came what has been referred to as the **narrative turn**. Scholars began to argue instead that social life itself, and not just accounts of it, is a matter of narrative, and that our identities and actions come into being through stories. This change in the way that scholars understood their task and their relationship to the material they analyzed – sometimes referred to as a shift in focus from representational to ontological narrativity – left its mark on research conducted across the spectrum of academia, in fields as diverse as sociology, political science, public administration, organization studies, anthropology, linguistics, gender studies, media studies, psychology, education, law, biology and physics.[1]

Scholars from this array of disciplines agree that narrative functions as a fundamental interpretive frame, helping us to organize our experiences and make the world comprehensible. Somers has stated this in no uncertain terms:

---

[1]See for example Bruner, 1991; Franzosi, 1998, 2010, 2012; Poletta, 1998, 2002; Czarniawska, 1999, 2000, 2004; Larsen, 2002; Porter et al., 2002; Feldman et al., 2004; Georgakopoulou, 2006; Bamberg, 2012; Feldman and Almquist, 2012; Holstein and Gubrium, 2012; Shuman, 2012; Hansen and Machin, 2013; and Udasmoro, 2013.

> People are guided to act in certain ways and not others on the basis of the projec-
> tions, expectations and memories derived from a repertoire of available social,
> public and cultural narratives. (Somers, 1994: 614)

Studying narratives thus provides insights into the formation and maintenance of identity (Lieblich et al., 1998; Mottier, 1999; Robertson, 2010, 2015). Stories not only provide scholars with information about something that has happened – one sort of primary source material in many case studies – they also provide insights into how individuals imbue those events and actions with meaning (Riessman, 1993: 19; Frank, 2012). Collectivities tell and share stories too. Cultures "work 'mentally' in common", through a process of "joint narrative accrual", according to Bruner. Continuity is provided by a "constructed and shared social history in which we locate our Selves and our individual continuities" (Bruner, 1991: 20). This means that the study of narrative is a way of gaining analytical purchase on the power dynamics that regulate understandings in society.

There are other reasons for studying narratives. For some it is a matter of good scholarship. Rather than producing sketchy accounts, often at high levels of abstraction, narrative attunes the analyst to nuance, helping us see things that would be overlooked in more technical readings, and making us aware of absences as well as presences (Robertson, 2000; Feldman and Almquist, 2012). The approach is valuable because it "deals with the particular and the specific, rather than the collective and statistical" (Kiser, 1996: 250) and privileges human agency. It ena-bles scholars to be more aware of and responsive to the voices of the marginalized in society, which otherwise tend to be drowned out by the powerful and the main-stream (Carlisle, 1994). Adoption of a narrative approach has also been considered to be a way of rebelling against the straightjacket of academic praxis (Clayton, 1994; Somers, 1994).

5.1.2 Narratives and their ingredients

The term **narrative** can be so vague and encompassing that Carlisle (1994) laments it is sometimes no use at all. The French semiologist Roland Barthes, for example, wrote unhelpfully that narrative is any form of communication:

> The narratives of the world are numberless. Narrative is first and foremost a prodi-
> gious variety of genres [...] narrative is international, transhistorical, transcultural:
> it is simply there, like life itself. (Barthes, 1977 [1966]a: 79)

Others have made more useful contributions. A familiar definition considers narrative as the organization of events into a plot (Bremond, 1966/1980: 390; Kozloff, 1992: 69–70). Todorov (1969) described it as the passage from one equi-librium to another – from stable situation to disturbance to a re-established stability. This concern with plot and organization translates into a focus on structure. It reflects the heritage of narrative analysis, which has its roots in literary analysis, coloured by Russian formalism, American new criticism, French structuralism and German hermeneutics.

It is rare to encounter a work on narrative that does not invoke *The Morphology of the Folktale*, written by the Russian formalist Vladimir Propp in 1928. A classic example of structural analysis, *Morphology* classified Slavic fairytales "according to their component parts and their relationship to each other and to the whole" (Propp, 1968 [1928]: 19). After having analyzed 100 tales, Propp was able to document a recurrence in storylines, characters (such as hero, villain, donor, helper), and what he referred to as **functions**, by which he meant both the actions of the characters and the consequences of these actions for the story. Propp claimed that despite the vast number of folktales in circulation, there were not more than 31 functions (which ranged from 'initial situation', 'violation' and 'hero's reaction' to 'pursuit', 'rescue', 'recognition', and 'punishment').[2]

Building on Propp, early structuralist approaches were based on two assumptions. The first is that while the structures of texts might seem different on the surface, similarities can be found on abstract levels. The second is that it is important to distinguish between two stories: the series of events, and the story as told by the author (De Fina and Johnstone, 2015: 153).

Improving on and streamlining Propp's formalist model, Labov and Waletsky (1967) analyzed narratives in terms of their formal properties and functions. He identified six common elements. Taken together, they provide a common definition of narrative.

The **abstract** is the summary of the narrative. As De Fina and Johnstone (2015: 154) put it, it "announces that the narrator has a story to tell and makes a claim to the right to tell it". The **setting**, comprised of the time, place, situation and participants or characters, is set out in the orientation, or the referential clause of the narrative. The **complicating action** (Todorov's **disequilibrium**) constitutes an additional element. The **resolution** tells what finally happens, and the **coda** reconnects the story with the present. The meaning of the action or series of events is commented on in the **evaluation**, or the 'story as told by the author' referred to above. Evaluative clauses are editorial and contain judgements. They "have to do with why the narrator is telling the story and why the audience should listen to it" (De Fina and Johnstone, 2015: 153). Laying bare the power of a narrative often involves discerning and documenting the techniques used by the teller of a story to show how their words should be understood.

Evaluation can be overt or covert. In its overt form, the narrator comments on the story from the outside ("a roar of outrage erupted from the crowd at the

---

[2]See Propp (1968 [1928]) or Herman and Vervaeck (2005) for a complete list.

injustice of the ruling"). In its covert form, the evaluation can be embedded in the story, for example in information given about the characters in the orientation ("he was known to be a fair man"; "she had a vindictive streak"). It could also be located in a comparison with alternative outcomes ("her dream of becoming a doctor and saving lives was thwarted by the senseless war").

A large body of narrative research builds on Labov and Waletsky's (1967) distinction between elements, and their insight that a story can have a referential or an evaluative function. They argued that the sequence of clauses is matched to a sequence of events, and that to move a narrative clause entails changing the order in which the events are understood to have occurred. It is thus known as a **formal approach** to the study of narrative, and has had a strong influence on scholars working within the tradition of discourse analysis, who have an interest in the linguistics and syntactic and semantic structures of narrative. But the ideas of Labov and Waletsky have also proved useful to researchers who enter the study of narrative from other disciplines, and approach discourse in a different way, who look for meaning in the way stories are told, and not just the way the component parts are assembled, and pay attention to the contexts of storytelling.

Chatman (1978) defines narrative as comprised of a story and a discourse. The **story (*histoire*)** is familiar from the structuralist take on narrative, comprised of the content of the tale or chain of events and the 'existents', or the characters and other components of the setting. Put differently, *histoire* is the 'what' of the narrative. The **discourse (*discours*)** in Chatman's construction of narrative is the 'how' – the means by which the content is communicated. (Note that the term is used with a slightly different meaning from 'discourse' in discourse analysis as presented in Chapter 8.) The distinction between story and discourse is helpful when it comes to conducting narrative analysis in practice. The component parts of story and discourse described above are given in schematic form in Table 5.1.

Table 5.1 The ingredients of a narrative

story (*histoire*)
referential clause
the 'what'

Abstract	summary of events	
	announces that the narrator has a story to tell	
	makes a claim that the narrator has a right to tell the story	
Orientation	sets out the time, situation, setting, participants	
Complicating Action	moves the story from equilibrium to disequilibrium	
Resolution	tells what finally happened	
Coda	returns to the present	

discourse (*discours*)		
evaluative clause		
the 'how'		
		the way in which the content is communicated
	Evaluation	the meaning of the action is commented on
		sense is made of the story

The operationalization of narrative advocated in this chapter combines several of the ideas presented above, arranged in a way that makes them amenable to empirical application. In keeping with Chatman, a narrative is defined here as an account comprised of an *histoire* or story (or a 'what' – the events and orientation referred to by Labov) and a *discours* or discourse (a 'how' – with a focus on the way a story is communicated, and not just its structure). It is thus a form of discourse in the sense that the way the story is communicated is influenced by social practices and generic conventions. It contains some, but need not contain all, of the elements and functions stipulated by structuralist theorists.

5.2 Analysis

Narratives can give different sorts of insights, depending on where they are found. For some scholars, such as those studying personal narratives, it is the unique experience (of gender or ethnic discrimination, for example) that affords insights. For others, such as those who study organizational narratives, it is their general currency, familiarity or repetitiveness that provides insights into a given culture (Czarniawska, 1999: 8). Some stories can have a single narrator; others can be multi-voiced. The approaches to analyzing them must be numerous, as are the narratives themselves. There is no, and must not be, 'one best method' of narrative analysis: what works best depends on the individual researcher, and the research questions guiding a given study.

5.2.1 Collecting data for narrative analysis

Researchers look for and find narratives in policy texts, leadership activity and policy formation, political theory, interview material such as oral accounts of critical, dramatic events in the lives of organizations, civic rituals and reconciliation commissions, political autobiography, life stories, illness narratives, novels, film, historical accounts, maps, news stories, scientific accounts, and symbols and myths.[3] Van Dijk finds them in the everyday, for example in conversations with ordinary people. But he says narratives are not to be found in a police report, a sociological analysis, a parliamentary debate or (because a narrative is something verbal) a picture (van Dijk, 1993: 123). Barthes, of course, would disagree with him, given that he viewed narrative as capable of being

> carried by articulated language, spoken or written, fixed or moving images, gestures, and the ordered mixture of all these substances; narrative is present in myth, legend, fable, tale, novella, epic, history, tragedy, drama, comedy, mime, painting [...] stained glass windows, cinema, comics, news items, conversation. (Barthes, 1977 [1966]a: 79)

In between these two extremes, students of narratives would be well-advised to look for texts that contain the features outlined in Table 5.1. These can be readily found in interview transcripts and media reports, for example, and for that reason examples of such primary source material will serve as illustrations later on in this section.

Before getting around to the actual analysis of narratives, many researchers face the task of generating them. This is particularly true when working with interview material. Lieblich et al. (1998: 9) advocate the use of narrative as a way of gathering valuable data (for example about experiences of discrimination) that would be impossible to get at otherwise. Certain kinds of open-ended questions are more likely than others to encourage narrativization, according to Riessman. It is preferable to ask questions that open up topics and allow respondents to construct answers, in collaboration with listeners, in the ways they find meaningful. In her experience, narratives often emerge when they are least expected (Riessman, 1993: 54–6).

---

[3]Specific examples are Mottier, 1999 and Garme, 2001 (policy texts); Shapiro, 1988 and Windslate et al., 1998 (leadership activity and policy formation); Banta, 1994; Coole, 1999; Herzog, 2001; Stephenson, 1999 (political theory); Czarniawska, 1999, 2000, 2004 (interview material such as oral accounts of critical, dramatic events in the lives of organizations); Chaney, 1986 (civic rituals and reconciliation commissions); Abell, 1987; Labov and Waletsky, 1967; Lieblich et al., 1982; McAdams, 1993; and White, 1987 (life stories); Riessman, 1993 (illness narratives); Dine, 1994; Goodsell and Murray, 1995; Shell, 1993; Sommer, 1991; and Zuckert, 1990 (novels); Chatman, 1990; Dine, 1994; Fishman, 1989 (film); Kiser, 1996; Mandelbaum, 1967; Miller, 1974; Mink, 1978 (historical accounts); Mottier, 1999 (maps); Barkin, 1984; Bell, 1994; Bennett and Edelman, 1985; Berger, 1997; Bignell, 1997; Dahlgren, 1995; Knight and Dean, 1982; Kozloff, 1992; Robertson, 2000, 2002, 2015; Smith, 1979; Tuchman, 1976 (news reports); Gjedde, 2000; Nash, 1994; Silverstone, 1984 (scientific accounts); Schirmer, 1993; Barthes, 1993; Levi-Strauss, 1963 (symbols and myths).

5.2.2 Identifying the object of analysis

It is necessary to be able to recognize a narrative in a given material. In some cases this can be relatively straightforward: a newsreader's lead-in, for example, usually signals the start of a news story. When narratives occur in interview situations, the researcher should be attuned to 'entrance and exit talk' that indicates the beginning and end of a story. **Entrance talk** is typically comprised of lexical signals to the audience that a story is about to be related ('well, I'll have to back up a bit to answer the question. You see, when I was on my way to…' or 'It happened like this'). **Exit talk**, like the coda in the structuralist schema, returns the listener or audience member to where they were before the story began and signals that the sequence of events has closed ('and that about sums it up' or 'and the rest is history'). Consider the following excerpt from an interview with a journalist working for a global news channel. When asked to explain how she decides which images to use in conflict coverage, the journalist begins by setting out the principles of the news outlet she works for, but then resorts to telling a story.

Box 5.1

Narrative Structure

Interviewer: When reporting a conflict, how do you decide what images to use?

Respondent: It's a question of taste. It's a question of what's right for the channel. Al Jazeera has historically had a higher threshold for gore than the BBC has – the BBC worries about offending its viewers, and in my view it often sanitizes all the impact out of its package, because they don't want to upset people too much. You know, there are horrible things happening out there, I want people to understand that, I want them to see it.

Interviewer: So those pictures out there – how gory are they?

Respondent: When I first filed from Syria back in March, we showed the body and face on an old man, lying on his kitchen floor dead. He had been shot by the Syrian army with a sniper, at random. The Syrian army has a sniper policy, it just puts guys up on the roofs, and all day they fire on to the civilian population. Not endless burst of machine fire, otherwise people wouldn't go out, it's random, and they do it because it's a terribly easy and cheap way of keeping an entire population completely terrorized, and it costs nothing. And no one knows when they leave their door in the morning if they'll come back in the evening, because a sniper could have just decided in the moment's impulse, I'll shoot that old man, or that small boy,

(Continued)

(Continued)

> or that woman going out shopping. So he was 70 something, laying in the family kitchen, and the whole neighbourhood had piled in. Family members were, it was heartbreaking, cradling his old face in their hands, and I wanted the tender cradling of the old man's face, and I had no problem with us running that. His face was not disfigured, it was peaceful in death, and they blanked the face out! So I ring the newsroom, and they argue back and I go 'this is a respectful shot, it's in a context, I'm sure you understand why we show this old guy's face, he's dead but he's not disfigured. Surely our viewers can handle a dead old man', and in the end they took the filter off.

(Source: Excerpt of unpublished interview with former Al Jazeera journalist Anita Mc-Naught by Kristina Riegert, for the Swedish Research Council funded project 'Europe as Other', Doha, September 2012, reported in Robertson, 2015)

We enter into the story from the end (what the journalist and her team ended up showing in their report) but also the beginning (when she first started reporting on the conflict in Syria). The 'entrance talk' ("when I first filed from Syria back in March") orients the listener by providing information about the time, the setting and the situation. The 'exit talk' ("in the end they took the filter off") is connected with the evaluation (the assessment that Al Jazeera viewers can handle distressing images). The orientation is rich and multi-layered, despite the brevity of the narrative: the time is the beginning of the respondent's assignment in Syria, in March 2011, but also an intimate moment in the life of a grieving family overlaid with an irate newsroom exchange.

It could be said that how a narrative is defined, and recognized in the empirical material that is being analyzed, depends on the nature of that material. Different sorts of material contain different sorts of narratives. The narratives that interest scholars are not always as concrete as a news report, film, or interview transcript. They can also exist at a more cumulative and thus abstract level, in the taken-for-granted assumptions upon which people operate. These are often elusive in empirical terms, but make such research worthwhile. It is thus important that each person undertaking narrative analysis is clear about what they mean by narrative, and how their usage relates to concepts like discourse, story, frame, theme, and so on. Are they synonymous? Are they subordinate, i.e. components out of which a narrative is created? Or are they something larger, to which several narratives contribute? How can a narrative be recognized when encountered in the particular primary source material being analyzed? Answers to such questions cannot be found in a handbook or methods textbook. Each researcher must create their own judgements and define their focus of analysis in a way that fits with their research question.

5.2.3 Organizing the material

Some researchers consider it important to engage with a narrative on its own terms. They warn against tendencies to read simply for content and reading a narrative as evidence for a prior theory. One way of avoiding such pitfalls is to begin with asking how the text is organized, and reflecting on why the narrator developed the tale in the way they did. Working with interview material, some start from 'the inside' (the meanings encoded in the form of talk), then explain outward, identifying the underlying propositions that make the talk comprehensible, including what is taken for granted (Riessman, 1993; Feldman and Almquist, 2012).

Taping and transcribing are absolutely essential to narrative analysis involving interviews. Riessman spends considerable time scrutinizing the rough drafts of transcriptions before going to the next level. It is here that she finds analytic induction most useful: a focus for analysis often emerges as she sees what respondents say. Some scholars find it useful, at this stage, to parse the narrative into numbered lines.

Lieblich et al. (1998) read, interpret and analyze narrative materials using the framework of two intersecting dimensions: holistic versus categorical and content versus form. The result of the meeting of the two dimensions is four modes of reading a narrative:

> **the holistic-content mode** of reading uses a complete story, like *The Hunger Games* trilogy or a *House of Cards* episode or the autobiography of a political leader, and focuses on the content presented by it. If the researcher analyzes separate sections (e.g. opening or closing sequences), he or she analyzes the meaning of the part in light of content that emerges from the rest of the narrative.

> **the holistic-form-based mode** of analysis usually involves looking at the plots or structure of complete stories. It asks whether the story ascends towards the present moment or descends towards it from more positive periods, and whether, for example, there is a turning point or climax which sheds light on the whole development (Lieblich et al., 1998: 13). Studies of decision-making in Swedish municipalities have identified organizational narratives as tragedies or romantic comedies, with one author reporting the results in the form of a script for a commedia dell'arte (Czarniawska, 2000: 26).

> **the categorical-content approach** is more familiar as 'content analysis' (see Chapter 2). Categories of the studied topic are defined, and separate utterances of the text are extracted, classified and gathered into these categories. This mode of reading focuses on the content of narratives as manifested in separate parts of the story, regardless of the context of the complete story (Lieblich et al., 1998: 16). Some authors use categories made up of single words; others use a broader category of 'event-explanation unit' in which narrators provide attributions to various events in their lives (Lieblich et al., 1998: 17). Researchers engaged in media analysis break news narratives down into themes or frames, for example, or, like Smith (1979), into actors and actants. In this mode, quantitative treatment of the narrative is fairly

common. It is possible to ask, for example how many times some aspect of a coun-try's relationship to the EU is framed as a problem or used with the word 'risk', or how many times a news report of a refugee crisis uses the imagery of a natural catastrophe, or the word 'failure'.

the categorical-form mode of analysis focuses on discrete stylistic or linguistic characteristics of defined units of the narrative. It can ask what kind of metaphors the narrator uses. Are elections depicted as horse races or football matches with winners and losers in public narratives, for example, or a politician's account of an election defeat? Defined instances of this nature are collected from a text or from several texts and counted, as in the categorical-content mode of reading (Lieblich et al., 1998: 17; see also Chapter 6).

Czarniawska (2004) provides pedagogical illustrations of how a narrative analysis can be conducted in keeping with the traditions of hermeneutics, struc-turalism, and poststructuralism (see under 'Suggestions for further reading'). The student who remains daunted at the prospect of an analytical framework with several intersecting dimensions should bear in mind that simplicity is gen-erally a virtue when it comes to research. As mentioned earlier, it is helpful to attend to Chatman's (1990) distinction between story and discourse – to separate the 'what' from the 'how' – and to pay particularly close attention to the for-mer or the latter depending on the nature of the material and the needs of the research question.

5.2.4 Analyzing talk: narrative analysis and focus group material

Work that builds on Labov and Waletsky's model tends, it has been said, to analyze narratives as texts without contexts. The model has also been criticized for failing to consider the contributions the audience may make to the telling of a story. In another strain of narrative research, scholars interested in 'everyday stories' have developed what are sometimes referred to as **interactional approaches to the study of narrative**. Their focus is on the work that stories do in social contexts, and on the involvement of audiences in the narrative act and the construction of sto-ries (Schiffrin, 1996; Ochs and Taylor, 1992; Ochs and Capps, 2001). This approach involves being aware of the way stories are adapted to the context in which they are told, are embedded in the conversations that surround them, and unfold in one way rather than another depending on the role of the participants. One variation on the interactional approach is what has been referred to as the 'small-stories' paradigm (Bamberg and Georgakopoulou, 2008). Its object of analysis is under-represented narrative activities such as the relating of ongoing events or talk about things that have yet to come and not least shared events. Given the emphasis on co-telling, focus group settings are a useful site for data collection.

The following excerpt provides an illustration. It was collected for research on **cosmopolitanism**, the 'sense of being at home in the world'. While cosmo-politanism at the elite level has long been the object of theorizing, less is known about 'everyday cosmopolitanism' and whether and how it can be observed in the discourse of non-elites. To find out more about this, and in particular about the intersection between their lived experience of the world beyond their national borders and their mediated experience of it as obtained through news reports, focus group interviews were undertaken with groups of people in the capital city of Stockholm and in a small town in a rural district of Sweden. The interview excerpted below was with a group of librarians who talked about their reactions to the news that the Swedish foreign minister Anna Lindh had been murdered.

Box 5.2

Reactions to news

Librarian 1: I was in England, you see, and it was awful. We were a group of librarians in England, who suddenly got the news. And we stood there and felt completely outside. We wanted to be home when it happened. And we cried together and it was … it was awfully strange. And then you saw all those pictures on TV, crying people, and you felt that that's where we should be. It was … strange.

Librarian 2: It's so strange when you see lots of people, because obviously, all that about 9/11, it's stuff you just stand and think about for a long, long, long time, about individual cases and so on. But otherwise it's war and so on, when you see that there are lots of people dying, and you aren't moved as much as when you see one single story, one person who tells it. You have to distance yourself.

Librarian 1: It feels so hopeless. I think you have to … I think you have to try to distance yourself and come back to your own little reality and try, well, do the best you can with your own little life. That's where we usually end up when we discuss things. Sometimes we discuss all the misery, but we try to do what we can in our own little library.

Librarian 2: The awful thing about television news is that you stop thinking. I mean, I've almost stopped looking at the news because of that. I think there is report after report after report, and I don't have a chance to react. That it's like that. So I much prefer to watch, you know, slower programmes and documentaries, that allow you to, like, keep up. Because it's … it's pure violence. I mean it's terror, terror, terror. And maimed people.

Interviewer: And you mean that it's not enough just to know what's going on, it's important to react somehow?

Librarian 1: Yes, for me it's important to react. Because I think sitting and being spoon-fed and not reacting, it's somehow … well, you feel numbed. And anything at all can happen without you reacting in the end.

(Source: Robertson, 2010: 70-2.)

This conversation can be broken down into the narrative elements set out by Labov and Waletsky, as shown in Table 5.2 below. But it also highlights the reason the model has been critiqued by narrativists interested in 'small stories', as there is not a single narrator. Two women participate in the telling, and use several stories to respond to a question about how the news helps them relate to world events.

Analyzing small stories and focus group conversations by attending to their component features, and both the 'what' and the 'how' of the narrative, makes it possible to discern patterns across a larger corpus of primary source material and compare texts such as transcripts of live interactions.

Table 5.2 Small stories in focus group settings, parsed into their narrative elements

Story	
Orientation	
time	the moment one speaker got the news that the minister had been killed
	'We ... suddenly got the news'.
place	far away from home, cut off from events
	'I was in England ... completely outside. We wanted to be home'.
participants	colleagues following the news
	'We were a group of librarians who suddenly got the news'.
situation	trying to make sense of deaths that the librarians learn about from the news
	'you saw all those pictures on TV, crying people... you see there are lots of people dying'
	'there is report after report after report'
Complicating action	
	The news does not engage the speakers in the plight of distant others as they think it should.
	'you see that there are lots of people dying, and you aren't moved as much'
	'You have to distance yourself'.
	'you stop thinking'
Resolution	
	The speakers decide not to deal with the misery of the world, or the news about it they get on television, but to do what they can in their own workplace.
	'We try to do what we can in our own little library'.
	One speaker decides to stop watching the news.
	'I've almost stopped looking at the news ... I much prefer to watch ... slower programmes and documentaries'.
Coda	
	From England and the death of the foreign minister, and from 9/11 and the deaths of many, the speakers return to their own small world.
	'you ... come back to your own little reality and try, well, to do the best you can with your own little life. That's where we usually end up'.
Discourse	
evaluation	The speakers feel the situation is hopeless, and unsatisfactory. They think it is a problem that they are not behaving like compassionate citizens, and television news is part of the problem.

Story	
	'for me it's important to react'.
	'It feels so hopeless'.
	'The awful thing about television news is that you stop thinking'.
	'you feel numbed. And anything at all can happen without you reacting in the end'.
how the story is told	The speakers emphasize and repeat certain words and phrases to underline the strength of their reactions and their distance from the world of news.
	'It was awful ... it was awfully strange ... It was strange'.
	'We wanted to be home ... we cried together ... that's where we should be'.
	'You aren't moved as much as when you see one single story, one person tells it'.
	'there is report after report after report'
	'it's pure violence ... it's terror, terror, terror'.
	'You have to distance yourself'. 'You have to try to distance yourself'.
	'You have to ... come back to your own little reality ... do the best you can with your own little life ... in our own little library'.

5.2.5 Analyzing media narratives: An example of television news analysis

Discourse analysts who study news stories, such as van Dijk (1993), have sought to show that the ways journalists structure or 'emplot' reports, and the ways they characterize protagonists, contribute to the dissemination of stereotypes and reproduction of power relations that disadvantage minority groups. Given that this research tradition privileges the written word, much of that research is based on press coverage. While newspaper texts are straightforward and easy to work with, the decline in the market and readership in many countries and the growth in the use of digital technologies suggests that it is worthwhile looking at other media for narratives. Scholars pursuing multimodal narrative analysis have been doing precisely this, studying narratives in television, social media (Page, 2011) and what De Fina and Johnstone (2015: 161) refer to as "the interaction of different semiotic resources" (or multimodal texts; see Chapter 7), i.e. sound, print, image and animation.

This section highlights television texts because they reflect this development and because they are particularly well-suited to studying the phenomena that narrative analysis seeks to explicate – power, identity, and the circulation of meaning in social contexts. Television is both a 'new' and an 'old' medium. It is new in that television news content is now broadcast on websites and YouTube. News stories are increasingly fashioned in packages and on platforms with the intention of making them easy to share. But television news is also 'old' in that it continues to purvey, as it has since at least the 1960s, "common, cultural references and thematic codes, incarnated in master or model narratives" that are often experienced as innocent, not because their intentions are hidden, but because they are naturalized (Barthes, 1993 [1970]: 131; Birkvad, 2000: 295). What narrative analysis can get at, and what tends to elude many other forms of media analysis, is the generation of these sorts of understandings – what we take for granted, what goes without saying.

The task facing the researcher here is to try to understand how these sorts of understandings appear natural while being so insidious and powerful. By paying attention to 'story', it is possible to study how certain themes and values can gain prominence through the repeated, conventional dramaturgy of the news report, and to compare hundreds of news texts. By paying attention to 'discourse' it is possible to study the techniques involved in telling those stories in one way rather than another, and thus giving the same events a different meaning.

Analyzing the 'story' is something that different researchers do in different ways, and with different degrees of formality. One way of going about the task is simply to leverage the elements outlined in Table 5.1 by turning them into code questions to be posed to the text (be it a newspaper or website article or television report). Analyzing the 'discourse' of the narrative is less formulaic and requires drilling down from the surface information or 'denotative content' of the text to examine its connotative content. **Denotation** refers to how things are explicitly or directly understood, without interpretation. The information that a participant in a narrative is the prime minister is denotative content. **Connotation** refers to the associations or secondary meanings imbued in a word, image or phrase. A headline in the Russian news channel RT referring to "Cameron's deceitful strategy to get UK Syrian involvement" (rt.com, 27 November 2015), for example, connotes that the British prime minister is dishonest and manipulative. Connotative content is often less subtle than this example, and examining it involves making behaviour visible that is otherwise invisible, i.e. the work of the audience. Chatman (1978: 41–42) calls this work the "reading out process", referring to our routinely employed abilities to decode from surface- to narrative structures. But while it may be routine, it is also skilled work. Illusions of verisimilitude, explains Brinker (1983: 254), are based on the viewer's "thoroughgoing familiarity with the conventions of representation" at work. Audiences recognize and interpret these conventions without being aware of them. People rarely give a thought to camera angles, but routinely and subconsciously decode the physical distance established by the filming and editing of a news story as associated with social distance. Politicians tend to appear in news bulletins at a respectable distance, while ordinary people tend to be shown at closer quarters, particularly if they are in distress. This convention has the effect of putting the average viewer in a more intimate relation to the sort of figures with which they are presumed to be on an equal social footing (see also Chapter 7). Unreliable figures can be looked up at if the journalist's intention is to depict them as menacing, and looked down on when they are shown as less powerful; filmed at an oblique angle, they are situated as 'other' (Graddol, 1994: 142).

Graddol identifies two traditions used in television journalism to tell stories about the world. The dominant one is **realism**, a term originally used to refer to a literary convention. The narrator in this tradition tends to be omniscient – "one who can see things which individual characters cannot see and who is in all places

Table 5.3 Coding scheme for analyzing the 'story' (*histoire*) of television news reports

Story

Abstract	How does the newsreader introduce the report? What do they say it will be about? What does the text at the bottom of the screen or behind the newsreader say the topic is?
Orientation	
time	Is it breaking news, or a report of something that happened earlier that day or the day before? Or is it actually about something that took place in the past (an assassination or clampdown or scandal, for example) that today's event (a funeral or the commemoration of the clampdown or a book published about the scandal) only serves as the 'news hook' for?
place	Where do the unfolding events take place?
	Typical answers to this question are 'at a press conference', 'outside the parliament' or 'at the scene of the earthquake'.
	Depending on the research question guiding the analysis, it can be worth noting whether the news story is set in a public or private space.
participants	Who speaks or acts in this story?
	In answering this question, distinctions can be made between:
	– 'real' people (the Russian president Vladimir Putin; the Ghanaian migrant Peter Bossman; the Bahraini activist Maryam al-Khawaja)
	– abstractions like states or collective actors ('Turkey shelled Kurdish forces in Syria', 'Washington recalled its ambassador', 'the party is divided')
	– characters (ruler, dissident, victim)
situation	What is the starting point or equilibrium?
	Here it can be useful to code for the institutional or political context of the story. Does it have to do with the local community, the nation, or with the European or world community?
	Is it a conflict or is the report about people's efforts to get along together? Is it about politics or the economy or society?
Complicating action	
	What happens to destabilize the equilibrium?
	For example, in a study of news coverage of migration, the starting point or equilibrium might be a national refugee policy that is in accordance with EU agreements and the country's humanitarian stance. A complicating action would then be: "the Swedish government announced today it would impose border controls to stem the flow of asylum-seekers, currently arriving at a rate of 10,000 a week".
Resolution	
	What finally happened?
	News reports are often about processes or ongoing events, so the question of what constitutes 'finally' must be connected to the 'time' coded above. But news reports tend to be formulaic, and the reporter's sign-off is a good place to look for the resolution.
	Examples:
	"Everything will come to a test this Friday, when it's likely that the protesters will go back to Tahrir Square. How the army will handle that remains to be seen."
Coda	
	How does the reporter return us to the studio and the rest of the broadcast, and how does the newsreader return viewers to the present?
	"We'll be hearing more from our correspondent in the days to come as we follow these ongoing developments in the field. Meanwhile ... "

at once" (Graddol, 1994: 140). Other characters can also contribute to the narrative, of course, but they are encompassed by the omniscient narrator's voice.

The other tradition is that of **naturalism**. Used more often in documentaries than in news bulletins, it provides "a representation of the world as it might be directly experienced by the viewer [...] From the naturalist perspective, a news report provides vicarious experience, an image of the world as we might expect to experience it if we were to stand where the reporter stands" (Graddol, 1994: 145). The objective, omniscient narrator's voice is absent from reports in which such narrative techniques are used.

The job of the narrative analyst is to create science out of the mundane, and make the conventions visible that render some narrative clauses evaluative. A useful way of approaching this task is to pose questions to the text. In Table 5.4 below,

Table 5.4 Coding scheme for analyzing the 'discourse' (*discours*) of television news reports.

how the story is told	What is the role of the reporter-narrator? Is he or she 'omniscient', in possession of all the facts and perhaps commenting on what is going through a participant's head? Or is the reporter a bystander, listening in on someone else's story before passing it on to us?	Is the reporter pictured in the centre of the field of vision, between the viewer and the participants? Or does the report use naturalist techniques that allow us 'direct' contact with the participants, i.e. by letting them tell the story in their own words?
	Is one side of the conflict silent or under-represented?	Are the participants on one side of the conflict only referred to, or are they pictured, and if so how? Are they in focus or behind a fence or at sea?
	Where is the viewer situated?	Do we see the conflict from behind the lines of the riot police, or from the middle of the protest march? Or do we watch events unfold from a rooftop?
	How is the audience addressed?	Are we invited, through the use of reporting conventions, to enter the room occupied by a participant? Does the journalist and camera operator place us in a position in which we can imagine conversing with the participant? Are we invited to react to what the participant or reporter tells us?
	Does the language used by the reporter-narrator suggest participants should be understood in one way rather than another? Does he or she refer to someone as being hostile, obstinate, or aggressive, or as conciliatory, heroic or victimized?	Is there metaphorical or symbolic content in view? Look for walls and fences, and sunrises and sunsets.
evaluation	How is the story to be understood?	
	What sense is to be made of these events, given the way they have been reported?	

Table 5.5 Transcription of 'Uganda child soldiers. Former fighter reunites with family', broadcast on Al Jazeera English, 3 May 2014

Story	Visuals
Newsreader:	
In Uganda, thousands of children were kidnapped and forced to fight for the Lord's Resistance Army led by Joseph Kony. Our correspondent reports from Kitgum on one former child soldier, who is finally heading home after 13 years in captivity.	
Reporter:	
When he was 10 years old, Dennis Ocan was abducted from his village in northern Uganda by rebels from the Lord's Resistance Army. That was in 2001. He was forced to become a child soldier, and to commit atrocities. It was 13 years before he could escape.	The report begins with a shot of an empty barracks, in which a young man, formally dressed, is packing his suitcase. The reporter is not in view.
Dennis Ocan (the young man):	
Many children were beaten to death. You have to follow the orders, or else they kill you. Children who tried to escape were killed. You have to follow orders until a chance to escape comes.	The young man is pictured sitting on the bed in the barracks. He is very still and speaks in a low voice.
Reporter:	
In recent weeks, this rehabilitation centre, run by the charity World Vision, has been his home. At the peak of the war, hundreds of child soldiers came through here every month. The murals they painted are still here. An estimated 10 thousand are still missing, most of them will never come home. But a trickle of former child soldiers do still escape, now grown adults. It's Christine Oroma's job to counsel them.	The reporter is not in view. Pan of walls with childlike, mural-size paintings of young people playing. Shot of piles of binders and papers, with more wall paintings in the background, of automatic rifles. Cut to a group of young men sitting on benches, in a ring, under a tree
Christine Oroma, Counsellor, World Vision:	
Such kind of killing is really a problem. Psychologically they keep on recalling.	Christine Oroma is alone on screen.

(Source: Webb, 2014)

the position of 'evaluation' is moved to the end of the coding scheme, as it tends to be a question best answered by the preliminary work of establishing how convention and connotation are being used to tell the story in one way rather than another. A column has also been added, in order to chart the interaction between the visual and verbal elements of the narrative.

The example above shows how a television news report can be transcribed, organized and analyzed using this framework (Table 5.5).

In the study that drew on the story of Dennis, as told by an Al Jazeera journalist, it was argued that the narrative resonates with an outlook that understands the world in terms of cosmopolitanism rather than conflict, because the report positions the viewer in the car beside the rehabilitated soldier, and beside him as he treads on eggshells and shakes the hands of other young men from the village. In so doing, the discourse of this particular narrative could be said to position the viewer – with the narrator witness – on the side of peace, freedom and reconciliation.

5.3 Critical Reflections

A good place to begin reflecting on the strengths and weaknesses of a narrative approach is with the television analysis presented above. The first point to make is that there are a number of narratives at work here, or rather narrative work taking place on different levels.

5.3.1 Questions of interpretation

On one level is the narrative of the original storyteller. Has the narrative of the journalist been 'read' the way he intended it to be read? Has it been 'read' the way the intended audience – perhaps a harassed parent, spooning meatballs into the mouth of their small offspring while the television news is on in the background – are likely to make sense of it?

5.3.2 Credibility

On another level, there is a separate narrative at work here: the narrative of the researcher. Doing research is a matter of dialogue – with the material being ana-lyzed, and with other scholars, be they world-renowned professors encountered at a conference, students in a classroom setting, or some other reader whom the student/researcher may never meet. For the dialogue to work, the analysis of the primary source material, i.e. the texts, must be transparent: the researcher should take the reader by the hand, as it were, and lead them through the mate-rial that has been analyzed the way an experienced traveller might introduce a tourist to a city or cathedral that the latter has never visited before. While the experienced traveller/researcher might have the advantage of knowing the place better than the tourist/reader, the two of them should be able to have a dialogue between equals as to what to make of it. Perhaps the traveller, who has been to the cathedral dozens of times, asserts that it is a fine example of, say, Gothic architecture. The tourist is looking at the cathedral for the first time, but may be an expert on cathedrals in another country, or on Gothic architecture in general, and is thus in a position to disagree with the traveller. Listening to the arguments of the tourist, it may become clear to the traveller that the familiar cathedral has unfamiliar features, and may have to be reconsidered. The point of the story (yes, another narrative!) is that the discussion could never have taken place had the traveller/researcher not taken the tourist/reader to the supposedly well-known cathedral. Substituting the cathedral with 'primary sources' or 'text', this means that the dialogue on which research is based cannot take place unless the researcher shares their material with the reader.

When the primary source material is comprised of hundreds of television news reports, all containing both words and pictures, or transcriptions of dozens of hours of interviews, or texts in a language not likely to be accessible to the reader, the business of sharing, and maintaining transparency in the reporting of results, can be challenging. Most researchers, lacking a better solution, resort to summarizing their material. Such summaries often take the form of a narrative. This approach to textual analysis can thus result in a narrative of a narrative.

Scholars approach their primary source material with their theoretical assumptions and research questions at the forefront of their minds. Those assumptions and questions may encourage them to see certain things in their material and to be blind to others. A BBC camerawoman expressed this rather more succinctly than Gadamer (see Chapter 1) when describing how she went about filming an event: "We see what we want to see. We film what we know" (Robertson, 2015: 145). The narrative of the researcher is thus not something to be taken at face value. As explained in Chapter 1, texts can be analyzed with either the understandings of the text producer or addressee in mind. What does that entail when a given text is interpreted in the context of the larger societal discourse?

5.3.3 Reflections on narrative analysis in general

Given these questions, it is hardly surprising that a recurrent criticism levelled at researchers using the narrative approach is that their analyses cannot be reproduced by other researchers. Not all agree that this is a problem. Bruner, for example, notes the eventuality of there being a difference between what is expressed in the text and what the text might mean, to return to issues raised at the beginning of the book. There is no ultimate solution to determining the meaning of a given text, he says: our best hope "is to provide an intuitively convincing account of the meaning of the text as a whole in the light of the constituent parts that make it up" (Bruner, 1991: 8). That in itself is a goal worth striving for. There is every reason to strive for reliability in narrative analyses and, where possible, for results that can be generalized.

Lieblich et al. (1998) agree that no reading is free of interpretation. Even at the stage of procuring the text (especially in the dialogical act of conducting an interview), explicit and implicit processes of communicating, understanding and explaining constantly take place. They refer to a dilemma that has to do with the role of theory in listening to and explaining an account: is the researcher a naïve listener attuned only to the phenomenological world of the narrator? Or does the researcher constantly question, doubt, look for gaps, contradictions, silences, the unsaid? They offer four criteria for assessing the quality of narrative research:

1. **comprehensiveness of evidence**: Like Riessman, they maintain that reports should be supported by numerous quotations, and alternative explanations should be discussed;
2. **coherence**: This has an internal and external dimension. Internal coherence can be evaluated in terms of how the parts or our analysis fit together; external coherence in terms of how they fit with existing theories and previous research;
3. **insightfulness**: A good study should be innovative or original in some way, in the presentation of the story and in the analysis of it;
4. **parsimony**: As with other research, a good narrative study should be able to fulfil the preceding three criteria with recourse to a small number of concepts. It should have elegance or aesthetic appeal (Lieblich et al., 1998: 173).

Essential to the work of evaluating narrative research is the point mentioned above: the sharing of results and interpretations with the relevant research community (be it fellow students or a tutor). Do they see the same patterns? Do they make sense of narratives differently? Do they follow the researcher's argument and find it compelling? Can they distinguish the researcher's voice from that of the narrators' in the primary source material? This is what Lieblich et al. refer to as **consensual validation**. In their view, it is particularly significant in narrative inquiry.

Czarniawska points out that the surge in interest in narratives has occasioned two kinds of warnings. First, some have questioned the legitimacy of work conducted by social scientists engaging in what is derogatorily referred to as 'literary work'. In this view, scholarship becomes literary criticism, and indeed a form of literary criticism that is inferior to that of literary theorists. Second, social scientists have to show that they are good not only at reading Barthes, but also at telling us something about organizations (in the case of Czarniawska's field of expertise) – or politics or culture or society or identity or power. Social scientists engaging in narrative work "have to move across lands belonging to someone else", and this is not without its hazards (Czarniawska, 1999: 37).

5.4 Narrative analysis and the study of power and other social phenomena

It was suggested earlier that people "work 'mentally' in common" (Bruner, 1991: 20) through the narratives circulating in society, and that the construction of such narratives thus places them in a shared social context. Because such construction work involves struggles over meaning, the study of narrative sheds light on power, and how we, as members of particular social formations, are more readily able to accept some "realities" than others and "sometimes become imprisoned by these realities" (Mumby, 1993: 7).

Narratives exist on different levels, or in different dimensions, and can be more or less abstract. The analytical instruments presented in this chapter have been used to explicate concrete narratives – the stories a librarian or a television journalist actually told and the words they used to tell them. But such analyses can only be interesting if they can give us insights into something larger or more general, and such generalization can only take place if specific micro-level narratives are related to accumulated or macro-level and recurrent narrative themes. These often take the form of taken-for-granted assumptions about how the world works referred to at the beginning of the chapter. These accumulated narratives go by different names. One is **public narratives**, which feature actors larger than the individual, like the 'working-class hero', the 'enemy within' or 'the market'. Another is **master narratives** (about Progress, Enlightenment, the triumph of Democracy and so on) in which some scholars claim we are embedded.

Narrativity is about making sense of our place in the scheme of things, and this takes place within certain political constellations. The study of narrative gives us a point of entry into the distribution of power in society, particularly in affording insights into phenomena that are constructed as 'natural'; it helps us to see what is not always visible and to hear 'that which goes without saying'.

Summary

The usefulness of a narrative approach

- the starting point for this chapter has been that narrative analysis provides useful insights into society and politics, and that social actors are better understood as 'narrative creatures' than as 'rational actors'
- the approach is characterized by considerable diversity, both conceptual and methodological. This can be a source of inspiration, but also of confusion and frustration
- practitioners of the approach differ when it comes to their starting points and assumptions; how they define narrative; and the uses to which narrative is put
- narrative is defined in this chapter as an account of something that has happened which is comprised of two parts: a 'story' and a 'discourse'
- contemporary narrative analysis has built on the work of the Russian formalists, French structuralists, and literary theorists
- narrative analysis is now used by scholars in fields as varied as political science, law, anthropology, gender studies, psychology and medicine
- by analyzing concrete narratives, such as those found in interview transcripts or media texts, it is possible get an analytical purchase on the more abstract narratives and taken-for-granted assumptions that have become so naturalized as to be almost invisible and which yet govern the way we make sense of the world.

How to go about doing it

- in collecting material, it is important to be clear about what you mean by narrative and how you will recognize one in your primary sources. When it comes to interviews, being attuned to entrance and exit talk is a useful method. Transcription is essential. Decisions about the amount of material to be analyzed should be governed partly by the nature of the research question and the material itself, partly by the researcher's ambition to focus on 'story' (in which more material can be accommodated) or 'discourse' (which is more time-consuming)
- when analyzing the narratives, it is useful to operationalize the features of the story (be they abstract, orientation, complicating actions, resolution or whatever) as questions to be posed to the text. When analyzing the 'discourse' of the narrative, it is useful to keep the question 'how' to the fore: how is this story being told so that its content leads to a given evaluation?

- when presenting results, bear in mind the importance of being able to have a dialogue with other (student)researchers about the findings of the study. This means sharing the material in some form or other – either by making original transcripts, texts or recordings available, or by summarizing the narratives and providing numerous quotes and examples.

Suggested Reading

Two textbooks on narrative can be recommended to the student who wishes to pursue the approach in more depth. Both distil the often complex ideas and obscure writing style of leading narrativists in an accessible, reader-friendly fashion. One of these is Holstein and Gubrium's (2012) anthology *Varieties of Narrative Analysis*.

In *Narratives in Social Science Research*, Barbara Czarniawska (2004) illustrates the various methods that can be encountered in the field of narrative analysis using material that the social science student should find it easy to relate to. There is also practical advice about how to incorporate a narrative approach in a larger project, and a glossary for the student who finds themselves confusing exegesis with mimesis and structuralism with poststructuralism.

The University of Nebraska Press has a series on narrative, and some of the volumes will be of interest to social scientists, such as the one edited by Brian Richardson (*Narrative Beginnings: Theories and Practices, 2008*) and the one entitled *Narrative across Media: The Languages of Storytelling* (Marie-Laure Ryan, ed., 2004). The *Routledge Encyclopedia of Narrative Theory* compiled by David Herman, Manfred Jahn and Marie-Laure Ryan in 2005 (paperback version 2008) is a valuable reference to me, should your library happen to have a volume. It has a helpful glossary and reader's guide. Some have found the chapter on discourse analysis in Tannen et al.'s *The Handbook of Discourse Analysis* (De Fina and Johnstone, 2015) to be helpful.

For those who find it especially important to focus attention on the linguistic features of narrative texts when analyzing evaluation, two texts are recommended: the chapter on narrative by Georgakopoulou in Zienkowski and Verschueren's *Discursive Pragmatics* (2011), and the chapter by Gimenez entitled 'Narrative analysis in linguistic research' in Litosseliti's *Research Methods in Linguistics* (2010). A good source of inspiration is the Narrative Inquiry journal. Visiting the http://wordpress.clarku.edu/mbamberg/ni website and reading the abstracts published there (even if the full articles may not be available to readers) provides a way of keeping abreast of developments in the field.

Exercise

A US rehabilitation programme: Angola Prison Rodeo

A few days after the story about the Ugandan boy soldier was broadcast, another report appeared on the same channel.

The task

Use the coding scheme given in Table 5.4 to get your analysis started. After you have coded this text, compare it to the boy-soldier narrative, and think about what the answers to the following questions might say about broader power relations in society.

1 In which way do the stories of the Ugandan boy-soldier and the Angolan rodeo differ? What can be said about those differences?
2 Are there important features of the primary source material (the text) that cannot be captured in the framework? If so, what additional or alternative questions could be posed to the text?
3 Are there elements in the framework that are absent from the material, and if so are they irrelevant or unarticulated?

You may also want to use the material to think more about the assumptions underlying the use of a narrative approach to the study of texts. Why study narrative?
   (After working with this exercise you can check the suggested analysis in Chapter 9.)

The text

The first part of the transcript of the report is reproduced below.[4]

Table 5.6   Transcript: US Rodeo Rehab, broadcast on Al Jazeera English on 8 May 2014

Story	Visuals
Newsreader:	
Rodeos are a big part of rural life in the southern US. But in the state of Louisiana, one show stands out. Our correspondent reports now from the Angola prison rodeo, which many say is the most controversial event in the world.	
Reporter:	Reporter not in view.
It's billed as the wildest show in the south, and for good reason.	Wild bull charges out of the pen and towards a group of black men sitting at a table in the middle of the dirt ring.
Take convict poker, an event that pits nerves against the raw power of the raging bull.	The table is demolished and the black men are scattered and thrown to the ground.
The last man sitting wins cash. But these aren't trained cowboys: they are inmates of one of Louisiana's most secure prisons.	The next shot shows a huge bull tossing a seated, unarmed man by the horns.

For the full text to analyze, please visit the companion website (**https://study.sagepub.com/boreusandbergstrom**).

---

[4]There is plenty of other material to practise on. A rich source of narratives can also be found on the Al Jazeera English website (www.aljazeera.com), if you search for 'Surprising Europe' (the exact address is www.aljazeera.com/programmes/surprisingeurope/). The units of analysis can be the individual episodes, the stories within those episodes, or the series as a whole. It can also be instructive to reflect upon how the narratives on these different levels relate to each other, and how these texts can be related to the study of such topics as cosmopolitanism, multiculturalism, post-colonialism and conflict.

6

Metaphor Analysis and Critical Linguistics

Kristina Boréus and Göran Bergström

6.1 Background

The following expressions appeared in different articles on the Internet in January 2015:

> 'Engage sick bags as stormy markets show no signs of calm.'[1]

> 'The market's ugly. You knew all that already. [...] But what you might not know is that there's a group of stocks that have sailed right through the turbulence.'[2]

> 'When the market's waters turn choppy and dark, unprepared investors who refuse to change course quickly find themselves capsized and underwater.'[3]

What views of the economy and markets do these sentences, with their metaphorical content, express and what does a reader learn about how markets function?

Chapters 3 to 5 demonstrated how the ideational aspect of texts can be analyzed by focusing on their argumentation, expressed ideas and the way stories

---

[1]Headline for article by Shawn Langlois, http://www.marketwatch.com/story/engage-sick-bags-as-stormy-markets-show-no-signs-of-calm-2015-01-12, published 12 January, 2015; accessed 19 September 2016.

[2]Matt Kranz: '9 stocks sail past the stormy market', http://americasmarkets.usatoday.com/2015/01/15/9-stocks-sailing-past-market-storm, published 15 January, 2015; accessed 9 September 2016.

[3]Glenn Curtis: 'Survival Tips For A Stormy Market', http://www.investopedia.com/articles/stocks/08/market-downturn.asp (accessed 19 September 2016).

are narrated. In this chapter we show how to analyze metaphorical language, grammatical structures and the choice of words in texts. The techniques presented here are more closely connected to linguistics as a broad discipline than are the methods presented in the rest of the book.

The strands of analysis presented are related by common theoretical assumptions. The kind of metaphor analysis shown here has its roots in cognitive linguistics – the branch of linguistics that studies how human thinking is related to linguistic expressions. By studying which metaphors are used in texts one might, according to the approach, learn something about our way of thinking that is not explicitly expressed. This analysis focuses on the ideational function of texts, while rhetoric, presented in Chapter 3, treats the usage of metaphors as a conscious way of a speaker to try and influence the listener, thereby focusing on the interpersonal function of metaphorical language. Analyzing grammar and lexicon (e.g. studying the vocabulary of a corpus) in the way demonstrated here has its roots in critical linguistics, an early form of discourse analysis.

The two approaches have different roots. Put simply, cognitive linguistics, out of which the metaphor analysis presented here has developed, takes its starting point in the human brain, while critical linguistics starts in society. Nevertheless, both approaches rest on certain common theoretical assumptions. Both take it for granted that our usage of language and how we experience the world are closely related. Language use is seen as an expression of only partly reflected ideas that affect how we experience the world we live in. No wonder then that cognitive linguistics and critical discourse analysis (CDA, presented in Chapter 8) which has adopted many of the methods used in critical linguistics have begun to cross-fertilize each other in regard to metaphor analysis (Goatly, 2007: 21). Thus, despite possible tensions between these approaches on a theoretical level, they can be used together in the broader frames of discourse analysis. One author who merges critical discourse analysis with the kind of metaphor analysis presented in this chapter is Charteris-Black (2004) who refers to his analysis as 'Critical Metaphor Analysis'. With a war metaphor of his own making he refers to the analysis of metaphors as "an important weapon in the armoury of the critical discourse analyst" (2004: 86).

6.2 Analysis

6.2.1 Metaphors we live by

To "see the light at the end of the tunnel" and to have "a long road ahead" might be (and usually are) metaphors. A metaphor describes something as something else that it is not, transferring meaning from one domain to another. This transfer is usually made from an area that is well known and tangible to what is less apparent to our senses and more abstract. If to "see the light at the end of the tunnel" is metaphorically meant, it refers to having found the solution to a difficult task or problem or that a difficult situation is coming to an end. The transfer here is probably of more than one aspect of the experience of moving in a tunnel: the darkness of the tunnel is the difficult or disturbing situation, the light at the end is the experience of knowing that things will be right again, while the idea of the tunnel itself might transfer the experience of confinement onto the experience of not getting away from struggling with a problem.

Figurative language

Metaphorical language is just one kind of **figurative language**. **Similes**, e.g. "families are like fudge", are close to metaphors but differ in that they state explicitly that there is a transfer of ideas. A **metonym** is an expression used for something that it is a part of or in other ways associated with. "The White House claims" is seldom a literal statement – it does not mean that a building has started to talk. When this phrase expresses that the president of the United States – or a spokesperson for the president – has uttered something, the function of the expression is not to claim that the president is like a big white building: the expression is not metaphorical either. A metaphor makes a transfer between areas that are not closely associated. It is sometimes difficult to tell a metonym apart from a metaphor and an expression can be both metaphorical and metonymical at the same time.

Metaphors are thoroughly studied in linguistics. A comparatively recent approach is that presented by the linguist George Lakoff and the philosopher Mark Johnson in their seminal *Metaphors We Live By* (1980). According to Lakoff and Johnson, metaphors are not a mere linguistic embellishment, as they were considered in earlier metaphor studies, but tools that we use, consciously and unconsciously, to grasp the world we live in. Our conceptual system, which affects both how we think and how we act, is metaphorical in nature. Because of that metaphors are not just phenomena at the surface of language, to use a suitable metaphor. They are important because they say something about more fundamental ways of seeing the world in a particular language community. If one has accepted a particular metaphor, one has also accepted a certain view of a phenomenon.

Metaphorical expressions and conceptual metaphors

Below we will distinguish between **metaphorical expressions** ('metaphors'), like the phrase to "see the light at the end of the tunnel" which is often used metaphorically, and **conceptual metaphors**.[4] Conceptual metaphors are collective ideas in a linguistic community according to which a phenomenon is conceptualized in terms of something it is not. Conceptual metaphors are expressed by metaphorical expressions in a language, both by set expressions, like the tunnel metaphor, and by freshly made up metaphors that are understandable exactly because they express shared ideas. Conceptual metaphors might also be expressed by non-figurative language.

---

[4]What we refer to as 'conceptual metaphor' can also be referred to as 'metaphor' (Lakoff, 1993: 209).

Lakoff and Johnson use metaphors in the English language to lay bare the conceptual metaphors that structure mundane activities in the English-speaking world (Lakoff and Johnson, 1980: 7–9). The conceptual metaphor TIME IS MONEY[5] is expressed in many different ways in English, e.g. "You're *wasting* my time", "How do you *spend* your time these days?", "That flat tire *cost* me an hour", "Do you *have* much time *left*?", "He's living on *borrowed* time". All these expressions speak about time as if it were money, an entity that we can save, spend etc. Several other languages use corresponding expressions which indicate that they too use the conceptual metaphor TIME IS MONEY. The expressions reveal a particular way of conceiving time that is related to how the concept of work has developed in modern cultures in which work is very often associated with the time it takes to carry it out, time is exactly quantified and one gets paid for work according to time units. These practices have not always existed but have emerged in modern industrialized societies. They strongly structure our everyday activities. We act as if time were a precious good, a scarce resource, and we understand it in that fashion.

Conceptual metaphors like TIME IS MONEY and the metaphors that express them highlight certain aspects of phenomena but hide others. They also direct our thoughts in certain directions. This is particularly important for the social sciences. Societal phenomena are far more abstract than natural phenomena like elephants or planets; for that reason we understand these to a large extent through conceptual metaphors. In many cases we are conscious about the conceptual metaphor being exactly that, but we are unable to state what would be a literal description. In that sense we are under the sway of metaphors. It then becomes important which metaphors are used in different contexts, what they highlight or conceal, and what they tell us about a phenomenon.

Take the metaphors for markets at the beginning of this chapter. According to them, markets can get *stormy* so that you might need a sick bag, stocks can *sail* on them and they have *waters* that might turn *choppy and dark* upon which investors might *capsize* and go *underwater*. Obviously markets are conceptualized as oceans and the conceptual metaphor MARKETS ARE OCEANS seems to be at work. Highlighted by that conceptual metaphor are qualities of markets such that when people invest in them they take risks because the markets are uncontrollable, like the stormy sea. Markets are like natural forces in relation to which humans can take precautions (bring the sick bag along) but which they cannot control. What this particular conceptual metaphor conceals is that, unlike a stormy ocean, what happens in the markets is the result of human actions. It also steers thought away from the fact that political decisions can regulate markets in a way that they cannot regulate oceans.

Dead, inactive and active metaphors

An important distinction in metaphor theory is that between dead, inactive and active metaphors. The process of making transfers in thought and language from

---

[5]Following the conventions of some linguistic literature, all conceptual metaphors in this chapter are typed in caps. The metaphors that express them are marked with *italics*.

tangible experiences or situations that are easy to grasp to what is abstract and complex is going on all the time. In the beginning, the metaphors are invented by writers or speakers, then some of them are taken up in language and over time become set expressions. Here we refer to expressions that average language users no longer understand as metaphorical, or where the meaning of the metaphor is no longer understood, as **dead metaphors**. We refer to metaphorical expressions that are set expressions but are seen as metaphorical after reflection as **inactive metaphors** and those freshly created as **active metaphors**. The terminology varies in the literature.[6] Despite terminological differences the central idea is the same: there is a scale along which the metaphorical aspect of an expression stands out more or less strongly.

Inactive metaphors are usually more interesting to study for the social sciences than are dead or active ones. They are conventional expressions whose metaphorical meaning is apparent to language-users, at least on consideration. Many of the metaphors that make a transfer from the human body to other physical things – 'mouth of the river', 'foot of a page', 'eye of the storm' – are of this kind. Moving from concrete reality to social reality we find lots of inactive metaphors, not least in journalism. In a big daily paper a president was reported to have

- bragged about an economic *turnabout* and claimed that
- *the shadow of crisis* had passed and to have
- *unveiled* a raft of proposals.

In the same paper a party was said to gain support by people who held a desire

- to support *clean politics*; yet
- the party was *facing* tough times and their economic policies were accused of having
- added to *the burden* of the common people.

The metaphors above might be more or less inactive: people will recognise some of them as metaphorical more easily than others and the judgment might vary slightly between language users.

The interesting thing about inactive metaphors is that they might tell us something about discursive patterns that are not fully conscious to language users. Active metaphors, in contrast, are the outcome of the creativity of particular language users and must be interpreted from the context in an active process by the addressees. Hence active metaphors are not as readily helpful to reveal cultural patterns (even though they might sometimes be interpreted as novel expressions of existing conceptual metaphors). Different strategies of interpretation are relevant

---

[6]Some authors refer to what we call inactive metaphors as 'dead metaphors'. The expressions 'conventional' versus 'creative' metaphor (Charteris-Black, 2004: 17) are also used. An author who makes a more detailed classification along the scale is Goatly (1997: 31–5) who distinguishes between "dead", "dead and buried", "sleeping", "tired" and "active" metaphors and suggests ways of telling these apart. In a later work (Goatly, 2007) he also distinguishes between '(accepted) conventional' and 'original' metaphors.

for inactive and active metaphors. When interpreting the established expressions of inactive metaphors one is using the discourse-oriented strategy of interpretation, while when interpreting an active metaphor one pays more attention to its particular creator, along with the producer-oriented strategy (see Table 1.1).

After presenting these theoretical background notions we will now move on to scrutinize a study in which the analysis of metaphors plays a crucial role.

6.2.2 A study of metaphors for sexual desire

Genevieve Patthey-Chavez, Lindsay Clare and Madeleine Youmans (1996) analyzed metaphors for sexual desire and heterosexual sexual activity in erotic romance novels for women, making use of the approach to metaphor theory presented above. The authors consider this approach to be a valuable way of revealing cultural models in societies. They analyzed 16 novels in the first erotic genre specifically directed at women, typical novels sold in North American book stores in the late 1980s and early 1990s.

The authors criticize another study in which metaphors associated with sexual passion in the United States were analyzed (Lakoff, 1987). The metaphors that Lakoff discussed reveal a conceptual system in which passion is conceptualized as hunger, heat, madness, games and war. People experiencing passion were animals or machines and passion was conceptualized as a physical force that takes over and alters the mind of individuals. The authors critique the interpretation of these conceptual metaphors as expressions of a common US cultural model while in reality they emanate from a male position in society (Patthey-Chavez et al., 1996: 82).

While pornography for men pictures women as objects for passion, erotic romance novels for women challenge women's objectification but in a complex and contradictory manner. While the stories in soft porn for men seemed to be there only to transfer the plot from one sex scene to the next, the analyzed novels for women presented entire fictional worlds in which sex was a passionate aspect of complex and dramatic relations. Novels had central stories in which the heroine travelled, met important and exciting people and helped to save someone or something from great danger. In the narratives for women sexual experiences were to a large extent described in terms of inner emotional experiences of pleasure while the narratives for men are dominated by descriptions of bodies, body fluids and physical experiences (1996: 80–1).

The central object of study was "the struggle between hegemony and sexual liberation in erotic fiction for women" (1996: 77), a problem the authors claim is inherent in the genre. On the one hand, there was sexual liberation in the sense that this new genre made a break with a historical pattern according to which erotic texts have been written for male consumption while women's sexual preferences have been made invisible or presumed to be in accordance with those of men. On the other hand, the analysts found deep-seated oppressive associations related to women's sexuality that they interpreted as hegemonic.

The analysis as a whole could be labelled critical discourse analysis (see Chapter 8) and was carried out with the help of different tools. Metaphors for sexual experience and passion were analyzed, as well as some key themes. Among those themes were rape, female sexual agency and how female and male protagonists were characterized. The results were analyzed in a discussion of the way the 'dangerous' liberating forces in the narratives were tamed into culturally acceptable forms. Here we will focus on the analysis of metaphors.

The authors read through a representative sample consisting of 16 novels and identified the sex scenes. The longer scenes were picked out to be the object of a more thorough study. They collected all expressions – metaphorical or expressed by other figurative language as well as literal – that referred to sexual experiences. The expressions were then categorized as expressing different conceptual metaphors. In the next step they compared usage of metaphors for female and male characters.

Several of the metaphors in use coincided with those found by Lakoff (1987). Lust was framed in terms of hunger, heat, war, animals and to some extent as insanity. Sexuality was also understood as an irresistible force. Other common metaphors in the novels were not mentioned by Lakoff: passion in terms of substances or experiences that affect consciousness, e.g. like a kind of hypnosis, an inability to think, primitiveness and water. In contrast to Lakoff's study, metaphors based on machines or sports were not found: sports and technology are apparently not erotic in this genre (Patthey-Chavez et al., 1996: 85).

Some cases showed no gender differences. The conceptual metaphor PASSION IS HEAT (fire) was used in relation to both women and men to the same extent. In other cases the researchers found gender differences that seemed to carry ideological weight. Expressions of the conceptual metaphor PASSION IS WET (water) ("With a force that left her breathless, a *wave* of pleasure *washed* over her" (1996: 89)) were more common in the descriptions of the heroines and were often used in the context of their passive responses to the heroes' thrusts.

The conceptual metaphor SEXUAL DESIRE IS A PHYSICAL FORCE also showed gender differences. For both women and men the force was an antagonist that they tried to fight off. But for male characters it was often the female body together with the force of passion that made them lose control, while for female characters it was their own bodies that 'betrayed' them.

SEXUAL DESIRE IS A PHYSICAL FORCE[7]
Female characters

- Where earlier she had fought against the *rising tide of excitement* within her own body, she now no longer struggled against the inevitable
- She gave in to the *longing that had stalked* her dreams for nights

---

[7]The authors' enumeration of the examples and their page notations for the novels from which quotes are drawn have been excluded here.

Male characters

- The firm flesh was like a *magnet*, drawing him ...
- The moist, welcoming heat of her body was unmistakable, a *silent command* that he come deeply within her

(Patthey-Chavez et al., 1996: 86)

The metaphor usage also constructed a conflict, a 'war between the sexes'. Violent language was often used in the description of sexual meetings. Here a rape-like undercurrent was found, most explicit in the many scenes where the heroine crossed the line between virginity and sexually initiated. In these sex scenes it was common that the heroes either forced the women to admit their own desire or to carry through the very sex act while the women were resisting.

MEN AND WOMEN ARE AT WAR

Men as invaders

- *She felt the invading* digits slipping between her nether lips
- The *vulnerable position* thrust her breasts up to him, and he swiftly bent to *capture* one

Men and women are at war

- Clare felt him tense and draw in his breath as if *readying himself for a dangerous feat of arms*
- He was a *war-horse* straining at the reins, all *leashed power* and trembling readiness

Women resisting invasion

- She *shoved*, but his strength was too much for her
- She *caught* his encroaching thigh between her legs

In this war of male conquest women were also conceptualized as land. Men were explorers and invaders, women the unknown continents to be explored and invaded. Women were also food that was consumed by the men. The most common of these metaphors were those based on war and conquest, in total 138 occurrences in the corpus (Patthey-Chavez et al., 1996: 91–2).

Thus the analysis of the metaphors points to a conventional view according to which women are subordinate to men: female desire was not quite accepted, hence they got 'betrayed' by their bodies when they felt it. Sex between women and men was conceptualized as men invading and conquering women who were then consumed.

The key themes also analyzed pointed in different directions: both towards 'liberation' and 'hegemony'. Almost all heroines were found to be strong and successful working women who often carried out some major rescue action (in the most extreme example she rescued her planet from destruction) and who were allowed a sexuality of their own. At the same time there were narrow limits for how women were allowed to express their sexuality. Next to all heroines were sexually inexperienced when they met the man that awoke their desire, while none of the heroes lacked sexual experience. The women showed their chastity by resisting the men's sexual 'attacks' for as long as possible, which explains a high frequency of what the authors call "rape imagery", defined as "[h]ero (or other male character) ignores female protagonist's verbal objections; uses some force to proceed; holds or pins female protagonist against the ground/bed/wall in order to proceed". This is to be distinguished from rape, a "clear, unambiguous instance of forced sex". Rape imagery appeared in 10 of the 16 novels. These pseudo rapes always 'forced' the women to great pleasure, which was what the hero was aiming for. After their sexual awakening these women did not go on experimenting: they did not find new lovers and had no erotic contacts with other women. Instead they married the hero.

Here we turn to a more general discussion of how to go about this kind of metaphor analysis, based on a closer look at different steps in the article but widening the discussion to modes of analysis relevant to other studies as well.

Analytical steps in metaphor studies

To start with, we want to point to the clear use of theory and discursive context of the study presented above. There is an explicit purpose presented, namely to examine the struggle between hegemony and sexual liberation in erotic fiction for women through a study of metaphors and a thematic study. The erotic romance novel is analyzed as a particular genre whose characteristics are described. To combine a study of metaphors with other ways of analyzing the texts is strongly recommended: no text can be understood solely from an analysis of its metaphors.

The first step in the analysis consisted of listing all expressions related to certain phenomena (desire, sexual intercourse) in selected parts of the corpus and then classifying these expressions. In this case the authors did not distinguish between literal and metaphorical expressions; other kinds of figurative language were also included. The reason for this was presumably that the conceptual metaphors used for classifying the listed expressions generated both literal and figurative expressions.

In some cases, however, it may be necessary for the purpose of one's study to tell figurative expressions apart from literal ones. Rosenblatt (1994: 25–7) gives advice on how this can be done. The general idea is to consider whether the expression may be used in totally different contexts and whether a literal interpretation of that expression would appear bizarre or false in the context: if that is the case, the expression is likely to be figurative. Obviously the expression to 'see the light at the end of the tunnel' could be used literally, e.g. by a person travelling by train. But if there is no real tunnel it is a metaphor. Furthermore, one can consider the implications of the literal expression. If the expression were literal it would mean that one could in principle touch the walls of the tunnel with one's hand, that the light would be dimmed if one put sunglasses on, and so on.

The second step for Patthey-Chavez et al. was to classify the listed expressions as being generated by certain conceptual metaphors. They do not comment on possible classification problems, which we think would have been an advantage. The classification was based on associations between expressions. These associations mostly appear self-evident, as when words like 'wave', 'ripple' and 'wash' are associated with water and classified as expressions of the conceptual metaphor PASSION IS WATER. Others are perhaps not as self-evident: is a 'silent command' a kind of physical force? We would also have liked to see a list of all analyzed expressions included in the article (perhaps as an appendix). It is also possible to argue for the existence of a particular conceptual metaphor by referring to other expressions in use in the linguistic community in question. Further, the authors provide an overview of the usage of different kinds of metaphors by presenting their frequency, both absolutely and in relation to the length of the texts. These frequencies are presented as tables. Such presentations add stability to the overall analysis.

The third analytical step after having listed the metaphors and classified them in accordance with conceptual metaphors, which will usually only be possible with some of them, is to interpret what the metaphors and conceptual metaphors reveal about the texts or the discourse under scrutiny. What interesting or important ideas about society and people do the metaphors and conceptual metaphors convey or what do they tell the analyst in regard to the research questions? This step would mostly involve a more average reading of the texts. Does the pattern of metaphors point in the same direction as the argumentation and other text content on a more explicit level? In the study by Patthey-Chavez et al. the answer was 'no', and in the Critical Reflection part of this chapter we discuss such possible tensions in more detail.

The fourth and last step is to interpret the result of the analysis in light of one's research questions. In the section on the relevance of the approach for questions on power etc. we return one last time to the article by Patthey-Chavez et al. to see how the authors interpreted their results on a societal level.

6.2.3 Analyzing grammar and lexicon

Critical linguistics is now mostly used as one of several ways of carrying out critical discourse analysis (CDA). A linguistic starting point is M.A.K. Halliday's **functional grammar** (Halliday and Matthiessen, 2014), which classifies linguistic structures according to the functions they fill in language use, and in expressing meaning.

Language and Ideology by Gunther Kress and Robert Hodge (1979) is an early book within critical linguistics. According to the authors the rules and system of categorization of any language are based on fundamental, often unconscious, views about the world we live in. Language is a social construction of fundamental importance for how we understand reality; the grammar of a language can be considered a theory of reality: "Language fixes a world that is so much more stable and coherent than what we actually see that it takes its place in our consciousness and becomes what we think we have seen" (1979: 5).

In a critical linguistic grammatical analysis the bottom line is that every language contains a number of thought models for how events and relations may be described. **Transitivity** is a term used to designate how grammar expresses choice of perspective when events and situations are described. Here, we will concentrate on descriptions of what happens, how change comes about. When one describes something that took place (or is taking or will take place) one chooses between existing models, and, by that, one also chooses a perspective on what happened.

A toolset for describing processes and participants

A conceptual toolset is used to refer to different grammatical elements. The concepts we present below are drawn from Fowler (1991: 70–80) but slightly adapted. This toolset cannot be used to break down and exhaustively describe the grammar of all sentences in a text, which could in principle be done if more categories than those presented in this chapter were used. We have chosen to focus on descriptions of *what goes on* since they are central to the interpretation of how an author or speaker makes sense of the social. Consider the following (slightly shortened) news item:

Box 6.1

Jet Airways flight with 59 on board makes emergency evacuation in Khajuraho

BHOPAL: A major accident was averted at Khajuraho airport when a Jet Airways plane carrying 59 passengers and 8 crew members developed some technical problems while landing and it had to be evacuated at runway on Monday afternoon.

For two days there will be no flight movement at the airport.

Sources said that flight 9W2423 that was coming from Varanasi, developed some technical problems with the hydraulic systems and had to be stopped at the runway. Emergency doors were opened and passengers were evacuated. [...]

Jet Airways issued an official statement on its Twitter handle at around 4.30 pm regarding the incident saying [...]

Director Khajuraho airport, Kamal Sharma told TOI, "It will take at least two days to resume flight movement at the airport. The plane is at the runway. It will have to be removed."

"All the passengers and crew members are safe," Sharma said.

(Source: *Times of India*, 13 April 2015[8])

---

[8]http://timesofindia.indiatimes.com/india/Jet-Airways-flight-with-59-on-board-makes-emergency-evacuation-in-Khajuraho/articleshow/46908133.cms (the Twitter statement by the airline has been left out.)

Obviously there are many alternative ways of describing what went on here and the toolset helps us to see what choices were made. Descriptions of this kind involve references to what took place – goings-on in the world – and to the participants involved. We start with the former, the **process**. A socially important difference is that between describing the process as an action, an event or a state. An **action** is deliberately carried out by a sentient being. Actions in the news item are "Sources said…", "Jet Airways issued an official statement…", "Kamal Sharma told TOI…", "…Sharma said". Jet Airways is not exactly a sentient being but everyone understands that there were humans formulating the tweet, so the issuing of the statement will have to pass as an action here.

Actions might be of different types. Here, we distinguish between those that are expressed by verbs that refer to material, to verbal and to mental actions. A **material action** is something tangible and external to a person, something done that could in principle be observed by somebody else. To make the point clear we exemplify such actions with a quote from a famous novel: "She spent hours on the riverbank. She smoked cigarettes and had midnight swims…" (Arundhati Roy: *The God of Small Things*). **Verbal actions** are referred to by verbs to do with speech and expressions, like in all the examples of actions described in the news story. The typical **mental action** is somebody imagining, thinking or believing something: "Writers imagine that they cull stories from the world. I'm beginning to believe that vanity makes them think so" (*The God of Small Things*).

A further useful distinction is that between whether or not it is stated that the action involved was directed at some other participant. In this text the actions (things were said and told and a statement was issued) are not reported to have involved other participants in the story apart from the verbal action described in "Director Khajuraho airport, Kamal Sharma told TOI" where *Times of India* has to pass as a participant in the process (we presume that Sharma has talked to a journalist from the paper). Physical actions might also involve other participants: "the crew evacuated the passengers" (which is not how the process is described in the article). Also mental actions might involve others: "he thought of his children".

In news language goings-on are often described as **events**,[9] as something that takes place that are not actions, not caused by somebody's deliberate doing. In this case, for instance, there "will be no flight movement" for two days at the airport (an event that will not take place). Interestingly, there are descriptions of things that went on that are described as events, even though without much pondering the reader understands that what took place must have been actions, the result of sentient beings deliberately doing something: the plane "had to be evacuated" and "had to be stopped at the runway" where "[e]mergency doors were opened and passengers were evacuated". Events, too, might be referred to as material, verbal or mental. The events described in the news item are all of the material kind. People's verbal interaction might actually be described as events, as in "issues were

---

[9]Referred to as 'processes' in Fowler (1991: 73).

Table 6.1 Processes: Ways of describing what takes place

	Actions					
	Material		Verbal		Mental	
	Involve other participants	Do not involve other participants	Involve other participants	Do not involve other participants	Involve other participants	Do not involve other participants
Example	'the crew evacuated the passengers'	'she swam at midnight'	'the airport director told TOI'	'sources said'	'he thought of his children'	'writers imagine'
	Events					
	Material		Verbal		Mental	
Example	'a major accident was averted'		'an argument was taking place'		'last night I dreamt'	
	States					
Example	'all the passengers and crew members are safe'					

argued about". Descriptions of mental events (when something happens inside people's minds without anybody deliberately doing something) are common, like when a person dreams or sees visions.

Both actions and events relate to changes in the world. Another kind of process[10] is called **state**, when verbs or adjectives imply no change: "The plane *is at* the runway", "[a]ll the passengers and crew members *are safe*", in which the words in italics indicate states. Table 6.1 summarizes the concepts presented so far with some of the examples used above.

From the descriptions of processes, we now turn to how the participants in the processes are described. A first distinction is between participants that do things themselves, referred to as **actors**, and those that have things done to them, who are referred to, with a term from critical linguistics, as **goals** in the process. A typical actor is the human **agent**, in the news item the sources and the airport director that carried out the verbal actions (and also the airline that issued a Twitter statement).

Grammatically speaking, there are also other actors in the text. The headline "Jet Airways flight with 59 on board makes emergency evacuation…" is expressed as if the flight were a sentient being that decided on and made the evacuation. Such an inanimate actor is called a **force**.

The participants that are the goals of the actors' doings are either human or non-human. Human goals are referred to with a grammatical term as **patients**.

---

[10]The term 'process' is used in critical linguistics although it is somewhat linguistically contra-intuitive to refer to the lack of change as a 'process' in ordinary language.

Table 6.2 Participants: ways of describing those involved in processes

	Actors		Goals	
	Agents (human)	Forces (non-human)	Patients (human)	Non-human goals
Example	'sources said'	'flight makes emergency evacuation'	'the crew evacuated the *passengers*'	'the crew opened the emergency doors'

Patients in the news item are the "passengers" that "were evacuated:. The plane, referred to as "it", is a non-human goal in the clause "it will have to be removed". Table 6.2 summarizes the terms used for classifying participants.

More elements could have been analyzed in the news item. One would be **circumstances**, referring to when something happened ("on Monday afternoon") and where it took place ("at Khajuraho airport" in "Bhopal"). More concepts could be invented. One would perhaps want to make a distinction between when an action affects somebody in a harmful or a good way – the possibilities are many and cells can be added to suit particular research questions. Tables 6.1 and 6.2 provide enough tools to carry out a meaningful analysis in many cases, as shown in the sample study by Sykes presented below.

Transformation and nominalization

A basic idea in critical linguistics is that the grammar of the analyzed text be compared with other possible ways of describing an event – that is the critical part of critical linguistics. The concept of **transformation** is used to express that descriptions of what takes place can be more or less complete. The most complete description includes the participants as well as the process. Even when it appears obvious that participants have been involved and that actions have been carried out or events occurred, elements can be suppressed in the description. A first transformation that allows for that is the use of **passive** instead of active verb forms. Examples from the news story are "[a] major accident was averted" and "it had to be evacuated". It is the use of the passive that makes it possible to state that something took place that apparently was the result of humans acting but without having to reveal the agents. If active forms had been used this would not have been possible: "... averted a major accident" calls for an agent and we need to designate one, such as "the crew", "an air-traffic controller" or "the pilot".

Another transformation of interest is **nominalization**, which refers to when verbs or adjectives that could have been used for a totalizing description are replaced by a noun. "Evacuation" is a nominalization. In a more complete description of the event there would have been both agents and patients and an active verb would have been used such as: "the crew evacuated the passengers".

Thus, the use of both passives and of nominalization has the effect that information which would have been part of a more totalizing description can be deleted. When participants are deleted from the description, the question of their responsibility does not arise as easily as when they are pointed out in the text. In the news item above we might actually have thought of praising some agent that averted an accident while in many other cases blame is closer at hand. Even though the effect of these transformations might be a certain mystification it does not necessarily mean that the author used transformations with the purpose of mystifying or hiding responsibility. The purpose might instead be to save space or the reason might be that actors are self-evident, irrelevant or unknown (Fairclough, 1994b: 82).

6.2.4 Lexicon

Critical linguists work with a lexicon as well, that is with systematically studying which words are chosen in texts. In the next section we show how a researcher studies which kind of verbs are chosen in a text, classifying verbs that indicate agency as different from those that do not. In Chapter 8 we give another example of how an author (Fairclough, 2000) uses a lexical analysis when studying with which other words ('new' and 'reform') tend to appear in a corpus of political texts. The purpose of the analysis is to learn more about the meaning and usage of important words by studying the company in which they appear.

Another way of studying a lexicon is to look for **over-wording**, "the proliferation of different words in the same area of meaning", which might indicate an ideological preoccupation with a topic, "suggesting that a particular area of meaning is especially significant or problematic" (Fairclough, 2000: 163). It might be difficult to tell when a text is 'over-worded' in referring to a topic, but the technique might be used to get a first hint of a subject being viewed as particularly important or thorny.

In the sample study presented in the next section, the author uses grammatical as well as lexical analysis.

6.2.5 A critical linguistic study of discrimination

Mary Sykes' article 'Discrimination in Discourse' (1985) deals with the identification of discrimination in discourse against minority ethnic or racial groups. According to Sykes, what a purely linguistic analysis can do is show what kind of textual treatment goes on, but whether the text's message is discriminatory needs to be argued for separately. We return to this issue towards the end of the chapter.

Some of the analyses carried out in the article will be summarized below. For that purpose we quote the entire text that was analyzed, a committee report on young homeless black people in the British city of Birmingham in the 1970s.

Box 6.2

Homelessness in Birmingham

The Commons Select Committee on Police and Race Relations concluded that there were approximately three hundred young blacks roaming the streets of Birmingham. Homelessness among black youngsters is a growing problem and daily more and more young people, both sexes, become homeless.

Case histories tell the same sad story – young black people find themselves overwhelmed by the problems of individual and ethnic identity. They get into trouble at school and then at work. Finally they find themselves at odds with their parents, and are asked to leave home. They feel rejected on all fronts. They begin to drift from place to place finding consolation only in unfortunate victims like themselves. These youngsters are usually between the ages of fourteen and nineteen and are often the products of broken homes. They are turned out into a complex world where slowly they begin to experience its hostilities. They become embittered and alone; unemployed and therefore become more and more alienated from society. They begin to sleep rough; in daytime they hang around arcades and amusement centres of Soho Road or drift into town in groups to their favourite haunt – the Bull-Ring centre.

Many of these youngsters drift into petty crime as a means of survival and are sent to remand homes for 'training'. On returning to the community social problems remain unchanged, homelessness is probably even greater, and prospects of employment greatly reduced.

(Community Relations Commission, 1974: 3, quoted in Sykes, 1985: 88-9)

Sykes goes about analyzing the attribution of responsibility or blame for the problem of homelessness by a transitivity analysis. She starts by counting the human participants that are identified in the text. They are:

1. Commons Select Committee (1 time)
2. young blacks (14 times when 'they' are included; 4 more times deleted like in 'Finally they find themselves at odds with their parents, and [they] are asked...')
3. parents (1 time)

Young black people are obviously the focus of the discussion, almost to the degree that other people are totally excluded. They are 8 times agents clearly taking action (e.g. they "begin to sleep rough"), 3 times agents that experience something (e.g. they "feel rejected") and 8 times patients (e.g. they "are sent to remand homes"). The youngsters are thereby described as clearly acting (not only experiencing) agents less than half of the times they are referred to. Further analysis shows that the kind of actions that they carry out is limited: these are all expressed by intransitive verbs (i.e. verbs without objects like "the girl is running" and not "the girl is kicking the ball" in which "the ball" is the object of the clause). Their actions involve only themselves ("roaming the streets"[11]). Their agency in social processes is further diminished by the lexicalization. Many of the verbs are rather inactive: "drift", "drift into petty crime", "get into trouble", expressions that avoid intentionality. No verbs that indicate mental actions are used about these participants. Sykes concludes:

> The causal role of young blacks in their own misfortunes has been minimized by denying them any significant agency in the processes leading to homelessness and crime. At the same time, however, other possible causal agents or processes have been deleted, obscured, or mystified by a series of transformations and substitutions ... (1985: 90)

The latter part of the conclusion refers to transformations that make the deletion of agents possible. Sykes continues:

> ... if agents were specified, readers might be more likely to ask questions about their role in the process. For example, if the second paragraph began "social workers tell the same story" [they are the ones that write the case stories], then readers might be prompted to ask why social workers were not doing something about the problem rather than just telling stories; or if young blacks get into trouble "with teachers", then questions might be asked about teachers' competence in accepting or handling cultural differences in the classroom. (1985: 92-3)

Thus, Sykes draws certain conclusions about the ideological effects of the message. That the interpretation follows the addressee-oriented strategy (see Table 1.1) is made clear from the references to effects on readers, exemplified in the last quote. Sykes also refers to certain studies of readers' and listeners' reactions to different grammatical manipulations with texts.

6.2.6 Improved digital possibilities

As described in Chapter 2, new databases and development of software have expanded the possibilities for conducting comprehensive content analysis. These developments are also highly relevant for the kinds of analysis introduced in this chapter.

The increasing number of full text databases, improved possibilities of creating one's own corpora, i.e. large collections of naturally occurring language data (Baker, 2006: 1) and the development of software have opened new doors, resulting in a growing interest in corpus linguistics. Charteris-Black (2004) demonstrates how corpus analysis of metaphors can be conducted. Parts of the analysis must be carried out manually. In a first step one reads a number of texts drawn from the context one

---

[11] "[T]he streets" is not the object or an affected participant, grammatically speaking, but a locative that tells us where the roaming takes place.

is interested in in order to identify possible metaphors. Words used to express these metaphors are then searched for in the corpus. After that it is necessary to read the expressions found to judge whether they are in fact metaphors (2004: 35–7).

Corpora are even more useful for studying lexical aspects of discourses, i.e. which words are used and how. Baker (2006) demonstrates different methods that can be used to describe linguistic patterns in a corpus. They might be used for studies inspired by critical linguistics and for other kinds of analysis, as pointed out in Chapter 2.

In a first step a corpus that is suitable for the study is identified or created. Sometimes existing full text databases are available. Examples are press text databases and the text databases for parliamentary debates that exist in many countries. Sometimes the solution is to build one's own specialized corpus. In that case the work consists in collecting texts already digitized from different sources or to scan texts so that they can be analyzed in a digitized format.

With the help of software for qualitative textual analysis (see Box 2.1) – there are several applications for Qualitative Data Analysis, QDA, also referred to as **Computer Assisted Qualitative Data Analysis Software, CAQDAS** – it is possible to analyze different lexical patterns in the text. Some applications have more features, some fewer, and you can also find useful freeware on the Internet. One of the techniques is to study **word frequency**. The software produces lists of the frequency of all the words in the corpus. The most common words are usually so-called **grammatical words** (or **function words**), such as pronouns ('I', 'her'), prepositions ('on', 'at') and conjunctions ('and', 'but'), while what is normally of most interest for the analysis are nouns, verbs, adjectives and adverbs. Software for the right language can sort the grammatical words out, if one wishes to put these aside. The applications often have certain functions – like recognizing grammatical words – that only work for one language (usually English) or perhaps for a few languages. Most functions, among them creating word lists according to word frequency, can be used for any language, and so-called **stop lists** that disregard words one is not interested in can be created manually. Word frequency can, for instance, be used to decide which topics are focused on in the corpus in the same way as in content analysis.

Dispersion of words can also be analyzed: in which texts in the corpus do different words occur and do they tend to appear in the beginning, in the middle or in the end of texts?

As pointed out in Chapter 2, the software can tell us nothing about the meaning of the words when they are used to analyze corpora that have not been tagged or annotated in regard to their meaning. Because of this it is often necessary to look at the words in context in a systematic way, which is the only way of analyzing their meaning. **Concordances** then become very handy. These list all occurrences of the word one wants to analyze with a chosen number of words before and after. The words are thus shown in context, improving the possibility of interpreting their meaning.

Another function of these applications is called **collocation**, which lists with what other words a particular word tends to occur in the corpus, i.e. next to or with only a few words in between. Baker (2006: Chapter 5) used this technique to study which words tended to occur in the vicinity of 'spinster' and 'bachelor', respectively. After disregarding a number of words of no interest and grouping the remaining words, he concluded that 'bachelor' collocated more frequently with words with a positive value, or words that themselves tended to collocate with words with a positive value, than did 'spinster'. The interpretation might be that the life of an unmarried man tends to be constructed in a more positive way than the life of an unmarried woman.

There are several other useful techniques, among them **keyness**, which is a way of measuring the frequency with which a word appears in one corpus compared to another. It is also possible to search for nominalizations (see Section 6.3.1).

For critical linguistic analysis in the social sciences or discourse analysis techniques of this kind are very useful, not least since social scientists often work with large numbers of texts so that it becomes impossible to perform a detailed analysis on all of them. The techniques facilitate finding patterns that point to characteristics of the discourse of which the texts are manifestations. They can be of great help in getting an overview of the texts. Not least the simple technique to let one's computer find the strings of words in which certain words occur (concordances) which proves very time saving. These computerized techniques are also good for avoiding drawing too strong conclusions on the basis of a few texts.

There are also limitations to these techniques that discourage their use as the sole basis for a discourse analysis in the social sciences. Among these limitations are issues discussed in the section on critical reflections in Chapter 2: that words appear out of context, that an important aspect of discourse analysis, namely to interpret the implicit, cannot really be done with QDA software alone, and that ideas can be expressed in so many different ways that it is often impossible to look for their expression by searching for particular words. Besides, working with corpora consisting of digitized texts means limitations from the outset (Baker, 2006): existing databases tend to have newer rather than older material, written texts rather than spoken, and texts from rich rather than poor parts of the world. Texts are taken out of context so that, for instance, newspaper articles might be reduced from being part of a newspaper page with illustrations and a particular layout to plain texts, lacking images, pullquotes or adverts. Thus, these techniques should be used with considerations for their limitations. It is, however, possible to combine these creatively, something that Baker (2006) exemplifies in several ways.

6.3 Critical reflections

A first question to ask regarding grammatical studies is what they actually tell us about implicit meaning that an ordinary reading of the same texts does not reveal.

6.3.1 Is hidden ideology really revealed?

Our answer to the headline question is that the point of this kind of systematic analysis is that it makes it possible to uncover meanings that might be just intuitively or not at all noticed by ordinary reading.

Taking Sykes' analysis of discrimination in discourse as an example, it seems as if an ordinary reading would not have done the same job. Perhaps it would have shown that the youngsters are portrayed as passive, but the analysis of grammar provides more systematic information. Neither is it obvious, practising ordinary reading, that other agents are hidden by the text's structure ('They get into trouble at school and then at work'). This conclusion, however, begs the question from whom is a message hidden? Sykes's analysis probably reveals things to an academic middle-class reader that would have been obvious for homeless youngsters in Birmingham without conducting specialized linguistic analysis. They know that they reflect and act and that they have experienced concrete interactions with the hidden agents.

6.3.2 Tensions

Analyzing different aspects of the same text can give results that point in the same direction or that seem contradictory. The explicit argumentation and the usage of metaphors might seem consequent and support the same message, something that supports the credibility of the analysis.

In other cases argumentation and metaphors point in different directions. This motivates further discussion but might not be an indication of a failed analysis. Texts might contain internal tensions as a result of tensions in or between the discourses of which they are manifestations. This was the case in the (1996) analysis by Patthey-Chavez et al. When key themes at the narrative level were studied it was found that women were portrayed as free and active people: goal-oriented and successful working women who had the right to pleasurable sex. Other themes pointed in other directions, while the metaphors for sexual relations between women and men constructed women as subordinate to and conquered or consumed by men. The authors interpreted this as the result of a tension between liberating and oppressive ideas harboured in the culture at the time.

6.3.3 The issue of reliability

Intersubjectivity is important for reliability. In the case of metaphors and their relation to conceptual metaphors, linguistic intuition and associations play a part. Good intersubjectivity depends on the associations made by the analyst not being too far from those of other language-users. This is often unproblematic: that metaphors which contain words like 'flood', 'wave' or 'wash' can be associated with a conceptual metaphor where water gets to stand for something else (in Section 6.2.2 for 'passion') should be easy to agree on.

The part of the analysis that necessitates classification into grammatical categories should not offer too great a challenge for intersubjectivity. It is not completely unproblematic, though: Sykes used her textual study for another article as well and came up with somewhat differing results (Sykes, 1988). The most important intersubjectivity problem is, however, how the grammatical patterns in the texts should be interpreted. What, for instance, do particular nominalizations express and how are they interpreted by primary addressees who do not read the text the way an analyst does?

6.3.4 Questions about language, reality and knowledge

Both critical linguistics and the kind of metaphor analysis presented here can be combined with a more or less constructivist/empiricist view of language in the world. If we imagine a scale from a radically constructivist to a radically empiricist view of language and reality we have clear epistemological views at each end. At the constructivist end we find ideas, according to which all our notions of reality – all we know – are based on the culture and the language world in which we live. This is a relativist view: different cultures hold different world views, none truer than the other. In a culture that recognizes the existence of magic and witches these phenomena exist, in a culture in which these are not recognized they do not. What the analysis can do is only to reveal the perspectives that different texts express; its task is not to relate these perspectives to some truer notion of reality than the version that the texts have provided.

At the other end of the spectrum, the radically empiricist, it is taken for granted that our senses as human beings make it possible for us to gain knowledge about the physical world we share, regardless of our cultures or languages. As long as there are clear definitions of the words 'magic' and 'witch', it is or it is not the case that the phenomena they refer to exist or have existed.

Cognitive linguistics, whose understanding of metaphors has been presented in this chapter, chooses a sophisticated position in between these endpoints in regard to the epistemological question of what can be known. The fact that we are humans with human bodies, brains and senses makes us share important experiences. As a consequence, there are certain general human ways to categorize (which is not the same as saying that the *categories* made in different language communities are the same: they are not). That, however, is less true for the social world, which is to a high degree a culturally and linguistically construed world. The following quote seems to make sense:

> We may feel that an elephant is obviously a "thing in the world", and that any people first coming upon elephants will give that species a distinctive name. But we will not feel the same security about stepsisters or trumps or mistakes. It is

difficult seriously to imagine human beings lacking such concepts one day "happening upon" a stepsister or a mistake and giving the phenomenon a name.

(Pitkin, 1972: 114)

This view does not solve the problem of what in the world is open to intersubjective knowledge. There is no easy way of telling the 'natural world', inhabited by creatures like elephants, and the 'social world' where everything is as relative as mistakes or trumps, apart. This view indicates that language and culture will have a more or less important role for what constitutes reality. It is likely that our common being in the world as humans sets more or less strict borders for the possible construction of social phenomena: perhaps stricter for how massacres can be constructed than for how freedom of the press or power can.

The 'truth' that language constructs our world is sometimes taken as a philosophical underpinning of discourse analysis. This assumption can, however, to some extent, be empirically tested. The problem of whether, how and to what extent our language affects our experiences of the world has long been disputed by linguists. Does language affect how we think? Do people with different native languages think in different ways? The idea that language affects how we think so that people who speak different languages think differently is referred to as the **linguistic relativity hypothesis**.[12] A large number of experiments in which people with different native languages have been made to solve cognitive tasks in different areas have been carried out. This is a lively research field. Developments in the last few decades indicate strongly that there is some evidence to support the linguistic relativity hypothesis. For a start, there is very large variety between the world's languages. Even though there are common grammatical patterns that can be found in many languages, some linguists are still struggling to find meaningful **linguistic universals**, i.e. patterns found in all languages (Everett, 2013: 48-9). This goes for all aspects of language. When it comes to tense, for instance, it feels natural to a native English speaker to think that verbs have three basic tenses that indicate if something happened in the past, is happening now or will happen in the future. The majority of the world's languages do not have three tenses, however. Many have two and make the distinction only between past and non-past events, or between future and non-future events. Likewise some languages have more tenses than three. Everett (2013: 56) exemplifies languages with two tenses with Karitiâna, a small langue spoken in the Amazon region of Brazil. In Yagua, spoken primarily in northeastern Peru, there are seven tenses.

Another difference is that while many languages conceptualize time as the past being behind us and the future ahead, there is at least one language, Aymara, spoken in the Andes, that reverses this order. This might be related to a notion that is wide-spread among the world's languages, namely that knowing is seeing.

---

[12]Also referred to as the **Sapir-Whorf hypothesis** due to it being formulated by the linguists Edward Sapir and Benjamin Whorf.

Understood that way, the Aymaran way of conceptualizing time makes better sense to speakers of other languages: we know about the past but not about the future; we see what is in front of us but not what is behind us (2013: 109).

Not only is there a wide diversity between existing languages, there is also strong evidence that language does affect cognition in many areas. In interviews with Aymaran speakers who knew no or little Spanish, it was found that the speaker pointed forward when referring to past events, while Aymarans who only spoke Spanish or had a poor understanding of the Aymaran language, tended to point backwards when talking about past events (as Spanish places the past behind us) (Everett, 2013). Another fascinating example is provided by Lucy (1992), who accounts for how the grammar of language affected people whose native language was English and Yucatec Maya (a Mexican language) differently when they were classifying objects and taking an interest in their qualities.

Experiments have shown the effects of language on cognition for several other areas as well, fairly strong for some, weaker for others. Fortunately this does not mean that we are helplessly caught in our local linguistic spider-webs. Even though our native languages teach us to think along certain lines, experiments also show that the influence is seldom absolute. People in experiments tend to favour certain ways of solving the cognitive tasks they are presented with, but not all speakers of the same language solve them in that way. People are also capable of learning other ways of seeing things in the experimental settings – they do not need to learn a new language to understand these (Everett, 2013).

6.4 Linguistic analysis and the study of power and other social phenomena

Both sample articles illustrate the usefulness of the methods discussed in this chapter for social sciences. Metaphor analyses of this kind often aim at uncovering a message whose meaning might not be fully conscious either for the author of the text or its readers. The idea is that the use of metaphors can tell the analyst something about patterns of ideas in a larger discourse. Patthey-Chavez et al. (1996) draw on the concept of cultural models (Holland and Quinn, 1987), claiming that the pattern of metaphors reveals patterns of thought in a society, in this case regarding female and male sexuality. For that reason they claim that their analysis does more than merely describe characteristics of the particular literal genre they studied, namely that it also casts light on more general ideas in the US at the time. What is the relation between such general ideas of a society and societal phenomena such a power or oppression? This is a theoretical as well as an empirical question. As stated by Patthey-Chavez et al.: "uncovering an existing cultural model is not sufficient for understanding the relationship between behavior and beliefs" (1996: 82). Other cultural models of female and male sexuality are also available. It is another task, they claim, to study how different cultural models are present, or absent, in real people's lives and their 'negotiations' in real relationships. Thus, nothing follows on directly about real women's power or oppression from an analysis of fiction, but presumably such an analysis says something that is relevant for power.

Sykes' analysis casts light on discrimination. To claim that ethnic/racial discrimination has taken place, she says, three things should be shown: (1) that two or more parties have been differentially treated; (2) that this is to the disadvantage of one of the parties; and that (3) the reasons for the differential treatment had to do with race or ethnicity. The analysis summarized above showed two things of importance for the issue of discrimination: that the black youngsters were described as lacking agency, which might be understood as demeaning, and that the role of other agents in creating the problem of homelessness was omitted from the story. The basis for considering the text discriminatory would be that racist practices contribute to the problems that the young people have, while the text conceals a lack of respect for their rights and instead emphasizes their special needs, thereby disadvantaging them. But, says Sykes, it is not certain that the differential treatment is due to these youngsters' skin colour. It is a pattern that is repeated in relation to other groups in precarious positions and in need of welfare, such as the unemployed or white youngsters in the same situation. Sykes thus uses her analysis to argue for the presence of discrimination, possibly ethnic discrimination. Her analysis is, in other words, obviously relevant for a societal issue and for a problem social sciences might deal with.

Both analyses are situated in times different from when this book was written. In both cases it would be interesting to compare here with what happened later (and with what happened earlier, for that matter). What turns have the ideas of female sexuality and heterosexual relations taken in the US with today's religious and moral trends, and how are they expressed in fiction? What has happened with regard to discriminatory discourse in relation to welfare issues in Britain since the 1970s?

Summary

On the usefulness of metaphor analysis and critical linguistics

- The methods presented in this chapter can be used to uncover perspectives and ideological messages that are not as explicit as those conveyed by literal language and argumentation.
- An analysis of metaphors or grammar does not always show more than ordinary ways of reading texts. Often, however, they give more substance to a message that is intuitively or vaguely captured by ordinary modes of reading.
- An analysis might point to tensions in texts that are revealed only if they are read in the ordinary way combined with an analysis of metaphors, grammar or lexicon, or if different methods are combined.
- The different methods can be combined with different kinds of interpretation strategies: with those related to the text producer, the addressee or the discourse. Active and inactive metaphors are more or less interesting in relation to different strategies of interpretation.

- Metaphor studies can be carried out on larger corpora and with the help of software, although part of the analysis still has to be manual.
- The kind of grammatical analysis shown here is work demanding and does not allow for the study of larger text corpora.
- Some kinds of lexical analysis are ideal for corpus linguistics and can be carried out with the help of QDA software.

How to go about doing it

- The methods presented here should be combined with 'ordinary reading' of some or all the texts to get at their messages at a more explicit level.
- One way to recognize a metaphor – a figurative expression that transfers meaning from one domain to another, stating that a phenomenon should be conceptualized as something it is not – is to ask whether the literal meaning of the expression would be false or bizarre in the context where it appears. If it would, it is probably figurative.
- Conceptual metaphors are collective ideas in a language community according to which a phenomenon is conceptualized as something that it is not. Conceptual metaphors are linguistically expressed by metaphors commonly used in the linguistic community – inactive metaphors – but might also be expressed by active metaphors or by literal expressions. The existence of a conceptual metaphor should be argued for by pointing to the concrete linguistic expressions that it generates.
- Conceptual metaphors highlight certain aspects of phenomena but hide others, something that can direct thought in certain directions. To point to what they highlight or hide might be part of a critical metaphor study.
- In the grammatical analysis of critical linguistics the descriptions of events and relations between participants are studied by taking apart and sorting the elements of sentences and by studying how these are related to each other.
- To study transformations means to analyze to what extent certain elements necessary to a process are deleted in a description.
- Nominalization takes place when nouns are used as replacements for formulations that describe processes in a more complete way, which has the effect that the description becomes vague and that participants can be deleted.
- The use of passives also allows for the deletion of participants.
- After the texts have been analyzed it remains to interpret the results in relation to one's research questions, whether or not the results point in one direction or at tensions in the texts. Tensions should be discussed.

––––––––––––––––––––– **Suggested reading** –––––––––––––––––––––

For those who want to deepen their theoretical understanding of the role of metaphors presented here Lakoff and Johnson (1980) is a good start, clear and well written. It demands some effort by a reader but it is well worth it, one of the rewards being to have read a classic of the genre. The book contains much more than what we have referred to here. An accessible introduction to this theory is Ungerer and Schmid (2006), overall a good introduction to cognitive linguistics.

There are many interesting studies of metaphors in relation to politics and other societal phenomena. Rigotti (1994; in German) studied political metaphors of different kinds, among them war, family and animal metaphors in politics and metaphors for power in certain political ideologies. Semino and Masci (1996) studied football metaphors in the rhetoric of Italian media tycoon and politician Silvio Berlusconi. Schneider (2008) compared the use of metaphors in mass media rhetoric that legitimizes (and delegitimizes) the political systems of the US and UK, while Drulák (same volume) analyzed the use of metaphors in discourses on EU reform. Schneider connects his analysis to a theoretical and methodological discussion about how legitimacy ought to be studied, while Drulák discusses how a study of metaphors in the scientific field International Relations should be developed methodologically. In Ahrens (2009) a number of authors present comparative studies of the metaphors female and male politicians in Germany, Great Britain, Ireland, Italy, the Netherlands, Singapore and the United States tend to use in their speeches. Goatly (2007) analyzes a large number of conceptual metaphors in English, among them SEX IS VIOLENCE, and discusses how they might be connected to cultural beliefs, ideologies and practices. An interesting idea, namely that Liberals and Conservatives in the USA understand society from different basic conceptual metaphors, is presented in Lakoff (1996).

Charteris-Black (2004), referred to above, demonstrates corpus analyses of religious and political texts and of sports and economic news reporting. He criticizes the rhetoric of New Labour in the UK (see further one of the examples in Chapter 8 in this volume). The author has also systematically analyzed metaphors and other rhetorical content in speeches by contemporary political leaders in the US and UK (Charteris-Black, 2005). Koller (2009) gives an example of a metaphor analysis carried out on a corpus with the help of particular software, studying religious and political metaphors in corporate discourse.

Fairclough (1994) treats critical linguistics and several other discourse analytical approaches and lexical analysis is taken to be one tool within the discourse analytical tool kit. Chapter 5 in Fowler (1991) gives a presentation of the grammatical and lexical analysis of critical linguistics that goes further than our introduction here. Halliday and Matthiessen (2014) give access to a larger set of concepts for analyzing which perspectives on the world are chosen in texts by presenting Halliday's functional grammar. Chilton (2004) offers many ways to approach texts with the purpose of studying political language critically, not least how implicit text messages might by analyzed.

An application of critical linguistic method on newspaper reporting on sexual violence is Clark (1998). The volume in which the chapter is included, Cameron (1998), contains several interesting chapters on feminist language studies and textual analysis. Another analysis inspired by Halliday's functional grammar and critical linguistics is Høigilt (2011) which studies Islamist rhetoric in Egypt.

The journal *Discourse and Society* regularly publishes studies based on linguistically inspired discourse analysis, among them studies of metaphors and critical linguistic studies.

Exercises

The Indian nation, metaphorically speaking

This exercise is about linguistic expressions of nationalism, a well-researched topic (see for instance Wodak et al., 2009). Modern political elites use public speeches to convince

(Continued)

(Continued)

people to rally round the flag and the national leadership and to convey the qualities of their nation to outsiders. This is done differently in different countries, due to countries' varying history and the ideas that dominate in the public spheres. The expressions of nationalism and of what the nation is and represents also vary over time and are often contentious within a country.

The task

In this exercise you will be examining some expressions of Indian elite rhetoric nationalism, expressed in political speeches, and have an opportunity to think of what a comparative nationalism study, focusing on figurative language, could look like. List all the metaphors for India and the nation that you find.

1 What are the conceptual metaphors for India and nation at work?
2 What do these conceptual metaphors highlight and what do they conceal?
3 Find speeches by politicians from similar occasions in another country. It can be an English-speaking country but the comparison might be more interesting if speeches in other languages are chosen. Answer the first two questions and discuss similarities and differences between the countries.

The texts

The texts to analyze are excerpts from speeches by Indian President Pranab Mukherjee on his assumption of the office as president and on the occasions of India's Independence Day and Republic Day. The quote below is drawn from the speech held on the president's assumption of office:

> Speech by ShriPranab Mukherjee on his assumption of office as President of India, New Delhi, 25th of July, 2012
>
> I am deeply moved by the high honour you have accorded to me. Such honour exalts the occupant of this office, even as it demands that he rises above personal or partisan interests in the service of the national good.
>
> The principal responsibility of this office is to function as the guardian of our Constitution. I will strive, as I said on oath, to preserve, protect and defend our Constitution not just in word but also in spirit. We are all, across the divide of party and region, partners at the altar of our motherland. Our federal Constitution embodies the idea of modern India: it defines not only India but also modernity. A modern nation is built on some basic fundamentals: democracy, or equal rights for every citizen; secularism, or equal freedom to every faith; equality of every region and language; gender equality and, perhaps most important of all, economic equity.

(Source: http://presidentofindia.nic.in/speeches-detail.htm?254, accessed 20 July 2016. For the full texts to analyse, please visit the companion website at **https://study.sagepub. com/boreusandbergstrom**.)

Indian political rhetoric on gender equality

A brutal rape - mentioned in one of the excerpts to be analyzed for the metaphor exercise above - that caused the death of a student in 2012 had made international news and led to nationwide protests and a debate on women's freedom and rights.

The task

Think of the exercise as a pilot study for research on Indian gender politics after these events (proper research questions would have to be formulated for such a study). Answer the following questions:

1 What problems does the president address in his speech?
2 What are the causes of the problems, according to him?
3 What are the proposed solutions?
4 What do the answers to the above questions reveal about Indian gender equality at the time?

Use both a simple content analysis (see Chapter 2) to answer the questions and a grammatical analysis where you use some of the analytical tools presented in this chapter. Use Tables 6.1 and 6.2 for ideas.

The text

The text to analyze is another address by the president of India, held on International Women's Day 2016 at the occasion of the presentation of the Nari Shakti Puruskar award, to "institutions and individuals who have rendered distinguished services for the cause of women", awarded by the Ministry of Women and Child Development. Here is part of that speech:

> The Nari Shakti Puraskar is, therefore, a token of the nation's appreciation of these women and institutions for their effort to make a difference and improve the condition of lives of women in our country.
>
> The awards are intended to also inspire others to contribute and give hope and succor to women - particularly the vulnerable or marginalized. To my mind, any effort, big or small, is equally valuable - it is the spirit and attitude that these initiatives inculcate within us - which I consider most important.
>
> I congratulate the proud recipients of this national honour and thank them for their contribution.
>
> I am filled with pride and happiness at seeing how the women of India are taking great strides forward, assuming leadership roles and challenging responsibilities in all spheres of life. But I am equally distressed and concerned that a converse dimension of our society has, of late, been revealing its grotesque nature - every now and then.

(Source: http://presidentofindia.nic.in/speeches-detail.htm?498 (accessed 20 July 2016.) For the full text to analyze, please visit the companion website at **https://study.sagepub.com/boreusandbergstrom.**)

7

Multimodal Discourse Analysis

Anders Björkvall

7.1 Background

The rationale for this book is that the analysis of texts is of key importance for our understanding of a number of issues in society at large. However, in many texts language alone does not create meaning. Instead images, illustrations and information graphics play key roles for the production and interpretation of meaning. This is obviously the case in contemporary mass media texts, on many websites and in advertisements, but also, for instance, in pamphlets and leaflets from political parties, governments and organizations as well as in textbooks and reports in various formats. Such texts are often referred to as *multimodal* texts. The concept of text is extended to include *modes of communication* other than just writing or speaking. Too strict a focus on the linguistic parts of these texts comes with the risk of missing out on other relevant meanings conveyed by other modes, such as images.

Figure 7.1 shows the cover of a report (Wallace, 2010) that the public interest group GeneWatch UK has produced for Greenpeace International. Figure 7.2 presents a page from a brochure produced by the Swedish Nuclear Fuel and Waste Management Company. Both texts deal with the same topic: the handling and disposal of nuclear waste and its consequences. In addition, images are of key importance for the communicative functions of both texts. But from the perspective of this chapter the differences between the two texts are more interesting. The texts present two totally different perspectives on the handling of nuclear waste, an increasingly present environmental, economical and societal challenge in many parts of the world. And it is through the combination of images, illustrations and language that these differences become most obvious.

Rock Solid?

A GeneWatch UK consultancy report

Figure 7.1   Cover of a GeneWatch UK report for Greenpeace

The Swedish Nuclear Fuel and Waste Management Company is responsible for the 'safe' disposal of spent nuclear fuel in Sweden, a country that has had nuclear power plants since the 1960s. The text in Figure 7.2 (Swedish Nuclear Fuel and Waste Management Company, undated) contains a schematic illustration of how different types of spent fuel are transported between power plants and their final disposal. Arrows in different colours systematically connect the different units. Such illustrations can give the impression of scientific precision and accuracy. In addition, this illustration is placed at the top of the page, thus setting a tone of 'technical reliability' for the rest of the page. Just below the illustration there is a caption which reads "Sweden has a well-functioning system for managing and disposing of various types of radioactive waste". The illustration of the nuclear waste management system and the verbal confirmation that the system is "well-functioning" complement each other: the illustration shows how the different units of the system are dynamically connected and writing is used to evaluate the functionality of the system. This relation between the illustration and the linguistic statement is what Roland Barthes called **relay** in one of the most influential papers ever written on image–language relations: 'Rhetoric of

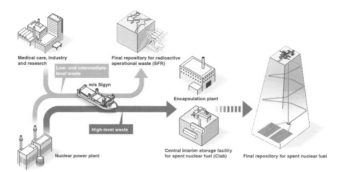

Sweden has a well-functioning system for managing and disposing of various types of radioactive waste.

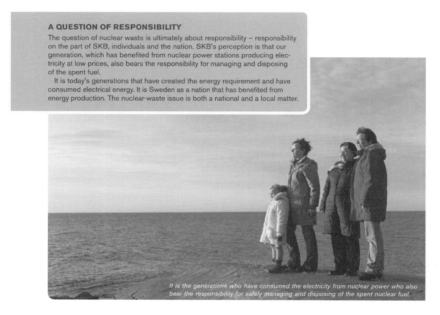

A QUESTION OF RESPONSIBILITY

The question of nuclear waste is ultimately about responsibility – responsibility on the part of SKB, individuals and the nation. SKB's perception is that our generation, which has benefited from nuclear power stations producing electricity at low prices, also bears the responsibility for managing and disposing of the spent fuel.

It is today's generations that have created the energy requirement and have consumed electrical energy. It is Sweden as a nation that has benefited from energy production. The nuclear-waste issue is both a national and a local matter.

It is the generations who have consumed the electricity from nuclear power who also bear the responsibility for safely managing and disposing of the spent nuclear fuel.

Figure 7.2   Page from a brochure by the Swedish Nuclear Fuel and Waste Management Company

the image' (1977 [1966]b). In other words, the illustration of the nuclear waste management system and the sentence that evaluates the system create a combined meaning at a higher level than if they were to be interpreted separately. This complimentary view of image–language relations is one of the cornerstones of the model for multimodal discourse analysis presented in this chapter.

The cover of the GeneWatch UK report for Greenpeace in Figure 7.1 presents a different view of the disposal of spent fuel. Despite the fact that this is a report presenting research findings – the subtitle of the report is "A scientific review of geological disposal of high-level radioactive waste" – there are no information graphics in the text. Instead, there is a sepia-coloured photograph of a stone with an inscription. There is also a question at the top of the page, "Rock Solid?", which is also the main title of the report, and the question is set in a colour that matches the sepia tone of the photograph. Colour is thus used as a means for emphasizing the connection between the critical question and the stone with the inscription. This top-placed question frames the rest of the messages found in Figure 7.1: can we really trust rock as a final repository for spent nuclear fuel? The inscription on the stone has a salient warning, "CAUTION–DO NOT DIG", followed by information saying that "radioactive material from nuclear research" is "buried" in the area. This danger of "buried" nuclear waste is further emphasized by the stone's visual resemblance to a tombstone. Is the human race digging its own grave when burying nuclear waste underground? This type of *semiotic sign* (see Chapter 1), based on resemblance, is what the founding father of semiotics, Charles Sanders Peirce, called an **iconic sign**.

Even though both Peirce and Barthes, who along with Ferdinand de Saussure and Umberto Eco are two of the most influential names in general semiotics, have been mentioned in the introduction to this chapter, the aim is not to present a classic semiotic account of the analysis of images. The chapter introduces **multimodal discourse analysis** as a means for text analysis in the social sciences, thus relating to the chapters on critical linguistics (Chapter 6) and discourse analysis (Chapter 8) in this book.

In everyday language 'text' usually refers to coherent chunks of written language, but in contemporary society many modes of communication, such as writing, images and colours, are combined into meaningful messages. As mentioned, this has been the case for many years in advertising, on election posters, and in many other media texts, but it is increasingly also the case in information from, for example, public authorities or in educational texts. Any student or researcher in the social sciences who is interested in conducting a more detailed analysis of texts may thus have use for analytical tools that connect to linguistic text analysis but at the same time go beyond the written parts of the text. Multimodal discourse analysis offers such tools.

The theoretical and methodological framework comes from the work by Gunther Kress and Theo van Leeuwen, mainly from their book *Reading Images: The Grammar of Visual Design* (2006). The basic assumption is that *discourses*, defined as "socially constructed knowledges of (some aspect of) reality" (Kress and van Leeuwen, 2001: 4), can be expressed in many shapes and forms – in many communicative modes – which calls for analytical frameworks that can handle multimodal texts. The major part of the concepts introduced in the chapter comes from Kress and van Leeuwen (2006). Not all of the concepts can of course be included in this chapter, and some analytical concepts have been merged, all in order to make the chapter accessible to readers that have little or no previous knowledge of discourse analysis and linguistics.

This chapter begins with an introduction to how symbolic *interaction* can be analyzed. This part focuses on the interactive potential set up between a sender of a text, or a depicted person, and the reader or viewer. The analysis relates to issues of power as well as exclusion and inclusion from social interaction. For instance, depicted persons can be presented as if they are inferior, superior or equals to the person looking at an image. They can also be depicted in a way that symbolically includes or excludes them from the social world or social group of the viewer. The analysis of such symbolic interactions can be performed in relatively close connection to what is described as the *interpersonal* function of texts in Chapter 1 of this book.

Then follows a description of how *representations* of on-goings in the world can be analyzed from a multimodal perspective. This analysis relates to what is called the *ideational* function of texts in Chapter 1 (Halliday and Matthiessen, 2014: 30), what is sometimes also referred to as the *content* function. Depicted persons, and sometimes objects, will be called *participants* in this analysis, and the participants can be represented as active or passive in texts. This dynamic, or the lack thereof, is expressed as *processes*: who does what to whom or what other type of relation is set up between participants represented in a multimodal text? The analysis of processes and participants can give insights on how different versions of goings-on can be construed in multimodal texts depending on, for example, the interests of the producers of texts and the dominating ideologies and discourses in various realms of society.

The last part of the analysis presented in the chapter deals with *composition*. One difference between verbal language and images is that images are *spatially* organized whereas language is primarily organized according to a *temporal* and *linear* logic. In other words, a linguistically oriented text analysis will often include answering the question of "in what order" since the linear order of words is highly meaningful. "Will I see you tomorrow?" has a different meaning from "I will see you tomorrow" just as "the protesters were threatening the police" is fundamentally different from "the police were threatening the protesters". In the analysis of the composition of images, the guiding question is "where". In other words, the placement of an element in an image, but also of elements on a larger page such as those in Figure 7.1 and Figure 7.2, carries meaning. It matters whether an element in a visual composition is placed high or low, to the left, to the right or in the centre. It also matters whether it is larger or smaller in relation to other elements in the composition.

The analysis of symbolic interaction, representations of goings-on in the world and composition all aim at identifying different types of meaning in multimodal texts. Such an analysis can form the foundation for further investigations into issues of gender, power or ethnicity: "How are masculinities, femininities and ethnicities construed in election pamphlets in India and Canada?", "Why are women construed as less active than men in advertising?", "Why are citizens positioned as powerless in texts from public authorities when they are supposed to be empowered?", or "Why are persons with certain ethnic backgrounds systematically idealised in the composition of certain multimodal texts and others left out?"

Even though the focus on meanings of multimodal texts can be rewarding when investigating issues in the social sciences, it requires careful epistemological and methodological considerations right from the start of the analysis. Meanings in and of texts are by no means static or given since they are intrinsically connected to the social, cultural and historical contexts of the texts and to the interests and interpretative strategies of the producers of texts and their readers. In multimodal discourse analysis, just as in critical discourse analysis and critical linguistics, **meaning potential** (or **semiotic potential**; see van Leeuwen, 2005: 4) is the preferred term when talking about texts. The assumption is that texts contain a number of potential meanings that the reader recognizes, does not recognize or, perhaps, chooses to ignore when interpreting the text. In order to know which of these meaning potentials are actualized when a reader meets a certain text, the processes of actual reading and interpretation have to be studied. That type of analysis requires different methodological tools from the text analytical tools presented in this chapter, such as interviews, questionnaires and ethnographic studies of how texts are brought into social practices. The point is that anyone who analyzes multimodal texts – or any text – based on the terminology introduced in this chapter must recognize that they can only identify potential meanings, rather than fixed meanings of texts that are relevant for anyone, anywhere, at any given point in time. For the sake of simplicity, the term *meaning* will still be used in this chapter, keeping in mind that the explanatory value of the analysis cannot go beyond potential meanings.

A short analysis of one of the features of the text from GeneWatch UK for Greenpeace in Figure 7.1 may illustrate the difference between meaning potentials and meanings that are actualized by readers of the text. The multimodal text has the headline 'Rock Solid?' and both the headline and the photo of the stone are sepia toned. The use of the same colour for many elements in a multimodal text can create *cohesion*, connecting the elements. More specifically, images and written elements that have the same colour have the meaning potential of "we belong together" or "we are connected"; this is referred to as **visual rhymes** in multimodal discourse analysis. In that way the critical question in the headline, "Rock Solid?", is connected to the image and its content. The critical question is explicitly supported by the image: radioactive material is detrimental to the environment and dangerous, or even lethal, to humans. At the same time it is by no means certain that all readers will acknowledge or notice this visual, colour-based connection between the headline and the image. For instance, to some readers the difference between the mode of writing and image will overshadow the meaning potential of colour as a cohesive resource. The fact that the solidity of the rock can actually be questioned just by looking back at historical nuclear experiments, in this case in the USA, is then a meaning potential of the multimodal text that may not be recognized or actualized by the reader.

Accordingly, the method for analysis presented in this chapter can result in reasonable interpretations of texts based on what we know from text and discourse analytical research regarding how texts are constructed, but also how they tend to be interpreted. Thus, the method can offer descriptions of preferred readings and interpretations, which do not in any way exclude other readings.

7.2 Analysis

Qualitative methods for analysis usually require a toolbox with many analytical concepts and terms, even though not all of them will become relevant for every single study. The sample analyses below contain a number of multimodal texts from different parts of the world, but only certain aspects of these will be analyzed, always with the aim of showing how the basic analytical concepts can be employed in order to answer questions that can be relevant to the social sciences.

7.2.1 Interaction

Many multimodal texts contain images of persons, and there is a potential for symbolic interaction between the depicted persons in an image and the person that actually looks at the image, located outside the image; this person will be referred to as the reader of a multimodal text.

The majority of relations between human beings involve power; this is also the case in the type of symbolic interaction discussed here. Power relations between depicted persons and a reader can be of three main types. First, the relation can be set up as if power is attributed to the reader. Second, power can be given to depicted persons, and, third, an equal power relation can be set up. *As if* is a key expression here, since the analytical interest is directed toward symbolic relations of power. We usually know very little about the actual power relations between the reader of a multimodal text (or of any text for that matter) and the people depicted in it.

The most important resource for expressions of *symbolic power relations* is the camera angle, what is sometimes referred to as the *perspective* of an image or another visual representation. There are three main vertical perspectives in images (Kress and van Leeuwen, 2006: 140–3):

- from above
- from below
- eye-to-eye

In the **from above perspective** the reader is symbolically placed in a position that looks down on the depicted person. This gives symbolic power to the reader. In the **from below perspective** power is attributed to the persons in the image. Finally, the **eye-to-eye perspective** is the perspective of 'equality'.

Figure 7.3 shows a multimodal text posted on a wall in central Cape Town, South Africa. Someone has glued a paper advertisement from the City of Cape Town, featuring the mayor Patricia De Lille, to the wall. De Lille is depicted slightly from below, thus attributing power to the mayor, but not too obviously. She is a democratically elected mayor, and it would possibly be too challenging to further increase the from below perspective in which the reader is positioned.

Figure 7.3 Patricia De Lille in a Cape Town street

In the case of the De Lille text, the vertical camera angle is used to underline the authority of the mayor in office, but at the same time she is addressing the citizens of Cape Town as part of a social group that she herself is or wants to be part of. If we for a minute disregard the adjustments (the speech bubble and the red marker blurring) that someone has made to the text in Figure 7.3, De Lille states that "I have a drug problem, and so do you" and that "we may not use them, but they still affect us". In the first statement the personal pronoun 'I' is matched with 'you' – the reader. In the second sentence De Lille and readers of the poster are grouped together as 'we' and 'us'.

The linguistically expressed meanings are matched with interactional meanings expressed in the image in Figure 7.3. These meanings have to do with symbolic *inclusion* and *exclusion* in a social group, and with symbolic *distance*. Whereas the vertical perspective in an image was described as the perspective of symbolic power, the horizontal perspective is that of inclusion or exclusion. Three main options are available (see 'involvement', Kress and van Leeuwen, 2006: 133–40):

- full frontal
- rear view
- side view

In the **full frontal perspective** the reader is placed in a horizontal position right in front of the depicted person. This is the perspective of 'social involvement' and it is illustrated by the full frontal image of mayor De Lille in Figure 7.3. The horizontal perspective of this image makes the reader look straight at the mayor, symbolically including her in their social group. This is in line with the visually most salient sentences in the text where the drug problem is described as something that affects all in the community, even the mayor. In this way, the interactive meanings expressed by the horizontal perspective in the image support the written statements.

The perspective of social involvement becomes clearer if compared with the two other perspectives that to various degrees exclude the depicted person from the reader's social world or group. The first example is the rear view perspective, the perspective of 'full detachment', in which the depicted persons are excluded from the reader's social group. It would of course be absurd to make the reader of the text in Figure 7.3 face De Lille's back, but it is not an uncommon perspective in media images. This perspective assigns full anonymity to the depicted persons, thus symbolically excluding them from the social world of the reader.

The side view perspective is also a perspective of exclusion, but of 'partial' rather than 'full' detachment. In this perspective the reader is placed in an oblique angle facing the depicted persons. This camera angle shows a certain interest in the depicted, but still partially excludes them from the social group of the reader. For instance, this perspective can be recognized from early anthropological photography where indigenous people where often depicted from the side view perspective, symbolically excluding them from the social world of the photographer and, accordingly, from that of the viewer of such images (see Kress and van Leeuwen, 2006: 133–5).

The lower image in Figure 7.2 from the Swedish Nuclear Fuel and Waste Management Company also positions the reader in the side view perspective. This may seem a little strange: why are the people in the image not fully included in the social group of the reader? When read together with the caption the reason becomes clearer: "It is the generations who have consumed the electricity from nuclear power who also bear the responsibility for safely managing and disposing of the spent nuclear fuel." In other words, the people in the image are part of the group that are responsible for the management and disposal of spent nuclear fuel. It is not assumed that the reader of the texts is or wants to be part of that social group. Another aspect of the image is that the depicted persons seem to look at something far away; perhaps they look toward the future. This, however, is a representation of a going-on in the world that will be discussed in the next section of this chapter.

There is another noticeable difference between the image of De Lille in Figure 7.3 and the group of people in Figure 7.2. The reader encounters the depicted persons at different distances with De Lille at a personal distance and the group of people at a longer distance. The category of **symbolic distance** in images (see 'Social distance', Kress and van Leeuwen, 2006: 124) is inspired by the theories of the anthropologist Edward T. Hall (1966). Put briefly, Hall suggested that the physical distances that human beings keep between each other in social life are directly related to the social relation between the persons involved in interaction. For instance, one can usually keep a closer physical distance to one's father than to one's superior at work. These physical distances vary between cultures and sub-cultures, and so does the enactment of social roles, but the point here is that Hall's way of thinking can be helpful when analyzing symbolic distances in multimodal texts.

Kress and van Leeuwen (2006: 124) suggest that *size of frame* is the main resource for expressing symbolic distance in images. Depending on how the image is cropped, the depicted persons stand out as more or less distanced from the reader. Figure 7.4 presents a number of different symbolic distances that can be expressed through size of frame. The figure is a simplification of the different distances presented by Kress and van Leeuwen (2006: 124–7).

The depicted persons are found at the centre of Figure 7.4. When a **personal distance** is expressed, the image of a person is cropped in a way that no more than the head and shoulders are visible, or sometimes even less such as the face or

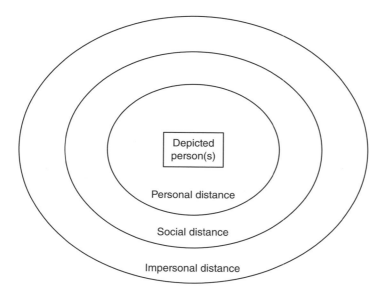

Figure 7.4 Symbolic distance in images

parts of the face only. In relation to Hall's description of enacted social distances this framing of an image would symbolically place the reader at a distance that we can keep only to persons that we know well, such as close friends or family.

At a **social distance** the depicted persons would be cropped at the waist or at the knees; the image can also be cropped in such a way that a person's entire body but not much more is shown within the frame of the image. Here, the reader is symbolically positioned as if they are at a farther distance from the persons in the image than in the case of personal distance. Social distance is the distance which in Western culture is usually upheld between, for instance, colleagues at a workplace. Finally, at an **impersonal distance** persons can also be depicted in full figure, but they will only occupy less than half of the total image space, and be presented as if they were strangers or more distant acquaintances.

The use of size of frame for expressing symbolic distance is illustrated in both Figure 7.2 and Figure 7.3. The lower image of a group of people in Figure 7.2 expresses impersonal distance between the reader and the depicted persons. They are all shown in full figure, but the persons occupy less than half of the space of the full image. This is actually in line with the interactional meanings expressed in the rest of this multimodal text. The text is dominated by rather formal statements that, for instance, lack personal pronouns that can sometimes give a text more of a dialogic, or interactive, character:

> It is today's generations that have created the energy requirement and have con-sumed electrical energy. It is Sweden as a nation that has benefited from energy production. The nuclear-waste issue is both a national and a local matter.

The persons in the photograph are not presented as friends of the reader or as someone who wants to be close to the reader; they are distant representatives of a generation that "have consumed electrical energy" and of "Sweden as a nation". It is probably also the case that the topic of the multimodal text – "the nucle-ar-waste issue" – is not a personal issue. At least it is not presented as such in the text. Rather, it is a present, but also future, responsibility for an entire generation of which the distant persons in the image are representatives.

In Figure 7.3, Mayor De Lille is depicted as if she were at a social, almost personal, distance in relation to the reader. As mentioned, the writing in this mul-timodal text directly addresses the reader through the use of personal pronouns and includes the reader in the social group of 'we' and 'us'. Thus, the less distanced interaction set up by the image is in line with the other choices made in the text, including the full frontal perspective. The topic, drug use, may also play a role here as something more personal and close, affecting members of the community in a more direct way than nuclear waste disposal.

The text in Figure 7.3 also illustrates the last feature of the analysis of symbolic interaction: *speech* and *image acts*. In **systemic functional linguistics**, the theory of language that underpins many of the analytical tools in, for instance, *critical linguistics* (see Chapter 6), a distinction between four basic speech acts is made (Halliday and Matthiessen, 2014: 135–8).

- statements
- questions
- offers
- commands

A *statement*, "Barack Obama won the election", implies that the speaker or writer *offers information* to the listener or reader. Information can also be *demanded*, "Did Barack Obama win the election?", which is a *question*. Not only information can be offered or demanded through the use of language, but also *goods* and *services*. To offer goods and services, "Please, have a look at the constitution of our party" is, not surprisingly, called an *offer*, whereas demanding goods and services is described as a *command*, "Give me a copy of the constitution".

There are a number of other, more specific, speech acts as well, for instance *warnings* or perhaps *insinuations*, but in principle these can all be sorted under one of the basic speech acts: the warning is a type of command, "watch out", and the insinuation is a type of statement, "I saw you with your ex-husband yesterday". However, from the perspective of the analysis of texts in the social sciences such semantic and to some extent grammatical categorizations are usually of lesser importance. More interesting is the fact that the basic speech acts presuppose a specific *response*, which is relevant for the type of interaction that a reader of a text is invited to. Statements presuppose some kind of *consideration* as a response, or at least an *acknowledgement* on the behalf of the listener or the reader, even if such an acknowledgement can be almost unnoticeable: "Barack Obama won the election" – "Oh, really". Questions presuppose *answers* whereas the preferred response to an offer would be an *acceptance*: "Please, have a look at the constitution of our party" – "Yes, I will". Commands require some kind of *action* that does not need to be verbally expressed, even though it can be accompanied by language or gesture: "Give me a copy of the constitution" – "Here you are".

These are all examples of preferred responses to the various speech acts, but again, it is difficult to know how an actual reader will react to a text that is dominated by, for example, questions or commands. It is any reader's privilege to 'read against' a text. What an analysis of speech acts in a text can provide is a description of its preferred response structure. Such a response structure can offer an indication of whether a text tends to be open for interaction – if it invites the reader through its response structure – or if it is more closed to interaction. A text dominated by statements has the lowest interactive potential in terms of response structure; it only presupposes that the reader acknowledges its offer of information. Offers (of goods and services) are slightly more interactive; the reader has to at least accept or reject these. Commands and questions are the most interactive speech acts since they presuppose actions and answers from the listener or reader.

Kress and van Leeuwen (2006: 116–24) argue that just as there are speech acts that can be expressed in speech and writing there are **image acts** that can be expressed in the visual mode. However, they also argue that the resources for expressing image acts are not as specified as those used for speech acts. The analysis of image acts is therefore less complex and only includes *offers* and *demands*. Offers are expressed in the visual mode when the gazes of depicted persons are not directed toward the reader, as in the lower image in Figure 7.2. In that image the reader is just offered to watch the persons; the interactive potential of the image is low.

In Figure 7.3 Patricia De Lille is looking straight at the reader and the image act of demand is expressed. Exactly what De Lille is demanding is hard to say, but perhaps she is demanding attention, or social interaction of some kind. The human gaze is a powerful interactional resource, and it would be difficult for any reader to totally avoid the demand character of this and similar images.

A brief analysis of the image act in Figure 7.3 together with the most salient speech acts in the text can show how image acts and speech acts combine in multimodal texts, but also how changing one single speech act may completely change the interactive meanings into an humoristic critical commentary. As mentioned, the text was posted on a wall in Cape Town and it is unclear whether the person posting the text actually made the changes to it or not. It could also have been a process of different people adding elements to the text once it was posted. Originally, the larger, top positioned and framed part of the text consisted of the demand image in which De Lille demands something from the reader along with the sentence "I have a drug problem, and so do you". The sentence is a type of statement that could be interpreted more specifically as a *confession*. The original preferred response structure thus implies that the mayor seeks attention visually and then verbally states facts that the reader is expected to acknowledge.

Three noticeable changes have then been made to the multimodal text: the 'do you' including the full stop has been blurred by a red marker pen; the 'd' in 'end' has been blurred in the same way; and a speech bubble has been added encircling the statement "I have a drug problem". The speech bubble further connects the statement to the mayor – there is no doubt that she is the speaker. From the perspective of speech acts and image acts the second part of the sentence is turned into a question: 'an so' (the reason for blurring the 'd' in 'and' is probably to turn the mayor's language into a slightly more vernacular version of English). This adjustment to the print also strikes out the 'you', the reader in this section of the text, and all the focus is directed toward the problems of the mayor. In the new multimodal ensemble of image and writing, the mayor still seeks attention through a visual demand, but then she produces the confession that she is a drug addict, which is completed with the 'an so' question, asking the reader what the problem is with that.

Thus, the text in Figure 7.3 is an example of how different visual and verbal resources can be combined in order to invite a reader to a specific kind of interaction. It also illustrates what can happen with the meanings of a text when other resources – in this case mostly visual resources – are added: information from a public institution such as the City of Cape Town can be turned into a critical commentary regarding the mayor's drug policy or into political caricature, making fun of a politician with power.

7.2.2 Representations of on-goings in the world

The second, broader type of meaning-making through multimodal texts has to with representations of goings-on in the world; of the dynamic actions or non-dynamic states that participants represented in a text are engaged in. It is important to stress the term *representation*. Multimodal discourse analysis is a *constructivist* approach to communication (see Chapter 1 of this book): in texts, versions of reality are created, and these versions depend on, among other things, the interests of the persons behind the text or normative discourses. In other words, a going-on in the world – for example an action by someone toward someone else – can be represented in many, sometimes contradictory, ways. The tools for analysis of representations presented below can be employed in order to say something about various representations rather than making statements about a 'reality' outside the texts.

The relation between *participants* in an image, for instance depicting US soldiers or Taliban fighters, can be represented in relation to *processes* of different types. A participant can be represented as an **actor** (called an 'agent' in Chapter 6) in an **action process**. An actor is a participant that initiates and is active in a dynamic going-on; a soldier can 'threaten' another soldier with a gun, and the threatened soldier is represented as the *goal* in the action process. An analysis of such and related representations can point to ideological choices in a text, for example, when people of a specific ethnicity or gender are always represented as actors and people of another ethnicity or gender are always represented as goals. This type of analysis of agency in texts was one of the more powerful tools in the field of critical linguistics in the 1970s and 1980s (see Chapter 6 in this book).

Even though they are not identical, the analytical tools presented here connect to the analysis of *transitivity* presented in Chapter 6 of this book (see Tables 6.1 and 6.2). Kress and van Leeuwen (2006: 45–113) have developed a detailed account of participants and processes that can be visually represented. A selection has been made for this chapter, based on the relevance for students in the social sciences when analyzing multimodal texts.

Although there can be no exact mapping between transitivity in language and in image, action processes are the visually expressed processes that are most similar to the *material actions* described in Chapter 6. These are processes that take place in the outer, material world and not, for instance, in the human mind. In language, the processes are expressed by verbs, most commonly a finite verb, in a clause: 'the solder *shoots* at the enemy'. In that clause 'the soldier' is the actor, 'shoots' expresses the process (a material action in the terminology of

Figure 7.5   Vectors in an action process

Chapter 6), and 'the enemy' is the goal. If a similar process were to be expressed in an image, this could be done as in the example in Figure 7.5, a screenshot from the popular computer game 'Call of Duty'.

The function of the finite verb in language, 'shoots', is carried by the rifle in Figure 7.5. The rifle functions as a **vector** (Kress and van Leeuwen, 2006: 46) and connects the actor – the soldier who 'shoots' – with the goal, the enemy in the building. A vector is formed by an arrow or a line in an image that creates dynamic meanings revolving around 'movement' and 'action'. Usually, but not always, vectors emanate in one participant, the actor, and point to another participant, the goal. An example would be when participants in a public rally or demonstration are represented as either actors, for example, raising their arms with the function of vectors in the direction of a goal, such as the police, or when the police (actors) are represented as pointing their weapons (vectors) at a protesting crowd of people (goals). There are less dramatic examples of action processes, of course, and also those that do not explicitly involve human participants. 'MS Sigyn', the ship at the top of the illustration in Figure 7.2 where it is explained how radioactive waste is transported, is dynamically connected to, for example, the "final repository for radioactive operational waste" and the "encapsulation plant" through the use of arrows. In other words, 'MS Sigyn' is represented as the actor that 'transports' the waste to the other, non-human, goals in this action process.

From the perspective of broader issues addressed in the social sciences it is relevant that the participant roles in action processes in images are the results of choices made by someone with a specific interest at a specific point in time. A public rally for whatever purpose can be represented as including active protesters or active law enforcement representatives. An analysis of such representations can say something interesting not only about power relations in a society, but also about access to the public sphere for different groups of people. Further, the action process of handling nuclear waste could be visually represented as a process involving human participants in the roles of actors or goals, but in Figure 7.2 it is not. Instead, all the participants are non-human, from the actor, the ship 'MS Sigyn', to the goals: "encapsulation plant", "final repository for radioactive operational waste" and ultimately "the final repository for spent nuclear fuel" (see Table 6.2). This may make the process seem safer and more controlled than what would have been the case if human actors had been explicitly represented in the illustration. Again, such an analysis can be broadened to ask questions of how 'risks' are handled and dealt with in different areas of society.

A few other types of participants in action processes need to be mentioned. If a vector does not point in a specific direction, or if it has the shape of a double-edged arrow, both emanating in and pointing to participants, it is hard to say if the participants are actors or goals. In such cases, and they are quite common, both the participants are called **interactors**. A typical example would be two heads of state photographed when shaking hands at the final press conference of a state visit. Again, from the perspective of representation of power, it matters whether a head of state is repeatedly represented as only a goal at the state visit, or as an interactor or actor.

In other cases a vector points at a goal but the participant in which it emanates is not in the image, or the origin of a vector in an image lies in an empty space. In other words, there is no actor that initiates the process. The vector still represents a dynamic process, but it represents an **event** rather than an action (see Table 6.1). Objects that 'fall' may for example leave speed lines; 'to fall' is not an action, but rather a dynamic process without an explicitly represented initiator.

Events, just like action processes, take place in an outer reality whereas **reaction processes** and **mental processes** take place on the inside of human beings, in their minds. In reaction processes, the human gaze functions as a vector, connecting depicted persons in a multimodal text. The participant that 'looks' is analyzed as a **reacter**, and the participant toward which the gaze is directed is the **phenomenon**. The participant doing the looking *reacts* to something in the world – the phenomenon; the gaze connects the outer world phenomenon with the inner reality of the reacter. In some cases, as in the lower image in Figure 7.2, the phenomenon is not in the image. The gazes of the depicted persons are directed towards an invisible phenomenon. This opens up for slightly more abstract interpretations. Are the persons in the image envisaging the future of nuclear power; are they looking at future generations, reflecting on the responsibility of their own generation?

Another example of reaction processes are the cases when two participants are looking at each other; they become **interreacters** (similar to interactors in action processes). This is illustrated in the image in Figure 7.6 that is part of

Figure 7.6 Gaze as vector in an interreaction process

a multimodal text that includes print ("Sexuality, it's not just about sex" and "Gender") and handwriting, for instance: "What is the difference between sex and gender?" and "It's still love".

The two men are represented as interreacters in a reaction process; they are reacting to each other. The multimodal text in Figure 7.6 is part of a number of texts that were exposed on the University of Cape Town campus in order to raise awareness about disability, gender and relationships. The reaction process in the image is used as a resource for normalizing love and sexuality between persons of the same gender.

However, it is difficult just from looking at the image in Figure 7.6 to interpret the exact content of the reaction process; we have to go to the context of the image and its relation to the written parts of the text in order to come to the conclusion that the reaction is probably best described as 'love'. Similarly, in Figure 7.2, we had to make a well-informed and contextually motivated guess at the more exact nature of the phenomenon as well as the reacters' reflections on it.

In *mental* processes the content of goings-on in the minds of represented participants are made explicit, just as it is possible to do in language, for example in 'the representatives of the present generation think about the future of nuclear power'. The visual resource for expressing such mental processes is the thought bubble in which the content is placed, either as writing or as another visual representation. In mental processes, the human participant from which the vector emanates is called a **senser** and the content in the thought bubble is called the **phenomenon**.

The thought bubble as a resource for expressing mental processes was developed and is most commonly used in comics, and the same is true for the last type of dynamic process to be introduced in this chapter: the *verbal* process (see Table 6.2). What can be expressed in language as "the representatives of the present generation say that nuclear power has done its duty" could be expressed visually by, for example, adding a speech bubble with the content "nuclear power has done its duty" next to the depicted persons at the bottom of Figure 7.2. In verbal processes there is a **sayer**, with the **utterance** represented in the speech bubble.

What all the processes presented so far have in common is that they are expressed through the use of vectors of different kinds, and that these vectors add some kind of movement and dynamics to the visual representation. Kress and van Leeuwen (2006: 45–78) call these **narrative representations**. However, there are also other types of visual representations of on-goings in the world that present the world as less dynamic, and that do not make use of vectors. These can be viewed as visual versions of verbally expressed *states* of affairs like "she *is* the CEO of a multinational company" rather than the more active and dynamic "she *directs* a multinational company" (see 'states' in Table 6.1). These processes represent what somebody or something *is* or *has*, and Kress and van Leeuwen (2006: 79–113) refer to them as **conceptual representations**. Such processes of 'being' and 'having' can be of two basic types that relate participants to each other in terms of, on the one hand, part–whole structures, and on the other, super- and subordination. The first type is called **analytical processes** and the second **classificational processes**.

Analytical processes actualize two participants: the **carrier** and the **attributes**. Maps are examples of multimodal texts that usually express analytical processes. In a map of Europe, for instance, Europe as a continent would be the whole – the carrier – and the different national states would be the attributes – the parts that make up the whole. Of course, analytical processes of this kind are often challenged. How big is Europe, and what should its attributes be? And in times of political turmoil and conflicts: what are the relations between the attributes? What counts as a country rather than a region in maps of Europe as a whole?

Representations of identities are commonly expressed in analytical processes. Such representations are often the results of ideological choices that draw on different types of normative discourses. In Figure 7.5, not only is an action process

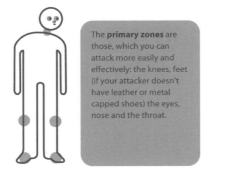
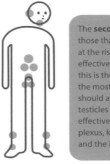

The **primary zones** are those, which you can attack more easily and effectively: the knees, feet (if your attacker doesn't have leather or metal capped shoes) the eyes, nose and the throat.

The **secondary zones** are those that you can attack but at the risk of not being so effective: testicles (because this is the area that is protected the most. In any case one should aim at the back of the testicles for the blow to be effective), ears, chin, solar plexus, kidneys, groin, shin and the instep.

Step 8: Learn how to react to any attack.

Figure 7.7   Analytical process: Self-Care and Self-Defence Manual for Feminist Activists

realized through the machine gun as a vector; the uniforms as well as the weapons are attributes that make up the carrier of 'soldier'. Another attribute is also visible in Figure 7.5. The head of the goal in the action process can be seen if one looks carefully. A head covered in a 'keffiyeh' – an Arab headscarf – is visible as a part of the analytical process that makes up the whole of the enemy's identity as 'Arab', or at least having a Middle Eastern identity. In this case the analytical processes are used as a means of assigning identities to participants in the multimodal texts, but probably also for promoting loyalty with one of the identities rather than another. How this is done, and above all why this is done in a particular way, could be questions for further research.

Analytical processes are sometimes connected to gendered discourses of the human body. For instance, the advertising business is often accused of representing women in analytical, static, processes as a set of bodily attributes to be evaluated by the male gaze. Men in advertising, on the other hand, tend to be represented as actors in action processes, with attributes that symbolize power (ties, suits) or activity such as sports equipment. A totally different analytical representation of men is shown in Figure 7.7.

The multimodal representation in Figure 7.7 comes from a publication on female self-defence from CREA (Creating Resources for Empowerment in Action). CREA is a feminist human rights organization that is based in India. In this illustration the body is represented as a carrier that is not made up of power attributes such as big muscles or expensive clothing; the attributes that make up the carrier – presumably a male aggressor – are the zones of the body that are most sensitive to physical attacks by a woman. In fact, it is interesting to see how the primary zones for a successful attack are so salient in the representation that they become the main attributes of the male body. Figure 7.7 shows how analytical processes in images can be used in order to empower a very large group of people – in this case women in the developing world – who face the risk of being attacked and sexually abused by men.

Another multimodal aspect of the representations in Figure 7.7 is that the illustrations and the written parts can complement each other because of their spatial and linear organization. If we look at the writing to the left in Figure 7.7, the linear organization of language allows for a definition of the body's '**primary zones**' (boldface in original), and these are the zones "which you can attack more easily and effectively: the knees, feet (if your attacker doesn't have leather or metal capped shoes) the eyes, nose and the throat." However, it is very difficult to use language in order to show *where* those body parts are located, so the visual representation that is spatially organized is used to do this 'showing', and it is done through an analytical process.

The final type of processes presented in this section is the classificational processes that represent super- and subordination rather than part–whole structures. Super- and subordination have to do with power and hierarchies, and these types of representations are often found when organizations, public authorities, corporations or businesses present their internal structure. The analysis of classificational processes can also be fruitful if one wants to, for example, compare how political systems are represented in different multimodal texts.

The tree structure is the typical shape of classificational processes. In Figure 7.8 the leadership structure of the Massachusetts Institute of Technology (MIT) is represented as an 'organization chart'.

The participants in classificational processes are *superordinate* and *subordinate*, concepts that capture the hierarchical and power infused nature of these types of representations. At the top of the tree structure in Figure 7.8 is the President of MIT, L. Rafael Reif, represented as a superordinate participant. His subordinates are the Chancellor, the Provost and the Executive Vice President and Treasurer. But these three are not only subordinates, they are also, in turn, represented as superordinate in relation to a number of other subordinates in the organization. The hierarchical nature of this multimodal text is also reflected in the writing at the lower right-hand corner in Figure 7.8, where additional information is given concerning who 'reports' to whom, with reference to other organizational charts of the MIT.

From the perspective of the social sciences it is important to remember that the classificational process in Figure 7.8 is a representation of a power structure. In other words, it is one of many possible ways to represent this power structure, but it is the one that MIT, for various reasons, wants to be the public one. However, it gives the impression that MIT is a hierarchical, top-bottom, organization. That may also be the case if one were to empirically study and analyze how power and control are employed at MIT, but such an analysis would most certainly also show that there are many hidden connections and structures that are not visible in the classificational process in Figure 7.8. For instance, some of the subordinates at the bottom of Figure 7.8 may have power over certain agendas that would, in practice, give them more power than is represented in the organizational chart. There would certainly be many informal decision paths going back and forth in ways that may be too complicated to be represented in a chart like the one in

Figure 7.8   Classificational process: MIT's organizational chart

Figure 7.8. However, comparing such actual decision paths and informal connections between employees in an organization with the classificational processes that often give only the official version of the power structures can give insights relevant to many different fields in the social sciences. And finally one may ask, why does MIT – a world-leading research and educational institution – want to present itself as a highly hierarchical organization?

7.2.3 Composition

Composition has to do with how parts of a multimodal text can communicate different meanings based on where they are placed on, for example, the cover of a magazine or a newspaper page. One implication is that when textual elements such as images, illustrations, headlines or written paragraphs are placed as part of a textual composition they are assigned other, complimentary, sometimes even contradictory meanings than the interactive and representational meanings that they communicate as separate elements. According to Kress and van Leeuwen (2006), elements placed toward the top of a page tend to be assigned meanings such as 'ideal' or 'general' whereas those placed toward the bottom can be assigned meanings like 'real' or 'specific'. There is also a left–right dimension that can be used to create meaning in multimodal texts, assigning meanings such as 'given' to elements placed to the left and 'new' to those to the right. The left–right dimension is related to the semiotic principle of reading and writing from left to right in Western cultures, and does not apply to cultures where this principle is not present. The analysis of the top–bottom and left–right dimension is called an analysis of **information value** (Kress and van Leeuwen, 2006: 194–201).

However, the composition of a multimodal text can be meaningful in other ways as well. **Framing** of elements in a text can create meanings of *connection* and *disconnection*. For example, in Figure 7.1 the sepia tone was used as a device that connected the heading and the image of the 'tombstone'. They were presented as if they belong together. A contrasting colour between the elements would have had the opposite effect, disconnecting the two elements semiotically.

The final analysis to be introduced here is that of **salience**. This aspect of composition relates to the extent to which different elements in a text are foregrounded in relation to other elements. This is related to meanings of 'importance': a more salient element in a multimodal text is presented as if it were more 'important' than other elements in the same text.

Returning to the analysis of information value, an understanding of the underlying assumptions behind that analysis is needed in order to strengthen its validity. Figure 7.9 presents a model for the information values of some multimodal texts.

The model in Figure 7.9 has an outer frame that should be read as the boundaries of a semiotic space: a newspaper page, an advertisement, or a cover of a brochure or a pamphlet. As shown, elements placed in the top space are assigned the information value of 'ideal', with related values of 'general' and 'abstract'. Elements

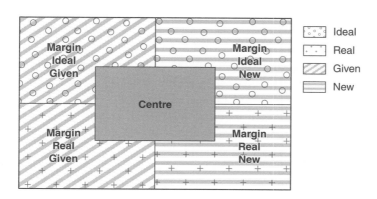

Figure 7.9　Information value (Adapted from Kress and van Leeuwen, 2006: 197)

placed toward the bottom are presented as if they are 'real', or 'specific' and 'down to earth'. Broadly speaking, the **ideal–real dimension** of multimodal texts has an *experiential* provenance in human environments. Whereas the sky is far away and difficult to touch, the earth is highly tangible and has a direct physical presence for human beings. These experiences of high and low are also used in texts, thus making possible a distinction between the information values of textual elements such as 'ideal', 'general' and 'abstract' vs. 'real' or 'specific'.

As mentioned, elements placed to the left in the semiotic space are assigned the information value of 'given' and those to the right 'new', following a linear principle of semiotic organization in language. Finally, there are the information values of 'centre' and 'margin'; elements that surround a centred element tend to represent aspects of the centred element – not necessarily subordinate in relation to the centred element – as when in an ice cream advertisement the centred image of the ice cream is surrounded by key words describing it as 'delicious', 'refreshing', 'produced locally in Vermont' or perhaps 'organically produced'.

In relation to the model in Figure 7.9, it should be pointed out that this is neither an absolute model of compositional meaning-making in multimodal texts nor a 'how to' guide to assigning specific meaning potentials to elements in a text. The model is an attempt to illustrate how elements are likely to be presented and interpreted in multimodal texts. There will be exceptions, and there are a number of text types for which the model is less relevant, such as, for instance, strictly linear texts and websites which show a different layout depending on how the reader scrolls them or the size of the device they are viewed on. In addition, it is important to remember that the dimensions of information value may or may not be realized through the composition of any given multimodal text. For the distinction between 'ideal' and 'real' and 'given and 'new' to be relevant there needs to be some kind of framing device, like a line or space, separating different elements in the semiotic composition. If there are no devices that distinguish, for example, left from right in a text, we would have to say that this potential of meaning-making was just not actualized.

In the text from the Swedish Nuclear Fuel and Waste Management Company in Figure 7.2 there are framing devices that separate top from bottom. It shows a text box with a darker background that emphasizes this distinction, and the white background of the illustration separates it from the photo at the bottom. In other words, there are framing devices that are put to use in order to realize the ideal–real dimension in this text. Thus, the top-placed elements – those that make up the illustration – and those placed at the bottom in the photo of persons from different generations are attributed with additional meanings other than their interactive and representational meanings. The technical process of handling spent nuclear fuel is presented as an 'ideal' whereas the depicted persons are presented as more 'real'.

Even if the text in Figure 7.2 may have the rhetorical aim of 'selling' the Nuclear Fuel and Waste Management Company as a competent actor to the public, it is above all an information brochure. In advertising, where selling products and services is

Figure 7.10 New Nordic advertisement, *Woman* magazine

always the final goal, persons and products in social environments of different types are usually idealized in the top position. Figure 7.10 shows an ad published in *Woman*, one of Britain's best selling magazines targeted at middle-aged women.

Just as in Figure 7.2, there is a framing device in Figure 7.10 that separates top from bottom, 'ideal' from 'real': the pink background at the top half of the ad creates a symbolic distinction in relation to the white background at the bottom. In other words, the personal, medical problem, "I felt my stomach was going to explode!", and the photo of a smiling woman at a symbolic distance between 'social' and 'personal' (see the section on interaction above) are presented as if they have the information value of 'ideal'. At the bottom of the page the 'real' information is presented: a written narrative about how 'Jane' developed stomach problems, the solution, a product called 'dida' (a food supplement), and a more technical description of the content and functions of 'dida'. There is specific information on where the 'dida tablets' can be purchased as well as telephone numbers and a website address. On the lower, 'real', space of the page there is also a photo of the package of the product.

The point with the two analyses of information value in Figure 7.2 and Figure 7.10 is to show that choices in terms of layout and composition are meaningful, sometimes ideological or at least argumentative or rhetorical. There is a difference between presenting technical solutions as an 'ideal', as in Figure 7.2, and presenting photos of persons and their personal problems as the 'ideal' as in Figure 7.10 and in many other advertisements.

Another example of how the ideal–real dimension can be used is found in Figure 7.7 where the two interreacters – the two men that look at each other – are presented as the 'ideal' through the layout of the multimodal text. The distinction is set up between the photo frame and the white background formed by the bed. The written parts, "Sexuality, it's not just about sex", "Gender" and other handwriting are presented as 'real', as a specification of the meanings in the photo of the two men. In addition, it may be relevant that the idealised relation in this South African text is that between a black and a white man.

To some extent the given–new (left–right) dimension is also actualized in the top section of the advertisement in Figure 7.10. There is no obvious framing device, but the mode of writing vs. the visual mode (the photo), creates a sort of distinction that is recognized from many other advertisements, not least from those that specifically target women. To the left a severe stomach problem is presented as a 'given' that many readers can identify with. In other words, it is assumed that at least some of the readers of *Woman* have experienced these problems. The 'new' in the ad is the image of a smiling, happy woman, presented as 'Jane' in the bottom part of the text. This is a 'new' woman that no longer has stomach problems. This type of use of the given–new dimension in multimodal texts is prototypically found in advertisements for weight loss products showing an overweight person to the left and a slimmer version to the right (which would be reversed in cultures where reading and writing is not done from left to right).

The pattern in Figure 7.10 relates to a more general compositional pattern of problem–solution that is to some extent related to issues of gender. In advertisements targeted at middle-aged women a physical 'problem' (often an aesthetic 'problem' or a medical one as in Figure 7.10) is often taken as a starting point, as a given for the entire ad that has to be worked on by women and solved with the help of the product advertised.

More generally, the given–new dimension relates to change, not only from 'medical problem' to 'solved problem' but, for example, from 'poor' to 'rich', from 'immigrant' to 'citizen', or from 'child' to 'adult'. This raises the critical question of what is presented as a desirable change in a text and what is not. Or, for example, whether the change is concerned with all members of a society, or only a selected few?

Returning to Figure 7.10, the 'given' stomach problem and the 'new' Jane are actually connected through an illustration of a female body that overlaps both the image of Jane and that of the 'dida' package. This is related to another aspect of composition that Kress and van Leeuwen (2006: 203–4) call **framing**. As mentioned, the top and bottom part of the ad in Figure 7.10 are disconnected through the use of **contrasting** backgrounds. Semiotically, they are presented as if they do not belong together – they have different information values. However, through the use of **overlapping**, this distinction is partially downplayed as the illustration of the female body connects the advertised product to the happy woman depicted in the top section. Through the layout of the advertisement the product is explicitly connected to the given–new dimension: the product is what made the transformation from problem to solution possible.

There are a number of devices that can be used to connect or disconnect elements in multimodal texts:

- overlapping
- framing
- visual rhyme
- contrast
- distance

All these devices can be used in order to present elements in a text as if they belong together or as if they do not. As mentioned, overlapping between elements was used to connect the photo of the smiling Jane to the product in Figure 7.10. In the same text there are also examples of framing devices used for disconnecting elements. For example, there is a framed rectangle with a pink background that separates the information under the headline "This is why dida™ is so good!" from the rest of the written elements at the bottom of the ad. This separation is probably motivated by the fact that the information in the rectangle is quite normative and gives a short version of the advantages explained more extensively elsewhere in the 'real' section of the ad.

At the same time the pink background sets up a *visual rhyme* with other pink elements in the advertisement. Visual rhymes are often used to symbolically connect elements in a multimodal text that are placed at some distance from each other. The use of the same type face, bold face, italics or other types of shapes also creates such cohesion between elements. In Figure 7.10, a pink colour is used to connect the lower rectangle with the short description of why 'dida' is so good, to the 'idealised' elements (the statement about the stomach problem and the happy Jane), and to the packaging of the product. Actually, it is possible to grasp the key points of the ad by just reading these rhyming elements. *Contrast* as a framing device has quite the opposite function as visual rhymes: elements in contrasting colours, typefaces or shapes are symbolically disconnected. Finally, a long *distance* between elements in a text can be used to disconnect these symbolically whereas short distances can connect elements.

The final aspect of the composition of multimodal texts is salience: is an element presented as if it is more or less important in relation to other elements in the same text? The main resources for creating relative salience are presented below (see Kress and van Leeuwen, 2006: 201–3):

- size
- colour
- overlapping
- contrasting typeface
- cultural symbols

Relative *size* is the most straightforward device for assigning salience to an element in a multimodal text: the larger the element, the more 'important' it is. In Figure 7.10 the largest elements are the top placed statement about the stomach problem and the image of the woman along with the photo of the product packaging. These elements are presented as the most 'important' ones. Other elements in the texts are smaller, and thus presented as 'less important', even though some of them are given salience through other layout choices. As mentioned, pink is used as a type of signal *colour* in the ad that gives salience to the rectangle explaining why 'dida' is so good, to other 'idealised' elements and to the package. In other words, these elements are not only framed as belonging together, they are also presented as quite 'important' in the advertisement.

Salience can also be given to an element by making it *overlap* other elements. For instance, the drawing of the female body in Figure 7.10 overlaps with both the photo of Jane and part of the packaging of the product, and it gains some salience through this. This is also the case for the golden rectangle in Figure 7.2 with the headline "a question of responsibility"; it overlaps the photo of the depicted persons at the bottom of the page. A *contrasting typeface* can also be used as a device to give salience to an element in a text. The use of bold face in headlines is perhaps the most obvious example. Finally, well-recognized cultural symbols tend to gain attention and thus become 'important' even if they are neither large, colourful nor overlapping. It is difficult to give examples of such symbols since they vary between cultures and sub-cultures, but religious symbols, flags or politically loaded symbols fall into this category.

7.3 Critical reflections

When the analytical tools presented in this chapter are combined they can be used to answer specific questions about multimodal texts, for example how ethnicity or gender is construed in advertising or social media. Perhaps more importantly, such an analysis can open up questions relevant for our understanding of, for example, power relations or other discursive formations at higher levels of abstraction. However, there are a number of aspects of the presented method that need to be critically attended to; a few of these are discussed below.

7.3.1 Language and image

This chapter has introduced an extended concept of text that includes, for example, writing, image, illustrations, information graphics, and colours. The discussion of the interactive as well as the representational function of images was related to how those functions can be expressed in language. This has at least one obvious methodological advantage: we can talk about meanings expressed in images in a similar way – with a similar terminology – as we can speak of meanings expressed in language. For example, we can talk about processes and participants in images as well as in linguistic clauses (see Chapter 6) and we can talk about combinations of image acts and speech acts when analyzing the interactive functions of multimodal texts.

But there are significant differences between how language and image can be used for meaning-making. One researcher who has pointed this out is David Machin (2007; 2014). Machin argues that images create meaning above all through their iconic resemblance to something else in the world as we know it. An image of a house means 'house' because we recognize the house from our experience of the world outside the image. Based on this assumption Machin argues that it can be problematic to deconstruct an image into components such as vectors, participants and compositional fields with various information values. When analyzing language, this type of deconstruction into components is motivated because language has a grammar that relies on, among other things, linear semiotic principles where one component follows after another. But if images are above all iconic representations that create all meaning at once, so to speak, can they really have a grammar similar to that of language?

This may seem like a semiotic discussion with less relevance to text-oriented researchers and students in broader fields of the social sciences, but it is important to consider the explanatory value of any method for analysis. The linguistically inspired and well-defined analytical categories may seem to give high reliability to the analysis of any multimodal text, but questions of validity must also be kept in mind. If one thinks that images, just like language, create meaning through combinations of different elements, an analysis of action processes in, for example, a history textbook, may provide high validity when examining how a certain type of participant is acting upon other participants. Vectors must be identified, and participants are then categorized as either actors or goals, and conclusions can be drawn.

On the other hand, if one believes that images create meaning above all through their direct resemblance to something in the world, and that they cannot be deconstructed into pre-defined, grammar-like categories, such an analysis would, of course, have a lower validity. It would then be better to base the analysis of the images on one's own experience of the world or to invite readers from a number of social groups in society into the interpretative process. For instance, based on one's knowledge of the world, an image of football hooligans could be interpreted as if they are actively 'threatening' other people even if they do not show any raised weapons or other vector-like objects.

Another point of critique is that the presented method does not offer concepts for the analysis of visual argumentation (see Chapter 6). Again, this is partially due to the different principles of semiotic organization of language and image. Argumentation, where a thesis is supported by a number of more or less connected arguments, is well-supported by the linear and temporal organization of language. Such argumentative flows are harder to achieve in image, if everything is shown at the same time (see Kress, 2010: 55–6). That being said, this method can be applied in combination with a more language-oriented analysis of argumentation, where some arguments are expressed through language and others visually (Kjeldsen, 2012). For instance, in the advertisement in Figure 7.10 the thesis (or issue expression) could be formulated as 'buy dida' and the image of the smiling woman along with a number of written elements function as arguments that together support the thesis.

7.3.2 Different types of multimodal texts

All the texts that have been presented in this chapter have in common that their semiotic space is limited by a rather predictable and stable format, for instance the front of the GeneWatch UK report for Greenpeace, the torn-out text from the City of Cape Town, the photo of the two men attached to a bed with writing on it, or the ad for stomach medicine. However, many texts do not have such stable boundaries. The format of a webpage displayed on a computer screen, for instance, depends on the size and settings of the web browser window. In relation to the analytical concepts presented in the chapter, this mainly becomes problematic when analyzing composition. Dimensions of high–low and centre–margin become relative to the size of the browser window – how it crops the displayed multimodal text or image – and how the reader scrolls it. Items placed at the bottom of the page may then not be visible at all, which invalidates the analysis of information value presented in this chapter (see Knox, 2007, for an alternative model for the analysis of web-based newspapers).

Another example would be longer, printed text such as textbooks or reports. These types of texts often make use of images, illustrations and information graphics, but the texts as a whole are dominated by the sequential and temporal principle of organization of writing. Images and illustrations are often placed next to the written parts that they are semiotically connected to. Again, the analysis of composition – especially information value – loses some of its explanatory value. An image placed at the top of such text may not at all have the information value of 'ideal', it is just connected to the chunk of written text that is placed there. For example, it would be misleading to say that a table showing the US annual deficits is 'idealised' just because it has been placed at a top position in one of the pages of the budget of the United States Government. Such issues require critical considerations on behalf of the researcher or student doing the analysis, all in order to not employ the presented method too mechanically, and in that way reduce its explanatory capacity.

7.3.3 Doing multimodal discourse analysis in practice

Initially, it may be challenging for a student in the social sciences to employ concepts of multimodal discourse analysis without any previous experience of discourse analysis (Chapter 8), critical linguistics (Chapter 6), semiotics or general linguistics. On the other hand, all of the concepts and terms presented in this chapter have been developed in order to be concrete rather than abstract concepts, allowing for a practical analysis of texts.

Further, multimodal discourse analysis is better adapted to the qualitative analysis of smaller rather than larger corpora of texts. As discussed above, a number of qualitative considerations are necessary throughout the process of analysis in order to keep the validity of the analysis at an acceptable level, and it is generally more rewarding to analyze texts from all of the perspectives presented above (interactive, representational and compositional), which is a time-consuming process. Then again, it is of course possible to select just one or two analytical categories and employ these in an analysis of a lager corpus of texts. An example would be to select the human gaze as a resource for expressing reaction processes in a large corpus of child care brochures from different cultures. Who is presented as the reactor and who is the phenomenon? Is the male or female parent more often the reactor with the child as phenomenon, and how does this differ between cultures? And why do such patterns differ between cultures? Some QDA applications now offer the possibility to code pictures, which is helpful when analyzing larger corpora.

7.4 Multimodal discourse analysis and the analysis of power and other societal phenomena

Even though all the text analytical examples in this chapter have dealt with power or other phenomena in society, they have done so through a quite detailed analysis, very close to the text itself. The main point of the analyses has been to offer ways to penetrate multimodal texts in a more systematic and perhaps also formal way than what is usually possible by just intuitively reading and interpreting without an arsenal of text analytical concepts at hand.

Issues of power can usually be analyzed directly through multimodal analysis of interactive meanings in texts. The chapter has shown how point of view in images can be used as a maker of power. Depicted persons can be represented as if they are superior or inferior to the reader, or as if they are included or excluded from the social world of the reader. Symbolic distance is another category which can be related to power, and so can the use of speech acts and image acts: is the reader asked to do something or not? And who is the depicted person that has the power to command or demand?

The analysis of representations of on-goings in the world and that of composition can also be connected to the analysis of power. Different representations depend not only on the power of text producers in relation to the readers, but also on the power of normative discourses to regulate what it is possible to represent in a text and what it is not. In other words, who does what against whom in a multimodal text is not randomly determined. The fact that the 'goal' in the action process in Figure 7.5 is wearing a 'keffiyeh' and sits in a building with a sign in Arabic is a result of discourses that construct Arabs as enemies and Western soldiers as good actors in many conflicts. Such discourses can be more systematically identified and dissected through a thoroughgoing analysis of recurring representations in multimodal texts.

In a similar way, the analysis of composition can point not only to what is regarded as 'ideals' in texts of certain types (information value), but also to what is presented as most 'important' (salience) and 'connected' or 'disconnected' (framing). The chapter has shown how the technical side of nuclear power is 'idealized' in the text from The Swedish Nuclear Fuel and Waste Management Company (Figure 7.2); a compositional choice that can have further relevance in the analysis of discourses around nuclear power in many societies. The analysis of the given–new dimension in the ad in Figure 7.10 showed how it related to a gendered problem–solution pattern that is relevant in many other domains of society where female problems continuously have to be worked upon, often through the use of commercial products. Finally, the rather straightforward analysis of salience can point to patterns in what is construed as if it is important in society: is it commercial products, beauty, freedom, liberty, gender equality? Thus, the analysis of salience can be a powerful tool for an analysis of value systems in cultures and sub-cultures. Framing can often say something about categorization: which social groups or categories of things or ideas are presented as belonging together, and which are symbolically separated? And what does that say about a society at a specific point in history?

Summary

On the usefulness of multimodal discourse analysis

- Multimodal discourse analysis can be used in order to analyze meanings in multimodal texts in a more detailed and less intuitive manner, grasping both the meanings expressed through language and those expressed through images and illustrations. It is possible to combine the method with that of linguistic text analysis presented in Chapter 6.

- Multimodal discourse analysis can also be combined with other approaches to the analysis of texts presented in this book, for example, discourse analysis (Chapter 8) and the analysis of argumentation (Chapter 3).
- By analyzing interaction represented in multimodal texts it is possible to draw conclusions about, for example, power, inclusion and exclusion.
- The analysis of visual representations of on-goings in the world can help to categorize texts as more or less dynamic and also to systematically identify who does what to whom. This analysis can be used to answer questions such as "how are relations between persons in an organization represented?", "how can maps be directly related to ideological and political tensions in a given part of the world?" or "what are the markers of identity in a given text and to whom are they attributed?"
- The analysis of the composition of multimodal texts can say something about the ideological motivations behind a certain layout. Elements placed to the left in a text are often presented as if they are 'given' in relation to elements placed to the right, but 'given' to whom and under which circumstances? Elements placed in a top position in a multimodal text are 'ideal' in relation to lower elements, but why is something idealized at the expense of something else? And why are certain elements salient, and thus presented as if they are important, while others are not? This type of analysis can give input to discussions about ideologically driven choices in multimodal texts.

How to go about doing it

- Only a restricted number of texts can be analyzed if all the three functions (interaction, representation and composition) are to be analyzed qualitatively. If only a few analytical categories are selected, the number of texts analyzed can be increased.
- Multimodal discourse analysis as a text analytical method is often successfully combined with research questions relevant to the fields of gender studies, poststructuralism, rhetoric and discourse analysis in general.
- Precision is of key importance, and so are consistency and clear definitions of the concepts applied in the analysis. This type of text analysis has to be detailed before it can be abstracted to a level that is usually required for making it relevant in the social sciences.
- It is important to have a clear aim for the analysis, and not to over-interpret the results. Multimodal discourse analysis is a method for analyzing and producing reasonable and well-founded interpretations of texts; it is not a method for making statements about how producers or interpreters of texts think.

Suggested reading

The main source for this chapter has been Gunther Kress's and Theo van Leeuwen's book *Reading Images: The Grammar of Visual Design* (2006). The book presents not only a detailed exploration of resources for meaning-making in multimodal texts, but also critical discussions of, for example, the differences between language and image. Machin (2007) is a comprehensive presentation of the core content of *Reading Images*, targeted mainly at students of journalism and media studies, with many illustrative and practical

(Continued)

(Continued)

examples. The book also contains a critical examination of some of the assumptions that Kress and van Leeuwen (2006) make. Machin and van Leeuwen (2007) focus on the tension between the global and the local in today's media landscape, and include a comparative, multimodal analysis of local versions of *Cosmopolitan* magazine.

Halliday (1978), Hodge and Kress (1988), van Leeuwen (2005), Kress and van Leeuwen (2001) and Kress (2010) are books that discuss **social semiotics**, the overarching theoretical framework for the concepts and methods presented in this chapter. The linguistic application of social semiotics – *systemic functional grammar* – is introduced in Halliday and Matthiessen (2014), a book that requires some previous knowledge of linguistics from its readers.

The Routledge Handbook of Multimodal Analysis (2014, edited by C. Jewitt) contains articles on multimodality from researchers in many different disciplines, including anthropology, education, linguistics, and cognitive science. The leading academic journals in the field of multimodality are *Visual Communication* and *Social Semiotics*.

Exercise

South African students' protests against a colonial statue

In March and April 2015 student protests took place at the University of Cape Town campus in South Africa under the slogan 'Rhodes Must Fall'. The slogan refers to a statue of the British colonialist Cecil Rhodes, placed in a central position in the university campus. The protesters in the 'Rhodes Must Fall' movement demanded the immediate removal of the statue. They were successful, and the statue was removed in April 2015. During the course of the student protests the university made available so-called 'Have Your Say' noticeboards on which students and staff could have their say regarding the future of the statue. The noticeboards were later removed because of a number of racist and defamatory comments, but before that they were filled with written comments, drawings and images.

The task

The multimodal texts to be analyzed present views or opinions that are related to the Rhodes statue and its possible removal. How can these views or opinions be identified through an analysis of the texts that focuses on the use of images and composition in combination with writing?

The texts

Figure 7.11 shows a section of one the 'Have your say' message boards containing two images, print and a few handwritten comments (which are hard to read here – both images can be accessed on the companion website at **https://study.sagepub.com/boreusand bergstrom**).

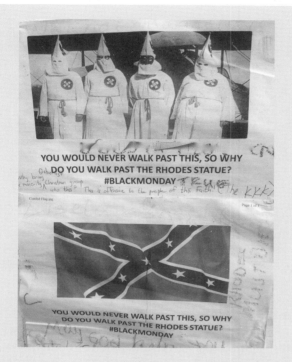

Figure 7.11 'Have Your Say' notice board, University of Cape Town

The second text to analyze is an article from the University of Cape Town student newspaper *Varsity*, which describes an on-campus meeting arranged by the university. It also contains an image of the Rhodes statue. For access to this article, please visit /http://varsitynewspaper.co.za/news/3984-setting-date/.

Aisha Abdool Karim

Setting a Date

Image: Aminu Ebrahim

ON MONDAY, March 16th the university hosted a discussion entitled "Heritage, Signage and Symbolism" as part of a planned series of talks on transformation, which were planned last year. During the introduction given by Professor Crain Soudien, Deputy Vice-Chancellor and Chair of the discussion, students requested that the order of speakers be rearranged so that Ramabina Mahapa, SRC President, could present

the university would still not be able to provide a date

his response first.

The request was granted and after Mahapa delivered his speech he, along with the majority of those present, left the room demanding that a date be set for when the statue would be removed. After the floor was opened to comments of whether or not the discussion should continue, it was decided that the discussion should be closed. Sally Titlestad, Spatial Historian and Heritage Management Consultant, commented that, should the decision be made to remove the statue, the university would still not be able to provide a date for the removal.

Titlestad noted the complexity of the issue and said that regardless of what the institution's decision is, there will first need to be a "heritage impact assessment for the removal

full heritage impact assessment will need to be conducted

of a protected piece of property involving full public participation". She then elaborated by saying that whilst this was procedure not always required, in this particular case it was made necessary "because there are so many stakeholders".

Titlestad said stakeholders such as funders, alumni, current students and staff, would all need to be consulted and participate in the process as they "care so much about the brand of UCT". The large number of people who are required to have a say in the final decision of what happens to the statue means that a full heritage impact assessment will need to be conducted. Titlestad also said that people could be charged if they failed to follow that process.

Considering the process that needs to be followed Titlestad said that a date could not be set, even provisionally, as the time taken to conduct these assessments varies. She raised the point that there are long waiting periods where "you put out notices and everyone gets a chance to comment back". Those comments are then compiled and brought back, which is what makes it difficult to provide an exact timeline for when the statue will be removed.

Titlestad emphasised that although stakeholder engagement

is important, the ultimate decision to remove the statue will depend on the research done into the issue and "It will still rest on the recommendation of the heritage impact assessment".

Titlestad also raised the example of the Cenotaph war memorial

"difficult to provide an exact timeline"

which was moved from Adderley Street, where it had been located since 1924, due to the addition of a MyCiti bus station. The process failed to consult stakeholders and this caused a delay in moving the memorial. Titlestad said that whether it is a demolition or relocation of the statue, it is still necessary to first conduct a heritage impact assessment.

After the discussion ended Dr Max Price, Vice-Chancellor, said that he could not provide a date for the statue's removal as that decision had to be taken by the Council. Price said that a special council meeting would be called on May 20th in which a decision would be made on whether or not the statue would be removed, as well as other issues of transformation. However, on March 18th an e-mail was sent out stating that the meeting had been moved to April 15th. Price stated that the program to address transformation at UCT had been accelerated due to the student protests which have taken place since March 9th.

Figure 7.12 Setting a date', *Varsity*, 24 March 2015

8

Discourse Analysis

Göran Bergström, Linda Ekström and Kristina Boréus

8.1 Background

In an earlier Swedish edition (Bergström and Boréus, 2000), this chapter began with a description of discourse analysis as a relatively odd duck within research in the social sciences and humanities. Today there is no basis for that assessment, since a significant number of studies in different disciplines are based on some form of discourse analysis. In addition, there are special textbooks which provide introductions to discourse analysis. However, both the prevalence of various approaches to discourse analysis and the fact that the very concept of discourse is defined in different ways justify an attempt to provide a more comprehensive account of the concept of discourse and what unites and distinguishes different approaches within discourse analysis. Despite its increasing proliferation, discourse analysis is still viewed as rather abstract, and we have, therefore, attempted to demonstrate the applicability of discourse analysis and present concrete arguments as to how to go about analyzing empirically different social science problems.

8.1.1 What is discourse?

The proliferation of the term 'discourse' has led to divergent meanings. While linguists can highlight certain features, French philosophers can highlight others; and while Anglo-Saxon discourse analysis employs the notion of 'discourse theory', which itself can also mean different things, within critical discourse analysis (CDA) yet other definitions are used. It is, therefore, important to deal with the question of what the term 'discourse' can mean.

An initial step towards increased precision is to distinguish between a narrow and a broad definition. This distinction is related to a division of discourse analysis into three different generations (Howarth and Torfing, 2005: Chapter 1). On the basis of the view of the **first generation**, 'discourse' is used in the narrow sense. This generation is related to the models of linguistic analysis that are presented in Chapter 6, and discourse means "samples of spoken dialogue, in contrast with written texts", or "spoken and written language" (Fairclough, 1992: 3). When 'discourse' is in this way imbued with the meaning of a cohesive chunk of written or spoken language, discourse analysis then primarily becomes the analysis of text without any connection to the context in which it occurs, which is not what we intend by 'discourse analysis' in this book.

Definitions used here can be said to originate instead from the second or third generation, definitions that include a consideration of more dimensions than merely the text (see, for example, Johnstone, 2008; Gee, 2011; van Dijk, 1997, 2013). CDA is an example of the **second generation** within discourse analysis, and the term 'discourse' is broadened to include linguistic aspects of social practice as well. In line with the **third generation**, discourses include all social phenomena, or "social systems of relations" (Howarth, 2000: 8). All creation of meaning occurs discursively, and the term 'discourse' includes even non-linguistic aspects of social practice.

Thus, according to the distinction between broad and narrow discourse definitions, the narrowest way of conceptualizing discourse is when the term refers to chunks of text without context, while the second broadest definition refers to linguistic practices, related to other kinds of social practice. The broadest definition includes linguistic as well as other kinds of social practice (see the example of university teaching as a discourse in Section 1.1).

There is also another kind of distinction between different uses of the term discourse in the literature. Sometimes 'discourse' refers to a particular perspective – an ideological view or a particular way of understanding – on a phenomenon. In accordance with this definition, what is expressed about a phenomenon at a particular time, in an institution, might be the expression of more than one, perhaps contradictory, discourses. But sometimes 'discourse' refers to the patterns for how a certain phenomenon tends to be talked and written about at a particular time in a particular context or institution. According to this latter kind of definition, a particular discourse might harbour internal contradictions and tensions.

8.1.2 Discourse analysis as philosophy and social theory

Discourse analysis offers an opportunity for a broader form of textual analysis that is based on a number of theoretical points of departure, which we present in this section. Under the subheading 'Critical reflections' we return to these theoretical preconditions.

First, discourse analysis embraces a view of language and language use which suggests that language is not conceived as a neutral instrument for communication. The view that language represents a given reality is rejected. Instead, the formative and constitutive side of language is emphasized: language always involves a perspective on the world. This does not mean that discourse analysis denies the existence of non-linguistic spheres: i.e. a "reality out there". Laclau and Mouffe (1990: 100–3) exemplify this with the example of a stone. That every object is viewed as discursively determined need not entail the view that the stone only exists when defined by a "system of socially constructed rules", it only means that the stone may assume different significations. For a stone-age warrior it might be a potential tool, for a settler it might be part of the foundation of a future dwelling and for some students it might be an archaeological discovery. Viewing language as constitutive entails that different interpretations of the stone create the basis for our knowledge, and the issue of power involves having certain knowledge accepted as the correct knowledge. Social life is not fixed, and the context for people's lives is continuously in the process of being constituted.

Second, discourse analysis often focuses on questions of power (Gee, 2005; Keller, 2013; van Dijk, 2013). An example can be who has the right to express themselves on a particular matter. If, for instance, certain social groups have been excluded in favour of experts in the formulation of a specific policy, this has consequences in terms of societal power. Fairclough calls this "**power in discourse**" (Fairclough, 2015: 27). Another way of looking at questions of power is to focus on "**power behind discourses**". On the basis of this perspective, the focus is instead on more comprehensive discourses that radically reshape social reality, a form of "hidden power" (2015: 27). An example can be new power relations that arise as a result of the marketization of European higher education policy, even if these are not directly visible to contemporary university students. Discursive power in this sense can be seen to bear some similarity with what has been called the third dimension or face of power (Lukes, 2005; see also Chapter 1 in this volume).

Yet another way of studying questions of power is to study competition between distinct discourses over the establishment of a particular understanding. This emphasis on the influence of discourses also underscores Foucault's point that power cannot be seen exclusively in negative terms. He states that power should also be viewed as a productive means, for example, that power can promote or produce specific understandings, suggestions and categories. Finally, the researcher's interest can also be focused on the effects that discourses can have and the ways in which specific groups can be advantaged or disadvantaged by those effects. Discourse-oriented policy theory has, for example, highlighted that discourses always have concrete implications via the conceptions and presumptions upon which they are based.

In this way, the first two theoretical starting points of discourse analysis are intertwined. Language is always part of, and constitutive of, special social practices, and these social practices always have implications for social relations and power relations (Gee, 2005: 33).

Third, within discourse analysis there is often an interest in the generation and change of social identities. These are viewed from the perspective of discourse analysis as mutable and unstable, and it is, therefore, interesting to study how social identities are formed within specific discourses. The notion that identities have a material existence is rejected. Identities such as 'woman', 'man', 'worker' or 'professor' are not given, do not exist 'out there'. In a similar way, discursive psychology, for example, emphasizes that identity construction is not entirely an internal process that occurs 'in there' within our individual psyches (Shotter, 1993; Billig, 1999; Potter and Edwards, 2001). Identity construction is viewed instead in terms of processes based on a coalescence of self-image and others' images. From this point of view, a specific identity is not possible unless it is placed in opposition to something else, 'the other', that the identity in question is considered not to be (see Hall, 1997). That is why discourse analysis often proceeds on the basis of distinctions such as 'us' and 'them' and focuses on how the creation of a 'we' always occurs in relation to the creation of a 'them'.

Fourth, discourse analysis does not focus on agents and underlying motives for the actions taken on the part of agents in the same way as is done, for example, in the analysis of ideas and ideology. In relation to this particular aspect, though, there are differences between various approaches within discourse analysis. While the discourse theory approach focuses on discourses themselves and their constitutive power, discursive psychologists, for instance, emphasize the role of agents as mediators and negotiators of discourses. This also applies to some extent to critical discourse analysis (CDA).

Fifth, discourse analysis is inherently interdisciplinary (Weiss and Wodak, 2003). Discourse analysis is marked by methodological and theoretical heterogeneity and discourse analytical work is being produced within a range of disciplines, for example within social psychology, critical linguistics and sociology (Hart, 2010: Chapter 1). This has led to an eclectic approach within the field, an approach that on the one hand has caused a risk of unsystematic analyses, but on the other hand has generated a dynamic which has been fruitful.

Above, we have provided an introductory presentation of the philosophical and theoretical elements of discourse analysis. In the following section, we will demonstrate how discourse analysis can be used to analyze texts. In order to use discourse analysis, it is necessary to proceed on the basis of a research question that is consistent with the philosophical perspectives and research focus that we have taken up in this section. For that reason, we will discuss which types of scientific research questions can be considered appropriate for discourse analysis. After that, some of the main traditions within discourse analysis will be presented, followed by the section 'Analysis' in which we provide concrete examples of how discourse analysis can be used.

8.1.3 Discourse analytic research problems and research focus

Michel Foucault is probably the person most strongly associated with discourse analysis. In his classic works, such as *Madness and Civilization: A History of Insanity in the Age of Reason* (2001 [1967]), *Discipline and Punish* (1977), *The Archaeology of Knowledge* (1972) and *The History of Sexuality: The Will to Knowledge* (1990), Foucault provided a number of examples of how questions of power, knowledge and discourse are placed at the centre of focus with the help of discourse analysis. Even if Foucault has been highly influential in the field in general, he did not develop any analytical tools for the detailed study of texts with which to carry out a concrete discourse analysis. We, therefore, deal with Foucault's analyses as a source of inspiration that can provide a general perspective for discourse analytic work rather than as a specific method for discourse analysis.

One interpretation of Foucault's concept of discourse is that he used the word to refer to "practices that systematically form the objects of which they speak" (Foucault, 1972: 49). A discourse can be described as a system of rules that legitimizes certain knowledge but not other knowledge and that indicates who has the right to express themselves with authority. Discourses also have a dynamic element, since the rule systems change. In addition, discourses include a number of preconceived notions regarding how we view the world and how these views result in people being controlled and organized on that basis. This occurs through a number of procedures that can be called **mechanisms of exclusion**. Examples of these kinds of mechanisms of exclusion are when something is prohibited, is defined as deviant or not deviant, is seen as a tradition or not a tradition, is viewed as right or wrong. Power is not something that is exercised by a subject or against a given subject but instead is developed in relations between people and entails limitations for some and opportunities for others.

A concept that, for Foucault, is strongly related to power is *knowledge*; primarily established knowledge. Established knowledge provides the impetus for the mechanisms of exclusion that have been described. Knowledge regulates what is acceptable to say, how this should be presented and who is allowed to say it. Knowledge contributes to creating **subject positions**, i.e. frameworks for human action that are created in the discourse. These discursively created positions, in turn, determine the space for the action freedom of subjects. A discourse on welfare policy thus says something that claims to be true for that topic. If there is a rule in the prevailing policy discourse that everyone should have the right to housing, or vice versa that society has no responsibility to guarantee housing for its citizens, the discourse creates power relations. Different subject positions are created for the homeless (for instance, a citizen that has not been granted fundamental rights versus an individual that has not been able to arrange their housing situation), depending on which rule emerges from the discourse.

Foucault can be seen to represent two different points of entry to discourse analysis, namely archaeology and genealogy. In the **archaeological** approach,

Foucault directs attention towards the inner form of discourses; he reveals the **episteme** (what is knowable) and systems of rules of different epochs, which together indicate something of essential importance about the views and experiences of a particular time. This method of working corresponds in part to 'normal' social science and historical research, since the researcher searches back to specific events at specific points in time. This differs from the **genealogical** method of working, which does not primarily proceed from the the the past. In studies inspired by this approach, the starting point is the present. The analysis begins with the help of some dimension of the theme in question that has been taken from a current discussion. A genealogical analysis entails tracing 'family relations' where various other discourses and practices create the preconditions for a specific discourse. Tied to the genealogical approach is also the purpose of studying the conditions of possibilities of the discourse: how a particular phenomenon has come to be problematized, has been made the object of study for different disciplines, and how it has led to different social practices or institutional solutions.

Finally, it can be noted that in the aftermath of Foucault, discourse analytic studies have often focused on (power related) questions of how particular knowledge is created, perpetuated and reproduced as well as which effects this knowledge can have. Interest can be directed towards how something can be identified as problematic, how certain social practices can become institutionalized in order to deal with topics that are conceived as problematic, and how these conceptions and institutions can constitute (in the sense of establishing different subject positions) and govern people. The discourse analytical tradition has in this way opened up for a range of alternative research questions that can be said to fall outside the scope of the other text analytical traditions covered in this book.

However, as has been stated previously, Foucault has not provided any detailed guidelines about how these themes can be studied empirically, and in the coming sections we will, therefore, turn to three traditions that have to a greater extent developed ways of carrying out empirical studies.

8.1.4 Discourse theory

The first tradition within discourse analysis is represented here by Ernesto Laclau and Chantal Mouffe. This approach has its roots in poststructuralism and post-Marxism. They focus their interest on power struggles on the macro level of society. The starting point is that these can be studied via the linguistic level and the continuously ongoing struggle over meaning in language. A central starting point for this approach is its view on the issue of the relationship between discourse and non-discourse: all social phenomena are treated discursively. Apparently, these authors use the broadest concept of discourse. In an oft-cited example, the authors try to clarify what they mean when they state that discourses even include non-linguistic aspects:

> Let us suppose that I am building a wall with another bricklayer. At a certain moment I ask my workmate to pass me a brick and then I add it to the wall. The first act - asking for the brick - is linguistic; the second - adding the brick to the wall - is extralinguistic. Do I exhaust the reality of both acts by drawing the distinction between them in terms of the linguistic/extralinguistic opposition? Evidently not, because, despite their differentiation in those terms, the two actions share something that allows them to be compared, namely the fact that they are both part of a total operation of building the wall [...] This totality which includes within itself the linguistic and the non-linguistic, is what we call discourse. (Laclau and Mouffe, 1990: 100)

Discourse theory is influenced by several different traditions. Initially, it is clearly influenced by semiotic language philosophy, which goes back to the Swiss linguist Ferdinand de Saussure's view of language as a system of signs. The starting point is the linguistic level and "the logic of signs" (Laclau, 1993: 434–5). As has been shown in Chapter 1, this entails that signs consist of two parts: the signifier (for example, the utterance 'cat') and the signified (the general idea of what cats are) and that the relationship between these two parts is unstable. The meaning of signs is thus an open question, and discourse theory is interested in this meaning-making process, in *when* signs assume meaning and *how*. The outcome of this meaning-making process is understood as the current discourse surrounding a particular field, and Laclau and Mouffe therefore define discourse as "the structured totality resulting from the articulatory practice" (Laclau and Mouffe, 1985: 105).

A concept that highlights this ambiguity of discourses and the ongoing meaning-making processes, is the concept of the **element**[1] since elements are seen as the signs that are subjected to continuous struggle and that remain ambiguous. Laclau and Mouffe also introduced the term **floating signifiers** for those elements within a discourse that are particularly contentious and open to different meanings. In political debates signs such as 'justice', 'equality' and 'change' seem to occupy a central place in completely different discourses, and there is a political struggle over filling the sign in question with meaning. This indicates that these elements can also be seen as floating signifiers.

Discourses are generally characterized by the fact that they reduce the ambiguity of signs, and discursification involves signs assuming a higher degree of fixity. In this context, another concept enters, that of **moment**, which refers to the **closure**, or locking, of the meaning of an element. A closure of this kind is also related to the term **articulation**, which refers to how a discourse is constructed. Articulation is a form of practice that creates a certain relationship between the elements that comprise the precondition for a discourse: "we will call articulation

---

[1]All the terms in this and the next paragraph are presented in Laclau and Mouffe (1985: Chapter 3).

any practice establishing a relation among elements such that their identity is modified as a result of articulatory practice" (Laclau and Mouffe, 1985: 105).

When a number of different elements from, for instance, economic, political and social spheres are articulated or written in a way that creates a specific meaning, this common and modified meaning can form the basis of a discourse (Smith, 1998: Chapter 3). This can be exemplified by how 'terrorism' in Argentina was articulated under the Argentinian military juntas. The regime came to equate terrorism with things that were not previously associated with terrorism, such as 'young nuns', 'crazy people', 'sickness' and 'chaos', while what was 'western' and 'good' was associated with 'peace', 'law' and 'order' (Zac, 2005).

In conjunction with a discursification and locking of meanings, other possible meanings are excluded. If a leftist-oriented education discourse, for instance, no longer contains the sign 'equality', it has been relegated to a **discursive field**, a kind of pantry filled with meanings and different leftovers from other discourses. The contents of this pantry create a potential threat to every discourse, given that each item in this pantry could sometime in the future challenge the prevailing discourse. However, its contents do not provide the discourse with any meaning right now, but instead create what discourse theory has called the **constitutive outside**. Since meaning, in this view, is always relationally constructed, the outside is also seen as something that assigns meaning to the inside. Our notions of a certain event or identity are thus also manifested through its binary opposition, in relation to what it is *not* expected to be (see, for example, Laclau, 1995: 151). To use a simple example: the way 'they' are denoted also assigns meaning to our understanding of 'we'.

When the range between possible meanings in a discourse is reduced in these various ways, and if stabilization also mitigates antagonism between discourses, we can speak of **hegemony** (Laclau and Mouffe, 1985: 142). This kind of stabilization can also be expressed as a form of "organization of consent" (Barret, 1991: 54). When the power dimension is so clearly included in discourse analysis in this way, it bears traces of the Italian Marxist Antonio Gramsci, whose work emphasized, in an unusually strong manner for Marxism, the role of ideas in societal change. Gramsci used the expression 'hegemony' to denote a state in which prevailing societal conceptions are not challenged, despite one class being subordinated to another.

A concrete way in which a discourse analysis based on discourse theory can be conducted is to construct so-called **chains of equivalence**. A sign is considered to be endowed with meaning through a system of distinctions. A certain element is written alongside of or linked to certain signs, at the same time as the element in question is distinguished from other signs. A discourse concerning Nazis, to take an example, cannot be understood unless 'Nazism' is studied in relation to both what it is considered to stand in opposition to and what it can be considered to be associated with. In a German Nazi discourse during the 1920s, there are, for example, a number of signs/elements that are contrasted with Nazism. These can be 'humanism', 'democracy', 'Americanism', 'Bolshevism', 'foreigners', 'Jews', etc. At the same time, there are elements that Nazism is positively related to, for example 'fatherland', 'honour', 'order'.

Taken together, one element in a discourse can have a special role, i.e. comprise a **node**. One sign in the Nazi discourse is unique, since it is related to all of the other signs: 'Jews'. 'Jews' has links to all of the other signs mentioned, sometimes in terms of a negative relation ('fatherland') and sometimes in terms of a positive relation ('Bolshevism'). 'Jews' is closely associated with 'Bolshevism' but with 'Americanism' as well. This node functions as a kind of hub in the discourse. It is through the node that a definite meaning for the signs that surround it are fixed. It could even be claimed that without the presence of 'Jews', this discourse could not have developed.

A discourse is generally characterized further by two different tendencies. We mentioned previously that the term 'moment' corresponds to a tendency to lock or fix meaning. The elements gain fixity, which is a precondition for the pattern of elements that comprise a discourse. **Antagonism** corresponds to a completely different tendency, since this serves instead to break up discourses. Theoretically, the concept of antagonism can be seen as an example of a Marxist legacy, and Marxism thus comprises another tradition that discourse theory bears traces of. On the basis of the Marxist conception of a fundamental conflict between social classes, Laclau and Mouffe take as a starting point that social life can be seen in terms of conflict. However, antagonism does not refer to a contradiction on the economic level, as in Marxism, but as something that can be described as a 'war' that involves meaning creation on a linguistic level (Laclau and Mouffe, 1985: 122–7).

An example of a study of a war over meaning of this kind is Bobby Sayyid's study of how the 'Shah's discourse' in Iran was challenged by an alternative discourse, namely that of Khomeini (Sayyid, 1994). The traditional discourse was based on a division into a 'white revolution' that was good and was associated with 'modernization', 'the West', 'nationalism' and 'Arabic', while the 'red revolution' was evil. The Khomeini discourse was able to break the monopoly of what characterized a 'good' revolution, since new elements, previously associated with 'evil', such as 'social equalization', were able to be integrated into the good alternative discourse. The discourse analysis here poses an interesting challenge to other theories with the ambition of explaining the fall of the Shah (see, for example, Halliday, 1979; Skocpol, 1982).

We mentioned previously that there is a discursive field that continuously comprises a potential threat to the prevailing discourse. This can be exemplified by the prevailing European education policy (Olssen et al., 2004), in which an equality discourse during the past decades has been challenged by a more neo-liberal discourse. The focus on equalization of social differences has thus been replaced by competition and a focus on the individual. However, the element 'equality', even if it has been temporarily placed in the pantry of the discourse, can come to challenge or disturb the logic of the new discourse in the future. Another term that corresponds to tensions and changes within discourses is **dislocation**. When discourses are characterized by dissolution, disturbance or dislocation, a new and more open situation arises. Disturbance can be seen as a failure, since the framework for action of the discourse no longer works, and subjects have to act under new and more open conditions (Howarth, 2000: 109–11).

The term **subject** corresponds to the concept 'subject position' in discourse analysis. For Laclau and Mouffe, the term has a somewhat different content than for Foucault. From the perspective of understanding, it is not without interest that a person is a worker in a factory, i.e. the structural position is not dismissed as meaningless. However, the person/subject occupies other positions in a discourse, subject positions such as 'Christian', 'woman', 'environmental activist', 'home town romantic', 'parent', etc. We live through these positions, and every subject position carries with it a kind of filter that we view the world through (Howarth, 1995: 123; Smith, 1998: Chapter 3). It is also through these subject positions that people's actions are both made possible and limited. In relation to Foucault's more structurally determined way of defining subject positions, Laclau and Mouffe's way of conceiving of these contributes to a clearer element of mutability in discourses. For Laclau and Mouffe the element of uncertainty is reinforced in this way even in the case of the concept of identity. On the basis of this perspective, **identity** thus stands for those fundamentally unstable subject positions that the 'I' attempts to identify with.

Table 8.1 summarizes the analytical concepts that are presented in this section and their function in analyses.

Table 8.1 Analytical concepts in discourse theory

Analytical concept useful for...	Analytical concept	Definition
mapping out discourses	sign	Designation and what is being designated (term and cognitive content)
	element	Sign that is under contention
	floating signifier	Sign that is especially contested and open to different meanings
mapping out discourses in terms of the position of actors	subject position	Discursively determined positions for people
	identity	Subject positions that the unstable 'I' seeks to identify with
mapping out the emergence and stability of discourses	moment	Sign that has been fixed and over which there is no longer a struggle
	articulation	Process in which different elements are brought together in a discourse

(Continued)

Table 8.1 (Continued)

Analytical concept useful for...	Analytical concept	Definition
	chain of equivalence	The way in which certain signs are linked to each other in order to thereby create a particular meaning
	constitutive outside	The binary opposition that provides meaning to the inside by means of the inside being contrasted with it
	nodal point	Sign that functions as a hub in a discourse
	hegemony	Discourse that is not challenged
mapping out the dissolution and instability of discourses	antagonism	Battle over meaning
	dislocation	Profound change of the conditions of a discourse due to an event that cannot be immediately incorporated into the discourse
	field of discursivity	What is temporarily omitted from the discourse. The 'pantry' of meanings that can potentially reoccur and contribute to a future disruption in the discourse

8.1.5 Discursive psychology

The second tradition, discursive psychology, is represented here primarily by the work of Margaret Wetherell and Jonathan Potter. Discursive psychology is based on a view similar to that of discourse theory in terms of the relationship between the discursive and the non-discursive. Wetherell and Potter state that discourse is *thoroughly constitutive*: "Discourse, in our view, is not partially constitutive or only constitutive under some conditions but is thoroughly constitutive. Our accounts of objects always construct those objects in certain ways and this construction is inescapable" (1992: 62).

However, discursive psychologists seem to place certain practices outside of discourse. They concur with Stuart Hall's point that events, relations and structures do have conditions of existence and real effects outside the sphere of the discursive, but that it is only within the discursive that they are constructed within meaning (Hall, 1988: 27, in Wetherell and Potter, 1992: 63). This position places them somewhere between Laclau and Mouffe's view of discourse as a totality that includes within itself the linguistic and the non-linguistic and Fairclough's separation between discursive and non-discursive practices.

The tradition of discursive psychology focuses primarily on talk and text, its analysis emphasizes meanings, conversations, narratives and anecdotes. Even though the authors are aware of the fact that aspects other than linguistic practices are important, they claim that even these aspects may be studied through a focus on discourse. They state that one "must also focus on institutional practices, on discriminatory actions and on social structures and social divisions. But the study of these things is intertwined with the study of discourse. Our emphasis will be on […] how forms of discourse institute, solidify, change, create and reproduce social formations" (Wetherell and Potter, 1992: 3).

The difference between discursive psychology and discourse theory is, however, more significant with regard to the definition of discourse. In contrast to Laclau and Mouffe's focus on the "large-scale discourses" of society that may dominate an entire sphere, discursive psychology highlights discursive variation and the fact that a given debate or sphere is commonly characterized by a number of competing understandings (Wetherell, 1998). In other words, these authors refer to discourses as perspectives on phenomena (see the distinction made in Section 8.1.1). This fragmented array of different meaning clusters surrounding a particular debate or policy field is captured by the analytical concept **interpretative repertoire**, defined as "a recognizable routine of arguments, descriptions and evaluations distinguished by familiar clichés, common places, tropes and characterizations of actors and situations. Such repertoires become evident through repetition across a corpus" (Edley and Wetherell, 2001: 443).

Edley and Wetherell's notion of interpretative repertoire also implies a different understanding of agency compared to Laclau and Mouffe. In line with the notion of multiple interpretative repertoires, individuals are considered to have greater possibilities to choose from among, or draw upon, competing understandings. This kind of discourse analysis thus sees individuals both as products of discourse and as producers of discourse, whereas Laclau and Mouffe tend to view individuals solely as subjects of discourse (Jørgensen and Phillips, 2002: 7). In this way, Wetherell and Potter stress that discourses are not to be seen as causal agents in their own right (Wetherell, 1998: 395) and that individuals use existing understandings flexibly in order to create, modify and reproduce a specific interpretative repertoire. This focus on more or less strategic use of different repertoires and on the ongoing struggle to make claims accountable is informed by rhetorical and conversation analysis (see, for example, Duranti and Goodwin, 1992; Sacks, 1992). Language use is thus seen as oriented towards social action and a desire to reach a certain end (see, for example, Widdicombe and Wooffitt, 1995, for a more detailed analysis of the use of rhetorical devices and strategic language use). This means that interpretative repertoires do not have the power to govern the condition of their use but are instead "available as resources to be used in a range of contrasting and sometimes surprising ways" (Wetherell and Potter, 1992: 93).

This understanding can be exemplified through Nigel Edley and Margaret Wetherell's study of how men construct feminism and feminists (Edley and Wetherell, 2001). They found two competing interpretative repertoires. The first is referred to as the liberal feminist repertoire, a repertoire that is bound up with recurrent and straightforward descriptions of women seeking equality. The second repertoire, the interpretative repertoire of feminism as extremism, is more complex and is composed of a larger array of recurrent themes. Therefore, in line with the rigorous empirical analysis of conversation analyses (Potter and Edwards, 2001), the analysis of this second repertoire requires giving attention to the detail of the talk and the interaction. Besides recurrent use of the notion of extremism, this more complex construction of feminism also points to irrationality and an abundance of emotions and anger. Together, these descriptions, arguments and evaluations create an understanding of feminism as something unacceptable or "too much", a position counter to a balanced, reasonable and healthy feminism (Edley and Wetherell, 2001: 446).

This second repertoire is also described as an embodied account in which a specific understanding of what feminists *are like* becomes important. This means that the repertoire works through an overt subject position constructed for feminists. By looking at how individuals associated with this understanding of feminism are constructed, we gain a deeper understanding of the second interpretative repertoire itself. When mapping the subject position associated with this interpretative repertoire, the researchers found recurrent descriptions of feminists as ugly women, lesbians and man-haters (Edley and Wetherell, 2001: 444), which enforce the equation of feminism with extremism.

It is thus important to note that the discourses are not seen to be in themselves determining subject positions (Wetherell, 1998: 401). The existence of a certain repertoire does not easily place individuals in ready-made subject positions, according to discursive psychologists, but instead subjects may draw upon different repertoires in unconventional ways and may actively negotiate the positioning of the self and others. This is what Wetherell means when she talks about subject positions in play (Wetherell, 1998). Even if an interpretative repertoire constructs feminists as ugly women, lesbians and man-haters, it is not evident that these positions are accepted. An existing discourse or interpretative repertoire may offer a certain subject position, but this position is always negotiated and sometimes also negated.

This view of agency and negotiation between a range of existing subject positions also takes individuals positioning themselves into account. An important point in discursive psychology is that when constructing, for example, feminism and feminists through descriptions and categorization, participants are at the same time representing themselves in certain ways. The same kinds of discursive processes that surround the construction of interpretative repertoires and subject positions take place when we construct notions of ourselves. Our identities and selves are viewed as constructed through the internalization of social dialogues, dialogues that are both comprised of discourses that position individuals in particular categories (Gergen, 1994) and of people's active use of available discourses. When analyzing existing self-representations, we must, therefore, focus on the rhetorical organisation of text and talk and on how subjects constitute or position themselves through existing linguistic resources. In the study of men's constructions of feminism and feminists, one interviewee tries, for instance, to distance himself from the interpretative repertoire while at the same time representing it. This offers him the possibility of positioning himself as a modern-day "reconstructed" man (Edley and Wetherell, 2001: 445) rather than as a potentially troublesome sexist.

Interaction, rhetoric and attempts at encountering conflicting versions of reality always take place within broader spheres of meaning. The interpretative repertoires and subject positions offered by the interviewees only become meaningful within a general form of intelligibility, which is bound up with or constituted from a negative or discriminating understanding of women. This implies a return to Foucault's broader understanding of the role of discourses in the construction of various realms of objects and subjects (Wetherell and Potter, 1992: 89).

Discursive psychologists have thus tried to occupy a middle position between highlighting regular patterns of shared sense-making resources, on the one hand, and the possibility for actors to use these creatively in specific contexts, on the other. This combination of more fine-grained conversation analytic and ethnomethodological approaches with Foucauldian and post-structuralist theories has been described in the following way:

> From the former [the conversation analysis] we take the emphasis on the action orientation of people's talk and the notion of social order as constituted intersubjectively as participants display to each other their understanding of what is going on, while from the latter [the post-structural tradition] we take the notion of discourse as organized by "institutional forms of intelligibility" which have a history and which imbricate power relations. (Wetherell and Edley, 1999: 338)

Discursive psychologists, at least those that have added the prefix 'critical' (see, for example, Edley, 2001), also take an interest in power relations. This means focusing on ideological effects that the use of different discourses or interpretative repertoires may have. Discursive psychology connects this understanding to Foucault's view of modern power as working through knowledge, for example through the identification of new categories of people (Wetherell and Potter, 1992: 83). Based on this understanding, discourses may have the effect of establishing, sustaining and reinforcing oppressive power relations with regard to those defined or categorized through the discourse (Wetherell and Potter, 1992: 70). In this way, ideologies are studied as practices or outcomes, which implies an interest in how exploitation is legitimized or how discriminated identities are reproduced from the particular use of different interpretative repertoires operating in a culture (Wetherell and Potter, 1992: 103). To return to the example of men's constructions of feminism and feminists, these constructions are related to the ideological effects they produce and the ways that they potentially maintain or challenge existing power relations. The interest is not one of finding a sexist ideology but of illustrating how certain interpretative repertoires may serve to legitimise or reproduce a disqualification of feminism and to reinforce discriminating identities for feminists.

8.1.6 Critical discourse analysis

The third tradition to be presented is critical discourse analysis (abbreviated as CDA). There are a number of different variants of CDA, although within the field three starting points have been highlighted: "CDA combines *critique* of discourse and *explanation* of how it figures within and contributes to the existing social reality, as a basis for *action* to change that existing reality in particular aspects" (Fairclough, 2015: 6; emphasis in the original). It can thus be stated that critical discourse analysis shares common ground with a tradition of social critique: "critical discourse analysis is an instrument whose purpose is to expose veiled power structures" (Wodak, 1996: 16). This section will be based primarily on Norman Fairclough's approach within critical discourse analysis, sometimes called the 'dialectical-relational approach', as opposed to a range of CDA-studies that focus more heavily on linguistic analysis (see, for example, van Dijk, 1997, 2013; Machin and Mayr, 2012).

A tradition of social theory that has been a source of inspiration for critical discourse analysis is the Frankfurt School and its critical theory. Similarities between critical theory and discourse analysis include critique of ideology (see Chapter 4) and that cultural phenomena are considered to be relatively autonomous phenomena which cannot be understood merely with the help of studies of the economic system. Discourses, in Fairclough's critical discourse analysis, have several different functions. In addition to constructing social identities, they perpetuate prevailing social relations. In terms of the view of discourses, such as that they contribute to maintaining prevailing power structures, there are influences from Marxist traditions, but above all there are similarities to Bashkar's critical realism, which makes a distinction between a "domain of the real" independent of our senses and a "realm of the empirical" that corresponds to what our senses can comprehend (Fairclough, 2010: 355). If Laclau and Mouffe stress the constitutive function of discourses, Fairclough also stresses the dependent function of discourses, i.e. that discourses are formed by a social structure that is characterized by "both a discursive and non-discursive nature" (Fairclough, 1992: 64).

When critical discourse analysis proceeds from the level of the text, the starting point is linguistic, with a focus on, among other things, grammatical structure. Discursive practice refers to how texts are produced, distributed and consumed. When Fairclough integrates social practice into the analysis, the discourse is situated in a broader social context. Discourse is related to both other discourses and to non-discursive areas. The model reflects well the overall purpose that characterizes CDA, namely to study the relationships between discourses and other social structures. In the remainder of this section, we provide examples of analytical tools that can be used on different levels.

CDA uses the narrow discourse definition – discourse as linguistic practice only – and differs from other perspectives on discourse analysis in that it makes use of linguistic tools on the **level of the text** to a greater degree. Syntax analysis entails a focus on different aspects of meaning-making, which coincides to some extent with what we have taken up earlier in relation to critical linguistics in Chapter 6. These kinds of linguistically-oriented discourse analyses are, for example, conducted by authors such as Teun van Dijk and Christopher Hart. In empirical analyses regarding the current migration issue, they have, based on analysis of propositions and metaphors, shown how discourses tend to be organized by a polarization: "negative properties of outgroups and positive ones of ingroups tend to be emphasized" (van Dijk, 2013: 194, see also Hart, 2010).

Returning to our general focus on Fairclough, the analysis of the level of the text can be exemplified by three techniques: the analysis of transitivity, nominalization and modality (Fairclough, 1992: Chapter 6). The first two analytical concepts are described in Chapter 6. **Modality** refers to the degree of certainty with which a text producer, such as a political leader, expresses themselves. There is a difference between a prime minister saying that "ill health related to the workplace *might need* to be investigated" and that "ill health related to the workplace *will be* investigated". In this example, it becomes evident that the use of almost similar wording might implicate a very different degree of certainty, promising the audience different things. In addition to studying grammatical structures in texts, the analysis deals with mapping out what is explicitly stated and what is implicitly understood.

In the analysis of **discursive practice** the focus is on how texts are produced, distributed and consumed. The techniques for this can include participant observation and some form of simple study of documents. The concept of **intertextuality** is used in CDA as an access point to the theme of production of the text and deals with how texts relate to each other: "intertextuality is basically the property texts have of being full of snatches of other texts" (Fairclough, 1992: 82). This can involve, to mention just one example, how part of the text of a government directive 'survives', i.e. how it can be found in the texts of national commissions of inquiry and the texts of subsequent legislation. In addition to intertextuality, a given text from a commission of inquiry or legislative proposal can very well contain **interdiscursive** elements. The Bologna discourse, which aims at reducing the differences between the higher education systems among different European countries, reveals the influence of various general social discourses. For example, it is possible to see the influence of a liberal social discourse that emphasizes growth, competition and interchangeability. Another influence comes from a regulative discourse with elements of a common educational structure for all of Europe (a three-year basic undergraduate degree, a two-year advanced – master – degree and a three-year doctoral degree) as well as a common grading system (ECTS).

The theme of distribution sheds light on how distribution varies between different types of text. For example, the texts of political leaders are distributed through certain institutional domains (media, reports and policy manifestos), while a disarmament agreement is distributed in other ways. The point is that different channels of distribution entail different kinds of consumption of the text in question (Fairclough, 1992: 79).

The theme of consumption in the study of discursive practice can be illustrated with the help of our discussion of different interpretive strategies in Chapter 1. One of these is called adressee-oriented. This kind of interpretive strategy characterizes studies that investigate, for instance, how different people understand (consume) a specific political manifesto. Fairclough himself has, however, not developed this aspect of discourse analysis.

When the analysis is broadened to include social practice as well, the discourse is placed in a social context, and the ambition of discourse analysis to be able to say something 'critical' about ideology and power becomes more pronounced. The analysis is broadened, since text as a manifestation of social practices is part of a greater structure. Fairclough uses the concept **discourse order** and means that a specific discourse must be related to other discourses. For example, if we are to understand how demands for gender equality work will be received and dealt with within a specific organization, this discursive practice need to be related to other discourses that exist within the organization. Within, for instance, a trade union, a focus on gender cannot simply replace a traditional focus on conflict between work and capital but must be represented in a way that is compatible with the traditional class-based discourse (see Mahon, 1996).

A clear difference in relation to Laclau and Mouffe is that discourses in CDA do not only constitute but are also constituted. In this context, the concepts of both ideology and hegemony become relevant. The concept of hegemony in Fairclough, however, does not entail a wholly deadlocked situation; social change is possible, since other ways of articulating text and discursive practices cannot be excluded. Just like Laclau and Mouffe, Fairclough envisions hegemony as including both contradiction and instability (Fairclough, 1992: 93). CDA itself does not provide any recipe for how social practice should be studied; social science is needed for this. At the same time, CDA, through its foundation in linguistics, offers a elaborate model for studies of text and discursive practice.

8.2 Analysis

In this section we will use three examples to show how texts can be studied with the help of discourse analysis in order to shed light on social science problems. The examples illustrate the approaches that we presented above. Discourse analyses that have been conducted in the social sciences hardly follow any specific methodological approach, and there are rarely any clear templates to rely on. Despite this, there are certain steps in the concrete process of analysis that all discourse analyses have to consider. We therefore conclude this section with a more concrete discussion of methodological approaches.

8.2.1 Discourse theory – the construction of a hegemonic discourse and the use of chains of equivalence

The political scientist Charlotte Fridolfsson uses discourse theory in her analysis of the social movement protests at the EU summit in Gothenburg, Sweden, in 2001 (Fridolfsson, 2004). This particular summit marked the end of the Swedish Presidency of the European Union, and, as was the case with other international political summits at the time (for example, Seattle in 1999, Prague in 2000 and Genoa in 2001), it was accompanied by massive demonstrations arranged by a coalition of various social movements and groups. Similar protests have also occurred since (for example, London and Brussels in 2013, and Paris in 2015), making this a relevant and ongoing issue for empirical analysis in the social sciences. In Gothenburg, the demonstrators called for "democracy, a sound environment and solidarity" (Fridolfsson, 2004: 80). However, the demonstrations were also characterised by material damage and violence. Several hundred civilians and police officers were injured, and three people were shot by the police. The events later came to be referred to as the 'Gothenburg riots', and in her analysis Fridolfsson analyzes the ideological package that followed on from this designation and the multiple meanings that were generated in relation to the summit (Fridolfsson, 2004: 80). In the following section, we wish to highlight how this was accomplished in the study, which employs several of the analytical concepts from discourse theory presented above.

Focusing on an elite discourse as manifested in printed and broadcasted media and government reports, Fridolfsson analyzes how the meanings of the events in Gothenburg are fixed. This fixation is of particular importance, since the events, according to Fridolfsson, can be seen as a dislocation within the discourse structuring the idea of liberal democracy and the related role of international summits (2004: 80). The violence and protests challenged the understanding of contemporary democracy as rational, legitimate and characterized by popular support, and thereby dislocated the previous understanding of prevailing liberal democracy as well as its functioning. Based on the massive protests, a new and open situation with regard to the understanding of contemporary liberal democracy was established, opening up the possibility for new and alternative processes of meaning-making. For this reason, the struggle to establish the taken-for-granted understanding of these events and to re-establish the discourse structuring the idea of liberal democracy and the related role of international summits became crucial.

This is associated with Fridolfsson's starting point that meaning-making is marked by uncertainty and struggle or antagonism. In the study, these understandings are developed through the concepts of hegemony and hegemonic intervention from discourse theory. These concepts are defined here as follows: "A hegemonic intervention is a process taking place in an uncertain context where the discourse is the result; hegemony is the new fixation of meaning" (2004: 81). By focusing on hegemonic intervention in relation to the existent dislocation,

Fridolfsson attempts to analyze how a certain understanding of the events, the understanding of the events as 'a riot', is constructed and established in a context in which other meanings had the potential of structuring the understanding instead. This understanding, or fixation of meaning, is seen as the discourse that structured the understanding of the events in Gothenburg.

In addition to focusing on the creation and establishment of the new meaning, the hegemony, the author also shows how alternative understandings of the events, referred to here as antagonistic discourses, are downplayed. These are understandings that could have structured the prevailing understanding of the events but that, as a result of the antagonism or conflict between the competing understandings, failed to do so.

Fridolfsson is also interested in how the notions of collective protest and social movements are shaped, used and reproduced through discourse (2004: 79). One starting point of the analysis of the notions of collective protest and social movements is that movement identities are far from fixed and are not entirely shaped by the movements themselves. Instead, consistent with Laclau and Mouffe, identities are seen as contingent, and the meanings attached to these movements are regarded as the result of the ever-present conflicts and antagonisms embedded in social relations. Drawing on structural linguistics, another starting point is that these identities are relationally constructed; they receive meaning only by diverging from other potential identities.

To be able to conduct an empirical study of how the notions of collective protest and social movements are fixated, Fridolfsson follows the logic of the analytical concept *chains of equivalence*. Fridolfsson's analysis thus shows how the notion of the 'protesters' is connected to a range of other concepts that, in line with the view of identities as relationally constructed, together construct the meaning associated with the notion of 'protesters'. In general, the demonstrators were largely subjected to descriptions connoting war, terrorism and criminal activity (2004: 90). This chain of equivalence between protesters, war, terrorism and criminal activity is central to the processes of meaning-making surrounding the protesters; the understanding of the protesters is infused with the meaning of the surrounding concepts.

In the material, this meaning-making process could be seen, for example, in statements that associated the protesters with hooligans. The local government commissioner, when talking about the events in a radio interview, stated: "Those you saw here on the Avenue, they are not demonstrators, they are hooligans" (2004: 89). The designation 'hooligan' was also found in the newspaper material. In one newspaper article, for example, Gothenburg is said to have been raped by hooligans (2004: 90). In a similar vein, in another newspaper article the protesters were described as "suspects, preparing to commit criminal activity such as vandalism and assault" (2004: 83).

Another central notion in this relationally constructed meaning of the protesters was that of 'youths'. The deviating troublemakers were perceived as being "young" (2004: 85). Consistent with such an understanding, activists were often made into "rascals" or "boys" (2004: 89). In the newspapers the demonstrators were described as, among other things, "adolescents that want to be noticed" (2004: 86), and Swedish public service television made a series entitled "Violence and youth" about the events in Gothenburg. On their website they wrote: "Youth uprising in the past is a recurring theme in all broadcasts – from the swing dancers in the 40s to today's hip-hoppers and globalization protesters" (2004: 85). The protests taking place in Gothenburg were thus seen as a repetition of prior youth revolts and thereby also as a cyclical occurrence relatively independent of the prevailing political context.

Through these fixations of meaning (the protesters as, for example, young hooligans), 'the violent protesters' could thus be seen as an element (a sign that is contested), which are transformed into a moment. Taken together, these ways of representing the protesters construct an understanding of them that neglects political messages and makes them seem incomprehensible as political actors. In terms of the ideological package that follows on from the designations analyzed, it can be noted that the protests are deprived of their political meaning, and the alternative globalization movement becomes de-politicized (2004: 91).

From a more general perspective, Fridolfsson also highlights how the hegemonic discourse structuring these protests diverts attention from broader questions about the organization of liberal democracy. Massive protest against the contemporary form of democracy and the international system could potentially call these systems into question. However, since the protests were understood as illegitimate and apolitical, this did not happen.

The absence of this critique can be understood in light of the previous discussions of relationally created notions, i.e. how the institutionalised political system is also constituted in terms of what it is regarded not to be. This point of departure is known as the *constitutive outside* in the terminology of Laclau and Mouffe. Since the constitutive outside in this case – the criminal, young hooligans – was perceived as an illegitimate threat to the political system, the political system is, consequently, defined as the legitimate, sound and appropriate way of doing politics. As Fridolfsson puts it: "Institutionalised politics thus constantly marks its own existence by deviating from the non-institutional forms of collective action, in order to retain its official status" (2004: 81). The demonstrators were thus, within this hegemony, not threatening or challenging the prevailing political system but were in fact constituting the summit and liberal democracy as "real politics".

8.2.2 Discursive psychology – mapping identities and the legitimation of exploitation

Margaret Wetherell and Jonathan Potter's study of racist discourse in New Zealand (1992) has received a considerable amount of attention and will be used here to exemplify a discourse analysis based on discursive psychology. In line with the approach of discursive psychology, the aim of the study is described as: "to map the broad sweep of sense making about race that goes right across a culture, to characterize the dominant discourses of majority group members in New Zealand and to indicate some of the most important ways in which these discourses are deployed" (Wetherell and Potter, 1992: 97–8).

The interest of the authors is thus in the production of meaning. The processes of meaning-making through which groups and identities are constructed are also seen as a result of people's active deployment of certain discourses. In order to map these discourses, the authors have conducted 81 interviews with white New Zealanders (referred to throughout the book as "Pakeha New Zealanders", following local parlance) and collected a sample of parliamentary proceedings, newspapers, magazine stories and transcripts of television reports. The fact that the authors use interviews, at least in part, is characteristic of discursive psychology. Inspired by conversation analysis, this tradition places an emphasis on everyday discourse, the situated use of language, interaction and variation, which is often especially well represented in this kind of study (1992: 89).

In the analysis of this material, the authors search for interpretative repertoires as a way of identifying shared sense-making about race in New Zealand. In line with their definition of interpretative repertoires, they look for repetition across the corpus, for example, of descriptions, metaphors and arguments in relation to the minority group. However, a key element in the use of this analytical concept is also the search for variation. Their narrow notion of discourse, together with their focus on fragmentation, leads the authors to search for conflicting ways of constructing events, processes and identities. Hesitation, ambivalence, contradiction and inconsistency may be indications of a shift between repertoires and are, therefore, important to observe in the search for variability (Edwards, 2005).

In a general perspective, the Māori people are understood primarily as a cultural group rather than a racial group. However, when looking closely at the descriptions, categorizations and evaluations, the authors were still able to find certain tropes, metaphors and images ("blood", "coffee-colored people", "brown skinned") dating from a previous race discourse intertwined in the current interpretative repertoires. Based on the presence of these recurrent metaphors and images, the authors claim that race persists as a kind of residual sediment (Wetherell and Potter, 1992: 123).

The authors further find that the majority population interviewees draw on two interpretative repertoires concerning the Māori people: culture as heritage and culture as therapy. In the culture as heritage repertoire, culture is seen as something unchangeable and traditional. Culture is described as something stable that one must "hang onto" when "everything else fade [sic] out" (1992: 129). In the latter repertoire, Māori culture is constructed as a psychological need that the Māori people are dependent on. The Māori people are described, for example, as a group that needs to "find their roots" (1992: 132), if they are not to "lose their identity" (1992: 133). More specifically, this analysis is based on quotes like these:

> ... you know the rootless young Polynesian is perhaps a little more obvious than the rootless young European although there's quite a few of those, and for the same reasons surprisingly, is still very visible in streets (mmhm). Um, and part of the recent upsurge in Māoritanga [the Māori culture, Māori way of life] has been to encourage many of them to go back and find their roots, and that's exactly what they needed. (1992: 132)

On the basis of a range of descriptions and evaluations of the Māori people, Wetherell and Potter thus show how the Pakeha New Zealanders construct an understanding of Māori people as possessing a particular cultural background, with which they must remain in close touch in order to live a full life.

The authors later go on to examine the subject positions that the interpretative repertoires, culture as heritage and culture as therapy, offer both the Māori people and the Pakeha population. The Māori people become bearers of their culture, and since it is important to preserve this culture and not end up "rootless", they are also given a duty to act as "museum keepers". They are, for example, not expected to take part in the society of the white New Zealanders, since this may risk leading to rootlessness. Problems that the group faces within society will, in accordance with this understanding, be framed as a psychological problem rather than as a political problem of inequality.

With regard to these subject positions, the Pakeha population is recognized as the norm, people without a particular culture who merely act in accordance with common sense. These representations also influence the group's leeway for action. In accordance with the interpretative repertoires of culture and cultural differences, for the majority group, culture can be seen almost as a playground (1992: 134). Since they are understood as standing outside of culture and are simply members of the common civilization, they are not obliged to take an active part in museum-keeping or cultural preservation. However, they have the choice to do so, if they wish. For them, culture is not a burden or an unavoidable duty but something that could potentially enrich their lives if they choose to take an interest in it. Taking an interest in Māori culture could also construct them as liberal, progressive and egalitarian, and thereby hide the condition of uneven development and domination by the majority group in society at large.

Another focus of interest is the particular ways that the majority population presents or positions itself in relation to the Māori people, using a range of rhetorical devices in order to lend validity and legitimacy to their claims. One example from this study is the attempt of the majority population to raise critical concerns about the Māori people while at the same time presenting those concerns in such a way that they are not associated with their own personal understandings.

Wetherell and Potter explain this dilemma for the Pakeha people as "the attempt to manage a highly racial and obnoxious account without being heard as racist and thus disqualified" (1992: 97). The influence of rhetorical theory is quite clear. This influence directs attention towards the way a particular argument is designed and the fact that arguments are constructed in opposition to competing alternatives (1992: 96).

In terms of the ideological effects of the culture-as-therapy repertoire, the problems faced by the Māori people are understood as psychological problems caused by their rootlessness (1992: 131–3). If only this group were made to feel "good about themselves" or proud of their cultural belonging, their social problems would disappear, according to this understanding. In these ways the exploitation of the Māori can continue, without any guilt being cast on the white majority and without drawing any attention to it or causing any debate.

To summarize the ideological work performed by both of these culture-based interpretative repertoires, differences between the groups are naturalized at the same time as tensions, designations and power relations are downplayed. The interpretative repertoires thus establish an understanding of the groups as naturally different, and all of the differences between the groups are, therefore, possible to understand as 'normal'. It is not the case that one group dominates the other according to this understanding; they are understood as just different and will thus 'naturally' end up in different places and positions in society. Issues that could potentially be understood as political and social are instead defined as cultural problems within these repertoires. Instead of demanding social and political change, the repertoires reproduce an understanding of the Māori people as a group facing a range of identity-based problems that they themselves are responsible for solving.

The authors go on to state that despite the aura of pleasantness and progressiveness that cultural discourse may have, it nonetheless assumes some of the same functions as race discourse previously. On the surface it might appear as if the cultural discourse underlines respect and tolerance of differences. However, at the same time it reproduces a colonial history through which cultural differences are constructed as a naturally occurring fact and inequality and exploitation are downplayed (1992: 137). Based on the understanding of ideological effects in discursive psychology, these interpretative repertoires may be seen as something that legitimizes the prevailing order and reproduces existing power structures.

8.2.3: CDA and the analysis of change

We will now look at an example of discourse analysis in which there is a focus on the details of what is said or written, at the same time as the text is integrated in a 'social practice'. In one of Fairclough's studies, the object of analysis is "The politics of New Labour" in the UK, or more specifically "the language and rhetoric of New Labour" (Fairclough, 2000: 5). Politics is defined as a struggle between different groups over essential values, which is also manifested in language. The power perspective is thereby present from the start in the study, which aims at both analyzing and changing:

> My interest in the politics and language of New Labour starts from my view that it is profoundly dangerous for my fellow human beings for this new form of capitalism to develop unchecked, because it dramatically increases inequality (and therefore injustice and suffering) and because it threatens to make life on earth ecologically unsustainable. I see my analysis of New Labour as within the tradition of critical social science – it seeks knowledge for purposes of human emancipation. (2000: 15-16)

In the study the question is raised as to whether it is possible, as New Labour believes, to continue a policy directed towards social justice and protection from the negative effects of the market while at the same time adopting various neo-liberal ideas. A symbiosis of that kind entails, according to Fairclough, problems both on a linguistic level and in practice.

The empirical material for the study is comprised of different types of New Labour texts (party manifestos, etc.), official publications and speeches primarily by Tony Blair, the party chairperson at that time. In this example, we will limit the presentation to that part of the study that deals with the changed political orientation of New Labour.

The detailed textual analyses use a number of techniques. There is, for instance, an initial sounding-out step in which the occurrence of words and their context are identified. After that, different analytical techniques are used, for instance, analysis of nominalization, metaphors, the use of 'we' and the occurrence of the passive form. Finally, the extent to which a text highlights actors is studied in connection with the description of social processes, and Fairclough also works with the logic of equivalences, i.e. tools that we have previously described in conjunction with the central concepts of discourse theory.

Initially, Fairclough entered a significant amount of New Labour texts and Blair's speeches into a computer application in order to extract key words in New Labour's discourse (see the description of what can be done with certain kinds of QDA applications in Chapter 6 of this volume). The following key words were produced through the data analysis: "We", "Britain", "people", "crime", "welfare", "partnership", "reform", "deliver", "promote", "new", "schools", "deal", "tough", "young", "business" (2000: 18).

The occurrence of certain words does not in itself necessarily say very much about content, but Fairclough studies additionally the occurrence of words in relation to each other (how they collocate, see Chapter 6) and the context in which they occur. The word 'new' occurs 609 times in a 50-page speech by Blair, and 'new' cannot be related to just anything at all for New Labour. 'New' occurs primarily together with 'Labour', 'Britain' and 'Deal'. It consistently involves the introduction of a new policy for British social democracy. An example of closely related words used in different contexts are 'modernisation' and 'reform'. Modernisation is primarily connected to the UK, while reforms are associated with the EU. The term 'reform' is consistently tied to the word 'economic' ('economic reform'), 'markets', and is more or less always used in an EU context. Modernisation is, on the contrary, not linked to 'economic' or 'market'. When Blair speaks about welfare policy in the UK, a divergence arises. Welfare questions are no longer discussed within the framework of 'modernisation' but instead as 'welfare reforms'. Fairclough, unfortunately, does not develop this observation systematically. This type of broadening of discourse analysis would otherwise be a good example of how social practice can be dealt with. However, Fairclough finds that welfare issues are a sensitive area for Labour, since they represent a core value for Labour's voters. The term 'reform' is, furthermore, exceptionally open and appeals to completely different groups of voters and can harmonise with divergent values on welfare policy. 'Reforms' within the welfare field could refer to both more and fewer economic redistributions. Fairclough's view is thus that the word 'reform' more likely masks than clarifies, since it makes no attempt to answer the question "is the welfare state being wound up or truly transformed?" (2000: 19).

Fairclough also analyzes the occurrence of nominalizations and metaphors in a speech by Tony Blair:

> I believe in this country, in its people and our capacity to renew Britain for the age in which we live. We all know this is a world of dramatic change. In technology; in trade; in media and communications [...] Add to this change that sweeps the world, the changes that Britain itself has seen in the 20th century [...] Talk of a modern Britain is not about disowning our past. We are proud of our history. This is simply a recognition of the challenge the modern world poses. [...] To make Britain more competitive, better at generating wealth, but do it on a basis that serves the needs of the whole nation - one nation. (Speech by Blair, in Fairclough 2000: 25-6)

In the above quote, the word 'change' assumes an almost metaphoric character through the clause 'change that sweeps the world'. Change is likened to a tidal wave and is made into something unavoidable that cannot be stopped. The word 'change' is not used as a verb but has been nominalized, which is significant for understanding. Change is often conceived of as a complex set of processes. Particularly in a traditional Labour discourse, cause and effect are pointed out in connection with the social changes being described. Through nominalisation what is the cause and what is the effect in New Labour's parlance are concealed at the same time as the changes are anonymized, since actors and the direction of change are concealed.

That actors are written out of the text is also seen in another analysis of nominalization and metaphors. Fairclough cites a New Labour document that presents technology as a subject, thereby leading other actors to disappear:

> in the increasingly global economy of today, we cannot compete in the old way. Capital is mobile, technology can migrate quickly and goods can be made in low cost countries and shipped to developed markets. British business must compete by exploiting capabilities which its competitors cannot easily match or imitate [...] knowledge, skills and creativity... (White Paper, in Fairclough, 2000: 23)

The metaphor that is employed here is "technology that can migrate" through which more traditional actors behind transformations of capital and technology are made invisible. Within the political left it is otherwise common in analyses of the global economy to take up a specific actor, namely multinational corporations. In New Labour's description of the global economy, multinational corporations are not explicitly present, which implies a change in relation to the traditional Labour discourse.

This brings us to the third part of Fairclough's methods of analysis, the study of which actors are highlighted and which chains of equivalence can be created. When multinational corporations are no longer identified as actors in the New Labour discourse, which actors are represented instead? According to Fairclough, there is one main actor represented in the New Labour discourse, namely the nation-state (Fairclough, 2000: 29). This is a significant change in relation to a more traditional Labour discourse. The UK and other nation-states are represented as competitors, which is made possible by 'Britain' being equated with 'British business'. Here Fairclough constructs a chain of equivalence in which, among others, the following links are included: 'Britain' = 'country' = 'people' = 'we' (2000: 30). What Fairclough wishes to show is that the New Labour discourse on the global economy presupposes that certain expressions can be tied to each other.

Taken together, these textual analyses have shown that the New Labour discourse actually diverges from a traditional Labour discourse on the question of the global economy. Furthermore, the discourse is characterized by significant vagueness and contradictoriness, which becomes apparent when competing values such as 'enterprise' and 'fairness' can be emphasized in the same sentence. This is related to yet another linguistically-oriented tool of analysis for Fairclough, one that draws attention to how binding words such as 'and' and 'as well as' can be used to modify previous meanings or positions. New Labour claims in this way to "go beyond" things that the traditional Labour discourse considered to be incompatible values. It is claimed, for instance, that the theme of free entrepreneurship is no longer in conflict with poverty. Further, in Fairclough's view, New Labour's political discourse is also characterized by the language being unstable and shifting, which could indicate a lack of fixity in the discourse.

Fairclough does not analyze the level of discursive practice in this study. This could, however, be done, since New Labour's political discourse is explicitly related to other discourses, such as Thatcherism, the earlier discourse of US president Bill Clinton, the 'New Democrats' in the US and some social democratic discourses in Europe. In this part of the analysis, he does not use linguistic tools. Instead the conclusions are based on rather general observations. One such is if the material explicitly refers to or is related to other texts with values or presuppositions, they can be said to influence the discourse. In the case of New Labour, the influence of the Thatcherian discourse in particular is very apparent. Despite this influence, there are still elements that can be tied to other, more leftist-oriented traditions, which make it reasonable to see the New Labour discourse as remarkably eclectic.

When social practice is integrated in discourse analysis, the analysis is broadened to something 'outside' of the texts related to New Labour. In addition to other discourses, non-discursive fields can also be included, for instance increased income differences between social groups or demographic changes. This type of analysis is, however, not done systematically but rather in a more ad hoc fashion in conjunction with the textual analyses. An example of this is when Fairclough, on the basis of the ambivalence that characterizes New Labour's political discourse, discusses this discursive instability within the framework of a broader social context.

8.2.4 Steps in discourse analysis

After formulating a research question that is consistent with a discourse analysis tradition, it is necessary to ponder over what materials are needed in order to answer the question. Unfortunately, it is not the case that the discourse to be studied is accessible to the researcher to observe directly in advance. Even if a decision has been made to study, for instance, the EU's education policy discourse, it cannot simply be 'fetched'. Discourses are primarily analytical delimitations, and, therefore, it is necessary to consider and argue for the manner in which manifestations of the chosen discourse are to be delimited and gathered.

An initial question to resolve is whether to use a concept of discourse that includes non-linguistic practices as well. Which ones, in that case, and how are they to be studied? Should, for example, participant observation of educational practitioners be included?

Second, even if limited to a focus on speech and written texts, a decision must be reached about the arenas in relation to which the discourse is to be delimited. In relation to the example of the EU's education policy discourse analyzed in the exercise for this chapter, it is necessary to consider which EU institutions might produce material of relevance to these issues, whether even different national arenas should be studied and, if so, which national authorities and institutions. It is important to state the reasons behind a given sample clearly and to present well-founded arguments for why that sample is representative for the discourse being studied.

Third, it is important to consider the temporal delimitations. How long a time period is needed in order to study a potential discursive change, and, conversely, how long a time span can be said to still reflect 'the present'?

Fourth, the texts that can be considered to reflect the chosen discourse need to be chosen. To look at, for instance, the general policy programmes that different

EU institutions have produced is, naturally, reasonable. However, without supplementary material, this could be too narrow to consider the corpus to reflect the discourse in question. If key material that would certainly say a lot about the discourse in question is not included, the question of validity arises. It is important that the researcher clarifies which considerations they have taken into account and which principles for selection they have applied.

Fifth, a way must be found to create themes or some overarching structure in the material. Otherwise, there is a risk of 'drowning' in the material. In line with Fairclough's study, it is possible to begin with, for example, an introductory computerized corpus analysis. Another way of creating order in the material is to work with analytic questions. These are questions that correspond to the general questions posed in the study but that are more operationalized and which together are expected to be able to provide answers to the general questions.

The sixth step involves the use of the analytical tools. As an example from Fairclough shows, analytical tools from different approaches can be combined. Of greatest importance in the choice of concrete analytical tools is that they are relevant to the research questions and appropriate for the material.

Seventh, and finally, in working with the material, it is important to be transparent. Working with quotes in order to exemplify the salient patterns that are considered to have emerged is a way both of presenting arguments in support of the conclusions and of increasing transparency in the study.

8.3 Critical reflections

In considering the advantages and disadvantages of discourse analysis, we return to some of the discussions under the subheading 'Discourse analysis as philosophy and social theory' (Section 8.1.2). We highlight here two characteristic traits of at least some discourse analyses that can also be seen as good reasons for discourse analysis. After that, we raise some critical issues, followed by a discussion of the problem of reliability in discourse analysis.

8.3.1 Advantages and challenges

The first reason in favour of discourse analysis is the interest in questions of power. Even if there are differences between the approaches presented here in terms of how they view power, power is generally understood as central to discourse analysis. This does not mean that the way in which power is dealt with in discourse analysis is without problems. With regard to a Foucault-oriented perspective, the very broad concept of power can be problematic. If power is everywhere, a reasonable question is: are there any situations without power?

A second reason is the multidisciplinary environment that discourse analysis is situated in. Social science and humanities faculties provide a wealth of different techniques for discourse analysis. Discourse analysis thereby contributes to the creation of a forum for innovations that can be an impetus for methodological development.

On a more general level, we will highlight two problems that afflict different types of discourse analysis to varying degrees. The first criticism is that discourse analysis, with the exception of CDA, can be perceived as relativistic. A common example used to illustrate the dangers with relativism concerns the Holocaust. The logic of the argument is that if relativism is accepted, we must also accept deniers of the Holocaust (see, for example, the discussion in Hacking, 1999). A possible response from a practitioner of discourse analysis is that even if the existence and meaning of an object must be seen discursively, this does not mean that we lack the possibility of determining what is true or false within a given discourse. Ultimately, truth is a matter of consensus within the scientific world and science is held together by the unwritten rules of the game that the research community is organized around (Kuhn, 1996).

On the basis of constructivism, another problem can also be formulated. For the practitioner of discourse analysis it may be difficult to position themselves outside the discourses. The perspective constructs both the observer and the observed. In general, this point is not the object of intense discussion within discourse analysis. Perhaps practitioners of discourse analysis should, to a greater extent, problema-tize the epistemological implications of more constructivist assumptions.

The second problem can be formulated in terms of discourse analysis, and espe-cially discourse theory, focusing only to a limited extent on agents or subjects in the form of people of flesh and blood. Discourse analysis does not offer any theory of individual people or of groups of people in society. On the basis of the example of the native population of New Zealand, we tried to show how discourse analysis can, on the other hand, increase understanding of how collective identities are constructed.

8.3.2 Questions of reliability

Reliability tends to be problematic in certain variants of discourse analysis, at least in the social sciences. Below we discuss these questions in regard to the approaches that have been exemplified.

A first discussion point involves the vagueness or ambiguity in (at least some of) the analytical tools for discourse analysis. For example, the analytical tools for discourse theory can be defined in an unclear manner, and there seems to be different understandings of the analytical concepts among different discourse theoreticians. On the basis of this kind of objection, it is of central importance that a researcher should clarify exactly what the analytical concepts mean.

Another objection involves shortcomings in the application of the chosen analytical tools. For example, in relation to the study in discursive psychology that was discussed, it would have been preferable for the authors (Wetherell and Potter, 1992) to have applied their own definition of the concept of interpretive repertoires in a stricter manner. They do not clarify in their study which specific parts of an interpretive repertoire they believe to have found in the material and what comprise the recurring definitions, metaphors and descriptions. They work in a strikingly open way and do not, as in other types of approaches to discursive psychology (see, for example, Horton-Salway, 2001), work with texts in a more detailed manner, which makes it difficult at times to see how the authors have arrived at their conclusions. Later discourse psychological studies have tried to overcome this issue by working even closer in line with the methodological principles of conversational analysis, thereby favouring more rigorous empirical analyses (Edwards, 2005; Potter and Edwards, 2001).

Third, and finally, there may be shortcomings in relation to working in a systematic fashion. As Fairclough's study showed, the systematic manner that characterized the analysis of the textual level was not reflected in the analysis of the social practice. The steps in this analysis are not as explicitly operationalized and as systematically carried out.

8.4 Discourse analysis and the study of power and other social phenomena

The examples we have presented here show that discourse analysis can be highly useful for studying power and other important social phenomena. In this section, we will thus briefly return to the ways in which questions of power were analyzed in those studies. In line with Laclau and Mouffe's focus on antagonism, Fridolfsson's study raises questions of power by focusing on the struggle over who gets to represent what has happened and who has behaved in a way that promotes democracy or anti-democracy. Questions related to power also arise when the potential challenge to the prevailing political system is delegitimized, which can lead to the legitimacy of the prevailing system being strengthened.

In the study in discursive psychology on how the native population of New Zealand is presented by the majority population, Wetherell and Potter (1992) are interested in how a multicultural "culture discourse" psychologizes and de-politicizes the problems that the native population meets. The focus on power thus equals a focus on the ideological effects that a given discourse has.

CDA studies also take on an explicit ambition to deal with questions of power through their connection with critical theory. In Fairclough's (2000) study of New Labour, the power perspective is intertwined with critical theory and its view of society as characterized by unequal conditions and different forms of exercise of power that favour some but disfavour more.

Summary

On the usefulness of discourse analysis

- Discourse analysis can be used for, among other things, studying debates, changes in viewpoints over time and their discursive preconditions. The approach can highlight either commonalities or tensions and antagonisms.
- Discourse analysis can be used for mapping out the construction of identities, for example, by analyzing subject positions ('the people', 'Swedes', 'Communists').
- Studies of identity construction can be integrated with issues of power. What leads to Group X being marginalized?
- Discourse analysis can also deal with issues of power by studying different kinds of order, such as cultural hegemony or gender power.
- Discourse analysis does not claim to explain phenomena in terms of cause and effect.
- Discourse analysis does not put societal actors centre stage in the analysis.

How to go about doing it

- The discourse or discourses that are to be studied need to be delimited. It is necessary to decide on a concept of discourse and a fixed time period.
- Both the choice of source material and the delimitation of the discourses are of central importance. The choice should always be discussed and justified.
- Ultimately, the method is determined by the research question. As we have seen, a study of identities can be conducted in different ways with the help of different discourse analysis designs. As always, it is important to formulate good reasons for the approach that you choose.
- Since discourse analysis strongly emphasizes the importance of language, that social relations are revealed through language, the material must be read very carefully. It often requires close reading. After gaining an overview of the material, it is necessary to work through the material a number of times.
- Within discourse analysis there are different ways of sorting the content in the text. For example, the textual content can be structured with the help of analytic questions or more quantitative techniques.
- In relation to the choice and use of concrete analytical tools, these can be combined on the basis of the different approaches in order to be appropriate for the research question and the material.

———————————————— Suggested reading ————————————————

Jørgensen and Phillips' (2002) *Discourse Analysis as Theory and Method* contains a comprehensive and useful account of all three of the approaches that have been presented in this chapter. Another illustrative introduction to the general discourse analytical field can be found in Reiner Keller's (2013) *Doing Discourse Research*. This book presents a broad range of discourse analytical approaches in a hands-on manner. In a similar vein James Paul Gee's *How to do Discourse Analysis: A Toolkit* (2011), Barbara Johnstone's *Discourse Analysis* (2008), Rodney Jones's *Discourse Analysis: A Resource Book for Students* (2012) and Brian Paltridge's *Discourse Analysis: An Introduction* (2006) present a toolbox for linguistically-oriented discourse analysis.

For those who wish to read more about the discourse theory approach, there is *Laclau and Mouffe: the Radical Democratic Imaginary* (Smith, 1998). Another broad and thorough review of different traditions in discourse analysis is Howarth (2000). In addition, there is an anthology published in the early 2000s, *Laclau: a Critical Reader* (Critchley and Marchart, 2004). Torfing (1999; see also Howarth and Torfing, 2005) also offers a thorough presentation of discourse theory in *New Theories of Discourse: Laclau, Mouffe and Žižek*. Lastly, one may also point to a prominent tendency within the field, namely the 'logics approach'. This approach to discourse theory has striven to give the discourse theory approach a more scientific status with explanatory ambitions, and has been developed by David Howarth and Jason Glynos (2007).

In relation to literature that deals with discursive psychology, a good starting point can be Jonathan Potter and Margaret Wetherell's book *Discourse and Social Psychology* (1987), which has played a central role in the development of discursive psychology. This particular form of discourse analysis was developed further in their book *Mapping the Language of Racism* (1992), which provides an account of one of the most extensive studies within discursive psychology.

A critique of discourse theory from the perspective of discursive psychology is developed in the article "Positioning and interpretative repertoires: Conversation analysis and post-structuralism in dialogue", in *Discourse and Society* by Margaret Wetherell (1988). In this article the author describes how discursive psychology tries to marry poststructuralism with conversation analysis and how their use of the concept of subject positions differs from that of Laclau and Mouffe.

In the anthology *Discourse as Data: A Guide for Analysis* (2001), Nigel Edley presents a pedagogical step-by-step model of how to conduct an analysis based on a discursive psychology approach. Mary Horton-Salway's chapter in the same book exemplifies an alternative type of discursive psychology approach. This approach leans more heavily towards the rhetorical dimension of text and talk in social interaction.

An up-to-date and easily accessible summary of Fairclough's version of CDA can be found in the introductory chapter in the third edition of *Language and Power* (Fairclough, 2015). Other introductions can be found in *Discourse and Social Change* and in *Critical Discourse Analysis*, in which there is also a fine presentation of critical discourse analysis. There is a revised and expanded edition of the latter work (Fairclough, 1992, 1995, 2010). *Analyzing Discourse* is a more recent work by Fairclough that is also a kind of introduction but one that is more clearly organized and pedagogic (Fairclough, 2003). For those who are interested in empirical studies of the economic crisis from a CDA perspective, there is also *Political Discourse Analysis* (2012), in which Fairclough and Fairclough integrate a clearer focus on argument analysis within a CDA study.

A hands-on guide to critical discourse analysis can be found in Machin and Mayr (2012). In a similar vein, Terry Locke's *Critical Discourse Analysis* (2004) is a brief but comprehensive introduction to CDA as a method.

An approach closely related to CDA is discursive linguistics. This is more historically oriented, and the critical perspective is less prominent. It is a form of corpus linguistics. A detailed presentation of a methodological model for how an analysis of this kind should be conducted is presented by Spitzmüller and Warnke (2011) in *Critical Discourse Studies*, 8(2).

—————————————— **Exercise** ——————————————

Conflicting values in EU education policies

Education policy has a growing importance at EU level. Different EU institutions formulate guidelines that will have an impact at a national level. But formulating policies in this specific field creates trade-offs between different values. The purpose of discourse analysis is often, as shown in this chapter, to identify contrasting and conflicting values or to find ways of making sense of a particular issue. These different values and representations are relevant to analyze since they are, according to a discourse analytical point of view, connected to wider ongoing power struggles.

The task

In the following example you are asked to search for different discourses structuring the EU's politics of education.[2] Thus, you are asked to use a narrow discourse definition according to which 'discourse' is linguistic practice, and the kind of definition stating that a discourse is a particular perspective on a phenomenon.

1   What discourses concerning education and the purpose of education can be found in the material?
2   What subject positions can be found in the material for, among others, students and citizens?
3   How are these discourses and subject positions related to relations of power and the struggle for hegemony?

(After working on this exercise you can check the suggested analysis in Chapter 9.)

The texts

The texts to be analyzed are two documents from two EU institutions, the EU Council and the European Parliament. These documents have been chosen with regard to three general principles. To begin with, they were picked because they can be seen as key documents regarding current educational politics within the EU. Secondly, they address the general educational field rather than a particular sub-field, such as higher education or teacher education. Thirdly, they are chosen because, at the time of designing this exercise, they were up-to-date and they structured the educational policy of the EU up until the year 2020. Therefore, the 'Council Conclusions on a strategic framework for European cooperation in education and training' ("ET 2020")and 'Recommendation 2006/962/EC of the European Parliament and of the Council on key competences for lifelong learning' are the selected material for the analysis of the EU's educational discourse.

---

[2]In the development of this example, we have been inspired by Lena Sjöberg's (2011) doctoral thesis on Swedish educational policies.

Council conclusions of 12 May 2009 on a strategic framework for European cooperation in education and training ("ET 2020")

1   In the period up to 2020, the primary goal of European cooperation should be to support the further development of education and training systems in the Member States which are aimed at ensuring:

   (a)   the personal, social and professional fulfilment of all citizens;

   (b)   sustainable economic prosperity and employability, whilst promoting democratic values, social cohesion, active citizenship, and intercultural dialogue.

2   Such aims should be viewed in a worldwide perspective. Member States acknowledge the importance of openness to the world at large as a prerequisite for the global development and prosperity which - through the provision of excellent and attractive education, training and research opportunities - will help the European Union achieve its objective of becoming a world-leading knowledge economy.

3   European cooperation in education and training for the period up to 2020 should be established in the context of a strategic framework spanning education and training systems as a whole in a lifelong learning perspective. Indeed, lifelong learning should be regarded as a fundamental principle underpinning the entire framework, which is designed to cover learning in all contexts − whether formal, non-formal or informal − and at all levels: from early childhood education and schools through to higher education, vocational education and training and adult learning. Specifically, the framework should address the following four strategic objectives (detailed further below):

   1   Making lifelong learning and mobility a reality.

   2   Improving the quality and efficiency of education and training.

   3   Promoting equity, social cohesion and active citizenship.

   4   Enhancing creativity and innovation, including entrepreneurship, at all levels of education and training.

You can find the URLs under 'Council of the European Union' (2009) and 'European Parliament and Council' (2006) in the bibliography. For the full text and the other document to analyze, please visit the companion website at **https://study.sagepub.com/boreus andbergstrom**.

9

Suggested Analyses

Kristina Boréus and Göran Bergström

9.1 Chapter 2, Content Analysis

There are many possible ways to work with this exercise. Below we suggest an analysis in which words are counted. The exercise could be part of a pilot-study for a comparative study about changes in the political rhetoric by British Labour after the late 1960s up until the mid-2010s when the winds of change were blowing through the party. We formulate two hypotheses to be tested.

H1: There will be the same changes of frequency of words between the two Labour manifesto corpora as found in the Swedish public debate: 'democracy', 'equality' and 'solidarity' would be less frequent in the later corpus, while 'justice'/'fairness' and 'freedom'/'liberty' would be more frequent.

There are also other words that could be hypothesized to become more or less frequent when the ideological debate moved focus. Frequencies of important terms like 'state', 'market' and 'business' could have changed, with references to the state being less common and references to market and business more frequent.

H2: 'State' will be less and 'market' and 'business' more common in the later compared to the earlier Labour manifesto corpus.

To test the hypotheses the coding scheme in Table 9.1 was constructed.

In a first step we compared the length of the corpora, finding that the second corpus was much larger than the first one: 16,510 words for the first two manifestos compared to 47,641 for the second two.

In a second step the selected words were searched. It was necessary to go through all the occurrences to sort out those words that, according to the instructions, should not be counted. This resulted in the first count for the word 'market' in the early corpus showing 14 occurrences, 8 for being part of the name 'the

Table 9.1 Coding scheme and instructions for a pilot-study on ideological change

1. Note the name of the source.
2. Note the number of occurrences of the following terms:

business

democracy

equality

fairness

freedom

justice

liberty

market

solidarity

state

Coding instruction: All forms of and compounds with these nouns, except for when they occur in names, should be noted. Thus note both 'equality' and 'inequality', 'market' and 'market forces' but not 'Social Democracy'. Note only nouns, thus not 'free', 'democratic' etc.

Common **Market'** and 1 for '**market**ing'. That the 8 occurrences in the name of the European Common Market should not be counted was already clear from the instructions. We also decided that 'marketing' should not be counted. Thus only 5 occurrences remained. The search for 'state' also gave rise to new decisions. It was clear from the outset that 'United **States**' should not be counted, being a name. It also seemed obvious that words like **state**ment and **state**d should not count; neither should e**state** and '**state** … of health'. It was also decided that 'Secretary of **State'** should not be counted, which meant that a new rule could be added to the original ones, namely that words in titles should not be counted. There were a few similar decisions made for other terms. For a wider study all these decisions should be added to the coding instructions which should then be tested again.

In a third step the relative frequencies, i.e. the number of occurrences of a term divided by the total number of words in each corpus, were calculated.

Just as in the Swedish corpus and in line with H1, the frequency of 'democracy', and 'equality' dropped, while 'freedom' increased. 'Solidarity' did not occur at all, which might reflect a difference between Swedish and British left-wing rhetoric. 'Liberty' occurred only once in the entire material (which does not make it reach 0.01% of the total number of words). While 'fairness' became slightly more common, 'justice' did not, which contradicts H1. This difference between the two countries might be related to the difference in the usage of 'equality', with the reason for the rise in the Swedish context perhaps being that the labour movement replaced it with the more neutral term 'justice', something that did not take place in the British Labour manifestos.

The differences between the corpora in relative frequency of the terms 'business' and 'market' support H2, indicating that business and markets had

Table 9.2 Relative frequencies of certain words in British Labour party manifestos

Term	Relative frequency in 1970+1974 corpus, %	Relative frequency in 1997+2001 corpus, %	Support or contradiction of H1 and H2
democracy	0.07	0.02	supp. H1
equality	0.06	0.01	supp. H1
fairness	0.00	0.02	supp. H1
freedom	0.00	0.04	supp. H1
justice	0.02	0.00	contr. H1
liberty	0.00	0.00	n/a
solidarity	0.00	0.00	n/a
business	0.00	0.16	supp. H2
market	0.03	0.10	supp. H2
state	0.01	0.12	contr. H2

become more important topics in the party rhetoric. We leave it to the reader to reflect over different possible reasons for the word 'state' not behaving in line with our expectations.

It should be kept in mind that only four manifestos have been examined and that larger corpora from the time periods should be compared for more stable conclusions to be drawn: there are many things that could affect the content of a single manifesto. Apart from widening the material, a study of the wording could, as a next step, analyze the words in context (which is easy with the concordance function included in packages like WordSmith or the freeware AntConc (see Box 2.1) but which can also be done with Word's search function). Have the terms perhaps changed meaning? Does 'democracy' for example refer to the same phenomena in the later corpus as in the earlier corpus?

In a content analysis of a more qualitative kind, a coding scheme for expressions of ideas could be developed and used. Another way would be to develop a set of more open questions about ideological change to pose to both corpora and use it to systematically compare policy areas. The coding could also be carried out inductively, starting in the manifesto texts and looking for differences of relevance in relation to the research questions.

9.2 Chapter 3, Argumentation Analysis

In a first step the argumentation is restructured in a pro et contra list. The issue expression is taken to be the claim that young people should not smoke. There are four pro arguments found while parts of the text cannot be related to that claim. The implicit premises for the pro arguments have been interpreted, as shown in Table 9.3.

The first part of the evaluation is the critical discussion of the tenability of the arguments. P1 seems to be relatively easy to believe – or could it perhaps be the

Table 9.3 Tobacco industry argumentation analysis: Pro et contra list

---

IE: Young people should not smoke

P1: Smoking has always been an adult custom.

(ɸP1): Young people should not follow adult customs.

P2: Even for adults smoking has become very controversial.

(ɸP2): Young people should not do what is controversial for adults.

P3: Even we as a tobacco company do not think it is a good idea for young people to smoke.

(ɸP3): Companies normally want people to use its products to make a profit so when they do not there must be a particularly strong reason.

P4: If you take up smoking just to prove you're an adult, you're really proving just the opposite.

(ɸP4): You should not take up smoking for the wrong reasons and acting immaturely is no good.

P5: You might not be old enough to smoke.

(ɸP5): If you are too young to smoke you should refrain from doing so.

---

case that almost as many non-adults as adults smoke? P2 is true given that 'controversial' is taken to mean that the habit has been criticized and warned against, while there are people that defend it (at least from the tobacco industry). P3 is difficult to test, unless one sees the advertorial as proof enough. The claim also needs precision: who exactly are 'we'; certainly not everyone working for the company. In what way can a company 'think'? P4 is an evaluation that seems difficult to prove as true or false. P5 really says very little. 'You' might be a person of any age capable of understanding the text and the claim begs the question at what age you are old enough to smoke. Thus, no argument is apparently false but some are quite vague.

The next step is the discussion of the relevance of the arguments, i.e. of the tenability of their premises. (ɸP1) is apparently a weakly supported claim as it stands: it seems to totally depend on the issue of whether we think that young people should do as adults do or not, thus the relevance of P1 could be seriously questioned. (ɸP2) has the same problem. There are, for instance, things that are controversial for adults to do that might not be seen as controversial if done by young people, such as living in a family without contributing economically. (ɸP3) appears as the strongest claim out of the premises but it says nothing about the reasons in this particular case. (ɸP4) is as difficult to prove as true or false as the argument it is a premise for, but it could be noted that it implies (in a weak sense; it does not follow logically) that there might be right reasons to take up smoking. (ɸP5) as it stands could well be supported by rather strong arguments about young people's health but no such arguments are provided.

By judging the tenability and relevance of the arguments, the degree of rational persuasiveness of the argumentation and thus the support of the issue expression appear modest. Was the intended effect of the text really to make young people refrain from smoking? When the third evaluation question is asked, whether all strong and relevant arguments for or against the issue expression have been included, this question becomes even more pertinent: it is obvious that the most relevant arguments in support of the claim that young people should not smoke – that smoking causes cancer and endangers the smoker's health in other ways and that it is addictive – have been left out of the argumentation.

Yet another doubt about the sincerity of the issue expression is formulated in van Eemeren's analysis: "… it is already clear from the start that the arguments that are put forward by Reynolds will not appeal to young people. It is more than doubtful [...] that considerations of age and convention will be decisive reasons for young people to decide not to smoke" (van Eemeren, 2010: 21).

The answer to question (1) is that the degree of rational persuasiveness of the argumentation is rather low, particularly since the most important arguments for the issue expression are left out.

A rhetorical perspective could shed more light on this text and help in answering question (2). The analysis showed that from a logos perspective the argumentation is not very persuasive. But texts of this genre are normally not based on logos. What seems to be at stake is instead the ethos of the tobacco company: it should not be seen as trying to persuade young people to smoke. This is but an educated guess, of course. In a wider study (in which broader research questions should be formulated) of this and other tobacco companies' reactions to the kind of criticism mentioned, more material should be analyzed and other means of collecting information, such as interviews, could be used.

9.3 Chapter 4, Qualitative Analysis of Ideas and Ideological Content

The first two questions dealt with the chapter on the policy area to end sexual violence (G6). As answers to the first two questions, I would suggest the following skeleton of practical reasoning in the chapter:

G6: 'End violence against women and girls'.

D6: 1) 'There is insufficient support and sanctuary … ',

2) 'low prosecution rate … '

3) 'special forms of violence…that need special expertise'

… and so on in aspects 4 and 5 of the policy area.

P6: 1) 'Sanctuary for those fleeing abuse!'

2) 'Prosecute violence against women and girls!'

3) 'Establish specialist support for Asian and black women'

… and so on in aspects 4 and 5 of the policy area.

Table 9.4 V-D-P triads in the WE party manifesto

	Values	Descriptions	Prescriptions
Fundamental level (I): Philsosophical (1. Based on political philosophy)	'Women´s achievement of their full potential' (V1) (explicit)	a) 'Nowhere in the world do women enjoy full equality' (explicit) (Dsit) b) Inequality hinders → the achievement of women´s 'full potential' (explicit) (Dme)	'Bring about equality for women!' (P) (explicit)
Fundamental level (II): Theoretical (2. Based on economic theory)	1. Top position for Britain in the competition on the world market (V2). (implicit)	a) Countries need 'talent' and 'potential' to compete on the world market (implicit-explicit) (Dsit) b) The lack of equality for women → is a waste of 'talent' and 'potential' (explicit) (Dme) c) 'Gender equality means a more vibrant economy' (explicit) (Dme)	'Bring about equality for women!' (P) (explicit)
(3. Based on political theory)	2. A society without internal strife (V3) (explicit)	Gender equality → 'means a society at ease with itself', that is, individuals not living 'at odds' with each other but in 'mutual respect'. (unclear but explicit) (Dme)	'Bring about equality for women!' (P) (explicit)
(4. Based on cheerful nationalist ideology)	3. Britain on top (V4) (implicit, but obvious)	Eliminating gender inequality → will make Britain 'take the lead' and 'not lag behind other countries' in gender equality (explicit) (Dme)	'Bring about equality for women!' (P) (explicit)

The other questions – on the additional fundamental values of the preamble page of the WE party manifesto – hinted to allude to Britain as a nation. Answering the third, fourth and fifth questions, I suggest in the table below four fundamental values and their accompanying four V-D-P–triads. I also suggest that they make up a combined inner structure of practical reasoning on the fundamental level of the party ideology.

Regarding the sixth question, one might possibly think of the inclusion of these four values and triads as a kind of argumentative overkill; as if the party's position would get stronger if it piled up heaps of attractive fundamental values. Another possibility is to regard these as a strategy for emphasizing the 'mainstream' character of the WE, attaching the party to established traditional tenets in the British political culture, shared by the main political parties. Deeper still, one could regard these formulations as a profound and cunning manoeuvre to attach and include *gender equality* as a new element in this British political culture. One could also regard them in the historical light of the liberal idea tradition itself. We shall not forget that liberalism in Britain (from 1830 onwards arguing for extended voting rights, for abolished corn tolls, later for a social welfare state) from the beginning presented the liberal ideas as the age-old national spirit of a free people, directed against the privileged positions of the powers of the old society (the Monarchy, the aristocracy and the Church). So the paradoxical appearance of 'the nation' in the preamble might turn out to be nothing less than old left liberalism in Britain, now implicitly adding patriarchy and gender inequality to the established row of reactionary political powers of the old society.

9.4 Chapter 5, Narrative Analysis

The exercise suggested for getting a feel for this approach was to analyze the 'Angola prison rodeo' report and then compare it to the narrative of the Ugandan boy-soldier used in Chapter 5. The first step of the analysis was done for you, by structuring the 'Angola' story in a table according to the coding scheme with the story in the left column and the visuals in the right column. The suggested solution outlined below sets out what could have been done after that.

First, the transcript of the Angola prison rodeo was parsed using the coding scheme presented in Chapter 5, which breaks down the report into its narrative components. This could be called the coding step.

Table 9.5   Narrative components of 'US Rodeo Rehab'

Abstract	*How does the newsreader introduce the report? What does he or she say it will be about? What does the text at the bottom of the screen or behind the newsreader say the topic is?*
	The newsreader introduces the report by telling us that in the American South, where rodeos are popular, one stands out because instead of cowboys, untrained black convicts compete. White Americans pay money to watch them get thrown off bucking broncos and trampled by bulls. An Al Jazeera reporter went to watch this very controversial event.
	The lead-in and heading of the event tell us the event is the 'Angola prison rodeo', not the 'Louisiana rodeo'. He says it will be about a popular, but controversial event.
Orientation	
time	The time is unspecified, but understood to be the present. We are told that this is an annual event, so we understand that this is not a one-off incident, but something that recurs.
place	*Where do the unfolding events take place?*
	The events take place on one site, but in many places.
	The newsreader's lead-in clearly indicates that the events take place in the South: the American South and, more precisely, the state of Louisiana. The entire report takes place at the rodeo held by the state prison. "Locally, the prison is known as Angola, or more simply, 'the farm'."
	So the events take place in:
	–the South
	–the American South
	–Louisiana
	–a prison called 'Angola'/'the farm'

participants	Who speaks or acts in this story?
	We listen to white men and women from Louisiana who have brought their families to the rodeo, and to the prison warden.
	We watch the black prisoners try to avoid being hurt or killed by stampeding bulls and bucking broncos.
	One black inmate, selling goods rather than competing, says he enjoys it and that his family comes every year.
situation	What is the starting point or equilibrium?
	The equilibrium is an annual festival that offers something to everyone. The local whites get an enjoyable day out with their families. The prison warden gets to implement his policy of rehabilitation. The inmates get a day out of prison and a chance to earn money: "For many, it's a highlight of life behind bars."
Complicating action	What happens to destabilize the equilibrium?
	It turns out that the prison competitors are untrained and without protective equipment, so place themselves in danger by taking part. Injuries are common.
Resolution	What finally happened?
	Unclear. We don't know what happens in the end: staff don't tell us how many people get hurt and we don't get close to talk to inmates/competitors. The last interview is with an inmate who says he enjoys it, but the last shot is of a man being thrown from a bucking bronco.
	"At Angola prison, the average sentence is 95 years. Most of these men will die and be buried here. For them, this rodeo is a taste of freedom. Even if it's only for a few seconds."
Coda	How does the reporter return us to the studio and the rest of the broadcast, and how does the newsreader return viewers to the present?
	The narrator returns the perspective to the present by commenting at the end that most of the competitors will die and be buried at Angola prison, because the average sentence is 95 years. The immediate present gives them a few moments of freedom.

Following this coding came the analysis. In this step, the two news reports ('Uganda' and 'Angola') were compared by reflecting on answers to the questions posed in the exercise about what can be said about the differences between the stories, whether there are important features of the news reports that evade the coding scheme, and whether there are features in the coding scheme that are absent or unarticulated in the news reports.

As explained in Chapter 5, narratives can be found on many levels. A news report is a narrative, often constructed from component narratives (the stories told by people interviewed in the report). Taken together, reports from one channel can be seen as part of the more general, overarching narrative of that channel – in this case, Al Jazeera English, which claims to represent the 'global south' and to give 'a voice to the voiceless'. What insights does a comparison of the two stories give us into that overarching Al Jazeera narrative?

Certain aspects of Table 9.5, found to be particularly relevant to these two texts, were transferred to a new table in which coding results from the two reports were placed side-by-side and developed to facilitate an answer to the first question.

In what way do the stories of the Ugandan boy soldier and the Angolan rodeo differ? What can be said about those differences?

Table 9.6 Comparison of 'US Rodeo Rehab' and 'Ugandan boy soldier returns home'

	Angola	Uganda
time	The time is now, but the event has happened before and will recur. On a connotative level, it is static.	On a connotative level, the time of this narrative is a time of transition, from a troubled past to a hopeful future.
place	We are confined in one place: the rodeo, which clearly divides black inmates and white spectators. The space of this narrative is guarded – by protective gates at the rodeo (restraining the raging bulls) and in intermediate shots, and barbed wire surrounding the penitentiary. The black men in need of rehabilitation are confined within these spaces, where they are watched by prison guards and members of the public who come to watch the spectacle.	The story unfolds in a liminal place, or a threshold. The rehabilitation centre is a halfway house, a respite or transit from captivity and darkness to home and warmth. It is marked by the traumas of the boys and men who have passed through it (the murals). But it is a place for them to leave those marks and move on. The moving car is also a narrative vehicle, connecting the past to the future.
participants	The reporting style is naturalist. The reporter is invisible and lets the white rodeo visitors tell him in their own words why they think it's fun to watch unarmed black inmates get charged by wild bulls. But it is the whites who come across as the Others, rather than the silent black inmates.	The reporting style is naturalist. The returning boy soldier is in the centre, not the journalist. A person who could be given the character of a villain, if not a monster, is given a human face and a name. The boy who has witnessed and committed atrocities is depicted as polite, quiet and well-dressed, and given the character of victim kidnapped as a child. The other person who speaks is the African woman who helps him on his way from one life back to the village; from captivity to a new existence, by helping him talk about and deal with his violent past.
situation	The starting point is a moment of freedom for black men who have committed a crime and will never be returned to society.	The starting point is the neutral space of the rehabilitation centre, and a young man now ready to leave it and return to society.
Complicating action	The moment of freedom may hurt the black criminals, who are unarmed and untrained.	The journey moves the narrative forward, taking Dennis away from the no man's land of the rehabilitation centre to the unknown territory of what was once home. The moving vehicle is a powerful image, and as Dennis and the viewer are situated in the back seat, they are not in control. The destination (home, or exile?) is unknown.

	Angola	Uganda
Resolution	Most of the competitors will die and be buried at Angola prison, because the average sentence is 95 years. The local whites are safe, but the blacks are stuck where they are, and not going anywhere.	Two phrases are key. 'He's safe,' says the reporter. It is an open statement, as whether Dennis is now safe from his former captors, or from himself and his troubled past, or safe from exile, is unclear. 'He arrives', says the reporter at the close of the report. This signals a beginning of a story, rather than the end.
Evaluation	The whites emphasize that the black offenders had a choice when they decided to commit a crime. The journalist tells us many were first-time offenders, but will never be released from prison. The story is told in such a way that the warden's claim this is rehabilitation seems both nonsensical and hypocritical. By presenting the Louisianan approach to rehabilitation, its opposite (although absent in this report) seems to make more sense. The white southerners in this report seem strange.	The resort to violence is not necessarily a matter of choice. Redemption and reconciliation are the way forward. This is our business. By placing the viewer beside Dennis on his journey, we are implicated in the transition from war (absent) to home (the pictured space of resolution).

By contrasting the 'Angola' method of rehabilitation with the more humane treatment by Ugandans of Dennis, it is the white Americans who come across as strange and inhuman. The space of Angola is closed and static – not open and forward-moving as in Uganda. The former is a space without hope or forgiveness. The latter is the opposite. The viewer is invited to reflect on which is the most fruitful approach.

The two Al Jazeera stories about the rehabilitation of black men who have committed violent crimes are examples of how otherness can be grasped in terms of contrasts, in the Saussurean sense (i.e. red is not-blue). Americans are 'other' in the piece about the rodeo, because the justice system can be seen to be unjust, and its rehabilitation measures as non-rehabilitation, when contrasted with the Ugandan method that Dennis, the former boy soldier, experiences. 'Proper distance' not only preserves *the other* through difference (the average viewer can never know what it means to be a child soldier who has been kidnapped and forced to commit atrocities), it also creates understanding through proximity (when the viewer is positioned by his side as he travels from the intermediate space of the rehabilitation centre home to the village, and invited to celebrate his return from the dead).

Are there important features of the primary source material (the text) that cannot be captured in the framework? If so, what additional or alternative questions could be posed to the text?

The strength of narrative is that it draws on our understanding of other stories, and students who have analyzed the report from Louisiana find themselves reminded of the inhabitants of Panem, the ruling class of the centre, who delight in the spectacle of The Hunger Games. An additional question could probe that intertextuality.

Are there elements in the framework that are absent from the material, and if so are they irrelevant or unarticulated?

The framework worked well for this analysis. Certain aspects of it, found to be particularly relevant to these two texts, were transferred above to a new chart in which the two reports were placed side-by-side. Just as you may wish to borrow only some items from the coding scheme, it is up to you to add elements or features that might do better justice to your own primary source material.

9.5 Chapter 6, Metaphor Analysis and Critical Linguistics

Metaphor analysis

India is conceptualized by the metaphors as a living creature, as in 'the day when modern India was born.' The most conspicuous metaphors for India are those that conceptualize the country not only as a living creature but also as a good mother and its inhabitants as her children:

INDIA IS A GOOD MOTHER AND THE INDIANS ARE HER CHILDREN
- We are all equal *children* before our *mother*
- *Mother* is our protection from evil and oppression, our symbol of life and prosperity

This conceptual metaphor highlights unity. India is one and all Indians are siblings. It also points to the need for obedience: children ought to obey good mothers since these are grown-up, know better than children and will act in the children's best interest.

Clashing interests are concealed when the nation is conceptualized as an individual, a person. This is emphasized in the expressions where India is described as a person, who makes requests and who strives for goals, a person with a will (but not necessarily a mother):

INDIA IS A PERSON
- India *asks* each one of us, in whatsoever role we play in the complex drama of nation-building, to do our duty with integrity, commitment and unflinching loyalty
- all that new India *strives for*

Thus, India is conceptualized as an individual who is the mother of the Indians and is protective and asks of her children that they be committed and loyal. This is drawn to a point where India is conceptualized as divine, a goddess with Indians as her worshippers, as in "We are all, across the divide of party and region, partners at the altar of our motherland".

Analyzing the metaphors for the nation, we find the individual person or a group of persons in "the Nation took a pledge". Through other metaphors, the nation is perceived of as a building:

A NATION IS A BUILDING

- A modern nation *is built on* some *basic fundamentals*
- nation-*building*
- The *foundations* [for the nation] *were laid* through our Constitution

Highlighted in this conceptual metaphor is stability and planned construction. Rapid unplanned change is downplayed.

Individual human beings, family and buildings – perhaps homes – are thus associations here. That unity and stability are conveyed in the message by the metaphors used by the president is not very surprising in a speech to the citizens of a large, multi-ethnic nation, with its history of domestic tensions and strife. A larger study would confirm whether this is common in Indian political elite rhetoric.

Metaphors of the nation as a person, or more specifically as a woman or a mother, are widespread. They are part of modern nationalism, and not only in India. The conceptual metaphor of the nation as a mother is used about the UK but also about many other nations in languages apart from English. The building metaphor is probably also quite common.

Take some time to discuss how the metaphors for nations found in the other corpus you have analyzed differ and resemble those found in the Indian president's speeches and how similarities and differences could be explained.

Critical linguistics

Making a simple qualitative content analysis, using the first three questions of the exercise, is a quick way to get an overview of the text content. The different parts of the text where the answers to questions 1–3 are offered can be highlighted. This part of the analysis is only exemplified below.

To answer the question "What problems is the president addressing in his speech?" the following parts of the text were coded:

> "It is intolerable that in this day and age, women are still being exposed to barbaric brutality and violence because they are women."

> "Violence or fear of violence reduces the freedom and development of everyone, particularly our women and children."

"But more than that, it diminishes our *society* when it allows such inhuman treatment of its women rather than guarantees their safety, security and equal rights."

"… addressing malnutrition, maternal mortality"

A few formulations implying the existence of problems in a vague way, like the statement about the award winners' "effort to make a difference and improve the condition of lives of women in our country", have not been coded.

Answering the second question, "What are the causes of the problems, according to [the president]?", gives a meagre result; the closest to a statement about causes is "… a converse dimension of our society has, of late, been revealing its grotesque nature – every now and then".

Using the third code question, "What are the proposed solutions?", reveals that much of the text deals with possible means to change conditions. There are some rather vague formulations like "[w]e must remind ourselves" that every society member has the right to live in security, peace and dignity, and that the mindset of "our people" must evolve to realize that it is in society's interest to create the conditions for women's free choice. There are also more concrete suggestions, like the proposal to use community programmes for the implementation of government policies and the concrete development programmes mentioned. Other proposals for how women should be empowered include that the government, the private sector and civil society organizations should cooperate, and there is mention of everyone working together to develop legal, administrative and other measures to "ensure the safety and security of our mothers and sisters". The president also advises women not to wait for others to "give" them what is their right but that the minds of "our women" should be empowered. He also assumes that gender equality is (part of) the solution, "a key driver" for economic growth and social progression.

The analysis so far shows, in sum, that the problems addressed are brutality and violence against women and children, which reduce individual freedom but also "diminish" society. Concretely, malnutrition and maternal mortality are also mentioned. No clear causes of the problems are formulated. The text emphasizes solutions that include the cooperation of various actors for the empowerment of women, which, in its turn, is seen as a way of promoting economic growth and social progress.

A critical linguistic analysis fleshes out the description above in important ways. In a first step, we list all the participants and the frequency with which they are referred to.

Some choices regarding the classification in non-obvious cases were necessary. The pronoun 'we' is, for instance, notoriously difficult to classify as it is often unclear to whom apart from the speaker/writer it refers. In this case all 'we's have been interpreted as referring to "us in India", which is likely but not self-evident

Table 9.7 Participants referred to in the president's address (in order of appearance)

I, the president	14
women	24
we (in India), us, ourselves	7
men	1
them (women and men)	1
institutions for the cause of women	2
the nation (of India)	1
others	1
recipients of the price, awardees	4
Ladies and Gentlemen	2
every society member	1
everyone	1
children	1
Government	3
civil society	1
the public at large	1
mothers	1
sisters	1
our people	2
girls	1
Ministry of Women and Child Development	2
the private sector	1
civil society organizations	1
Swami Vivekananda	2
a nation, country	4

for all instances. We have chosen not to include deleted actors in the way Sykes does in the sample study.[1]

The groundwork should always be done carefully but in this case some results are so striking that small classification inconsistencies will not cause important reliability problems. The most striking result is that women are in total focus, while men are hardly mentioned. The second most prominent participant is the

---

[1] In most studies of this kind there will be classification problems. This is not a drawback for the study as long as the analysis is consistent and the choices of classification are not linguistically contra-intuitive. Choices that are not self-evident should be commented on, particularly if another choice would have affected the answers to the research questions.

president, the holder of the speech. The main participants in the processes referred to in this speech on women's conditions in India are thus the president-speaker and women. We also have a conspicuous absence: that of men who are only mentioned in "the achievements of exceptional women and men".

As found by the content analysis, violence against women is described as an important problem. Analyzing, in a second step, nominalizations, "violence" is revealed to be one: it is violence that "reduces the freedom and development" of women and others and "diminishes our society". It is obvious that the violent agents have been deleted from the sentences and replaced by violence as a force. In another sentence the passive form is used with this effect of deletion: "women are still being exposed to barbaric brutality and violence". The only perpetrator referred to is the "converse dimension of our society" that has been "revealing its grotesque nature".

An analysis of agency further reveals that women (unlike the president who only refers to himself as an agent) are, like the black young people in Sykes' article, in the large majority of cases not agents in the processes. This goes for their empowerment and bettering of their positions as in "The awards are intended to also inspire others to contribute and give hope and succor to women", "it is in society's own interest to create the conditions for their women to freely exercise choices" and "All nations have attained greatness by paying proper respect to women".

What this analysis adds to the answers to the questions reached by the content analysis is that men are completely deleted as agents in the violence that Indian women suffer, which is formulated as a pressing problem in the address. Men or men's actions are not even pointed at as part of the problem.

The solution to many problems is the empowerment of women, according to the speech. But although women are urged to demand their rights, they are in the majority of cases not referred to as agents.

What does the analysis above reveal about Indian gender equality politics at the time, the fourth research question? An analysis of one speech can only reveal that much information, in this case that the president of India (perhaps together with his speech writers) found it convenient at this occasion to exclude men from the problem picture of men's violence against women and to portray women as passive recipients of their own empowerment. An enlarged analysis of more texts could provide a basis for conclusions of whether this expressed his own mindset, the mindset of a leading political elite, or if it reflected the expected frames of public elite discourse at a national level at the time. It could be combined with a study of actual changes – or the lack thereof – in laws and legal practices that affect Indian women's rights.

9.6 Chapter 7, Multimodal Discourse Analysis

From the perspective of composition, the most salient elements in the 'Have Your Say' noticeboard text in Figure 7.11 are the images of four members of the Ku Klux Klan (KKK) and the Confederate battle flag; they are presented as 'important'. These elements gain their salience through being large in size and, perhaps more importantly, by being culturally loaded symbols. Both of them make reference to slavery in the American South. In that way, the issue with the Rhodes statue in South Africa is intertextually connected to racism in another time and another location.

The representation of especially the KKK members can be further analyzed as a process. There are no obvious vectors in the image, with the exception of the human gaze that has more of an interactive function here. The represented process is a conceptual one, more specifically a symbolic process in which the persons in the image are represented as carriers and their clothes have the function of attributes. The attributes make up their identity as a whole. The specific robes marked with the characteristic cross and the sharply pointed hoods with eyeholes attribute the depicted participants with the identity of Klansmen.

From an interactive point of view, the depicted Klansmen are looking straight at the viewer; they are demanding something, at least the attention of the reader. This demand character of the top image in the multimodal composition is matched by demands for information – questions – in the printed parts: "You would never walk past this, so why would you walk past the Rhodes statue?" These are questions directed at the readers of the text, who are also addressed as 'you'. 'This' in "you would never walk past this" makes direct reference to the image of the KKK members and the Confederate flag, respectively.

The text in Figure 7.11 is both verbally and visually very explicit in its critique of the Rhodes statue through its overt use of culturally loaded symbols that connect the statue to slavery and other types of oppression. Its high interactive potential symbolically draws the reader into a dialogue about the similarities between Rhodes, the KKK and the American South.

Whereas the text from the 'Have Your Say' noticeboard in Figure 7.11 was published with no editorial control, the text in Figure 7.12 was published in the official student newspaper of the University of Cape Town, which has been published since 1942. Thus the contexts are different, and the *Varsity* text has to conform to the journalistic standards of the paper, including a certain amount of neutrality when reporting events.

The text provides a relatively detailed report of a meeting under the headline of "Heritage, Signage and Symbolism" at the university, and it describes a sequence of events: the question of the removal of the Rhodes statue was raised, a number of people left the meeting, a consultant described the procedures that have to take place before the possible removal of the statue, and the Vice-Chancellor presented the time plan for further meetings and discussions. From an interactive perspective, statements dominate this written part of the text. As representations of goings-on in the world, most of these statements contain verbal processes: "Titlestad said", "Price said", "Mapha delivered his speech" and so on. None of the statements are explicitly questioned, evaluated or challenged by the journalist, Aisha Abdool Karim, who aligns with the 'objective' and 'neutral' norms of this type of reporting journalistic discourse.

However, an analysis of the composition and the visual interaction in the text may modify this description. In terms of information values, the text realizes a centre–margin structure (see Figure 7.9) in which the centre element is the photo of the Rhodes statue. The centred photo is salient through size, but also through its uses of colour in this black and white textual environment. The other salient elements are the headline, "Setting a Date", and the following quotes from the article, all making reference to the problems with setting a date for the removal of the statue: "the university would still not be able to provide a date", "full heritage impact assessment will need to be conducted", and "difficult to provide an exact timeline". Through the composition, the Rhodes statue is presented as the centre around which all these quotes regarding the timeline revolve. These compositional choices could point to an interpretation such as "they are deliberately delaying the decisive meetings and assessments and by doing so they are also delaying the possible removal of the statue".

An interactive analysis of the image of the centred Rhodes statue in Figure 7.12 shows that Rhodes is depicted from the side, from a perspective of 'partial detachment'. Rhodes is partially excluded from the social group of the readers. In addition, through the non-frontal perspective of the image, the readers are offered to view Rhodes; he does not look at the readers. Thus, they are in no way obliged to give him attention; he can no longer demand anything from them. It would have been possible to choose another photo of the Rhodes statue, in which he was depicted as demanding something from his viewers, as a member of the same group as the viewers and so on, but the image in Figure 7.12 creates meanings that are quite the opposite. Thus its interactive meanings contribute to a critical touch that is also supported by the compositional choices.

In the text in Figure 7.11, the arguments against the Rhodes statue are made very explicit, verbally and through the images. But images as part of multimodal compositions can also create meanings in more subtle ways as in Figure 7.12, presenting a critical view by using the implicitness of some images and compositional choices as resources for expressing opinions in a newspaper genre that promotes 'neutral' reporting. Both the powerful, explicit side of images and their more subtle meaning-making potential are important in the analysis of multimodal texts.

9.7 Chapter 8, Discourse Analysis

These texts are characterized by two conflicting discourses or ways of writing about and making sense of education and the purpose of education. From a discursive psychologist's point of view, this difference could also be understood as two conflicting interpretative repertoires. In the following we illustrate how these discourses, which may be called a globalization discourse and a democratization discourse, may be analyzed through a range of different discourse analytical tools. We use a combined approach to illustrate how the three different discourse analytical traditions would conduct the analysis, but also to signal that it may be fruitful to combine tools from different traditions.

In the search for the nodal point, one may look for the sign that seems to induce meaning to the other elements. In this case, competitiveness is seen as the nodal point since the logic of competitiveness seems to influence the meaning of the other elements in the discourse. The general logic of competitiveness is evident since the proposed educational reforms are described as crucial for Europe "to achieve its ambition to become the most competitive and dynamic knowledge-based economy in the world" (Council of the European Union, 2009 [henceforth 'Strategic Framework Conclusions']: 2). The other document (European Parliament and Council (2006), henceforth 'Key Competences') also highlights a range of strategies and competencies needed for business in order "to remain competitive".

In the following discussion we highlight a range of elements (contested signs) that are tied to the globalization discourse through the ways they are given meaning in relation to the previously described logic of the nodal point, and thereby are also being transformed into moments.

High Quality – One of the strategic objectives is to improve the quality and efficiency of education and training. However, this is supposedly needed first of all since it may be a way to secure Europe's role in the global economy: "High quality education and training systems which are both efficient and equitable are crucial for Europe's success and for enhancing employability" (Strategic Framework Conclusions, 2009: 3).

Partnership – In both articles partnership is generally linked to parts of the labour market, and especially to the private sector. It is through a closer cooperation with these particular partners that the education system is expected to improve: "Partnership between the world of enterprise and different levels and sectors of education, training and research can help to ensure a better focus on the skills and competences required in the labour market and on fostering innovation and entrepreneurship in all forms of learning" (Strategic Framework Conclusions, 2009: 3).

Mobility – Travelling across borders is seen as an important way of improving the asset (people) in the knowledge-based economy: "As an essential element of lifelong learning and an important means of enhancing people's employability and adaptability, mobility for learners, teachers and teacher trainers should be gradually expanded with a view to making periods of learning abroad – both within Europe and the wider world – the rule rather than the exception" (Strategic Framework Conclusions, 2009: 3).

Creativity – Enhancing creativity is one of the strategic objectives that are put forward in the Key Competences document. However, it is a particular form of creativity that is linked to entrepreneurship and economic growth that is supposed to be integrated at all levels of education and training: "As well as engendering personal fulfilment, creativity constitutes a prime source of innovation, which in turn is acknowledged as one of the key drivers of sustainable economic development. Creativity and innovation are crucial to enterprise development and to Europe's ability to compete internationally" (Strategic Framework Conclusions, 2009: 3).

It may also be of importance to look at the relations between these elements, how the logic of the discourse is developed through the particular way these elements are discussed in relation to each other. How this relation is established, may be visualized through the following chain of equivalence: education – improved quality – partnership – mobility – entrepreneurship/creativity – competitiveness – economic growth. This chain of equivalence thereby illustrates the general logic of the discourse: how improved quality of education means a developed partnership between the education system and the private sector within the labour market, together with an increased focus on mobility and creativity (in the sense of focusing on teachers' need to migrate to find work and new competencies and students' needs to focus on economical entrepreneurship).

This discourse can also be seen as an interpretative repertoire from a discourse psychological perspective. As described above, such a repertoire can be characterized as "a recognizable routine of arguments, descriptions and evaluations distinguished by familiar clichés, common places, tropes and characterizations of actors and situations" (Edley and Wetherell, 2001: 443). One such recurrent description and argument that can be found is the description of education as a "key measure in Europe's response to globalization and the shift to knowledge-based economies" (Key Competences, 2006: 2). Another frequently used characterization of actors and situations is the notion of flexibility. People are for example asked to be able to "adapt flexibly to a rapidly changing and highly interconnected world" (Key Competences, 2006: 4) and one also wants to establish "more flexible learning pathways" (Strategic Framework Conclusions, 2009: 3).

This interpretative repertoire also becomes visible through the characterizations of agents, or the described subject positions. One frequently used position is that of "low-skilled people" (Key Competences, 2006: 2) or the "Low achievers in basic skills" (Strategic Framework Conclusions, 2009: 5). These "risk-groups" in need of extra attention and support are described as people with "low literacy, early school leavers, the long-term unemployed and those returning to work after a period of extended leave, older people, migrants, and people with disabilities" (Key Competences, 2006: 4). These individuals are the ones not acting in line with the preferred logic of this discourse (being interested in lifelong learning and mobility) and are thus represented as a threat towards the overall goal of economic growth and Europe's intent to retain a strong global role.

These individuals are thus the ones that are being problematized, and the aim is therefore to encourage these groups to become more like the "mobile life-long learners", another frequent subject position in this discourse. This characterization underlines the need for individuals to be mobile and ready to move to places where job opportunities exist within the global knowledge-based economy (Strategic Framework Conclusions, 2009: 3).

However, as stated above, there are also traces of another discourse in the material, and the material is thus characterized by antagonism. Besides the goal of competitiveness and economic growth, education is also highlighted in relation to democracy and human rights:

> In the period up to 2020, the primary goal of European cooperation should be to support the further development of education and training systems in the Member States which are aimed at ensuring: [...] sustainable economic prosperity and employability, whilst promoting democratic values, social cohesion, active citizenship, and intercultural dialogue. (Strategic Framework Conclusions, 2009: 2)

The nodal point in this discourse is the "active citizenship", that is being linked to elements such as "personal fulfilment", "social cohesion" (Strategic Framework Conclusions, 2009: 2) "tolerance" and "social and cultural diversity" (Key Competences, 2006: 2). According to this logic, education is thus a way of granting individuals the means of developing and enjoying their democratic citizenships.

This alternative discourse is, however, subordinate in relation to the globalization discourse. This could be seen both in relation to their relative strength and visibility in the material, and in the ways these are described in relation to each other. Elements connected to the democracy discourse are not as frequent, and this discourse is generally only visible as a secondary goal and as something that is achieved together with the globalization discourse:

> Efficient investment in human capital through education and training systems is an essential component of Europe's strategy to deliver the high levels of sustainable, knowledge-based growth and jobs that lie at the heart of the Lisbon strategy, at the same time as promoting *personal fulfilment, social cohesion and active citizenship*. (Strategic Framework Conclusions, 2009: 2; our emphasis)

In line with Fairclough's linguistic focus and the strategy of looking at wording, one may emphasize a recurrent use of the words "together with" when linking the discourses to each other. In this way the discourses are portrayed as compatible and potential conflicts between the discourses are concealed.

These conclusions also bring us to the last research question and the focus on hegemony and power issues within social practice. When democratic values are incorporated into the globalization discourse, and these alternative values are highlighted only when they further the overall aim of economic growth, the general liberal hegemony is reproduced. Ideological effects from this reproduction can further be seen on different levels. On an institutional level one may expect the educational institutions to structure their education around the demands of knowledge-based economies. Quality of teaching is hereby measured as the ability to increase employability and economic entrepreneurship. On an individual level students and teachers are expected to be mobile lifelong learners, who are willing to transfer to places where job opportunities exist. Those not willing, or not able to do so, are left behind and identified as problematic and non-productive.

References

Abell, P. (1987) *The Syntax of Social Life: The Theory and Method of Comparative Narrative.* Oxford: Oxford University Press.

Adams, I. (2001) *Political Ideology Today* (second edition). Manchester: Manchester University Press.

Adams, M.B. (1990) 'Eugenics in the history of science', in M.B. Adams (ed.), *The Wellborn Science: Eugenics in Germany, France, Brazil, and Russia.* New York, Oxford: Oxford University Press.

Ahrens, K. (ed.) (2009) *Politics, Gender and Conceptual Metaphors.* Basingstoke: Palgrave Macmillan.

Almond, G. and Powell, G. Bingham Jr. (1966) *Comparative Politics: A Developmental Approach.* Boston, MA: Little, Brown and Company.

Almond, G. and Verba, S. (1965 [1963]) *The Civic Culture: Political Attitudes and Democracy in Five Nations.* Boston, MA: Little, Brown and Company.

Anscombe, E. (1957) *Intention.* Cambridge, MA: Harvard University Press.

Apter, D.E. (ed.) (1964) *Ideology and Discontent.* New York: The Free Press of Glencoe.

Archer, M. (1995) *Realist social Theory: The Morphogenetic Approach.* Cambridge: Cambridge University Press.

Archer, M. (2000) *Being Human: The Problem of Agency.* Cambridge: Cambridge University Press.

Arnold, N.S. (1990) *Marx's Radical Critique of Capitalist Society: A Reconstruction and Critique.* Oxford: Oxford University Press.

Åsberg, C., Koobak, R. and Johnson, E. (eds) (2011): 'Special Issue: Post-humanities', *NORA– Nordic Journal of Feminist and Gender Research,* 19 (4).

Audi, R. (2010) *Epistemology: A Contemporary Introduction to the Theory of Knowledge* (third edition). London and New York: Routledge.

Aune, B. (1970) *Rationalism, Empiricism and Pragmatism: An Introduction.* New York: McGraw-Hill.

Austin, J.L. (1975) *How To Do Things With Words.* J.O. Urmson and M. Spisà (eds). Oxford: Clarendon.

Baker, P. (2006) *Using Corpora in Discourse Analysis.* London: Continuum.

Ball, T. and Dagger, R. (2011) *Political Ideologies and the Democratic Ideal* (eighth edition). Boston, MA: Longman.

Bamberg, M. (2012) 'Why narrative?', *Narrative Inquiry,* 22(1): 202–210.

Bamberg, M. and Georgakopoulou, A. (2008) 'Small stories as a new perspective in narrative and identity analysis', *Text & Talk*, 28: 377–96.

Banta, M. (1994) *Taylored Lives: Narrative Productions in the Age of Taylor, Veblen and Ford*. Chicago: University of Chicago Press.

Barad, K. (2003) 'Posthumanist performativity: Toward an understanding of how matter comes to matter', *Signs*, 28 (3): 801–31.

Barker, C. (2000) *Television, Globalization and Cultural Identities*. Buckingham: Open University Press.

Barkin, S.M. (1984) 'The journalist as storyteller: An interdisciplinary perspective', *American Journalism*, 1 (2): 27–33.

Barret, M. (1991) *The Politics of Truth: From Marx to Foucault*. Cambridge: Polity Press.

Barthes, R. (1977 [1966]a) 'Introduction to the structural analysis of narratives', in R. Barthes (ed.), *Image–Music–Text*. London: Harper Collins, pp. 79–124.

Barthes, R. (1977 [1966]b) 'Rhetoric of the Image', in R. Barthes (ed.), *Image–Music–Text*. London: Harper Collins, pp. 32–51.

Barthes, R. (1993 [1970]) *Mythologies*. London: Vintage.

Bell, A. (1994) 'Telling Stories', in D. Graddol and O. Boyd-Barrett (eds), *Media Texts: Authors and Readers*. London: Open University Press, pp. 100–18.

Bennett, W.L. and Edelman, M. (1985) 'Toward a new political narrative', *Journal of Communication*, 35: 156–71.

Berger, A.A. (1997) *Narratives in Popular Culture, Media and Everyday Life*. London: Sage.

Berger, A.A. (2014) *Media Analysis Techniques*. London: Sage.

Berger, P. and Luckmann, T. (1966) *The Construction of Reality: A Treatise in the Sociology of Knowledge*. New York: Doubleday.

Bergström, G. and Boréus, K. (2000) *Textens mening och makt: Metodbok i samhälls-vetenskaplig textanalys*. Lund: Studentlitteratur.

Berman, S. (1998) *The Social Democratic Moment: Ideas and Politics in the Making of Interwar Europe*. Cambridge, MA: Harvard University Press.

Berman, S. (2006) *The Primacy of Politics: Social Democracy and the Making of Europe's Twentieth Century*. Cambridge: Cambridge University Press.

Bhaskar, R. (1978/2008) *A Realist Theory of Science*. New York: Harvester Press.

Bhaskar, R. (1986) *Scientific Realism and Human Emancipation*. London: Verso.

Bignell, J. (1997) *Media Semiotics: An Introduction*. Manchester: Manchester University Press.

Billig, M. (1995) *Banal Nationalism*. London: Sage.

Billig, M. (1999) *Freudian Repression: Conversation Creating the Unconscious*. Cambridge: Cambridge University Press.

Birkvad, S. (2000) 'A battle for public mythology: History and genre in the portrait documentary', *Nordicom Review*, 2: 291–304.

Björklund, S. (1970) *Politisk teori* [Political Theory]. Stockholm: Aldus/Bonniers.

Block, E. (1984) 'Freedom, Equality, Et Cetera: Values and Valuations in the Swedish Domestic Political Debate, 1945–1975', in G. Melischek, K.E. Rosengren, and J. Stappers (eds), *Cultural Indicators: An International Symposium*. Wien: Verlag der Österreichischen Akademie der Wissenschaften, pp. 159–76.

Boréus, K. (1994) *Högervåg: Nyliberalism och kampen om språket i svensk debatt 1969–1989*. Stockholm: Tiden.

Boréus, K. (1997) 'The shift to the right: Neo-liberalism in argumentation and language in the Swedish public debate since 1969', *European Journal of Political Research,* 31: 257–86.

Boréus, K. (2006) 'Discursive discrimination of the "mentally deficient" in inter-war Sweden', *Disability & Society,* 21 (5): 441–54.

Bracher, K.D. (1984) *The Age of Ideologies: A History of Political Thought in the Twentieth Century.* New York: St Martin's Press.

Brecht, A. (1959) *Political Theory: The Foundations of Twentieth Century Political Thought.* Princeton: Princeton University Press.

Brekke, T. (2012) *Fundamentalism: Prophecy and Protest in an Age of Globalization.* Cambridge: Cambridge University Press.

Bremond, C. (1966/1980) 'The logic of narrative possibilities', *New Literary History,* 11: 387–411.

Brinker, M. (1983) 'Verisimilitude, conventions and beliefs', *New Literary History,* 14: 253–67.

Brulle, R.J. (2014) 'Institutionalizing delay: Foundation funding and the creation of U.S. climate change counter-movement organizations', *Climate Change,* 122: 681–94.

Brune, Y. (2004) *Nyheter från Gränsen: Tre studier i journalistik om 'invandrare', flyktingar och rasistiskt våld.* Gothenburg: JMG.

Bruner, J. (1991) 'The narrative construction of reality', *Critical Inquiry,* 18: 1–21.

Bunge, M. (1988) *Philosophy of Science, Volume l-ll.* New Brunswick and London: Transaction Publishers.

Burke, E. (1790) *Reflections on the Revolution in France.* Oxford: Clarendon Press. Available from http://www.econlib.org/library/LFBooks/Burke/brkSWv2Cover.html (accessed 13 July 2016).

Butler, J. (2007) *Gender Trouble: Feminism and the Subversion of Identity.* New York: Routledge.

Cameron, D. (ed.) (1998) *The Feminist Critique of Language: A Reader.* London and New York: Routledge.

Campell, A., Converse, P.E., Miller, W.E. and Stokes, D.E. (1960) *The American Voter.* Chicago: The University of Chicago Press.

Carlisle, J. (1994) 'Introduction', in J. Carlisle and D.R. Schwarz (eds), *Narrative and Culture.* London: University of Georgia Press, pp. 1–12.

Carnarp, R. (2002 [1928]) *The Logical Structure of the World and Pseudoproblems in Philosophy.* Chicago, IL: Open Court.

Carpenter, D.R. (2003) 'Phenomenology as Method 51', in H.J. Streubert and D.R. Carpenter (eds), *Qualitative Research in Nursing: Advancing Humanistic Imperative* (third edition). London, New York: Lippincott Williams & Wilkins.

Chalmers, A.F. (1990) *Science and its Fabrication.* Minnesota: University of Minnesota Press.

Chalmers, A. F. (1999) *What is This Thing Called Science?* Buckingham: Open University Press.

Chaney, D. (1986) 'A Symbolic Mirror of Ourselves: Civic Ritual in Mass Society', in R. Collins, J. Curran, N. Garnham, P. Scannell, P. Schlesinger and C. Sparks (eds), *Media, Culture and Society: A Critical Reader.* London: Sage, pp. 247–63.

Charteris-Black, J. (2004) *Corpus Approaches to Critical Metaphor Analysis.* Basingstoke, New York: Palgrave Macmillan.

Charteris-Black, J. (2005) *Politicians and Rhetoric: The Persuasive Power of Metaphor.* Basingstoke, New York: Palgrave Macmillan.

Chatman, S. (1978) *Story and Discourse: Narrative Structure in Fiction and Film.* Ithaca, NY and London: Cornell University Press.

Chatman, S. (1990) *Coming to Terms: The Rhetoric of Narrative in Fiction and Film.* Ithaca, NY: Cornell University Press.

Chilton, P. (2004) *Analysing Political Discourse: Theory and Practice.* London, New York: Routledge.

Clark, K. (1998) 'The Linguistics of Blame: Representation of Women in the Sun's reporting of Crimes of Sexual Violence', in D. Cameron (ed.), *The Feminist Critique of Language: A Reader.* London and New York: Routledge, pp. 183–97.

Clayton, J. (1994) 'The Narrative Turn in Minority Fiction', in J. Carlisle and D.R. Schwarz (eds), *Narrative and Culture.* London: University of Georgia Press, pp. 58–76.

Coleman, J. (2000a) *A History of Political Thought: From Ancient Greece to Early Christianity.* Oxford: Blackwell.

Coleman, J. (2000b) *A History of Political Thought: From the Middle Ages to the Renaissance.* Oxford: Blackwell.

Collier, A. (1994) *Critical Realism: An Introduction to Roy Bhaskar's Philosophy.* London: Verso.

Connolly, W.E. (1983) *The Terms of Political Discourse.* Oxford: Martin Robertson.

Coole, D. (1999) 'Narratives, Maps and the Theatre of Politics'. Paper presented at ECPR Joint Sessions in Mannheim, March. Available at https://ecpr.eu/Filestore/PaperProposal/2a78aefb-eb4f-4b9e-a58f-de8e37b75240.pdf (accessed 17 July 2016).

Council of the European Union (2009) 'Council conclusions of 12 May 2009 on a strategic framework for European cooperation in education and training ("ET 2020")' (2009/C 119/02), *Official Journal of the European Union,* available from http://eur-lex.europa.eu/legal-content/EN/TXT/?uri=uriserv:OJ.C_.2009.119.01.0002.01.ENG (accessed 25 July 2016).

Critchley, S. and Marchart, O. (2004) *Laclau – a Critical Reader.* London and New York: Routledge.

Crowley, S. and Hawhee, D. (1999) *Ancient Rhetorics for Contemporary Students* (second edition). Boston: Allyn and Bacon.

Czarniawska, B. (1999) *Interviews, Narratives and Organizations.* Gothenburg: GRI Report 1999: 8.

Czarniawska, B. (2000) *The Uses of Narrative in Organization Research.* Gothenburg: GRI Report 2000: 5.

Czarniawska, B. (2004) *Narratives in Social Science Research.* London: Sage.

Dahl, R. (1989) *Democracy and its Critics.* New Haven and London: Yale University Press.

Dahl, R. (1998) *On Democracy.* New Haven and London: Yale University Press.

Dahlgren, P. (1995) *Television and the Public Sphere: Citizenship, Democracy and the Media.* London: Sage.

De Fina, A. and Johnstone, B. (2015) 'Discourse Analysis and Narrative', in D. Tannen, H. Hamilton and D. Schiffrin (eds), *The Handbook of Discourse Analysis,* (second edition). New York: John Wiley & Sons, pp. 152–167.

Dine, P. (1994) *Images of the Algerian War: French Fiction and Film, 1954–1992.* Oxford: Clarendon Press.

Dovring, K. (2009) 'Quantitative Semantics in 18th Century Sweden', in K. Krippendorff and M.A. Bock (eds), *The Content Analysis Reader.* Los Angeles, London, New Delhi, Singapore: Sage, pp. 4–8.

Drulák, P. (2008) 'Identifying and Assessing Metaphors: Discourse on EU-reform', in T. Carver and J. Pikalo (eds), *Political Language and Metaphor: Interpreting and Changing the World.* London: Routledge, pp.105–18.

Duranti, A. and Goodwin, C. (eds) (1992*) Rethinking Context: Language as an Interactive Phenomenon.* Cambridge: Cambridge University Press

Duverger, M. (1966) *The Idea of Politics: The Uses of Power in Society.* London: Methuen.

Easton, D. (1971 [1953]) *The Political System: An Inquiry into the State of Political Science* (second edition). New York: Alfred E. Knopf.

Edley, N. (2001) 'Analysing Masculinity: Interpretative Repertoires, Ideological Dilemmas and Subject Positions', in M. Wetherell, S. Taylor and S.J. Yates (eds), *Discourse as Data: A Guide for Analysis.* London: Sage, pp. 189–228.

Edley, N. and Wetherell, M. (2001) 'Jekyll and Hyde: Men's constructions of feminism and feminists', *Feminism & Psychology,* 11(4): 439–57.

Edwards, D. (2005) 'Discursive Psychology', in K.L. Fitch and R.E. Sanders (eds), *Handbook of Language and Social Interaction.* Mahwah, NJ: Lawrence Erlbaum Associates, pp. 257–73.

Ellis, R.J. (1998) *The Dark Side of the Left: Illiberal Egalitarianism in America.* Lawrence, KS: University Press of Kansas.

Esposito, J.L. (2011) *Islam: The Straight Path* (fourth edition). New York: Oxford University Press.

European Parliament and Council (2006) 'Recommendation 2006/962/EC of the European Parliament and of the Council of 18 December 2006 on key competences for lifelong learning', *Official Journal of the European Union.* Available from http://eur-lex.europa.eu/legal-content/EN/TXT/?uri=uriserv:c11090 (accessed 25 July 2016).

Evans, V. (2009) *How Words Mean: Lexical Concepts, Cognitive Models and Meaning Construction.* Oxford: Oxford University Press.

Everett, C. (2013) *Linguistic Relativity: Evidence Across Languages and Cognitive Domains.* Berlin, Boston: de Gruyter.

Fairclough, I. and Fairclough, N. (2012) *Political Discourse Analysis: A Method for Advanced Students.* London and New York: Routledge.

Fairclough, N. (1992) *Discourse and Social Change.* Cambridge: Polity Press.

Fairclough, N. (1994a) 'Power and Change', in R.E. Asher (ed.), *The Encyclopedia of Language and Linguistics* (vol. 6). Oxford: Pergamon Press, pp. 246–50.

Fairclough, N. (1994b) 'Power and Language', in R.E. Asher (ed.), *The Encyclopedia of Language and Linguistics* (vol. 2). Oxford: Pergamon Press, pp. 940–9.

Fairclough, N. (1995) *Critical Discourse Analysis: A Critical Study of Language.* London: Longman.

Fairclough, N. (2000) *New Labour, New Language?* London: Routledge.

Fairclough, N. (2003) *Analyzing Discourse: Textual Analysis for Social Research.* London and New York: Routledge.

Fairclough, N. (2010) *Critical Discourse Analysis: A Critical Study of Language* (second edition). London: Longman.

Fairclough, N. (2015) *Language and Power* (third edition). London, New York: Routledge.

Feldman, M.S. and Almquist, J. (2012) 'Analyzing the Implicit in Stories', in J.A. Holstein and J.F. Gruber (eds), *Varieties of Narrative Analysis.* London: Sage, pp. 207–28.

Feldman, M.S., Sköldberg, K., Brown, R.N. and Horner, D. (2004) 'Making sense of stories: A rhetorical approach to narrative analysis', *Journal of Public Administration Research and Theory,* 14 (2): 147–70.

Feldman, R. (1999) *Reason and Argument.* Upper Saddle River, NJ: Prentice Hall.

Finnis, J. (1998) *Aquinas: Moral, Political and Legal Theory.* Oxford: Oxford University Press.

Fishman, E. (1989) *Likely Stories: Essays on Political Philosophy and Contemporary American Literature.* Gainesville, FL: University of Florida Press.

Foucault, M. (1972) *The Archaeology of Knowledge.* London: Tavistock Publications.

Foucault, M. (1977) *Discipline and Punishment: The Birth of the Prison.* Harmondsworth: Penguin Books.

Foucault, M. (1980) *Power/Knowledge: Selected Interviews and Other Writings 1972–1977.* Brighton: The Harvester Press.

Foucault, M. (1990) *The History of Sexuality (vol. 1): The Will to Knowledge.* Harmondsworth: Penguin.

Foucault, M. (1994) *Essential Works of Foucault 1954-1984. Vol. 3: Power.* V. Marchetti and A. Salomoni (eds). London, New York: Verso.

Foucault, M. (2001 [1967]) *Madness and Civilization: A History of Insanity in the Age of Reason.* London: Routledge.

Fowler, R. (1991) *Language in the News: Discourse and Ideology in the Press.* Abingdon: Routledge.

Francis (Pope [Jorge Mario Bergoglio]) (2015) 'Address of the Holy Father. United Nations Headquarters, New York Friday, 25 September 2015'. Available at http://

w2.vatican.va/content/francesco/en/speeches/2015/september/documents/papa-francesco_20150925_onu-visita.html (accessed 16 July 2016).

Frank, A.W. (2012) 'Practicing Dialogical Narrative Analysis', in J.A. Holstein and J.F. Gruber (eds), *Varieties of Narrative Analysis*. London: Sage, pp. 33–52.

Franzosi, R. (1998) 'Narrative analysis - or why (and how) sociologists should be interested in narrative', *Annual Review of Sociology,* 24: 517–54.

Franzosi, R. (2010) *Quantitative Narrative Analysis*. London: Sage.

Franzosi, R. (2012) 'On Quantitative Narrative Analysis', in J.A. Holstein and J.F. Gruber (eds), *Varieties of Narrative Analysis*. London: Sage, pp. 75–96.

Fridolfsson, C. (2004) 'Political protest and the threatening outside: A discourse analysis of events at an EU summit', *Distinktion,* 8: 79–92.

Friedman, M. and Friedman, R. (1979) *Free to Choose*. New York: Avon Books.

Friedrich, C.J. (1963) *Man and his Government: An Empirical Theory of Politics*. New York: McGraw-Hill.

Gadamer, H.-G. (1975) *Truth and Method*. New York: Seabury P.

Gadamer, H.-G. (1986) *The Relevance of The Beautiful and Other Essays*. Cambridge: Cambridge University Press.

Gadamer, H.-G. (1989) *Truth and Method* (second edition). New York: Crossroad.

Garme, C. (2001) *Newcomers to Power: How to sit on someone else's throne. Socialists conquer France in 1981; non-socialists conquer Sweden in 1976*. Uppsala: Uppsala University.

Gauthier, D.P. (1963) *Practical Reasoning: The Structure and Foundations of Prudential and Moral Arguments and their Exemplification in Discourse*. Oxford: Clarendon Press.

Gee, J.P. (2005) *An Introduction to Discourse Analysis Theory and Method*. London and New York: Routledge.

Gee, J.P. (2011) *How to do Discourse Analysis: A Toolkit*. London and New York: Routledge.

Geertz, C. (1964) 'Ideology as a Cultural System', in D.E. Apter (ed.), *Ideology and Discontent*. New York: The Free Press of Glencoe, pp. 47–76.

Georgakopoulou, A. (2006) 'Thinking big with small stories in narrative and identity analysis', *Narrative Inquiry* 16 (1): 122–30.

Georgakopoulou, A. (2011) 'Narrative', in J. Zienkowski, J. Östman and J. Verschueren (eds), *Discursive Pragmatics*. Amsterdam and Philadelphia: John Benjamins Publishing, pp. 190–207.

George, A.L. (2009) 'Propaganda Analysis: A Case Study from World War II', in K. Krippendorff and M.A. Bock (eds), *The Content Analysis Reader*. London: Sage, pp. 21–7.

Gergen, K.J. (1994) *Realities and Relationships: Soundings in Social Construction*. Cambridge, MA: Harvard University Press.

Giddens, A. (1984) *The Constitution of Society*. Cambridge: Polity Press.

Gimenez, J.C. (2010) 'Narrative Analysis in Linguistic Research', in L. Litosseliti (ed.), *Research Methods in Linguistics*. New York: Continuum, pp. 198–215.

Gjedde, L. (2000) 'Narrative, genre and context in popular science', *Nordicom Review,* 21 (1): 51–7.

Goatly, A. (1997) *The Language of Metaphors*. London, New York: Routledge.

Goatly, A. (2007) *Washing the Brain: Metaphor and Hidden Ideology*. Amsterdam: John Benjamins Publishing Company.

Goodsell, C. And Murray, N. (1995) *Public Administration Illuminated and Inspired by the Arts*. Westport, CT: Praeger.

Gough, I. (1979) *The Political Economy of the Welfare State*. Basingstoke: Macmillan.

Graddol, D. (1994) 'The Visual Accomplishment of Factuality', in D. Graddol and O. Boyd-Barrett (eds), *Media Texts: Authors and Readers*. London: Open University Press, pp. 136–57.

Grbich, C. (2013) *Qualitative Data Analysis: An Introduction*. London: Sage.

Gregor, A.J. (2000) *A Place in the Sun: Marxism and Fascism in China's Long Revolution*. Oxford: Westview Press.

Gregor, A.J. (2003 [1971]) *Metascience and Politics: An Inquiry into the Conceptual Language of Political Science*. New Brunswick and London: Transaction.

Gregor, A.J. (2005) *Mussolini's Intellectuals: Fascist Social and Political Thought*. Princeton and Oxford: Princeton University Press.

Grondin, J. (ed.) (2007) *The Gadamer Reader: A Bouquet of the Later Writings*. Chicago: Northwestern University Press.

Habermas, J. (1984) *The Theory of Communicative Action* (vols. 1–2). Cambridge: Polity Press.

Habermas, J. (1989 [1962]) *The Transformation of the Public Sphere: Inquiry into a Category of Bourgeois Society*. Cambridge: Polity Press.

Hacker, A. (1961) *Political Theory: Philosophy, Ideology, Science*. Toronto: Macmillan.

Hacking, I. (1996) *The Social Construction of What?* Cambridge and Massachusetts: Harward University Press.

Hall, E.T. (1966) *The Hidden Dimension*. Garden City, NY: Doubleday & Company.

Hall, S. (1988) *The Hard Road to Renewal: Thatcherism and the Crisis of the Left*. London: Verso.

Hall, S. (1994) 'Encoding/Decoding', in D. Graddol and O. Boyd-Barrett (eds), *Media Texts: Authors and Readers*. London: Open University Press, pp. 200–211.

Hall, S. (1997) 'The work of representation', in S. Hall (ed.), *Representation: Cultural Representations and Signifying Practices*. London: Sage, pp.13–74.

Halliday, F. (1979) *Iran Dictatorship and Development*. London: Penguin.

Halliday, M.A.K. (1978) *Language as Social Semiotic: The Social Interpretation of Language and Meaning*. London: Edward Arnold.

Halliday, M.A.K. and Hasan, R. (1976) *Cohesion In English*. London: Longman.

Halliday M.A.K. and Matthiessen, C.M.I.M. (2014) *Halliday's Introduction to Functional Grammar* (fourth edition). Abingdon, New York: Routledge.

Hampshire, S. (1959) *Thought and Action*. London: Chatto and Windus.

Hansen, A. and Machin, D. (2013) *Media and Communication Research Methods*. Basingstoke: Palgrave.

Hart, C. (2010) *Critical Discourse Analysis and Cognitive Science*. Basingstoke: Palgrave Macmillan.

Haug, W. (1987) *Critique of Commodity Aesthetics: Appearance, Sexuality and Advertising in Capitalist Society*. Minneapolis: University of Minnesota Press.

Hayes, J. and Knox-Hayes, J. (2014) 'Security in climate change discourse: Analyzing the divergence between US and EU approaches to policy', *Global Environmental Policy*, 14(2): 82–101.

Hedström, P. (2005) *Dissecting the Social: On the Principles of Analytical Sociology*. Cambridge: Cambridge University Press.

Herman, D., Jahn, M. and Ryan, M.-L. (eds) (2008) *Routledge Encyclopedia of Narrative Theory*. London and New York: Routledge.

Herman, L. and Vervaeck, B. (2005) *Handbook of Narrative Analysis*. Lincoln, NE and London: University of Nebraska Press.

Hermansson, J. (1992) 'Rousseau on Justice: In search for an Argument', in R. Malnes and A. Underdal (eds), *Rationality and Institutions: Essays in Honour of Knut Midgaard*. Oslo: Universitetsforlaget, pp. 255–77.

Herrick, J.A. (2013) *The History and Theory of Rhetoric: An Introduction*. Boston, MA: Pearson.

Herzog, A. (2001) 'The poetic nature of political disclosure: Hannah Arendt's storytelling', *Clio*, 30 (2): 169–95.

Heywood, A. (2007) *Political Ideologies: An Introduction* (fourth edition). Basingstoke and New York: Palgrave Macmillan.

Hirschman, A.O. (1991) *The Rhetoric of Reaction: Perversity, Futility, Jeopardy*. Cambridge: Harvard University Press.

Hobsbawm, E.J. (1990) *Nations and Nationalism since 1780: Programme, Myth, Reality* (second edition). Cambridge: Cambridge University Press (2nd edn 1992).

Hobsbawn, E.J. and Ranger, T. (eds) (1992) *The Invention of Tradition*. Cambridge: Cambridge University Press (1st edn 1983).

Hodge, R. and Kress, G. (1988) *Social Semiotics*. Cambridge: Polity Press.

Høigilt, J. (2011) *Islamist Rhetoric: Language and Culture in Contemporary Egypt*. London, New York: Routledge.

Holland, D. and Quinn, N. (1987) *Cultural Models in Language and Thought*. Cambridge: Cambridge University Press.

Hollis–Brusky, A. (2015) *Ideas with Consequences: The Federalist Society and the Conservative Counterrevolution*. Oxford: Oxford University Press.

Holloway, J. and Piciotto, S. (eds) (1978) *State and Capital: A Marxist Debate*. London: Edward Arnold.

Holstein, J.A. and Gubrium, J.F. (eds) (2012) *Varieties of Narrative Analysis*. London: Sage.

Horton-Salway, M. (2001) 'The construction of M.E.: The discursive action model', in M. Wetherell, S. Taylor and S.J. Yates (eds), *Discourse as Data: A Guide for Analysis*. London: Sage, pp. 147–88.

Howarth, D. (1995) 'Discourse Analysis', in D. Marsh and G. Stoker (eds), *Theory and Methods in Political Science*. Basingstoke: Macmillan Press, pp. 115–33.

Howarth, D. (2000) *Discourse*. Buckingham, Philadelphia: Open University Press.

Howarth, D. and Glynos, J. (2007) *Logics of Critical Explanation in Social and Political Theory*. Abingdon: Routledge.

Howarth, D. and Torfing, J. (2005) *Discourse Theory in European Politics: Identity, Policy and Governance*. Hampshire: Palgrave Macmillan.

Hsieh, H.-F. and Shannon, S.E. (2005) 'Three approaches to qualitative content analysis', *Qualitative Health Research*, 15 (9): 1277–88.

Inglehart, R. and Norris, P. (2003) *Rising Tide: Gender Equality and Cultural Change around the World*. Cambridge: Cambridge University Press.

Inglehart, R. and Welzel, C. (2005) *Modernization, Culture Change and Democracy: The Human Development Sequence*. Cambridge: Cambridge University Press.

Intergovernmental Panel on Climate Change (IPCC) (2014) 'Synthesis Report: Summary for Policymakers', http://www.ipcc.ch/pdf/assessment-report/ar5/syr/AR5_SYR_FINAL_SPM.pdf (accessed 12 July 2016).

Israel, J. (2014) *Revolutionary Ideas: An Intellectual History of the French Revolution from 'The Rights of Man' to Robespierre*. Princeton and Oxford: Princeton University Press.

Jameson, F. (1989) *The Political Unconscious: Narrative as a Socially Symbolic Act*. London: Routledge.

Jensen, A. (2007) *Theological Hermeneutics*. London: SCM Press.

Jewitt, C. (ed.) (2014) *The Routledge Handbook of Multimodal Analysis* (second edition). London and New York: Routledge.

Johnstone, B. (2008) *Discourse Analysis* (second edition). Oxford: Blackwell.

Jones, R. (2012) *Discourse Analysis – A Resource Book for Students*. Abingdon: Routledge.

Jørgensen, M. and Phillips, L. (2002) *Discourse Analysis as Theory and Method*. London: Sage.

Judt, T. (2010) *Ill Fares the Land: A Treatise on Our Present Discontents*. London: Penguin Books.

Keller, R. (2013) *Doing Discourse Research: An Introduction for Social Scientists*. London: Sage.

Kinsella, E.A. (2006) 'Hermeneutics and critical hermeneutics: Exploring possibilities within the art of interpretation', *Forum: Qualitative Social Research* 7 (3): Article 19. http://www.qualitative-research.net/index.php/fqs/article/view/145/319 (accessed 7 July 2016).

Kiser, E. (1996) 'The revival of narrative in historical sociology: What rational choice theory can contribute', *Politics and Society*, 24 (3): 249–71.

Kitcher, P. (2002) 'Scientific Knowledge', in P.K. Moser (ed.), *The Oxford Handbook of Epistemology*.Oxford, New York: Oxford University Press, pp. 385–407.

Kjeldsen, J.E. (2012) 'Pictorial Argumentation in Advertising: Visual Tropes and Figures as a Way of Creating Visual Argumentation', in F.H. van Eemeren and B. Garssen (eds), *Topical Themes in Argumentation Theory: Twenty Exploratory Studies* (Argumentation Library, 22), pp. 239–55.

Klein, N. (2013) 'How science is telling us all to revolt', *The New Statesman*, 29 October. http://www.newstatesman.com/2013/10/science-says-revolt (accessed 12 July 2016).

Klein, N. (2014) *This Changes Everything: Capitalism vs. the Climate*. London: Penguin Books.

Kleinnijenhuis, J.A., de Ridder, J.A. and Rietberg, E.M. (1997) 'Reasoning in Economic Discourse: An Application of the Network Approach to the Dutch Press', in C.W. Roberts (ed.), *Text Analysis for the Social Sciences: Methods for Drawing Statistical Inferences from Texts and Transcripts*. Mahwah, NJ: Lawrence Erlbaum Associates. pp. 191–207.

Knight, G. and Dean Knight, T.D. (1982) 'Myth and the Structure of News', *Journal of Communication,* 32: 144–61.

Knox, J. (2007) 'Visual–verbal communication on online newspaper home pages', *Visual Communication*, 6(1): 19–53.

Köhler, J. (2000) *Wagner's Hitler: The Prophet and his Disciple*. Cambridge: Polity Press.

Koller, V. (2009) 'Missions and Empires: Religious and Political Metaphors in Corporate Discourse', in A. Musolff and J. Zinken (eds), *Metaphor and Discourse*. Basingstoke: Palgrave Macmillan, pp. 116–34.

Kopperschmidt, J. (1985) 'An Analysis of Argumentation', in T.A. van Dijk (ed.), *Handbook of Discourse Analysis, Vol. 2*. London: Academic Press, pp. 159–68.

Kozloff, S. (1992) 'Narrative Theory and Television', in R.C. Allen (ed.), *Channels of Discourse, Reassembled: Television and Contemporary Criticism*. London: Routledge, pp. 67–100.

Kress, G. (2010) *Multimodality: A Social Semiotic Approach to Contemporary Communication*. London and New York: Routledge.

Kress, G. and Hodge, R. (1979) *Language as Ideology*. London: Routledge & Kegan Paul.

Kress, G. and van Leeuwen, T. (2001) *Multimodal Discourse: The Modes and Media of Contemporary Communication*. London: Arnold.

Kress, G. and van Leeuwen, T. (2006) *Reading Images: The Grammar of Visual Design* (second edition). London & New York: Routledge.

Krippendorff, K. (2013) *Content Analysis: An Introduction to its Methodology*. London: Sage.

Krippendorff, K. and Bock, M.A. (eds) (2009) *The Content Analysis Reader*. London: Sage.

Kuhn, T. (1996) *The Structure of Scientific Revolutions* (third edition). Chicago: University of Chicago Press.

Labov, W. and Waletzky, J. (1967) 'Narrative Analysis: Oral Versions of Personal Experience', in J. Helm (ed.), *Essays on the Verbal and Visual Arts*. Seattle: University of Washington Press, pp. 12–45.

Laclau, E. (1993) 'Discourse', in R. Goodin and P. Petit (eds), *A Companion to Contemporary Philosophy*. Oxford: Blackwell Publishing, pp. 431–7.

Laclau, E. (1995) 'Subject of politics, politics of the subject', *Differences: A Journal of Feminist Cultural Studies*, 7(1).

Laclau, E. and Mouffe, C. (1985) *Hegemony and Socialist Strategy: Towards a Radical Democratic Politics*. London: Verso.

Laclau, E. and Mouffe, C. (1990) 'Post-Marxism without Apologies', in E. Laclau (ed.), *New Reflections on the Revolution of Our Time*. London, New York: Verso, pp. 97–134.

Lakoff, G. (1987) *Women, Fire, and Dangerous Things: What Categories Reveal about the Mind*. Chicago, London: The University of Chicago Press.

Lakoff, G. (1993) 'The contemporary theory of metaphor', in A. Ortony (ed.), *Metaphor and Thought*. Cambridge: Cambridge University Press, pp. 202–51.

Lakoff, G. and Johnson, M. (1980) *Metaphors We Live By*. Chicago, London: The University of Chicago Press.

Lane, R.E. (1962) *Political Ideology: Why the American Common Man Believes What He Does*. New York: The Free Press.

Larsen, P. (2002) 'Mediated Fiction', in K.B. Jensen (ed.), *A Handbook of Media and Communication Research*. Abingdon: Routledge, pp. 117–37.

Larsson, R. (1970) *Theories of Revolution: From Marx to the First Russian Revolution*. Stockholm: Almqvist & Wiksell.

Lasswell, H. and Kaplan, A. (1950) *Power and Society: A Framework for Political Inquiry*. New Haven and London: Yale University Press.

Laver, M. (ed.) (2001) *Estimating the Policy Positions of Political Actors*. London, New York: Routledge.

Laver, M. and Garry, J. (2000) 'Estimating policy positions from political texts', *American Journal of Political Science*, 44 (3): 619–34.

Laver, M., Benoit, K. and Garry, J. (2003) 'Extracting policy positions from political texts using words as data', *The American Political Science Review*, 97 (2): 311–31.

Lee, A.S. (1994) 'Electronical mail as a medium for rich communication: An empirical investigation using hermeneutic interpretation', *MIS Quarterly*, 18 (2): 143–57.

Lepague, H. (1978) *Tomorrow Capitalism*. London: Open Court.

Letwin, S.R. (1992) *The Anatomy of Thatcherism*. London: Fontana.

Levine, R.A. (1963) *The Arms Debate*. Cambridge, MA: Harvard University Press.

Levi-Strauss, C. (1963) 'The structural study of myth', in *Structural Anthropology*. Harmondsworth: Penguin, pp. 206–31.

Lieblich, A., Tuval-Mashiach, R. and Zilber, T. (1998) *Narrative Research: Reading, Analysis and Interpretation*. London: Sage.

Lindberg, H. (2009) *Only Women Bleed? A Critical Reassessment of Comprehensive Feminist Social Theory* (Örebro Studies in Political Science 24). Örebro: Örebro University.

Lipset, S.M. (1959) *Political Man: The Social Bases of Politics*. New York: Doubleday.

Locke, J. (1964 [1690]) *An Essay Concerning Human Understanding*. Oxford: The Clarendon Press.

Locke, T. (2004) *Critical Discourse Analysis*. London, NY: Continuum.

Loris, N.D. (2015) 'The many problems of the EPA's clean power plan and climate regulations: A primer', *Backgrounder*. http://www.heritage.org/research/reports/2015/07/the-many-problems-of-the-epas-clean-power-plan-and-climate-regulations-a-primer (accessed 12 July 2016).

Losurdo, D. (2011) *Liberalism: A Counter History*. London: Verso.

Lucy, J.A. (1992) *Grammatical Categories and Cognition: A Case Study of the Linguistic Relativity Hypothesis*. Cambridge: Cambridge University Press.

Lukácz, G. (1971 [1923]) *History and Class-Consciousness: Studies in Marxist Dialectics*. Cambridge, MA: The MIT Press.

Lukes, S. (2005) *Power: A Radical View* (second edition). London: Palgrave Macmillan.

Lyotard, J. (1984) *The Postmodern Condition: A Report on Knowledge*. Minneapolis: University of Minnesota Press.

Machin, D. (2007) *Introduction to Multimodal Analysis*. London: Hodder Arnold.

Machin, D. (2014) 'Multimodality and Theories of the Visual', in C. Jewitt (ed.), *The Routledge Handbook of Multimodal Analysis* (second edition). London and New York: Routledge, pp. 217–26.

Machin, D. and Mayr, A. (2012) *How to do Critical Discourse Analysis*. London: Sage.

Machin, D. and van Leeuwen, T. (2007) *Global Media Discourse: A Critical Introduction*. London and New York: Routledge.

Mahon, R. (1996) 'Women wage earners and the future of Swedish unions', *Economic and Industrial Democracy,* 17(4): 545–86.

Majone, G. (1989) *Evidence, Argument and Persuasion in the Policy Process*. New Haven and London: Yale University Press.

Mandelbaum, M. (1967) 'A note on history as narrative', *History and Theory,* 6: 413–19.

Mann, M. (2012) *The Sources of Social Power* (vol. I). Cambridge: Cambridge University Press.

Manning, D. (1976) *Liberalism*. London: Dent.

March, L. (2013) *Radical Left Parties in Europe*. Abingdon: Routledge.

Marshall, T.H. (1965) *Class, Citizenship, and Social Development*. New York: Doubleday.

Marx, K. and Engels, F. (1848/1969) *Selected Works*, Vol. 1. Moscow: Progress Publishers, pp. 98–137.

McAdams, D. P. (1993) *The Stories we Live By: Personal Myths and the Making of the Self*. New York, London: Guildford Press.

McCombs, M.E. and Shaw, D.L. (2009) 'The Agenda-Setting Functions of Mass Media', in K. Krippendorff and M.A. Bock (eds), *The Content Analysis Reader*. London: Sage.

McLaughlin, J. (2003) *Feminist Social and Political Theory*. Basingstoke: Palgrave Macmillan.

McMillan, S.J. (2009), 'The Challenge of Applying Content Analysis to the World Wide Web', in K. Krippendorff and M.A. Bock (eds), *The Content Analysis Reader*. London: Sage, pp. 60–7.

McQuail, D. (2010) *McQuail's Mass Communication Theory*. London: Sage.

Miliband, R. (1972) *The State in Capitalist Society*. London: Weidenfeld & Nicolson.

Miller, J.H. (1974) 'Narrative and history', *Journal of English Literary History,* 41: 455–73.

Mink, L. (1978) 'Narrative Form as a Cognitive Instrument', in R. Canary and H. Kozicki (eds), *The Writing of History: Literary Form and Historical Understanding*. Madison, WI: University of Wisconsin Press, pp. 129–49.

Moore, B. Jr. (1965) *Soviet Politics – The Dilemma of Power: The Role of Ideas in Social change*. New York: Harper & Row.

Moser, P. K. (ed.) (2005) *The Oxford Handbook of Epistemology*. Oxford: Oxford University Press.

Mott, C. (1992) *A Christian Perspective on Political Thought*. New York and Oxford: Oxford University Press.

Mottier, V. (1999) 'Narratives of National Identity: Sexuality, Race, and the Swiss "Dream of Order"'. Paper presented at the ECPR Joint Sessions of Workshops in Mannheim. Available at https://ecpr.eu/Filestore/PaperProposal/8f02e5e3-7d04-47fa-8596-175c8e6c6a00.pdf (accessed 17 July 2016).

Müller, J.W. (2011) *Contesting Democracy: Political Ideas in Twentieth Century Europe*. New Haven and London: Yale University Press.

Mumby, D. (1993) *Narrative and Social Control: Critical Perspectives*. London: Sage.

Myrdal, G. (1944) *An American Dilemma: The Negro Problem and Modern Democracy*. New York: Harper & Row.

Myrdal, G. (1990 [1929]) *The Political Element in the Development of Economic Theory*. New Brunswick and London: Transaction Publishers.

Næss, A. (2005) *Communication and Argument: Elements of Applied Semantics* (vol. VII in *The Selected Works of Arne Næss*). A. Drenson (ed.) Dortrecht: Springer.

Næss, A., Christophersen, J.A. and Kvalø, K. (1956) *Democracy, Ideology and Objectivity: Studies in the Semantics and Cognitive Analysis of Ideological Controversy*. Oxford: Blackwell/Oslo: Oslo University Press.

Nash, C. (ed.) (1994) *Narrative in Culture: The Uses of Storytelling in the Sciences, Philosophy and Literature*. London: Routledge.

Norris, P. and Inglehart, R. (2011) *Sacred and Secular: Religion and Politics World Wide* (second edition). Cambridge: Cambridge University Press.

Nussbaum, M.C. (2000) *Women and Human Development: The Capabilities Approach*. Cambridge: Cambridge University Press.

Oakshott, M. (1939) *Social and Political Doctrines of Contemporary Europe*. Cambridge: Cambridge University Press.

Obama, B. (2015) 'Remarks by the President in announcing the clean power plan'. https://www.whitehouse.gov/the-press-office/2015/08/03/remarks-president-announcing-clean-power-plan (accessed 12 July 2016).

Ochs, E. and Taylor, C.E. (1992) 'Family narrative as political activity', *Discourse and Society* 3: 301–40.

Ochs, E. and Capps, L. (2001) *Living Narrative*. Cambridge, MA: Harvard University Press.

O'Connell, M. (1999) 'Is Irish public opinion towards crime distorted by media bias?', *European Journal of Communication*, 14 (2): 191–212.

Ogden, C.K. and Richards I.A. (2013 [1923]) *The Meaning of Meaning: A Study in the Influence of Language upon Thought and of the Science of Symbolism.* Mansfield Centre, Connecticut: Martino Publishing.

Olssen, M., Codd, J. and O'Neil A.-M. (2004) *Education Policy: Globalization, Citizenship and Democracy.* London: Sage.

Oreskes, N. and Conway, E.M. (2010) *Merchants of Doubt: How a Handful of Scientists Obscure the Truth on Issues from Tobacco Smoke to Global Warming.* New York, Berlin, London: Bloomsburg Press.

Page, R. (ed.) (2011) *New Perspectives on Narratives and Multimodality.* London: Routledge.

Paltridge, B. (2006) *Discourse Analysis – an Introduction.* London: Continuum.

Parsons, T. (2012 [1951]) *The Social System.* New Orleans: Quid Pro.

Parsons, T. and Shils, E.A. (eds) (1951) *Toward a General Theory of Action.* New York: Harper & Row.

Patthey-Chavez, G.G., Clare, L. and Youmans, M.(1996) 'Watery passion: The struggle between hegemony and sexual liberation in erotic fiction for women', *Discourse & Society*, 7 (1):77–106.

Peck, J. (2010) *Constructions of Neoliberal Reason.* Oxford: Oxford University Press.

Phillips, D.P. (2009), 'Airplane Accident Fatalities after Newspaper Stories about Murder and Suicide', in K. Krippendorff and M.A. Bock (eds), *The Content Analysis Reader.* London: Sage.

Pitkin, H.F. (1972) *Wittgenstein and Justice: On the Significance of Ludwig Wittgenstein for Social and Political Thought.* Berkeley, CA, London: University of California Press.

Plamenatz, J. (1970) *Ideology.* London: Praeger.

Polanyi, M. (2009 [1973]) *The Tacit Dimension.* Chicago: Chicago University Press.

Poletta, F. (1998) ' Contending Stories: Narrative in social movements', *Qualitative Sociology,* 21(4): 419–446.

Poletta, F. (2002) 'Plotting Protest: Mobilizing Stories in 1960 Student Sit-Ins', in J.E. Davis (ed.), *Stories of Change: Narrative and Social Movements.* Albany: State University of New York.

Polkinghorne, D. E. (1987) *Narrative Knowing and the Human Sciences.* Albany: State University of New York.

Popper, K. (2003 [1945]) *The Open Society and its Enemies* (vol 1-2). Abingdon: Routledge.

Porter, M.J., Larson, D.L., Harthcock, A. and Nellis, K.B. (2002) 'Re(de)fining narrative events: Examining television narrative structure', *Journal of Popular Film and Television,* 30: 23–30.

Potter, J. and Edwards, D. (2001) 'Discursive Social Psychology', in P. Robinson and H. Giles (eds), *The New Handbook of Language and Social Psychology.* Chichester: Wiley. pp. 103–18.

Propp, V. (1968 [1928]) *Morphology of the Folktale.* Austin: University of Texas Press.

Putnam, R. (1993) *Making Democracy Work: Civic Traditions in Modern Italy.* Princeton: Princeton University Press.

Rawls, J. (1993) *Political Liberalism.* New York: Columbia University Press.

Richardson, B. (ed.) (2008) *Narrative Beginnings: Theories and Practices.* Lincoln, NE: University of Nebraska Press.

Richardson, H.S. (1994) *Practical Reasoning About Final Ends.* Cambridge: Cambridge University Press.

Riessman, C.K. (1993) *Narrative Analysis.* London: Sage.

Rigotti, F. (1994) *Die Macht und ihre Metaphern: Über die sprachlichen Bilder der Politik.* Frankfurt, New York: Campus Verlag.

Roberts, C.W. (ed.) (1997) *Text Analysis for the Social Sciences: Methods for Drawing Statistical Inferences from Texts and Transcripts.* Mahwah, NJ: Lawrence Erlbaum Associates.

Robertson, A. (2000) 'Europa erzählt: Erzählanalyse und Fernsehnachrichten über Europa', in J.W. Deth and T.König (eds), *Europäische Politikwissenschaft: Ein Blick in die Werkstatt.* Frankfurt: Campus Verlag, pp. 87–111.

Robertson, A. (2010) *Mediated Cosmopolitanism: The World of Television News.* Cambridge: Polity.

Robertson, A. (2015) *Global News: Reporting Conflicts and Cosmopolitanism.* New York and London: Peter Lang.

Rorty, R. (1995) 'Feminism, ideology and deconstruction: A pragmatist view', in S. Žižek (ed.), *Mapping Ideology.* London: Verso.

Rorty, R. (1999) *Philosophy and Social Hope.* New York: Penguin Group.

Rosenblatt, P.C. (1994) *Metaphors of Family Systems Theory: Toward New Constructions.* New York, London: The Guilford Press.

Roy, A. (1997) *The God of Small Things.* London: Flamingo.

rt.com (2015) 'Cameron's "deceitful" strategy to get UK Syrian involvement', https://www.rt.com/op-edge/323561-david-cameron-isis-strategy/ (accessed 18 July 2016).

Ryan, M.-L. (ed.) (2004): *Narrative Across Media: The Languages of Storytelling.* Lincoln, NE and London: University of Nebraska Press.

Sabine, G. and Thorson, T. (1973[1937]) *The History of Political Theory.* (fourth edition). Hinsdale, IL: Dryden Press.

Sacks, H. (1992) *Lectures on Conversation* (vol. 1). Oxford: Blackwell.

Sand, J. (2000) *Arguing well.* London: Routledge.

Sartori, G. (2009) 'Guidelines for Concept Analysis' in D. Collier and J. Gerring (eds) *Concepts and Methods in Social Science. The Tradition of Giovanni Sartori.* Abingdon: Routledge.

Saussure, F. de (1959 [1916]) *Course in General Linguistics.* New York: The Philosophical Library.

Sayyid, B. (1994) 'Sign o'Times: Kaffirs and Infidels Fighting the Ninth Crusade', in E. Laclau (ed.), *The Making of Political Identities.* London: Verso, pp. 264–86.

Schiffrin, D. (1996) 'Narrative as self-portrait: Sociolinguistic constructions of identity', *Language in Society,* 25: 167–203.

Schirmer, D. (1993) 'At the Site of the "Common European House": How a Symbol structures Political Discourse', in M. Abélès and W. Rossade (eds),

Politique symbolique en Europe/Symbolische Politik in Europa. Berlin: Duncker and Humblot, pp. 179–89.

Schleiermacher, F. (1998) *Hermeneutics and Criticism and Other Writings,* translated and edited by A. Bowie. Cambridge: Cambridge University Press.

Schmandt, H.J. (1960) *A History of Political Philosophy*. Milwaukee, WN: Bruce Publishing Company.

Schneider, S.G. (2008) 'Exploring the Metaphorical (De-)construction of Legitimacy', in T. Carver and J. Pikalo (eds), *Political Language and Metaphor: Interpreting and Changing the World*. London: Routledge, pp. 83–101.

Schreier, M. (2014) 'Qualitative Content Analysis?', in U. Flick (ed.), *The Sage Handbook of Qualitative Data Analysis*. London: Sage, pp. 170–83.

Schurmann, F. (1968) *Ideology and Organization in Communist China* (second edition). Berkeley, CA: University of California Press.

Searle, J. (1997) *The Construction of Social Reality*. New York: The Free Press.

Seliger, M. (1976) *Ideology and Politics*. London: George Allen & Unwin.

Semino, E. and Masci, M. (1996) 'Politics is football: Metaphor in the discourse of Silvio Berlusconi in Italy', *Discourse & Society*, 7 (2): 243–69.

Shannon, L.W. (1954) 'The opinions of little orphan Annie and her friends', *Public Opinion Quarterly*, (18): 169–79.

Shapiro, G. (2009) 'The Future of Coders: Human judgments in a world of sophisticated software', in K. Krippendorff and M.A. Bock (eds), *The Content Analysis Reader*. London: Sage, pp. 234–42.

Shapiro, G. and Markoff, J. (1997) 'A Matter of Definition', in C.W. Roberts (ed.), *Text Analysis for the Social Sciences: Methods for Drawing Statistical Inferences from Texts and Transcripts*. Mahwah, NJ: Lawrence Erlbaum Associates, pp. 9–34.

Shapiro, M.J (1988) *The Politics of Representation: Writing Practices in Biography, Photography and Policy Analysis*. Madison, WN: University of Wisconsin Press.

Shell, M. (1993) *Children of the Earth: Literature, Politics and Nationhood*. Oxford: Oxford University Press.

Shotter, J. (1993) *Conversational Realities*. London: Sage.

Shuman, A. (2012) 'Exploring Narrative Interaction in Multiple Contexts', in J.A. Holstein and J.F. Gruber (eds), *Varieties of Narrative Analysis*. London: Sage, pp. 125–50.

Silverman, H.J. (ed.) (1991) *Gadamer and Hermeneutics*. New York: Routledge.

Silverstone, R. (1984) 'Narrative Strategies in Television Science – a Case Study', *Media, Culture and Society*, 6: 377–410

Simpson, P. (1993) *Language, Ideology and Point of View*. Abingdon: Routledge.

Simpson, P. (2004) *Stylistics: A Resource Book for Students*. Abingdon: Routledge.

Sjöberg, L. (2011) *Bäst i klassen? – lärare och elever i svenska och europeiska policytexter*. Göteborg: Acta Universitatis Gothoburgensis. https://gupea.ub.gu.se/bitstream/2077/24101/1/gupea_2077_24101_1.pdf (accessed 3 August 2016).

Skinner, Q. (1988a) 'Meaning and Understanding in the History of Ideas', in J. Tully (ed.), *Meaning and Context: Quentin Skinner and his Critics*. London: Polity Press, pp. 29–67.

Skinner, Q. (1988b) 'Language and Social Change' in J. Tully (ed.), *Meaning and Context: Quentin Skinner and his Critics*. London: Polity Press, pp. 119–34.

Skinner, Q. (2002) *Visions of Politics* (vol. I). *Regarding Method*. Cambridge: Cambridge University Press.

Skocpol, T. (1982) 'Rentier State and Shi'a Islam in the Iranian Revolution', *Theory and Society*, 11(3): 265–83.

Smith, A.-M. (1998) *Laclau and Mouffe – the Radical Democratic Imaginary*. London, New York: Routledge.

Smith, R.R. (1979) 'Mythic elements in television news', *Journal of Communication*, Winter, 29 (1): 75–82.

Swedish Nuclear Fuel and Waste Management Co (undated). *Final repository for spent nuclear fuel*. Stockholm: Swedish Nuclear Fuel and Waste Management Co.

Söder, M. (1978) *Anstalter för utvecklingsstörda: En historisk-sociologisk beskrivning av utvecklingen* (vol. II). Stockholm: ALA.

Somers, M.R. (1994) 'The narrative constitution of identity: A relational and network approach', *Theory and Society*, 23: 605–49.

Sommer, D. (1991) *Foundational Fictions: The National Romances of Latin America*. Berkeley, CA: University of California Press.

Spitzmüller, J. and Warnke, I.H. (2011) 'Discourse as a "linguistic object": Methodical and methodological delimitations', *Critical Discourse Studies*, 8(2): 75–94.

Stedman Jones, D. (2012) *Masters of the Universe: Hayek, Friedman, and the Birth of Neoliberal Politics*. Princeton and Oxford: Princeton University Press.

Stephenson, S. (1999) 'Narrative, Identity and Modernity'. Paper presented at the workshop on 'The Political Uses of Narrative' at the ECPR Joint Sessions of Workshops in Mannheim, 29-31 March 1999. Available from https://ecpr.eu/Filestore/PaperProposal/37fe9dc5-6ad9-4a73-b35a-704d8265ecb0.pdf (accessed 17 July 2016).

Stone, D. (2001) *The Policy Paradox: The Art of Political Decision Making* (revised edition). New York and London: W.W. Norton.

Stone, I.F. (1988) *The Trial of Socrates*. London: Cape.

Streeck, W. (2014) *Buying Time: The Delayed Crisis of Democratic Capitalism*. London: Verso.

Sutton, F.X. Harris, S., Kaysen, C. and Tobin, J. (1956) *The American Business Creed*. Cambridge, MA: Harvard University Press.

Sykes, M. (1985) 'Discrimination in Discourse', in T.A. van Dijk (ed.), *Handbook of Discourse Analysis* (vol. 4). London: Academic Press, pp. 83–101.

Sykes, M. (1988) 'From "Rights" to "Needs": Official Discourse and the "Welfarization" of Race', in G. Smitherman-Donaldson and T.A. van Dijk (eds), *Discourse and Discrimination*. Detroit: Wayne State University Press, pp. 176–205.

Tännsjö, T. (2002) *Understanding Ethics: An Introduction to Moral Theory*. Edinburgh: Edinburgh University Press.

Therborn, G. (1980) *The Ideology of Power and the Power of Ideology*. London: Verso.

Tingsten, H. (1939) *Konservatismens idéer [The Ideas of Conservatism]*. Stockholm: Bonniers.

Tingsten, H. (1973 [1941]) *The Development of the Ideas of the Swedish Social Democracy* (vol. 1-2). Totowa, NJ: Bedminster Press.

Todorov, T. (1969) 'Structural analysis of narrative', *Novel*, 3: 70–6.

Torfing, J. (1999) *New Theories of Discourse: Laclau, Mouffe and Žižek*. Oxford: Blackwell.

Tosh, J. (2015) *The Pursuit of History: Aims, Methods and New Directions in the Study of History* (sixth edition). Abingdon and New York: Routledge.

Toulmin, S.E. (2003 [1958]) *The Uses of Argument* (updated edition). Cambridge: Cambridge University Press.

Tuchman, G. (1976) 'Telling stories', *Journal of Communication* 26 (4): 93–7..

Udasmoro, W. (2013) 'Symbolic power in everyday narratives: Gender construction in Indonesian television', *Asian Journal of Social Sciences & Humanities*, 2 (3): 155–65.

Uhr, J. and Walter, R. (eds) (2014) *Studies in Australian Political Rhetoric*. Canberra: Australian National University Press.

United Nations (UN) (n.d.) 'The universal declaration of human rights'. http://www.un.org/en/universal-declaration-human-rights/ (accessed 15 July 2016).

Ungerer, F. and Schmid, H.-J. (2006) *An Introduction to Cognitive Linguistics*. Harlow: Addison Wesley Longman.

van Dijk, T.A. (1993) 'Stories and Racism', in D.K. Mumby (ed.), *Narrative and Social Control: Critical Perspectives*. London: Sage, pp. 121–42.

van Dijk, T.A. (1997) 'The Study of Discourse', in T.A. van Dijk (ed.), *Discourse Studies: A Multidisciplinary Introduction. Part I: Discourse as Structure and Process*. London: Sage, pp. 1–34.

van Dijk, T.A. (1998) *Ideology: A Multidisciplinary Approach*. London: Sage.

van Dijk, T.A. (2006) 'Discourse and Ideology', in T. van Dijk (ed.), *Discourse Studies* (2nd edn). London: Sage, pp. 279-407-

van Dijk, T.A. (2009) *Society and Discourse: How Social Contexts Influence Text and Talk*. Cambridge: Cambridge University Press.

van Dijk, T.A. (2013) 'Ideology and Discourse', in M. Freeden et al. (eds), *The Oxford Handbook of Political Ideologies*. Oxford: Oxford University Press, pp. 728–40.

van Dyke, V. (1995) *Ideology and Political Choice: The Search for Freedom, Justice, and Virtue*. Chatham, NJ: Chatham Publishers.

van Eemeren, F.H. (2010) *Strategic Maneuvering in Argumentative Discourse: Extending the Pragma-dialectical Theory of Argumentation*. Amsterdam and Philadelphia: John Benjamins Publishing Company.

van Eemeren, F.H. and Grootendorst, R. (1992) *Argumentation, Communication, and Fallacies: A Pragma-Dialectical Approach*. Cambridge: Cambridge University Press.

van Eemeren, F.H. and Grootendorst, R. (2004) *A Systematic Theory of Argumentation: The Pragma-Dialectical Approach*. Cambridge: Cambridge University Press.

van Eemeren, F.H. and Houtlosser, P. (2005a) 'Introduction', in van F.H. Eemeren and P. Houtlosser (eds), *Argumentation in Practice*. Amsterdam/Philadelphia: John Benjamins Publishing Company, pp. 1–10.

van Eemeren, F.H. and Houtlosser, P. (eds) (2005b) *Argumentation in Practice*. Amsterdam/Philadelphia: John Benjamins Publishing Company.

Van Leeuwen, T. (2005b) *Introducing Social Semiotics*. London and New York: Routledge.

Vedung, E. (1977) *Det rationella politiska samtalet: Hur politiska samtal tolkas, ordnas och prövas*. Stockholm: Aldus.

Vedung, E. (1982) *Political Reasoning*. London: Sage.

Vedung, E. (2000) *Public Policy and Program Evaluation*. New Brunswick and London: Transaction.

Vincent, A. (2010) *Modern Political Ideologies* (third edition). Chichester: Wiley-Blackwell.

von Beyme, K. (2013a) *Liberalismus: Theorien des Liberalismus und Radikalismus im Zeitalter der Ideologien 1789–1945*. Wiesbaden: Springer.

von Beyme, K. (2013b) *Konservatismus: Theorien des Konservatismus und Rechtsextremismus im Zeitalter der Ideologien 1789–1945*. Wiesbaden: Springer.

von Beyme, K. (2013c) *Sozialismus: Theorien des Sozialismus, Anarchismus und Kommunismus im Zeitalter der Ideologien 1789–1945*. Wiesbaden: Springer.

von Feilitzen, C., Strand, H., Nowak, K. and Andrén, G. (1989) 'To Be or Not to Be in the TV world: Ontological and methodological aspects of content analysis', *European Journal of Communication*, 4: 11–32.

Walberg, H.J., Arian, G.W., Paik, S.J. and Miller, J. (2001) 'New methods of content analysis in education, evaluation, and psychology', in M.D. West (ed.), *Theory, Method, and Practice in Computer Content Analysis*. Westport, CN: Ablex Publishing, pp. 143–58.

Wallace, H. (2010) *Rock Solid? A scientific review of geological disposal of high-level radioactive waste. GeneWatch UK consultancy report for Greenpeace International*. Buxton, Derbyshire: GeneWatch UK.

Walsby, H. (1947) *The Domain of Ideologies: A Study of the Origin, Development and Structure of Ideologies*. Glasgow: William MacLellan.

Walton, D.N. (1990) *Practical Reasoning: Goal-driven, Knowledge-based, Action-guiding Argumentation*. Savage, MA: Rowman & Littlefield.

Weber, M. (1972[1921]) *Wirtschaft und Gesellschaft: Grundlagen einer verstehenden Soziologie* (fifth edition.) Tübingen: J.C.B. Mohr. (Eng. transl. in Parsons, T. (ed.) (1947) *Max Weber. The Theory of Social and Economic Organization*. New York: The Free Press.)

Weber, M. (2009), 'Towards a Sociology of the Press: An Early Proposal for Content Analysis', in K. Krippendorff and M.A. Bock (eds), *The Content Analysis Reader*. London: Sage, pp. 9–11.

Webb, M. (2014) 'Uganda child soldiers. Former fighter reunites with family' (video), embedded in http://www.aljazeera.com/indepth/features/2014/05/uganda-former-child-soldiers-from-lord-resistance-army-ret-2014539240489470.html (accessed 18 July 2016).

Weinsheimer, J. (1985) *Gadamer's Hermeneutics: A Reading of 'Truth and Method'*. New Haven: Yale University Press.

Weiss, G. and Wodak, R. (eds) (2003) *Critical Discourse Analysis: Theory and Interdisciplinarity.* Basingstoke: Palgrave.

Weston, A. (2009) *A Rulebook for Arguments.* Indianapolis, IN: Huckett.

Wetherell, M. (1998) 'Positioning and interpreting repertoires: Conversation analysis and post-structuralism in dialogue', *Discourse and Society,* 9(3): 387–412.

Wetherell, M. (2012) *Affect and Emotion: A New Social Science Understanding.* London: Sage.

Wetherell, M. and Edley, N. (1999) 'Negotiating hegemonic masculinity: imaginary positions and psycho-discursive practices', *Feminism and Psychology*, 9(3): 335–56.

Wetherell, M. and Potter, J. (1992) *Mapping the Language of Racism: Discourse and the Legitimation of Exploitation.* New York: Harvester Wheatsheaf.

White, H. (1987) *The Content of the Form: Narrative Discourse and Historical Representation.* Baltimore: Johns Hopkins University Press.

Widdicombe, S. and Wooffitt, R. (1995) *The Language of Youth Subcultures: Social Identity in Action.* New York: Harvester Wheatsheaf.

Widfeldt, A. (2014) *Extreme Right Parties in Scandinavia.* London and New York: Routledge.

Wiebe, J.M. and Bruce, R.F. (2001) 'Probabilistic classifiers for tracking point of view', in M.D. West (ed.), *Theory, Method, and Practice in Computer Content Analysis.* Westport, London: Ablex Publishing, pp. 125–42.

Wiercinski, A. (2011) *Gadamer's Hermeneutics and the Art of Conversation.* Münster: LIT Verlag.

Windslate, J., G. Monk and A. Cotter (1998) 'A narrative approach to the practice of mediation', *Negotiation Journal,* 14, (1.8).

Wodak, R. (1996) *Disorders of Discourse.* London: Longman.

Wodak, R. and Meyer, M. (2009) 'Critical discourse analysis history, agenda, theory and methodology', in R. Wodak and M. Meyer (eds), *Methods of Critical Discourse Analysis.* London: Sage, pp. 1–33.

Wodak, R., de Cilla, R., Reisigl, M. and Liebhart, K. (2009) *The Discursive Construction of National Identity.* Edinburgh: Edinburgh University Press.

Wolin, R. (2004) *The Seduction of Unreason. The Intellectual Romance with Fascism from Nietzsche to Postmodernism.* Princeton, NJ: Princeton University Press.

Women's Equality Party (WE) (2015) 'Policy Document', https://d3n8a8pro7vhmx. cloudfront.net/womensequality/pages/405/attachments/original/1445332098/ WE_Policy_Launch.pdf?1445332098 (accessed 16 July 2016).

Zac, L. (1995) *The Narratives of Order, the Discourse of Argentinean Military Regime (1976-1983).* University of Essex, PhD thesis.

Zuckert, C. (1990) *Natural Rights and the American Imagination: Political Philosophy in Novel Form.* Savage: Rowman & Littlefield.

Index

Page references followed by b=box; f=figure; n=note; t=table